AF497379

AN INDEX TO THE
EARLY PRINTED BOOKS
IN THE BRITISH MUSEUM. BY ROBERT PROCTOR

PART II. MDI—MDXX
SECTION I. GERMANY

London: Kegan Paul, Trench, Trübner & Company, Limited

Dryden House, Gerrard Street, Soho : MDCCCCIII

OXFORD   PRINTED BY
HORACE HART AT THE
UNIVERSITY PRESS

PREFACE.

THIS instalment of the Index to the Early Printed Books in the British Museum is the first division of the second part. It corresponds in contents with the first two hundred and twenty pages of the first part, and deals with the books printed in Germany during the first twenty years of the sixteenth century. The reason for choosing the year 1520 as the limit is similar to that which has prompted the cataloguers of early english printed books to stay their hand at the year 1640, to wit, the vast stream of pamphlets and other ephemeral matter which in each case swamped the more literary output of the press, and was caused by the outbreak of the struggle, in the sixteenth century for religious and in the seventeenth for political freedom. A glance at Weller's Repertorium will show what this means in the period we are here concerned with, and though his book is a mere supplement, the proportion may be taken as tolerably correct. For the years 1501 to 1517 inclusive Weller registers some eleven hundred books in all, an average of sixty-five a year; for 1518, 1519 and 1520 six hundred, or two hundred a year; from 1521 to 1526, some two thousand four hundred, or four hundred a year.

Other reasons have led to the publication of this section of the Index as a self-contained work. Though incomparably more easy and straightforward than the italian or french divisions are likely to be, it has occupied during four years the greater part of a constantly diminishing leisure; and the prospect of completing the other countries in any reasonable time is so small that it seemed undesirable to keep the german section back for several years in order to issue the whole at one time, as was done with the first part. The most notable disadvantage of the method which has been adopted is the exclusion of the german books printed at Basel or in Austria-Hungary, whether with or without imprint; and it must be constantly borne in mind by those who consult the Index that the absence from the following pages of a german book sine nota does not necessarily imply that it is wanting in the Museum collections.

I have striven to make this part of my work less inaccurate than its predecessor, though from the greater rarity of sixteenth-century books, and the fact that (unlike the incunabula) they have never been deliberately bought by the Museum as specimens of printing, it must inevitably be still more incomplete. But the first part was compiled in a hasty and light-hearted fashion, many things being taken for granted which proved to be blunders; and the german section, which was first done, suffers even more from this cause than the rest, owing to inexperience, the development of my plan as the work went forward, and the greater difficulties to be overcome in the later parts, which made an increased amount of care essential. A fruitful source of error has been eliminated by the exclusion of the books in the Bodleian Library, and, more than all, I have had the great advantage of the help of Herr Konrad Burger, who has had the kindness and patience to read the proof-sheets and correct my references to Panzer and Weller throughout; his wide knowledge and un-wearying care have enabled me to avoid many mistakes.

It should be made clear to begin with that this book does not profess to be a complete history of German printing during the period it covers; it aims only at supplying material from a single library, more or less exhaustive as regards that library, towards such a history: the information given, though often supplemented from such outside sources as were easy of access, is mainly derived from the books themselves, and is not the result of research in other libraries, nor is it gathered from out-of-the-way sources. The plan adopted is as a whole the same as that of the first part, and I do not propose to repeat here the explanations as to arrangement and other details which were given in the preface to that. It will be enough to point out one by one the chief modifications of the original scheme under each head as they occur, whether in the way of omissions or additions.

In the list of towns (page 17) a distinction is made between those which are repeated from part i. and those which are first found here. Of the former only those are given which had presses at work during the years 1501–1520. Two changes have been made in the order and numbering; one is in the position of Erfurt, an alteration due to my ignorance of the Petrusberg press of 1479 when part i. was written: the other involves a change in the number-ing from Freiburg onwards, owing to Herr Burger's discovery of a book printed at Zweibrücken in 1492. But even the present list is not free from error; for Meissen, where Lotter the Elder printed a single book in 1520, hitherto considered the first production of that city, had a press as early as 1483, though the source from which Hain copied his entry (no. 3859) ingeniously omitted the decisive words which show it. I owe my knowledge of this fact also to Herr Burger's kindness.

The list of presses at the head of each town is similarly arranged as a con-tinuation of the earlier lists, a distinction being made between the presses of the fifteenth century and those of the sixteenth by the omission of any date to those which have already appeared in part i. Here again a few changes in the numbering will be found, notably in the case of Leipzig, Erfurt, München and Regensburg; partly by the fusion of presses wrongly divided, as Werman and Bötticher at Leipzig, partly by the division of one press into two (Conr. Kachelofen at Leipzig), but chiefly by the inclusion of new fifteenth-century presses, as at Erfurt, München and Regensburg.

Then we come to the information given in small type at the head of each press; and here the changes made have been far greater. The types are numbered as before according to the date at which they first appear, but variations which occur in a single type are distinguished according to the nature of the changes made. Thus an asterisk (1^*) always implies a recast, and therefore a change of body; while the use of superior letters (1^B, 1^C) refers to variations involving only the addition or subtraction of individual letters and not affecting the fount as a whole. Such types as were identified too late to be included in the numerical order without dislocation are numbered

thus: 1 bis, 2 bis, and so on. For the same reason a few types will be found
to be numbered out of their order of date, where a book containing a particular
fount at an earlier date than any previously recorded has come to light as the
sheets were passing through the press; Knoblouch 13 is an instance of this.
The references given to similar or parallel types are here made by means of
the printer's name, an easier method for the reader than the use of numbers
as in part i.: but the use of references of this kind at all is rendered much
less necessary by the type register, in which all the latin and german founts
in this volume are grouped according to their several styles and affinities.
The greek, hebrew and other oriental types are then given, with an independent numbering in roman lowercase figures. To most of the types is
added the measure of twenty lines of their body when unleaded. It is important to note however that this is not done as in part i. by measuring from
the top of the short letters to the bottom of the short letters in line 20, but
it represents the full body of the type. But in the case of very large types,
where the measurement refers to a single line only, the measure given is always
that of a short letter such as n. At the end of the list of types of each press
I have added references to analogies in the figures or facsimiles appended
to the type register, of which I shall speak later. The asterisk prefixed to
the number of the type in these references indicates that the facsimile has
been made from this actual fount: in other cases the resemblance is not
necessarily more than general, and the reference is often intended only to
help the student to determine roughly what kind or style of type he is to
expect.

The rest of the information given in the small type is wholly new, and is
not represented by anything in part i. First comes an enumeration of the
borders, which were at this period a very important feature in a printer's
stock, and are often of great value as giving clues to the identification of
books sine nota. These borders, whether used as frames for the titlepage
or in other parts of the book, if the four sides are cut on one block, or if the
design is continuous when more blocks than one are used, are numbered
consecutively in the order of their first appearance by means of roman capitals
(A, B, &c.). But such borders as are made up of four or more blocks, dis-
connected in design and therefore subject to constant variation, are called X
where they surround the whole page. In a few cases, where the variations
are few and afford definite data useful to the student, they are registered
by superior numbers (X^1, X^2, X^{1a}, X^{1b}). When odd border-pieces are used
singly, or to flank three or two sides only of the page, or if four pieces are
used to surround a cut or any matter that occupies only part of a page, then
such pieces are denoted by the letter Y. References are given to such
facsimiles of borders as are to be found in well-known and easily accessible
works of reference, such as Butsch, Muther or the Heitz series. Border-
devices (which are seldom X borders) are borders which contain the device
of the printer in some part of them. They are shown by the addition to the
number of the border (as A) of the number of the device (as c), thus: Ac.

This means that the printer's first border (in order of date) contains in it his third device.   But such a combination as Xc is never used.

These devices or printer's marks, usually found independent of borders at this period, though the influence of Froben made the border-device very common towards the end of it, are indicated by roman lowercase letters (as a, b, c) ; the devices are numbered in order of date, and references are given to modern facsimiles (not to such books as Rothscholtz) where such are available.

Lastly come the initials, shown in a similar fashion by greek lowercase letters (α, β, γ, &c.).   About these it is to be noted, first, that these letters refer only to sets of initials, meaning by a set three letters or more of the same style and size.   Where only two initials of a sort are found, and yet on account of marked individuality are counted as a set, the fact is always noted. Otherwise such initials, and all single letters not belonging to any recognised set in the hands of a printer, are covered by the general designation of Δ. Secondly, it is to be remembered that the ordinary lombardic letters common to a large proportion of the books of 1501–1520 are left out of consideration altogether.   Thirdly, and this is a defect, though one of no great extent, and avoidable only at the cost of a good deal of time and labour, the initials of sets used only before 1500 by printers who overlap the two centuries (most notably of course Ratdolt and the elder Schönsperger) are omitted, and the numbering begins with 1501, fifteenth-century initials being numbered only in so far as they are used after 1500.

To make the numbering of borders, devices, and initials clearer, it may be well to give an imaginary instance and elucidate it before passing on.   Thus if we find the following combination of letters : AcBX^{1}Y ; b ; $\alpha_1\Delta$: it means that in the book in question are used the printer's first and second borders, the first containing his third device ; likewise the first variation of a composite border, which is found in two or more definite combinations in various books ; also odd border-pieces.   Besides the third device (in border A) the printer's second device is found, and initials from his first and third sets, as well as odd initials unconnected with any set of his.

We come now to the separate entries of books, which form the nucleus of the text.   Concerning the entries as a whole, four things must be borne in mind.   The first is that (as I mentioned above) no books from the Bodleian Library are entered here.   I had no complete material for these, and the proportion of books not in the Museum was so extremely small in that which was in my hands (some two-thirds of the whole) that it seemed not worth while to undertake the wearisome task of reading through the hundred or more remaining volumes of the Bodleian catalogue for what was like to prove so poor a result.   Secondly, the undated books are distributed as far as possible according to their date, which can at this time almost always be determined within a year or at most two years, and are not, as was usually done in part i., placed together in a mass after the dated books.   When an approximate date is given in square brackets it is always based on some evidence, internal or typographical.   Thirdly, I have omitted all mention of duplicate copies

unless one of the copies is printed on vellum and the other on paper, or the two
copies have well-marked variations in their setting-up, such as a different
colophon.   Fourthly, books which were included in part i., though printed
after 1500, are always repeated in part ii., with a reference to the original
number, when they were ascribed in part i. to a wrong press; but if rightly
there ascribed, they are repeated here only in exceptional cases, where I had
some particular reason for doing so.

The numbers assigned to the entries are continuous with those of the first
part for greater ease of reference.   The intercalated numbers (as 9898A)
represent books accidentally omitted, or, more often, bought while the Index
was in the printer's hands.   These numbers must be distinguished from
those marked with a small letter (9941a, b), which is used in the case of
such books as are shown by a general titlepage (often an afterthought) or
by continuous signatures to form one whole, though they have sectional
titlepages as well; the parts are often found separately and quoted as
complete books, and it seems well to mark their proper relations to one
another in some way not likely to mislead.

About the dates there is little more to say than has been said in my preface
of 1898.   The only new feature is the appearance in certain Lutheriana of a
date within a parenthesis.   This is adopted for tracts which have either on
the titlepage or at the end a date concerning which it is impossible to decide
whether it is the date of writing or of printing, or if it is merely copied from
an original edition.   It is in fact another aspect of the same problem that con-
fronts us in those tracts that bear the name of Wittenberg in a prominent
position, only it takes a more insidious form; for the types always enable us
to decide whether Wittenberg was or was not the place of printing, while it
is often impossible to be sure of the date within a year or two.   The books
of Melchior Lotter the Younger are by far the most puzzling instance of this
difficulty; it is complicated in his case by a border which is constantly showing breaks that (if they are worth anything at all as evidence) very often
conflict with the alleged date of printing.   Another point may be noted.   In
the preface to part i. (page 16) I said that I had always treated a date
within the Kalends of January as belonging to the outgoing, not to the
incoming year.   As this was questioned by high authorities, I kept a note of
such instances occurring in the books of 1501 to 1520 as made a decisive
conclusion possible.   The examples I have found do, I think, justify my
original position.   In only one book included in the present volume does the
date necessarily refer to the incoming year, namely no. 11363; this is dated
1516, but it is a reprint of the undated Nürnberg edition, no. 11118, and like
the original edition it contains Pirkheimer's preface of 4 kal. Ian. 1516, which
must therefore mean December 1515.   One or two books of Froben's printing follow this rule, and an Isocrates, De regno gubernando, printed at Wien
by Vietor and Singren, 1514 Feb. 13, has a preface dated pr. kal. Ian. 1514,
that is necessarily December 1513.   But for Germany proper the bulk of the
evidence bears the other way.   Thus no. 9960 has a colophon dated 13 kal.

Ian. 1501, while the preface is dated 14 kal. Dec. 1501.   No. 10299 has no
date of printing, but has two dates in the text, the first Id. Dec. 1520, the
second, necessarily later, 8 kal. Ian. 1520.   No. 11292, a speech delivered 3
non. Oct. 1511, with a brief of Julius ii. dated 1511 Oct. 24, has a preface by
Christoph Scheurl dated 15 kal. Ian. 1511.   This opposite practice of two
scholars such as Scheurl and Pirkheimer is certainly curious.   No. 11569 is
dated : Lipsiae ex musaeo nostro, nono Calen. Ianuarias. Anno. M.D.XX.,
but it refers to the bull against Luther of 15 June 1520.   No. 11548 was
published 1520 Jan. 27, but the Peroratio is dated 17 kal. Ian. 1519.   No.
11847 has the date 1519 at the end, and a preface by Eck of 4 kal. Ian.
1518 referring to Bodenstein's Conclusiones of July 1518.   These instances
will, I hope, be enough to show that my position, if a wrong one, has at least
some ground to justify it.   For if the scholars of the Renaissance followed
the incorrect method, printers of thirty years earlier, with no tradition other
than the mediaeval, are hardly likely to have been better informed.   About
actual mistakes it is more difficult to be certain, as they seldom involve any
large difference ; but no. 11291 throws some light on a not uncommon and
rather puzzling blunder.   It is dated Saturday, 26 kal. Apr. 1511 ; the mention
of the day of the week shows this to be meant not, as one might suppose, for
a day in March, but for 26 April.

The references need a word of mention.   It is in these that the change
from the comparative light of the fifteenth century to the gross darkness of
sixteenth-century bibliography is most conspicuous.   In one way, it is true, this
is less felt in Germany than elsewhere, so far as the registration of books in
the vernacular goes, owing to the labours of Weller and others, but the
typographical side has been altogether neglected, except by Charles Schmidt,
whose method was not systematic enough to yield many good results, and
whose work was confined to the printers of a single city.   For the latin
books I have given references generally to Panzer's Annales, and to a few
special works, such as Schmidt's series on the Strassburg printers or
Böcking's bibliography of Hutten ; for the german books to Panzer's
Deutsche Annalen and to its supplement, Weller's Repertorium.   But I have
refrained from overloading the entries by many references to obscure books
of reference.   For the same reason, when a latin book is entered two or three
times over in Panzer's Annales, I have as a rule been content with a reference to the first entry, even though that in the supplement may be much
fuller ; unless the original entry is so far wrong as to be misleading.   Again,
many books in latin and german (such as vocabularies or Cato's Disticha) are
entered in the Annales and again in the Deutsche Annalen or in Weller : I
have not felt bound to give references to both.   A large number of books
entered in Weller's Repertorium as of 1520 or circa 1520 are demonstrably
later when brought into connexion with other books, for instance W. 1474
and 1478 (see page 40), and these are altogether omitted, unless there is
some good reason to the contrary ; to such as are doubtful I have usually
given the benefit of the doubt; those assigned by Weller to a year earlier

than 1520, but probably after 1520 (for instance, no. 11187), are given with a note of their true date. I have been very slow to admit books ascribed by Weller to a date later than 1520, and there are probably not more than two or three of these (no. 10319 is one) in the whole volume.

The typographical information which follows the references is arranged to correspond with the small type at the head of each press. This has been already fully dealt with, but two new features in founts of this period remain to be noticed. In some cases a book may contain only the capitals of a particular type which consists as usual of both upper and lower case. Such a fact is always indicated. But some founts, almost always sets of large capitals, have no lower case, and are used exclusively for headings and initials. It is to these types that the enclosure of the number referring to them within a parenthesis applies, and the use of such a parenthesis shows that in the particular book in question these capitals are used as initials only. Following the numbers of the types comes a mention of the woodcuts and diagrams (including those made up of rules) in any book which contains them. The words sometimes found in square brackets at the end of the entry mostly explain themselves ; they usually refer to the use of woodcut letters in place of type ; the readings (as in no. 10263–4) occasionally given are intended to be used in connexion with the title index of sine nota books, so that two editions which have titles worded in exactly the same way may be thereby distinguished.

At the end of each town is given a list of the books which have the place of printing but no printer's name, with an indication of the number under which they are entered. Though now and then, notably in the case of Johann Stuchs and Jobst Gutknecht, it is impossible to find any variation or peculiarity which enables some of the unsigned books by one of two printers to be assigned definitely to either of them, yet there is only one book (no. 11570) which has the place of printing given that I have been unable to assign to any known press. Books without place or printer are placed under their presses, if these can be identified; if this is impossible, but the place of printing is certain though not given, such books are grouped together at the end of each town; those in regard to which there is any doubt are placed all together at the end of the text (no. 11986–12004), first the groups, and then the single books. The types of these last are numbered consecutively, whereas in part i. the numbering began afresh for each book. This change makes it easier to arrange the books, and to obtain a general view of them when arranged.

The tables and registers are of far greater proportionate bulk than in the first part, but I hope that they will help to make the use of the Index easier in a corresponding degree. First comes a list showing what books were printed for stationers. It is of course absurdly small compared with what a similar list would be for Italy or France ; but it must be remembered that many books were printed in Italy and Switzerland for German publishers ; and that stationers who were also printers, such as Knoblouch, are not entered here, but the books printed for them by others will be found referred to in their place among those which they printed themselves. The second table is a title index to all books without place or printer, which is intended to enable any one who knows the exact title of a book to find the entry in the text relating to it. This index is divided into two parts, the first for dated, the second for undated books. The Luther tracts bearing dates which may or may not be the date of printing are entered in both divisions. In a few cases a reference is made to two numbers. This shows that there are two editions with identically the same title, and on looking them up in the text a note will be found at the end of each entry giving a reading from some other part of the book which serves to distinguish them from one another. The arrangement of this index is rather unusual. It begins with the first word, whether an article or not, partly because the various spellings Ain, Ayn, Ein, Eyn, are of help in breaking up a long series of similar titles; and the alphabetical arrangement is wholly independent of word-division.

Next comes the type register, which contains, grouped in their several classes, every fount of type described in the text, with measurements and other data whereby they may be identified. This is, I believe, the first time such a register has been made, and any usefulness it may have is largely due to the fact that at the date with which we are now concerned type-founding had become a regular industry, and the tendency for founts to follow a few stock models was constantly on the increase. It is amusing to see the way in which experiments such as Schöffer's archaistic or revived roman, the Lotter schwabacher, the Froben italic, the Schönsperger fraktur, were caught up and copied far and wide by enterprising founders, just as the types of William Morris have been imitated in the Amerikanischer Triumph-Gotisch, the so-called Jenson roman, and similar atrocities in our own day. For the obvious and manifold imperfections of this register I can only claim indulgence as being inherent in a first attempt. The necessary explanations for its use are given in the note which precedes the register itself. The sixty-seven facsimiles which follow it are meant to illustrate the register by showing specimens of the greater number of its more important groups: I have so far as possible refrained from reproducing types of foreign origin, unless their use was widespread in Germany. The presswork of the period was usually so execrable that in no circumstances could these blocks have been good ones: that they are not as good as they might have been I know well, but I believe that they will serve their purpose of giving a clue to the sort of fount which any prominent group-designation given in the register is intended to cover.

The index of printers and towns and the index of authors come last. Of the first little need be said. I have endeavoured to give both the first and last dates of a printer's work if it ended before 1520; a blank in place of a final date is to be taken as meaning that he issued dated books after 1520. The publishers are not included in this table. The only difficulty connected with the index of authors has to do with the anonymous books. I have entered these, usually more than once for each book, under catch-titles and prominent words.   But if the book is one which appears in the title index, and if one of the secondary headings is the same as the first word of the title, under which the book appears in the title index, it is generally not repeated under that heading in the index of authors.

CONTENTS.

ADDITIONS.

9915A. 1509. Iac. HENRICHMANNVS: prognostica ludicra. 4°. P. VI. 44. 147; SG. 113. Types 22, 25; cut.

9917A. 1509 Sept. 1. Ioh. Franc. Picus: deprouidentiadei.[PICO.]F°.P.VI.43. 144; SG. 105. Types 22, 28, gk. i; cut; βɼε. [Wants last leaf.]

9936A. 1515 Sept. 7. Ioh. GEILER: sermones de tempore et sanctis (de arbore humana, etc.) F°. P. VI. 69. 355; SG. 146. Types 17, 19, 25, 27; cuts; C; εθικ.

9996A. n.d. [b. 1517.] HORTVS sanitatis. F°. H. 8943? (Part i. no. 1448.) Types 4, 10, 13, 15, 20, 21 [see below]; cuts; βɼδн.

10052A. [n.b. 1507 Jan. 5.] Bernardus: in symbolum apostolorum. [BERNARD.] 4°. P. VI. 38. 95; SK. 26. Type 7.

10150A. n.d. [1519–20.] LUTHER: Unterricht auf etliche Artikel. 4°. W. 1592. Types 10, 12; X; δε.

10167A. 1509 Jan. Gerson: sermo de passione domini. [CHARLIER.] 4°. SSr. 12. Types 2, 3; cut. [Cf. no. 10176.]

10168A. 1510 Mar. 25. Sabellicus: exemplorum libri decem. [COCCIUS.] F°. P. VI. 46. 165; SSr. 16. Type 1, gk. i; a.

10228A. [a. 1515 Oct. 17.] Dion. CATO: disticha de moribus, etc. ab Erasmo recognita. 4°. P. VI. 75. 403; SSr. 167. Types 1, 4, gk. iij; C; ɼ.

10243A. 1516 Oct. Dion. CATO: disticha, etc. 4°. P. VI. 81. 459; SSr. 196. Types 1, 4, (12), gk. iij; C; e.

10377A. 1504 mid May. Wimpheling: AVISAMENTVM de concubinariis non absoluendis. 4°. P. VI. 354. 60. Types 6, 7, 9, 10, 12; a.

10383A. 1504. IACOBVS Gaudensis: textus dominicae passionis. 4°. Types 5, 6, 7, 9, 10, 12, 13, 14, gk; aΔ. [Woodcut hebrew.]

10483A. 1518. HENRICVS de Hassia: speculum animae. 8°. Types 5, 9, 10; cut.

10495A. n.d. [c. 1510.] HENRICVS de Herpf: collationes tres notabiles. 8°. Types 2, 4, 5; cut; Y.

10675A. 1509. FORTUNATUS. 4°. DA. 662. Type 24; cuts.

10691A. 1513 Nov. 24. Wurzgärtlein der andächtigen Seele. [HORTVLVS.—For Hans Auslasser, Schwaz.] 8°. W. 761. Types 14, 18, 26; cuts.

11191A. 1505. SECTA monopolii. 4°. Types 5, 6.

CORRECTIONS.

p. 26. Strassburg, Joh. Prüss the elder. Type 20 is first used at a much earlier date, namely in H. *8941 (before 1497 Oct. 21).—Type 21 (see above, no. 9996A), perhaps not used by the elder Prüss; text gothic like Knoblouch 2ᴮ, but the us is larger and falls lower; double hyphen. 83 mm.

p. 29. Strassburg, M. Hüpfüff. Type 3 bis, apparently the same as Grüninger 19, is used on the title of Hüpfüff's Mandeville, August 1501.

p. 40. Strassburg, M. Schürer.   The letter by Laz. Schürer dated 1520 March 1 in his edition of Sapidus, epigrammata, P. X. 27. 18, states that M. Schürer was dead at the time when Lazarus set up his press at Schlettstadt in the autumn of 1519, and that the Sapidus was his first book.   Both statements are difficult to reconcile with facts.

p. 54. Köln.   On page V of his work, Der Buchdruck Kölns bis zum Ende des xv. Jahrhunderts (Bonn, 1903) Dr. E. Voulliéme has called attention to a volume of Carthusian tracts, one of which contains the words: Impresserunt fratres domus colonie.   He deduces thence the existence of a press at this period (1514–1516 or later) in the Carthusian house at Köln. No. 10497, 10498 seem to belong to this series; there is a volume in the Bodleian containing three others of the same sort; but all are printed in the types of Landen, and it is more probable that these books were printed by him on commission for the Carthusian monks.

p. 62. Köln, Martin of Werden.   Cut 3 is found in at least one book (Buschius, hecatostichon) printed in type 4 with mixt hyphens, and therefore presumably not later than 1501 Jan.

p. 65. Ruloff Spot.   Type 2 is the same as that used by Zel in his undated S. Dorothea passio, etc.   Facs. in the Zeitschrift für Bücherfreunde, June 1901; see also Voulliéme, Der Buchdruck Kölns bis zum Ende des xv. Jahrhunderts, p. X.

p. 65. Joh. Helman.   He was father-in-law to H. Quentell, and at one time associated with him in business (Voulliéme, ubi supra, p. XLV); it is therefore at least possible that the book referred to in the text is a production of the Quentell printing-office.

p. 99. Nürnberg press 21.   I have made one press of these books in order to mark their close connexion with one another, but the evidence tends to show that, even though printed by one printer, the two groups may have been produced in different houses.   The imprint of no. 11030 makes it likely that the press of 1505–10 was in Pinder's own house.   The book mentioned in the Allgemeine deutsche Biographie, art. Pinder, as being printed by Peypus in Pinder's house is a Sanctae Vrsulae fraternitas, in quarto, and may be of the same date as the German edition (DA. 752) dated 1513.   But at this time Peypus was certainly the owner of an independent press.   At any rate the latter book disproves the assertion of the ADB. that Pinder died in 1509.   Nor if Peypus was printing large books for Pinder in 1505 can he well have been born in 1485, as is asserted in the ADB., art. Peypus.

p. 172. Meissen.   The right place for this town is between Metz and Heidelberg, as printing there dates from 1483 (Hain 3859).   Lotter's press is no. 2, not no. 1.

LIST OF BOOKS REFERRED TO
IN A SHORTENED FORM.

B. Ed. Böcking, Index Bibliographicus Hut-
    tenianus.   Leipzig, 1858.
Bauch. Gustav Bauch, Drucke von Frankfurt
    an der Oder (Centralblatt für Bibliotheks-
    wesen, 1898, p. 241 ff.).
BBZ. P. Heitz, Basler Büchermarken bis zum
    Anfang des 17. Jahrhunderts.
                          Strassburg, 1895.
Burger. K. Burger, Monumenta Germaniae et
    Italiae Typographica.   Berlin, 1892 ff.
    [Cited as B. in the Type-Register.]
Butsch. A. F. Butsch, Die Bücher-Ornamentik
    der Renaissance., vol. 1.   Leipzig, 1878.
Claudin, HIF. A. Claudin, Histoire de l'Im-
    primerie en France, vol. 1–2. Paris, 1900–2.
DA. G. W. Panzer, Annalen der ältern deut-
    schen Literatur, vol. 1 and Zusätze.
                          Nürnberg, 1788–1802.
Druckschriften. F. Lippmann and R. Dohme,
    Druckschriften des 15. bis 18. Jahrhunderts
    in getreuen Nachbildungen. Berlin, 1884 ff.
EBM. P. Heitz, Elsässische Büchermarken.
                          Strassburg, 1892.
H. Ludwig Hain, Repertorium bibliographi-
    cum.   Stuttgart, 1826 ff.
Heitz. Paul Heitz, Der Initialschmuck in den
    elsässischen Drucken. Strassburg, 1894–7.
KBM. P. Heitz and O. Zaretzky, Die Kölner
    Büchermarken.   Strassburg, 1898.
Kr. Paul Kristeller, Die strassburger Bücher-
    illustration.   Leipzig, 1888.
MT. J. W. Holtrop, Monuments Typographi-
    ques des Pays-Bas au XVe siècle.
                          La Haye, [1857–]1868.

Muther. Richard Muther, Die deutsche
    Bücherillustration der Gothik und Früh-
    renaissance.   München, 1884.
P. G. W. Panzer, Annales Typographici, 11
    vol.   Norimbergae, 1793–1803.
R. D. Reichling, Das Doctrinale des Alexander
    de Villa Dei.   Berlin, 1893.
S. C. Schmidt, Répertoire bibliographique
    strasbourgeois.   Strassburg, 1893–6.

SB.	Beck.	SM.	Morhard.
SF.	Flach fils.	SPa.	Prüss père.
SG.	Grüninger.	SPb.	Prüss fils.
SH.	Hüpfüff.	SS.	Jean Schott.
SK.	Knoblouch.	SSf.	Schaffener.
SKer.	Kerner.	SSr.	Schürer.
SKis.	Kistler.	SW.	Wähinger.

So. Moriz Sondheim, Die ältesten Frankfurter
    Drucke.   Frankfurt, 1885.
St. Karl Steiff, Der erste Buchdruck in Tübin-
    gen.   Tübingen, 1881.
TFS. Publications of the Type Facsimile
    Society.   Oxford, 1900 ff.
TP. Otto Thierry-Poux, Premiers Monuments
    de l'Imprimerie Française au XVe siècle.
                          Paris, 1890.
W. E. Weller, Repertorium typographicum.
                          Nördlingen, 1864 ff.
WP. Woolley Photographs. Photographs of
    early types, designed to supplement
    published examples.   (Lond. 1899 ff.)
Wz. T. Wierzbowsky, Bibliographia Polonica
    XV ac XVI ss.   Varsoviae, 1889 ff.

ABBREVIATIONS.

a.	after.	facs.	facsimile.	n.a.	not after.
b.	before.	ff.	leaves.	n.b.	not before.
bs.	broadside [1].	imp.	imperfect.	n.d.	no date.
c.	circa (about).	l., ll.	line, lines.	n.p.	no place of printing.
caps.	capital letters (majus-cules).	l.c.	lower case letters (mi-nuscules).	n.p.d.	no place or date.
				obl.	oblong [2].
cf.	confer (compare).	mm.	millimetres.	w.f.	wrong fount.

[1] An unfolded sheet in which the letterpress runs from foot to head, i.e. along the chain-lines. Open
F° is an open sheet printed in the same fashion as an ordinary folio, i.e. along the wire-lines.
[2] Used to denote single leaves less than a sheet, in which the breadth is greater than the height.

LIST OF TOWNS

1.	Mainz	(1454).
2.	Strassburg	(1459).
3.	Bamberg	(1461).
4.	Köln	(1466).
6.	Augsburg	(1468).
7.	Nürnberg	(1470).
8.	Speier	(1471).
10.	Ulm	(1473).
14.	Lübeck	(1475).
15.	Breslau	(1475).
17.	Rostock	(1476).
20.	Würzburg	(1479).
21.	Erfurt	(1479).
22.	Reutlingen	(1479).
23.	Magdeburg	(1480).
24.	Memmingen	(1480).
28.	Leipzig	(1481).
29.	München	(1482).
30.	Metz	(1482).
31.	Heidelberg	(1485).
33.	Regensburg	(1485).
35.	Münster (Westphalen)	(1486).
37.	Ingolstadt	(1487).
39.	Hagenau	(1489).
40.	Hamburg	(1490).
44.	Freiburg im Breisgau	(1493).
50.	Tübingen	(1498).
51.	Danzig	(1499).
52.	Pforzheim	(1500).

LIII.	Landshut . .	[n.b. 1501]
LIV.	Frankfurt an der Oder .	1502.
LV.	Wittenberg .	1503 Jan. 18.
LVI.	Wessobrunn .	1503 Aug. 11.
LVII.	Oppenheim .	1503 ?
LVIII.	Worms. . .	1504 Apr. 15.
LIX.	Konstanz . .	1506 Jan. 26.
LX.	Dutenstein .	1506 (Mar. 26).
LXI.	Schneeberg .	1506 Apr. 28.
LXII.	Braunschweig	1506 July.
LXIII.	Ottobeuren .	1509 Sept. 1.
LXIV.	Frankfurt am Main . . .	1511.
LXV.	Baden-Baden	1511 Nov. 20.
LXVI.	Durlach . .	1512.
LXVII.	Lahr . . .	1514 Nov. 1.
LXVIII.	Halberstadt .	1519.
LXIX.	Schlettstadt .	1519 Nov.
LXX.	Meissen . .	1520 Feb. 14.
LXXI.	Halle . . .	1520.
	[Zwiefalten . . .	1504
	Mindelheim . .	1518
	Stechelberg . .	1519 Sept.]

I. MAINZ.

3. Peter Schöffer, the elder
10. Johann Schöffer   1503 April 8.
12. Friedrich Heumann   1509 July 17.
13. Peter Schöffer, the younger, first press   1512 Feb. 24.

---

iij. PETER SCHÖFFER.

TYPES : see part i.

DEVICE. a, the two shields, as in the fifteenth century.

9842. 1502 Dec. 20. Psalterium. [BIBLE.] F°. P. VII. 406. 2. Types 1, 2; a.

[For continuation see press 10.]

x. JOHANN SCHÖFFER.

TYPES. Type 1 = iij. 5, the type of 1462 bible, Burger 74; 118-119 mm.—Type 2 = iij. 6, law commentary type of 1468, WP. 1; 92 mm.—Type 3 = iij. 8, first schwabacher, Burger 75; double hyphen, D tipt over, much mixture of sorts from 2; 91 mm.—Type 4 = iij. 9, smaller than 5, but like it; church text; 147 mm. Many letters from 5 in it at this period.—Type 5 = iij. 7, broad church text; facs. Druckschriften 27, Butsch I. 81. Large ¶ in and after 1515. 5*, used in 1520, is a recast on a kerned body.—Type 6 = iij. 2, larger psalter type of 1457; short letters 9 mm. Cf. Lacher 1.—Type 7, second text schwabacher, like Flach jun. 12, Knoblouch 18, etc.; ¶ with the last stroke turned back round the foot; 94-95 mm. Facs. Butsch I. 81, Druckschriften 27.—Type 8, latin text gothic, 80 mm.; open V like Flach jun. 3.—Type 9, small latin text gothic, style of Quentell 5, but has round h; cf. Hüpfüff 6, Knoblouch 9, Gran 5, &c.; 71-72 mm.—Type 10, small german type like Kirchheim ij. 2, Hüpfüff 3, Bumgart 5, &c.; 82 mm.—Type 11, large text latin gothic, kerned.—Type 12, middle german roman, as Prüss sen. 14, Hüpfüff 10, &c.; hyphen double at first, mixt in and after 1518, except in the Valerius Probus (no. 9878) which is probably after 1520; at first has greek form of colon and ę only, but œ; ℭ too small; 87 mm. Facs. Butsch I. 80.—Type 13 = iij. 1; smaller psalter type of 1457; short letters 7 mm.—Type 14, small schwabacher, like Knoblouch 6, Schott 6, &c.; probably about 78 mm.—Type 15, large roman capitals, thick, like M. Schurer 13; 8 mm. Facs. Butsch I. 80.—Type 16, small german roman like Grüninger 23, Prüss sen. 16, Quentell 13, &c.; long double hyphen; 66 mm.—Type 17, small gothic like Quentell 6, but round h; double hyphen; cf. Prüss sen. 10, Knoblouch 4, &c. —Type 18, small aldine roman like Anshelm 11, &c.; 88 mm.—Type 19, text roman, archaistic in style; very like a fount of Adam Petri, but has double hyphen; 112 mm.—Type 20, medium large, like Ratdolt 9 (Burger 5, colophon), &c.—Type 21, small italic, like Knoblouch 22, Heil 6: 88 mm.—Type 22, very large roman caps., 13 mm., as M. Schürer 12, Knoblouch 17, &c.—First greek type, 1515; second, 1520; both resemble those of Knoblouch.

Type 7, see fig. 53; 8, fig. 38; 9, fig. 45; 10, fig. 64; *12, fig. 8; 14, fig. 63; *15, fig. 1; 16, fig. 11; 17, fig. 46; 18, fig. 9; *19, fig. 5; 20, fig. 32 (1); *21, fig. 13.

BORDERS. A, folio, historical scenes.—Bc, an octavo border-device, white open style.— Cd, quarto border-device, similar to Bc, but architectural: Butsch I. 81.—In Nov. 1518 is used a fine X border with the arms of Albrecht v. Brandenburg (Butsch I. 80); the others (from 1514) are mostly black-grounded pieces with degraded grotesques.

DEVICES. a = Peter Schöffer; the two shields hung on a bough.—b, found in an initial D of set β used in the Livy of 1514 (e.g. on ff. cxxxvi[b], cccxciii[b]).—c, see border B.— d, see border C.

18

9843. 1503 Apr. 8. HERMES Trismegistus: de potestate dei. 4°. P. VII. 406. 3.
Types 1, 2; a. [One copy on vellum.]

9844. 1503. Informatio de genealogia S. Barbarae. [BARBARA.] 4°. P. VII. 407. 4.
Types 3, 4.

9845. 1505 March 6. Römische Historie aus Tito Livio gezogen. [LIVIVS.] F°.
DA. 559. Types 5, 6, 7; cuts; a.

9846. 1506 April 11. EXERCITIVM puerorum grammaticale. 4°. P. VII. 407. 5. Types
5, 6, 8, 9; cut.

9847. 1507 Sept. 1. Missale Moguntinum. [LIT.] F°. P. VII. 407. 6. Types 4, 5,
6, 8; cuts.

9848. 1508 April 2. Bambergische Halsgerichtsordnung. [BAMBERG.] F°. DA.
616. Types 5, 6, 7, 10 ; cuts.

9849. 1508. Joh. ESSLER; speculum astrologorum. 4°. P. VII. 408. 9. Types 5, 6,
8; diagr.; a.

9850. 1508. Directorium missae Moguntinum. [LIT.] 4°. P. VII. 408. 10. Types
5, 6, 9; cut.

9851. 1508 Oct. 28. Bambergische Halsgerichtsordnung. [BAMBERG.] F°. DA.
618. Types 5, 6, 7; cuts; a.

9852. 1509 May 16.   Reformation der Stadt Frankfurt a/M. [FRANKFORT.] F°.
DA. 648. Types 5, 7; cuts ; a; Δ.

9853. 1510 Aug. 10. Bambergische Halsgerichtsordnung. [BAMBERG.] F°. DA.
677. Types 5, 6, 7; cuts.

9854. n. d. [1511 ?] Joh. PFEFFERKORN: Handspiegel wider die Juden. 4°. DA.
693. Types 6, 7, 11.

9855. [a. 1512 Sept. 11.] Achtserklärung gegen Emich zu Leiningen. [GER-
MANY.] bs. W. 722. Type 7; Δ.

9855A. 1514 March 14. HORTVLVS animae. 8°. [Not DA. 770 = W. 835.] Types
6, 8; cuts; X; αβ.

9856. 1514 Aug. 23. Römische Historie Titi Livii. [LIVIVS.] F°. DA. 788.
Types 5, 6, 7; cuts; Y; b; αβΔ.

9857. [a. 1515 Apr. 24.] Ausschreiben der Stadt WORMS wider Franz von Sickingen. 4°. W. 877. Types 5, 6, 7; cut.

9858. 1515 July 12. TRITHEIM: annales regum Francorum. [For Joh. Haselberger.] F°. P. VII. 409. 20. Types 5, 6, 12, gk. i; cuts; a; α.

9859. 1516. Psalterium. [BIBLE.] F°. Types 6, 13; αΔ.

9860. 1516. Joh. Hartlieb; de generibus ebriosorum. [GENERA.] 4°. P. IX. 115.
93. Types 5, 6, 12, 14; cut.

9861. 1517 Aug. 21. Heinrich STROMER: Regiment. 4°. DA. 844. Types 5,
6, 7, 14; X; β.

9862. [n. b. 1517.] Des Römischen Königs Verantwortung auf die Klage so der
König von Frankreich über ihn gethan hat. [MAXIMILIAN.] 4°. W. 398.
Types 5, 6, 7.

MAINZ. x.
J. Schöffer.

9863. 1518 Nov. to 1519 March 15. LIVIVS: ab urbe condita libri. F°. P.VII.
     411.29. Types 12,15,16; A X; ┌δε⸴.
9864. [a. 1519 March 1.] Ulr. von HUTTEN: Dialogus oder ein Gespräch
     Febris genannt. 4°. W.1195. B.xxi b. Type 7.
9865. 1519 April. Vlr. de HVTTEN; de guaiaci medicina. 4°. P. VII. 411. 30.
     B.xxiii. 1. Types 12,15,16; cuts; ┌.
9866. 1519 Sept. Vlr.de HVTTEN: inuectiuae et opuscula. 4°. P.VIII.299. 1. B.
     xxiv.1. Types 12,15,16 [caps.]; ┌.
9867. 1520 Feb. FLORILEGIVM ex diuersis opusculis. 4°. Types 5,7,13,15,16
     [caps.],17,18, gk.ij; β.
9868. 1520 March. De unitate ecclesiae conseruanda. [HENRY IV.] 4°. P.VII.
     412.34. B.xxv. 1. Types 12,15,16 [caps.]; a; α┌.
9869. 1520 March. Conr. PEVTINGER: inscriptiones uetustae in Aug. Vind. F°.P.
     VII.413.37. Types 15,16 [caps.],19; cuts; A; a.
9870. 1520 March. TERENTIVS. 8°. Types (15),16, gk.ij; Bc X; a.
9871. [a. 1520 March 7.] ERASMVS: das Sprüchwort, Man muss entweder ein
     König oder ein Narr geboren werden. 4°. W.1364. Types 5,5*,7,20;
     Cd; α┌.
9872. 1520 Apr. Vlr. de HVTTEN: dialogi. 4°. P.VII.412.36. B.xxvi.1. Types
     12,15,16 [caps.],gk.ij; cut; ┌.
9873. 1520 [a. May 1]. In Edu. Leeum Erphordiensium epigrammata. [LEEVS.]
     4°. P.VII.413.40. Types 15,19,21; X; a.
9874. [a. 1520 May 27.] Vlr. de HVTTEN: de schismate exstinguendo. B.xxix. 1.
     4°. Types 15,16 [caps.],19; ┌. [Leaves 1–12 only.]
9875. 1520 Aug. Ioh. HVTTICHIVS: collectanea antiquitatum Moguntiae reperta-
     rum. F°.P.VII. 412. 35. Types 15, 16 [caps.], 19, 21, 22; cuts; A; a.
9876. [a. 1520 Oct. 22.] Beschreibung der Einreitung und Krönung Karls V.
     [CHARLES V.] 4°. DA. 995c. Types 7, 20.
9877. 1520. ERASMVS: die Sileni Alcibiadis verteutscht. 4°. DA. 978. Types
     5, 7, 14; X; ┌.
9878. n. d. [a. 1520?] Valerius PROBVS: de literis antiquis opusculum. 4°. P.IX.
     194. 354 ? Types 12, 15, 21 [caps.]; Δ.

APPENDIX.

   Type 1 = J. Schöffer 5.—Type 2 = J. Schöffer 8, with an additional I and two sorts of double
hyphen; in all the books except the Breviary a round comma and a strange sort of semicolon
are found; 80–81 mm. Cf. Knoblouch 2.—Type 3 = J. Schöffer 9; two kinds of double
hyphen, one, very large, used by Schöffer; ¶; 72–73 mm. Caps. of type 4 are found mixt in 3.
Cf. Knoblouch 9.—Type 4 = J. Schöffer 17; round h, double hyphen; 64 mm. Cf. Knoblouch 4.

   Border pieces (Y) the same as some of those in Schöffer's books c. 1514–1520.

   Initials. α, like Prüss H; 29 mm. A, Q only.—Δ, a B of Strassburg style, 19 mm.

9879. n.d. Breuiarium ad morem Seueriani collegii Erphordiensis, pars hiemalis.
     [LIT.] 8°. Types 1–4; Δ.
9880. n.d. Ordinarius Benedictinorum obseruantiae Bursfeldensis. [BURSFELD.]
     4°. H. 12059. Types 1, 2; cut; Y; α.
9881. n.d. Martyrologium ordinis s. Benedicti. [BENEDICTINES.] 4°. Types 1, 2, 5.
9882. n.d. Caeremoniale Benedictinorum obseruantiae Bursfeldensis. [BURS-
     FELD.] 4°. H. 4883. Types 1, 2, 5; cut; Y; α.
9883. n.d. Regula ordinis s. Benedicti. [BENEDICT.] 4°. Types 1, 2,5; cut; Y; α.

xij. FRIEDRICH HEUMANN.

No book by Heumann dated in any year other than 1509 is recorded. See DA. 651 (W. 511), 664; W. 486, 498, 4075; P. VII. 409. 14, 15; ix. 538. 12b (the earliest book), and ix. 540. 111 b.

TYPES. Type 1, square church text; some capitals are copied from the type of the 36-line bible.—Type 2, latin text gothic, like Quentell 7, Gran 8, &c. (fig. 37); double hyphen, thick ¶; V as Quentell, notas Flach 3 or Joh. Schöffer 8; 81–2 mm.—Type 3, small type, like Heinrich von Neuss 4 or Köbel 2; about 63–4 mm.; tailed h; cf. Jac. Schmidt 5.—Type 4, schwabacher like Schott 12, or Köbel 8; about 95 mm.—Types 1, 4 were afterwards used at Speier by Jacob Schmidt, and the lombardic initials also passed into his hands.

INITIAL. An initial I, containing the Crucifixion, 38 mm.; called α.

9884. 1509 Aug. 29. Gabr. BIEL: sermo passionis dominicae. 4°. P. VII. 408. 13.
     Types 1, 2, 3; cut; α.

9884A. 1509. Regimen sanitatis salernitanum, lat. et germ. [ACAD.] 4°. DA.
     651; W. 511. Types 1–4; cut.

[9884B. n. d. See no. 3273 (part i; types 1, 2).]

xiij. PETER SCHÖFFER, THE YOUNGER.

[See Weller 737 (15 Feb. 1512), 791 (1513 March 1), 783 (1513 Dec. 20), &c. See also below: Worms.]

II. STRASSBURG.

12. Johann Reinhard, of Grüningen, called Grüninger.
14. Johann Prüss, the elder.
15. Printer of Jordanus de Quedlinburg.
20. Georg Husner, second press, or an anonymous successor.
21. Matthias Hüpfüff.
22. Bartholomaeus Kistler.
25. Johann Knoblouch (1504 July 3 the first certain date).
26. Johann Schott, first press.

29. Martin Flach, the younger	1501 Jan. 8.
30. Johann Wähinger	1502 Aug. 31.
31. Wilhelm Schaffener, from Dutenstein, third press	1508 March 15.
32. Matthias Schürer	1508 June 8.
33. Johann Schott, from Freiburg i/ Br., third press	1510 May 24.
34. Reinhard Beck, first press	1511 Sept. 12.
35. Reinhard Beck, from Baden-Baden, third press	1512 March 18.
36. Johann Prüss, the younger	1512.
37. Wilhelm Schaffener, from Lahr, fifth press	1515 Aug. 31.
38. Conrad Kerner	1517.
39. Ulrich Morhard	1520 Sept.

xij. JOHANN REINHARD, CALLED GRÜNINGER.

TYPES. Types 4 (very minute); 5 (german text; in and after 1516 this type has roman letters from type 22 in it, and on 28 Aug. 1520 has flourishes in the Teuerdank style; facs. Kr. Abb. 22, 24; Butsch I. 72; Muther 238–247); 17 (middle large round, short letters $4\frac{1}{2}$ mm.; gradually a pointed ſ comes in, at first in st only (Coccinius, 1506), but in full measure, together with a pointed f, in the Caesar of March 1507; about the same time the curly-tailed h and a new V come in (23 Mar. 1507); when type 31 appears, the square ſ is again found in places; facs. Kr. Abb. 22, 24 lines 3–4; Muther 139–143); 19 (rounded canon; short letters $8\frac{1}{2}$ mm.; facs. Kr. Abb. 22, 24, lines 1–2; Muther 138; Butsch I. 72); 22 (middle roman, narrow; double hyphen, 89 mm.); 23 (small german roman, 63–64 mm.; facs. Muther 140, 143); 25 (latin text gothic like 13, except the capitals; 80 mm.); for all these see part 1.— Type 25* = 25, trimmed and recast on a smaller body with kerning; 77 mm.—Type 26, text roman; 105 mm.; facs. Muther 139–143.—Type 27, large text, face rather smaller than 14; usually kerned, 90 mm.; elsewhere (perhaps leaded) 10 ll. = 57 mm.—Type 28, very small gothic, with quasi-roman caps. (once with caps. of 29); 55 mm.—Type 29, small gothic, lyonnese in character; smaller face than 15; 60–61 mm.—Type 30, another small quasi-French fount, face rather larger than 15; like Knoblouch 20; tailed h; 66 mm.—Type 31, large type, rounder and more open than 17; caps. mostly like Ratdolt 9, partly as type 17 above; has square-ended ſ, but the pointed ſt from 17 is often used in it. 10 ll. = 79 mm. Facs. Butsch I. 72.—First greek type (gk. i), small and poor; second greek (gk. ij), finer and larger.— Small hebrew (hb. i.); 99 mm.; larger (hb. ij.) two letters only found in Feb. 1504.

Type 5, see fig. 54; 17, see fig. 28; 23, see fig. 11; 26, see fig. 3; 30, see fig. 48.

BORDERS. A, quarto, white ground; two winged boys at foot.—B, folio, style of A; facs. Kr. Abb. 22.—C, large quarto, perhaps border-device, dotted ground; wodows at foot, owl at top; facs. Kr. Abb. 24.—D, size of C; stripy ground; at top four dancing boys under arches.

—E, folio, style of Silv. Otmar B ; facs. Butsch I. 72.—F, size of C, D : at foot a half-woman ; two men drag a rope from her around pillars.

DEVICES.   Device b [1494], see EBM. pl. I. no. 4 ; c, EBM. I. 1 ; d, EBM. I. 3.   See also border C.

INITIALS.   α (40–50 mm.), β (24–26 mm.), Γ (17–18 mm.), δ (14–15 mm.), see Heitz, alphabet 1, 2, 3, 4 respectively ; the I of these sets are mostly found on his pl. XII (XII. 7 = β ; XII. 8 = α).—ε, black ground with floral ornament ; letters shaded ; size varies from 24 mm. (D) to 34 mm. (I)—ζ, similar to ε, but 14 mm. only.—н, similar to ζ, but 10 mm. only.— ꟻ, whole words (Tityre, Quia, Quid, Arma virumque cano), 18–25 mm., dotted ground.— θ, Strassburg style ; animals and flowers ; dotted black ground ; 26–29 mm.—ι, a series rather than a set, Strassburg style, with dotted or black ground (the dotted ground often prints black, being clogged with ink) ; there is a very large number of varieties, and the size varies from 20 to 26 mm., with many sizes between ; the smaller tail off into those called κ, so it is often scarcely possible to distinguish them.   See Muther 238–247.—κ, like ι, but 17–18 mm. only : often hardly distinguishable from ι.—λ, twenty-seven very large initials with scenes from the gospels (25–101 mm.) ; first used in the Evangelibuch of 1515 ; in this and other books 25 are found ; 18 of D, 3 of A and I, and one E.   Facs. of one D, Kr. p. 40, Abb. 18.—м, white ground, 41–42 mm. ; D, with two lovers ; I, Adam and Eve, no other letters.—ν, large, Strassburg style, dotted ground, 43 mm.   Facs., Heitz, alphabet 5.—ξ, large, ground faintly dotted, style resembling ε ; A, 46 mm. ; W, 40 × 45 mm. ; no other letters ; Cf. Prüss sen. ζ. ο, style of α–δ, 27 mm.

9886.   1501 Aug. 25.   BOETHIVS : de consolatione philosophiae. F°. P. VI. 27. 5 ; SG. 57.   Types 4, 17, 19, 22, 23, 26 ; c ; αβΓδ.

9887.   [a. 1502 Aug. 23.]   WIMPHELING : defensio Germaniae.   4°.   P. VII. 62. 32. Types 17, 22, 23, 26 ; cut ; βΓ.   [Impressum Fribu.]

9888.   1502 Aug. 28.   Vergili opera. [VIRGILIVS.]   F°. P. VI. 27. 12 ; SG. 60.   Types 4, 17, 22, 23, 26, gk. i ; cuts ; Y ; c ; αβΓδ.

9889.   1503 Mar. 18.   TERENTIVS : comoediae sex. F°. P. VI. 29. 24 ; SG. 61.   Types 4, 17, 19, 23, 26, 27, gk. i ; cuts ; Y ; αβΓδ.

9890.   1504 Feb. 3.   BOLLANVS : tractatus de conceptione B.V.M. 4°. P. VI. 30. 36 ; SG. 65.   Types 17, 25, 27 ; cuts ; c ; βΓ.

9891.   1504 Feb. 23.   Greg. REISCH : margarita philosophica. 4°. P. VI. 30. 37 ; SG. 66.   Types 17, 23, 26, gk. i, hb. i, ij ; cuts, diagr. ; βΓδ.

9892.   1504 Aug. 3.   Ioh. HVG : quadriuium ecclesiae.   F°. P. VI. 30. 38 ; SG. 67. Types 17, 19, 25, 26 ; cuts ; c ; αβΓε.

9893.   1504 Sept. 9.   Ioh. HVG : der heiligen Kirche und des R. Reichs Wagenfuhre. F°. DA. 550 ; SG. 68.   Types 5, 17, 19, 25 ; cuts ; αβδ.

9894.   n. d. [c. 1504.]   Hier. VEHVS : boemicus triumphus.   4°. SG. 69.   Types 26, gk. i ; cuts.

9895.   1505 Mar. 4.   Ioh. Garson : de miseria humana. [GARZONI.]   4°. P. VI. 32. 50 ; SG. 70.   Types 17, 19, 26 ; c ; βε.

9896.   1505.   Ioh. BERKEN : uita ss. Geruasii et Prothasii.   4°. P. XI. 356.   49 b ; SG. 73.   Types 5, 17, 25 ; cut ; βε.

9897.   n. d. [c. 1505.]   Iac. LOCHER : apologia contra Georgium Zingel. 4°.   Types 17, 26, gk. i ; cut ; Γ.

9898.   n. d. [c. 1505.]   Barthol. de Vsingen : figurae Donati. [DONATVS.] 4°.   Part i. no. 780.   Types 17, 25.

9898 A.   n. d. [c. 1505 ?]   Ein Hausrat. [JAHR.]   4°.   SH. 88.   Types 5, 17 ; cuts ; δ.

9899.   1506 June 23.   Paulus de CITADINIS : tractatus iuris patronatus.   4°. P. VI. 34. 66 : SG. 76.   Types 17, 25 ; cut ; βΓδζ.

9900.   [a. 1506 July 17.]   Mich. COCCINIVS : de imperii a graecis ad germanos translatione.   4°. P. VI. 33. 64 ; SG. 77.   Types 15, 17, 26, gk. i ; βε.

9901. 1507 Mar. 7.   Iulius der erste römische Kaiser, von seinen Kriegen.
  [CAESAR.] F°. DA. 594; SG. 78. Types 5, 17, 19, gk. i; cuts; Y ; αβε.
9902. 1507 Mar. 23. Römische Historie aus Tito Livio. [LIVIVS.] F°. DA. 593;
  SG. 79. Types 5, 17, 19; cuts; Y; αβſε.
9903. 1507 Aug. 26. Alcimus AVITVS: libri sex. 8°. SG. 81. Types 23, 28; d; н.
9904. [nb. 1507.] Gualterus LVDD: speculi orbis declaratio. F°. SG. 85. Types
  17, 25, 27, gk. i; diagr.
9905. n.d. [c. 1507–8.] Manuale Vergilianum. [VIRGILIVS.] 8°. Types 23 [caps.],
  28; cuts; βϱнſ.
9906. 1508 [a. Mar. 1]. Ioh. Adelphus Mulichius: margarita facetiarum. [MU-
  LICH.] 4°. P. VI. 39. 109; SG. 97. Types 5, 22; βſδεϱ.
9907. 1508 Mar. 31. Greg. REISCH: margarita philosophica. 4°. P. VI. 39. 107;
  SG. 87. Types 5, 15, 17, 19, 22, 25*, gk. i, hb. i; cuts, diagr.; βε.
9908. 1508 Apr. 8. PLAVTVS: comoediae. 8°. P. VI. 39. 106; SG. 88. Types 23
  [caps.], 28; cuts; d; ϱн.
9909. 1508 [a. May 17]. Geruasius SOVPHERVS: Henrici iv. Imp. bellum contra
  Saxones heroico carmine descriptum. 4°. P. VI. 39. 110; SG. 99. Types
  15, 22, gk. i, βε.
9910. 1508 [a. July 23]. Vdalr. ZASIVS: quaestiones de paruulis Iudaeorum bapti-
  zandis. 4°. P. VI. 40. 113; SG. 98. Types 15, 17, 22; ε.
9911. 1508 Sept. 1. Hug Schapler. [HUGH Capet.] F°. DA. 626; SG. 93. Types 5,
  17, 19; cuts; αβε.
9912. 1508 Sept. 8. HANS von Bühel: von eines Königs Tochter von Frankreich.
  F°. DA. 627; SG. 94. Types 5, 17, 19; cuts ; c; βſε.
9913. 1508. Der FREVDANK. 4°. DA. 627b; SG. 95. Types 5, 15, 17, 19; cuts.
9914. 1509 Mar. 18. Von der neuen Welt und fremden Inseln. [VESPUCCI.] 4°.
  SG. 101. Types 5, 17; cuts; βε.
9915. 1509. HYLACOMYLVS: cosmographiae introductio. 4°. P. VI. 44. 150; SG.
  109. Types 17, 25; diagr.; βſε.
9916. 1509. Ioh. Adelphus Mulichius: margarita facetiarum. [MUELICH.] 4°. P.
  VI. 44. 148; SG. 112. Types 17, 22; βε.
9917. 1509 Aug. 31. GLOBVS mundi. 4°. P. VI. 44. 149; SG. 104. Types 17, 25;
  cuts ; ε.
9918. 1509 Sept. 7. BOCCACCIO: Cento novella, das Buch der hundert Historien.
  F°. DA. 661 ; SG. 107. Types 5, 17, 19; cuts ; Y; αβε.
9919. 1509 Dec. 29. MVRNER: logica memoratiua, chartiludium logicae. 4°. P.
  VI. 43. 146; SG. 108. Types 17, 19, 22, 25; cuts, diagr; d; αβε.
9920. [a. 1509 Dec. 29.] Murner: MODVS practicandi. 4°. Types 17, 22; β. [Appen-
  dix to no. 9919.]
9921. 1511 Feb. TERENTIVS: comoediae. 8°. P. XI. 359. 210b; SG. 119. Types
  23 [caps.], 28 [29]; cuts; d; н.
9922. 1511 Apr. HYLACOMYLVS: introductio manuductionem praestans. 4°. P.
  VI. 52. 213; SG. 121. Type 22.
9923. [a. 1512 May 1.] Mich. COCCINIVS: de rebus in Italia gestis. F°. P. XI. 508.
  83b. Types 17, 22, 25, 30; εϱ.
9924. 1512 May 31. REISCH: margarita philosophica. 4°. P. VI. 55. 244; SG. 124.
  Types 5, 17, 22, 25, 29, gk. i, hb. i; cuts, diagr.; A; βεϱ.
9925. 1512 Aug. 23. GEILER: das Schiff des Heils. F°. DA. 708; W. 684; SG.
  125. Types 5, 17, 19; cuts; βεθΔ.

9926. 1512 Sept. 7. GEILER: Predigt der Himmelfahrt Mariae. F°. DA. 709;
SG. 126. Types 5, 17, 19; cuts; βϝεζθΔ.

9927. 1512 Nov. 24. Herm. von SACHSENHEIM: die Mörin. F°. DA. 735; SG.
127. Types 5, 17, 19; cuts; βεζθΔ.

9928. [a. 1513 Oct. 5.] Triumphus Emanuelis regis de infidelibus. [EMANUEL.]
4°. Type 22; κ.

9929. [a. 1513 Nov. 14.] GEILER: Passion des Herrn Jesu. F°. DA. 746 (cf. W.
827). Types 5, 17, 19; cuts; Y; βεθιΔ.

9929A. 1514 Feb. 25. Historie von Kaiser Karolus Sohn Loher. [LOTHAIRE.] F°.
DA. 788c; SG. 133. Types 5, 17, 19; cuts; βεθι.

9930. 1514 Mar. 24. GEILER: sermones. F°. P. VI. 64. 317; SG. 135. Types 17,
19, 25; cuts; αβεθι.

9931. 1514 Mar. 25. GEILER: das irrige Schaf. F°. DA. 773; SG. 136. Types
5, 17, 19; cuts; βεθιΔ.

9932. 1514 Aug. 5. MURNER: andächtige geistliche Badenfahrt. 4°. DA. 798;
SG. 137. Types 5, 17, 30; cuts.

9933. 1514 Aug. 10. Chr. Druthmari expositio in Matthaeum. [BIBLE.] P. VI.
64. 318; SG. 138. Types 17, 22, 25, 27, 30, gk. ij; cuts; αεθι.

9934. 1514 Sept. 4. Der weise RITTER. F°. W. 850; SG. 140. Types 5, 17, 19;
cuts; αβεθιΔ.

9935. 1515 Jan. 24, Mar. 19. REISCH: margarita philosophica. 4°. P. VI.
69. 353; SG. 142. Types 5, 17, 22, 25, 27, 29, 30; cuts, diagr.; A;
βζικ.

9936. 1515 Aug. 29. Ein kurzweiliges Lesen von Tyll EULENSPIEGEL. 4°. SG.
145. Types 5, 17; cuts; εθικΔ.

9937. 1515. Das Evangelibuch. [BIBLE.] F°. DA. 815; W. 894; SG. 147. Types
5, 17, 19; cuts; αεθιλ.

9938. 1516 Feb. 1, 24. GEILER: die Ameise. F°. DA. 834c; W. 996; SG. 149.
Types 5, 17, 19; cuts; Y; εθιλ.

9939. 1516 July 16. Der heiligen Altväter Leben. [VITAE.] F°. DA. 837; SG.
151. Types 5, 17, 19; cuts; Y; αβεθι.

9940. 1516 Sept. 20. Hübsche Historie von eines Bürgers Sohne aus Cypern
geboren. [CYMON.—For Joh. Haselberger.] F°. DA. 853b; W. 1000;
SG. 153. Types 5, 17, 19; cuts; ει.

9941 a. 1517 Feb. 4. GEILER: zwanzig Sermonen und Predigten (A–T).
b. 1517 Mar. 24. id.: die Brosämlein (a–v). F°. DA. 865; SG. 154. Types
5, 17, 19; cuts; B; εθι.

9942. 1517 Aug. 28. Evangelia mit Auslegung Joh. Geilers. [BIBLE.] F°. DA.
862; SG. 156. Types 5, 17, 19; cuts; BY; αεθικλ.

9943. n. d. [c. 1517–18.] Epistulae obscurorum uirorum. [GRATIVS.] 4°. P. IX.
174. 127. Types 25, 29; cut; κ. [Impressum Bernae.]

9944 a. 1518 Jan. 27. GEILER: Das Buch der Sünden des Mundes (A–P). Types
15, 17, 19; cuts; B; εθι.
b. 1518 Mar. 6. id.: Alphabet in 23 Predigten (a–g). F°. DA. 894; W.
1049; SG. 157. Types 5, 17, 19; cuts; αιμνξΔ.

9945. 1518 Aug. 1. GEILER: sermones et uarii tractatus. F°. P. VI. 86. 502; SG.
159. Types 17, 19, 25, 27, 31; cuts; C; αθικμνξοΔ.

9946. 1518 Sept. 7. Henr. STROMER: obseruationes aduersus pestilentiam. 4°. P.
VI. 87. 503; SG. 161. Types 17, 25, 27, 30; A; ικ?

STRASS-
BURG.
xij. Joh.
Reinhard.

9947. n.d.[c. 1518.] IOANNES de S. Wandalino: Verkündung von dem Kloster zu
S. Marien der alten bei Trier. 4°. W. 120. Types 5, 17; cut; ι.

9948. n.d.[c. 1518.] IOANNES de S. Wandalino: fidelis narratio de monasterio B.
Mariae ad litus martyrum. 4°. Types 17, 25, 30; cut; ι.

9949. 1519 Feb. 1. GEILER: sermones de arbore humana, etc. F°. P. VI. 90. 532;
SG. 162. Types 17, 19, 25, 31; cuts; DY; εθικο.

9950. 1519 Mar. 24. BOCCACCIO: Cento Nouella. F°. DA. 963; SG. 163. Types
5, 17, 19; cuts; Y; αεικο.

9951. 1519 July 24. Lor. FRIESS: Tractat der Wildbäder. 4°. DA. 938; W. 1255;
SG. 165. Types 5, 31; cut; ικ?

9952. 1519 Aug. 28. Hieronymus von BRAUNSCHWEIG: Distillirbuch (composita).
F°. DA. 935; SG. 167. Types 5, 19, 31; cuts; ικο.

9953 a. 1520 March 17. Hans von Wildeck: Frage und Antwort der Zehn Gebote
(A–K). Types 5, 19, 31; cuts; F; ικ.

b. 1520 Aug. 31. Marcus von Weida: nützliche Lehre wie man beten soll
(L–S). F°. W. 1384; SG. 171. Types 5, 31; cuts; ικ. [Print Room.]

9954. 1520 Mar. 18. GEILER: Predigt von den drei Marien. F°. DA. 968 d; W.
1392; SG. 170. Types 5, 19, 31; cuts; ι.

9955. 1520 Aug. 23. GEILER: Narrenschiff. F°. DA. 968; SG. 172. Types 5,
19, 31; cuts; DY; ιλ.

9956. 1520 Aug. 28. Ioh. ADELPHVS: Barbarossa. F°. DA. 998; SG. 173. Types
5, 19, 31; cuts; ιοΔ.

1520 Aug. 31. See 1520 March 17.

9957. 1520 Nov. 24. Murner: von Doctor Luthers Lehre und Predigten.
[LUTHER.] 4°. DA. 987; SG. 175. Types 5, 31: A; ι.

9958. 1520 Dec. 13. Murner: von dem Papsttum wider LUTHER. 4°. DA. 988;
SG. 177. Types 5, 31; A; ι. [Imp.; A–E only.]

9959. 1520 Dec. 24. Murner: an den Adel deutscher Nation wider LUTHER. 4°.
DA. 989; SG. 178. Types 5, 31; A; ι.

xiv. JOHANN PRÜSS, THE ELDER.

TYPES. Types 4 (square canon, short letters 9 mm.); 10 (small, like Quentell 6, but round
h and single hyphen; 65 mm.); 11 (small text, like Knoblouch 9; round h, double hyphen
different from that in the Caepolla of 1490, and capitals of 10 mixt in it; 71 mm.);
12 (schwabacher text with single hyphen, D like S reversed till 1508; afterwards a new
A and D like those of Kistler 1, Joh. Schott 1, and a comma sloping backwards; in the Missale
of 1508 both sorts of D are used; 95 mm.); 13 (square church text like Quentell 10; short letters
5 mm.); 14 (middle german roman, double hyphen at this period; 86 mm.); 15 (square church
type larger than 13, seemingly the same as Joh. Schott 3; short letters 6½ mm.: cf. G. Stuchs
10); for all these see part i.—Type 16, small german roman, single hyphen, ę and æ; like
Knoblouch 13; 75 mm.—Type 17, smaller square church text, many Mainz caps., short
letters 4 mm.; cf. Quentell 14.—Type 18, text german roman, like Grüninger 26, Knoblouch 8;
double hyphen; 100 mm.—Type 19, large text schwabacher like Joh. Otmar 17; comma sloping
backwards; cf. Beck 2. 106 mm.—Type 20, large text, as xx. 10; E differs from xv. 7, Grüninger
20, Gran 10, &c.; 87 mm.—Greek type, like ij. of press 12.

Type *4, see fig. 15; 10, see fig. 46; 11, see fig. 45; 12, see fig. 54; *13, see fig. 18; 14, see fig. 8;
*15, see fig. 16; 16, see fig. 11; *17, see fig. 20; 18, see fig. 3; 19, see fig. 52; 20, see fig. 34 (different E).

DEVICES. a (1507) EBM. VIII. 3; b (1508) EBM. VIII. 2; c (1509) EBM. VIII. 1.

INITIALS. α, a pictorial set designed for a psalter and missal, 61–62 mm.: B (Beatus uir),
C (Cantate), D (Dixi custodiam), D (Dixit insipiens), E (Exultate deo), S (Saluum fac), T (Te
igitur); to these must be added A (Ad te domine leuaui), though 50 mm. only. Compare

Furter's set with the same subjects.—β, calligraphic versals, 29 mm.—Γ, white Maiblumen, 20 mm.—δ, ditto, 27–30 mm.—ε, ditto, 52–54 mm.—ζ, black ground, large; same style as H, but the letters shaded as in Grüninger ε; 45–47 mm.—H, like Grüninger ε, black ground, but no shading on the letters; 31–3 mm.—θ, black Maiblumen, 27–28 mm. Δ initials include a canon T in the Fyner style (62 mm.), with plain white ground (used 1505, 1508, and 1509).

STRASS-
BURG.
xiv. Joh.
Prüss sen.

9960. 1501 Dec. 20. BEROALDUS: declamatio de tribus fratribus. 4°. P.VI. 27. 6; SPa. 32. Types 13, 14, 15; cuts.

9961. 1502 [a. Jan. 3]. Iod. BADIVS: nauiculae stultiferae. 4°. P.VI. 28. 16; SPa. 36. Types 13, 14, 15; cuts.

9962. 1502 Jan. 14. Vocabularius variorum terminorum. [DICT.] 4°. P.VI. 28. 17; SPa. 33. Types 13, 14, 15; cuts.

9963. 1502. Die heimliche Offenbarung Iohannis. F°. W. 238. Types 12, 13, 15. [Gedruckt durch Iheronimum Greff den Maler. Fragments in Print Room.]

9964. [c. 1502.] Apocalypsis cum figuris Hieronymi Greff. F°. Types 12, 13, 15. [Fragments in Print Room.]

9965. 1503 Jan. 29. TERENTIVS: comoediae sex. 4°. P.VI. 29. 25; SPa. 37. Types 13–16; cuts.

9966. [a. 1503 Feb. 13.] Wig. TREBELLIVS: concordia curatorum et fratrum mendicantium. 4°. SPa. 38. Types 15, 16.

9967. 1503 Mar. 23. Baptista Mantuanus: bucolica seu adulescentia. [SPAGNU-OLI.] 4°. P.VI. 29. 26; SPa. 39. Types 14, 15, 16; cut.

9968. 1503 Sept. 7. Alb. de EYBE: margarita poetica. 4°. P.VI. 29. 27; SPa. 40. Types 14, 15, 16.

9969. 1503. MAGNINVS: regimen sanitatis. 4°. P.VI. 29. 28; SPa. 41. Types 14, 15, 16.

9970. n.d. [c. 1503?] Missale speciale. [LIT.] F°. Types 4, 12, 13, 15, 17; cuts; αβ.

9971. n.d. [c. 1503–4?] Psalterium chorale Constantiense. [BIBLE.] F°. Types 4, 13, 15, 17, music; cut; αβ.

9972. 1504. Petrus de Aliaco: tractatus super libros metheororum. [AILLY.] 4°. P.VI. 31. 41; SPa. 47. Types 13, 14, 16.

9973. 1505 Mar. 11. Cornelius NEPOS: uita Catonis, etc. 4°. P.VI. 32. 51; SPa. 49. Types 13, 14. [Imp.; A—G only.]

9974. [a. 1505 July 31.] WIMPHELING: apologetica declaratio in librum suum de integritate. 4°. P.VI. 33. 57; SK. 15. Types 13, 14, 15; Γ.

9975. 1505. Gemma gemmarum. [DICT.] 4°. P. VI. 32. 54; W. 345; SPa. 51. Types 4, 10, 13, 15; δ.

9976. 1505. Missale ordinis hierosolymitani. [LIT.] F°. P.VI. 32. 53; SPa. 50. Types 4, 13, 14, 15, 17, music; cuts; βδεΔ. [Imp.]

9977. [a. 1506 Jan. 21.] Wimpheling: de uita et miraculis Ioh. Gerson. [CHARLIER.] 4°. SK. 25. Types 13, 14, 15; Γ.

9978. [a. 1506 Feb. 9.] Conr. PEVTINGER: sermones de mirandis Germaniae antiquitatibus. 4°. P.VI. 34. 70; SPa. 54. Types 14, 15; Γζ.

9979. 1506. Perottus: cornu copiae. [MARTIALIS.] F°. P. VI. 34. 68; SPa. 57. Types 14, 16, 18, gk.; βΓδζH.

9980. 1506. Psalterium, lat.-germ. [BIBLE.] 4°. P.VI. 36. 82; DA. 562; SH. 51. Types 11, 12, 13, 15; cut; αΓβδεΔ. [Durch Mathis Hüpfüff.]

9981. 1507 Jan. 12. Rodericus Zamorensis: speculum uitae humanae. [SANCIVS DE AREVALO.] F°. P.VI. 36. 89; SPa. 59. Types 15, 18; H.

27

D 2

9982. 1507 Mar. 14. DIONYSIVS NESTOR: uocabula. F°. P.VI. 36. 88; SPa. 60. Types 14, 16, 18, gk.; ϡн.

9983. 1507. Henr. BEBEL: ars uersificandi, etc. [S—Z, AA—DD.] 4°. SPa. 64. Types 14[caps.], 15, 16, gk. i.; α; н.

9984. n. d. [c. 1507?] WIMPHELING: ad Iulium ij. querulosa excusatio. 4°. SPa. 63. Types 13, 15, 16; н.

9985. 1508. Iac. de Theramo: Belial zu teutsch. [PALLADINVS.] 4°. DA. 604; SPa. 70. Types 4, 11, 12; cuts; b; ϡн.

9986. 1508. Franc. Marius Grapaldus: de partibus aedium. [GRAPALDI.] 4°. P. VI. 40. 115; SPa. 68. Types 14, 16, gk.; b; βϧ.

9987. 1508. Missale speciale. [LIT.] F°. Types 4, 12, 13, 15, 16, 17; cut; βδеΔ.

9988. 1509 Jan. 14. Missale Hamburgense. [LIT.—For Hermann (Barkhusen?) of Emden.] F°. P. VI. 45. 153; SPa. 76. Types 4, 12, 13, 15, 16, 17; cuts; βеΔ.

9989. 1509 Mar. 17. LVCANVS: Pharsalia. 4°. P. VI. 44. 151; SPa. 71. Types 14, 15, 16; b; н.

9990. 1509. Laur. Iustinianus: Unterrichtung eines geistlichen Lebens. [LAWRENCE.] 4°. DA. 635; SPa. 77. Types 12, 13, 15; cuts.

9991. 1509. Friedr. Riedrer: Spiegel der wahren Rhetorik. [CICERO.] F°. DA. 646; SPa. 78. Types 12, 13, 15, 16; cuts; βϧ.

9992. n. d. [c. 1509–10?] Historie von den vier Ketzeren Prediger Ordens. [MARY.] 4°. W. 503. Types 12, 13; cuts.

9993. [a. 1510 July 28.] WIMPHELING: defensio theologiae scholasticae. 4°. SSr. 45. Types 13–16; cuts; Y.

9994. 1510 Aug. 29. Nicolaus von WYLE: Translationen. F°. DA. 685: SPa. 80. Types 13, 15, 19; cuts; βδϧθ.

9995. 1511 Jan. 16. GEILER: nauicula fatuorum. 4°. P. VI. 54. 232; SSr. 48. Types 11, 13–16, 20; cuts; Y.

9996. 1511 Mar. 1. Breuiarium Argentinense, pars aestiualis. [LIT.] 8°. P.VI. 52. 216; SPa. 85. Types 10, 11, 13, 14, 15, 16, 19; cut; ϝδ.

xv. PRINTER OF JORDANUS DE QUEDLINBURG, 1483.

Division B continued.

TYPES. Types 1, 2, 3, 4, as in part i.: types 2, 3 both measure 91 mm.; type 4 (text like Quentell 7) is 79 mm. It has an additional E and thick ¶.—Type 6 = Grüninger 12.— Type 7 = Grüninger 20; 90 mm.; the E differs from Prüss sen 20.—Type 8, square canon type; short letters 9 mm.

Types 1–3, see Burger 149; 4, see fig. 37; 6, see fig. 45; 7, see fig. 34; 8, see fig. 15.

BORDER. A, a copy of one used by Higman; see TP. XII. 1.

9997a. 1502 Apr. 28. DIONYSIVS Areopagita: operum pars ij. P.VI. 29. 21. Types 1, 2, 3, 4; A; diagr.

b. 1502 June 15. id. pars iij. P.VI. 29. 22. Types 1, 2, 4.

c. 1503 Jan. 21. id. pars i. F°. P.VI. 30. 29. Types 1, 2, 4, 6–8.

9998. 1502 Dec. 20. IACOBVS de Voragine: legenda aurea. F°. P.VI. 28. 20. Types 1, 2, 4.

xx. GEORG HUSNER, SECOND PRESS.

TYPES. Types 5 (large round = Gran 4; in 1514-5 kerned); 6 (= Gran 8; text, double hyphen like Knoblouch 2, mixt C; 79 mm.); 7 (= Gran 9, small type like Prüss sen. 10, Knoblouch 4; round h, double hyphen, 63 mm.); for these see part i.—Type 9, round large text like xv. 2; the same as Gran 12.—Type 10 = Gran 10; as Grüninger 20, except E; cf. Prüss sen. 20.

Type 5, see fig. 24; 6, see fig. 37; 7, see fig. 46; 10, see fig. 34 (different E).

9999. [a. 1502 Nov. 9.] Germaniae Wimphelingianae defensio aduersus Murnerum. [GRESEMVNDVS.] 4°. SK. 2. Types 5, 6, 7, 9. [Ioh. Strosack impressit.]

10000. 1503 Jan. 24. IACOBVS de Voragine: legenda aurea. 4°. P. IX. 107. 9. Types 5, 7, 9.

10001. 1503 Nov. 16. PETRVS Comestor: historia scholastica. F°. P. VI. 30. 33. Types 5, 6, 9.

10002. 1504 Sept. 7. Vocabularius breuiloquus. [DICT.] 4°. P. VI. 32. 48; SPa. 44. Types 5, 7, 9, 10.

10003. 1505 Aug. 11. BARTHOLOMAEVS Anglicus: de proprietatibus rerum. F°. P. VI. 33. 62. Types 5, 6.

xxi. MATTHIAS HÜPFÜFF.

TYPES. Types 1 (large = Kirchheim ij. 1, like Prüss sen. 13 with different capitals; short letters 5 mm.) and 2 (German text, but without the square D shown in Burger's facsimile. In no. 10005 the A used is that of 2^C, and the C is mixt); for these see part i.—Type 2^B uses reversed S for D (this is also occasionally found later, e.g. in no. 10040), and different L and hyphen. 2^C reverts to the original D and L, has a new A as Beck 13 (found already in 1503; see above), a different hyphen, h of schwabacher form mixt with the other, and a thin ¶ (it is thick in 2, 2^B, 2^D). These features are not all found in no. 10040, where 2^C has additions (e.g. L and H) from 2^D in certain pages; but the hyphen, h, and ¶ do not vary. 2^D has new B, C, E as Beck 13, L as 2^B, ¶ as 2^B, A as 2^C, a new H mixt with the old, no schwabacher h, and again a different hyphen.—Type 3, small schwabacher = Kirchheim ij. 2; 82 mm.; cf. Bumgart 5.—Type 4, square canon type like Prüss sen. 4; short letters 9–10 mm.—Type 5, remarkable archaic german text, recalling Augsburg or Nürnberg founts; 112 mm. Facs., TFS. 1902b. The same type is used for a Plenarium sine nota, which is certainly earlier than 1504, and seems not to be by Hüpfüff.—Type 6, small text latin like Prüss sen. 11; single hyphen, round C as well as square; 70 mm. 6^B has double hyphen, new comma, no round C or the lombardic capitals found in 6.—Type 7, text latin, like G. Stuchs 12 but smaller; many wrong-fount caps., mostly from 3, 6 (but not the V); there is also a wrong-fount f; double hyphen; 82 mm.—Type 8, large round type like Flach jun. 1; short letters nearly 6 mm.—Type 9, small latin text like Koberger 19; 72 mm.—Type 10, middle german roman like Prüss sen. 14; double hyphen; 87 mm.—Type 11 = Prüss sen. 13, distinguished from 1 by its caps.; has V of 8 for its W. Facs., Kr. Abb. 31, line 1.—Type 12, large text schwabacher with ¶, comma sloping backwards, and double hyphen. Cf. Prüss sen. 19, &c. 106 mm. Facs., Kr. Abb. 31, lines 2, 3.—Facs. of types 2^C or 2^D, 4, 6 or 6^B, and 11, Butsch I. 69.

Type 1, see fig. 19; *2^B, see fig. 54; 3, see fig. 64; 4, see fig. 15; 6, see fig. 45; 7, see fig. 36; 8, see fig. 63, line 1; 9, see fig. 44; 10, see fig. 8; 11, see fig. 18; 12, see fig. 52.

BORDER. A, see device b.

DEVICES. a, EBM. VII. 1; b (= border A), EBM. VII. 2, Butsch I. 69.

INITIALS. Most of Hüpfüff's initials are odd ones. α, open white, twig design; D in 1503, 37 mm.; I in 1511, 52 mm.; A in 1514, 39 mm.; no other letters.—β = Prüss sen. H. —Γ, open white, rather like Grüninger Γ; two D (1512, 1514) an E (1506), and V (1515) found; 21–22 mm.—δ, two kinds of D with half-length figures of men; fifteenth century style; 40 mm. —ε, Strassburg style, 25 mm.—ζ, Strassburg style, 19 mm. Among the odd (Δ) initials are copies of a S of Grüninger α (used in 1518 by Knoblouch), and of an I and S from Grüninger β; letters of Prüss sen. β; also in the Seelenwurzgarten, 1511, and the Kalender of 1515 several curious varieties of I used by Kistler in 1497.

10004. [a. 1501 May 13.] Die Ordnung zu Ofen wider den Türken gemacht. [STATES OF THE CHURCH.] 4°. DA. 531. Types 1,3; cuts; a.

10005. 1503. Joh. VIRDUNG: Practica teutsch. 4°. DA. 544b; W. suppl. i. 17; SH. 25, 33. Types 1,2; cuts, diagr.; Y; αΔ.

10006. 1504 June 5. Teutsch Kalender. [EPH.] 4°. W. 277; SH. 32. Types 1–5; cuts; Y.

10007. 1504. Der Brunnen des Rats. [MELIBEE.] 4°. DA. 549b; W. suppl. i. 18; SH. 34. Types 1, 2, 4; cuts; β.

10008. 1504. Datus: elegantiolae. [DATI.] 4°. SH. 30. Types 1,4,6; cut.

10009. [c. 1504.] Hans GLASER: Spruch von dem Krieg. 4°. Not W. 283? Types 1, 2; cut.

10010. 1505 June 7. BEROALDVS: oratio prouerbiorum. 4°. SH. 37. Types 1,6; β.

10011. 1505 [a. Aug. 1]. De ora antarctica. [VESPUCCI.] P. VI. 33. 60; SH. 41. Types 1,4,6; cuts, diagr.; β.

10012. 1505 Aug. 30. Iac. HARTLIEB: defide meretricum in suos amatores. 4°. SH. 39. Types 1, 2, 4; cuts; Y; β.

10013. n. d. [c. 1505 ?] Von des Endkrists Leben. [ANTICHRIST.] 4°. H. 1150; SH. 29. Types 2, 4; cuts; Δ.

10014. 1506. Honorius: Historie von dem Meister Elucidario. [ELVCIDARIVS.] 4°. W. 356; SH. 59. Types 1, 2, 4; cuts; ꞁΔ.
1506. Psalterium, lat.-germ. See no. 9980.

10015. 1506. Somniorum interpretatio luculentissima. [SOMNIA.] 4°. P. IX. 355. 82b. Types 1, 2, 4; cuts.

10016. 1506. Ioh. TRITHEIM: de purissima conceptione uirginis Mariae. 4°. P. VI. 36. 80; SH. 57. Types 1, 4, 7; cuts.

10017. 1506. WIMPHELING: elegantiarum medulla. 4°. P. VI. 35. 78; SH. 55. Types 1, 4, 6; β.

10018. 1506. WIMPHELING: epistula excusatoria ad Sueuos. 4°. P. VI. 35.79; SH. 54. Types 1, 4, 7.

10019. n. d. [c. 1506 ?] Von dem christlichen Streit kürzlich geschehen zu Lisbona. [CHRISTIANS.] 4°. Not DA. 568? Types 2, 4; cut; Y; β.

10020. [a. 1507 Apr. 28.] Das Einnehmen und Einreiten und Empfahen des Königs von Frankreich in Genua. [LOUIS XII.] 4°. Types 1,2,4; cuts; Δ.

10021. [n. b. 1507.] Wimpheling: AVISAMENTVM de concubinariis non absoluendis. 4°. P. VI. 38. 103. Types 1, 4, 6; cut.

10022. 1508. Ioh. TOLLAT: margarita medicinae. 4°. DA. 620b. Types 2[B], 4 [caps.], 8; cut.

10023. (1508–9.) Ioh. ROSSSCHWANTZ: ein neu abenteuerlich Practica. 4°. Types 2[B], 4 [caps.], 8; cut; Y.

10024. 1509. Hübsche Legende von S. Anna. [ANNE.] 4°. DA. 643. Types 2[B], 4 [caps.], 8; cuts; Y.

10025. n. d. [n. b. 1509.] Joh. Kurtz: von dem venediger Krieg. [VENICE.] W. 479. Types 2[B], 4 [caps.], 8; cuts; δ.

10026. [a. 1509 May 31.] Ioh. VETTER: de quattuor heresiarchis ordinis praedicatorum. 4°. Types 1, 10; cut.

10027. 1510 Aug. 23. Ulr. TENGLER: Laienspiegel. F°. DA. 676; SH. 78. Types 2[B], 4, 8, 9, 10; cuts, diagr.; Δ.

10028. 1511 Feb. 20. Seelenwurzgarten. F°. W. 633; SH. 83. Types 1,2[C],4; cuts; Y; αβΔ. [Print Room.]

10029. 1512. ARNALDVS de Villa noua; von Bereitung der Weine. 4°. DA.730; STRASS-
  SH. 101. Types 2^C, 11; cut.

10030. 1512. Mich· SCHRICK: Büchlein von den ausgebrannten Wassern. 4°.
  [Cf. SH.22.] Types 2^C, 11; cut.

10031. 1512. Wahrhaftige Sage oder Rede von dem Rock J.C. [JESUS.] 4°. W.735;
  SH. 98. Types 4, 11, 12; cuts; Y; ɾδΔ.

10032. 1512. BRANT: das Narrenschiff. 4°. DA. 736; SH. 96. Types 2^C, 4,
  11; cuts; Y.

10033. n. d. [c. 1512?] Ringbüchlein. [BUECHLEIN.] 4°. W. suppl. i. 10. Types
  2^C, 4, 11; cuts. [Imp.]

10034. 1513 Jan. 25. Das Buch der Altväter. [VITAE.] F°. DA. 751; SH. 103.
  Types 2^C, 4, 11; cuts; Y; Δ.

10035. [a. 1513 June 6.] Abdruck eines lateinischen Sendbriefs von der eroberten Stadt Malacha. [EMANUEL.] 4°. DA.758 note? W. 756. Types
  4, 11, 12; cut; eʒ.

10036. 1513. Passio domini nostri. [BIBLE.] F°. P.VI.61.288; SH.109. Types
  10, 11; cuts.

10037. 1514 Mar. 20. Geschichte des grossen Alexanders. [EUSEBIUS.]
  F°. DA. 787; SH. 112. Types 2^C, 4, 11; cuts; B; αδeʒΔ.

10038. 1515. Die vier Angeltugenden. [BOETHIUS.] 4°. W.955; SH.128. Types
  2^C, 11; cuts; ʒ.

10039. 1515. Kalender. [EPH.] 4°. Types 2^C, 4, 11; cuts; Y; eʒΔ.

10040. 1515 Mar. 18. GEILER: Doctor Keiserspergs Paternoster. F°. DA.806;
  SH. 117. Types 2^C, 2^D, 4, 11; cuts; Y; ɾeʒ.

10041. 1515. WIMPHELING: adulescentia. 4°. P. VI. 72. 378: SH.119. Types
  2^D, 6^B, 11; Ab; ʒΔ.

10042. 1515. Vocabularius lat.-germ. 4°. P. VI. 73. 382; W. 972; SH. 122.
  Types 4, 6^B, 11; Ab; eʒ.

10043. 1516. Martyrologium, VIOLA sanctorum. 4°. P. VI. 79. 439; SH. 137.
  Types 4? 6^B, 11; Ab; Δ. [Wants ff. 1–4.]

xxij. BARTHOLOMAEUS KISTLER.

TYPES. Types 3 (like Hüpfüff 1; cf. Knoblouch 3^B) and 4 (schwabacher text like
Knoblouch 5^C, Joh. Schott 1; same H, N); for these see part i.—Type 5 = xxviij. § 3, type 4
(see part i); cf. Knoblouch 14, Landen 4.
Type 3, see fig. 19; 4, see fig. 55; 5, see fig. 39.

10044. 1501. Legenda de Sancta Anna. [ANNE.] 4°. P.VI.27.7; SKis.16. Types
  3, 5; cuts; Y.

10045. 1501. (Legende von S. Anna.) Leben Eucharii, etc. [See no.760.] 4°. W.
  154, 145; SKis. 17. Types 3, 4; cuts; Y. [Part 2 only.]

10046. 1502 Aug. 23. Caoursin: Der vermaledigsten unfrommen Türken Anschlag wider die Christenheit. [TURKS.] 4°. W. 247; SKis. 20. Types
  3, 4; cuts; Y.

xxv. JOHANN KNOBLOUCH.

TYPES. Type 1, large round, the same type as Beck 11 and Schott 9; but the lines of type are usually kerned on to one another. This fount, though varying a good deal from time to time, seems to keep its identity throughout.—Type 2, middle text like Flach jun. 3; open V; 81 mm. Single hyphen till 1509, then double; but single again from 1 June 1514; in and after 1508 the V of 10 is used exclusively. From 24 Jan. 1513 the type is much mixed with letters, especially caps., of type 14; it is called 2^B in this state. Thin ¶ as a rule, but occasionally a thick one is used. 2^C is the same type germanised (1509 only) by the addition of another d, w, h, ů, ů, &c.—Type 3, large church type, like Prüss sen. 13 or Hüpfüff 11, but more spiky: the dot of the i is a curve with the hollow facing left. Facs., Kristeller, Abb. 34, line 2. Used first in 1504; when next used, in 1507–8, it has different caps. like those of Hüpfüff 1, though it is not the same fount (3^B; facs. Muther 218); 3^B is used till 1513; in and after 1516 the earlier caps. are again used (D of both kinds); this is called 3^C. Cf. Burger 43, middle type.—Type 4, small type like Prüss sen. 10; thin ¶; 64 mm.—Type 5, text schwabacher, like Prüss sen. 12, but low L; D like S reversed; single hyphen; 93 mm. 5^B has high L as Prüss, D like that of Hüpfüff 2^C, double hyphen, and thick ¶. 5^C has a new double hyphen (one of those used with type 2 in 1509), low L (as 5), tall A and C like Hüpfüff 2^D, new N and H like Schott 1. 5^D has ¶ and hyphen as 5^C, but normal N; D level with line instead of below; low A and C, and H as in 5; L low as in 5, 5^C; new schwabacher h. Cf. Gran 13.—Type 6, small schwabacher like Schott 6, J. Schöffer 14, or Flach jun. 11; 78 mm.; has thick ¶ in 1508.—Type 7, middle roman, double hyphen, thin ¶; 87 mm.; ę at first, but from 1510 with æ mostly; in Aug. 1515 the round comma comes in, and the hyphen is mixt (single and double). Marginal quotes are used with it in no. 10092. Cf. Schott 7, Gran 16, &c. Type 8, larger text german roman, like Schott 5*; ę, double hyphen; 100 mm.—Type 9, small text like Prüss sen. 11; round h, double hyphen; 71 mm. 9^B (on and after 1513 Jan. 14) has some capitals from a type like Hüpfüff 9. In this state the type seems = Beck 8. ¶ and ⁋ in 1516. —Type 10, small text, like Flach jun. 2; tailed h, single hyphen; 74 mm.—Type 11, large text = Strassburg xxviii. § 3, type 2 (see part i); 105 mm. Cf. type 14 below.—Type 12, square canon type, as Hüpfüff 4 or Schott 10; rather rough; short letters 9½ mm. Facs., Kristeller Abb. 34, line 1; Muther 218.—Type 13, small german roman, single hyphen, thin ¶; 76 mm. Cf. Schott 4*, Gran 14, &c.—Type 14 = Kistler 5 (xxviii. § 3, type 4); see type 11 above. Usually mixt with type 2.—Type 15, small type, like 9, but a different fount; two sorts of double hyphen; thin ¶ and ⁋; 70 mm.—Type 16, medium large, like Ratdolt 9, but some caps. differ; tailed h.—Type 17, very large roman capitals, 14–15 mm.; cf. Schott 13; used only for initials in these books.—Type 18, second text schwabacher, like Joh. Schöffer 7 or Flach jun. type 12; 92 mm. Facs., Kristeller Abb. 34, lines 3–6.—Type 19, large roman caps., smaller than 17, thin and graceful; 7 mm. Cf. Schott 14. Facs. Kristeller Abb. 34 (date).—Type 20, small text type of French style, as Grüninger 30; double hyphen, tailed h, ⁋; 71 mm.—Type 21, large text schwabacher, with long comma sloping backwards, as Prüss sen. 19, Hüpfüff 12 and Beck 2; 108 mm.—Type 22, italic, like Joh. Schöffer 21; 92 mm. Not as Schott 15.—First greek, older style (cf. Schott); second, very cursive, 87 mm.; both are like Joh. Schöffer's first and second founts respectively.—Facs. of types 1, 7, 11, Butsch I. 68; of 1, 12, ib. 70; of 8, 19 (caps. only), ib. 71.

Type 1, see fig. 24; 2, see fig. 38; 3, see fig. 18; 3^B, see fig. 19; 4, see fig. 46; 5, see fig. 54, 55; 6, see fig. 63; 7, see fig. 8; 8, see fig. 3; 9, see fig. 45; 12, see fig. 15; 13, see fig. 11; 14, see fig. 39; 16, see fig. 32^1; *18, see fig. 53; 19, see fig. 2; 20, see fig. 48; 21, see fig. 52; 22, see fig. 13.

BORDERS. A, quarto, S. John the Evangelist, signed by H. Baldung Grün; used 1513 March 14 and 1519; Butsch I. 71. Cf. M. Maler B.—B, quarto, stripy ground, at foot arms of empire and label: Cum priuilegio imperiali. B^2 has these words cut out. Facs. Butsch I. 68. Used also by Schott in both states (B, B^2).—C, signed by H. Baldung Grün, folio; at foot emperor seated.—D, folio = Beck D; facs. Butsch I. 70. Cf. Val. Schumann B.—E, quarto, four-piece, but in one style, white ground; not variable in these books; facs. of top and bottom pieces, Kristeller, Abb. 34.—F = Flach jun. A. To these must be added a border and cut in one piece used in no. 10118.

X-borders. Besides E, properly an X-border, one (X^5) is used in no. 10126, identical with a border of Flach (king in procession at base). 17 other pieces are found; 1–4 (X^1) in no. 10087; 5–8 (X^{2a}) in no. 10088; 5–7, 9 (X^{2b}) in nos. 10089, 10090, 10101, 10108 and 10109;

after this these passed into H. Gran's hands, being used by him (for Knoblouch) in Dec.
1518. 10–13 (X³) are used in no. 10117; 14–17 (X⁴) in no. 10124.

DEVICES. a, EBM. ix. 4; b, EBM. ix. 1; c (1507), EBM. ix. 3.

INITIALS. α, white, Maiblumen style, like Prüss sen. γ; 21–22 mm. C and V only
are found; probably strays.—β, large black, resembling Prüss sen. ζ; letters shaded, some
have figures in them; 48–50 mm.—γ, style of β, partly identical with Prüss sen. η; 30–33
mm.—δ, similar to α, but 17–18 mm. only.—ε, same set as Schott β; P with Annunciation,
55 mm.; G, Death of Our Lady, 53–4 mm.; stripy ground. Cf. Beck Δ.—ζ, Strassburg
style, 23–25 mm.—η, Strassburg style, 18–20 mm. Each of these last appears to be two or more
sets mixt; the earlier appear by themselves only in the Wimpheling of 1513; the later are
partly identical with Hüpfüff ε and ζ.—θ, like ζ, but 29 mm.

Among odd (Δ) initials may be mentioned: a C like xiv. δ (June 1507); the D of Hüpfüff
α (1507 Oct. 21); black C on a white ground, like a painted letter, 54 mm. (ib.); curious
large calligraphic H, 60 mm. (1509 Feb.); a large black Maiblumen C, 41 mm. (1515 Nov.
19); a large black-ground H with arabesque ornament, 40 mm. (1516 Apr. 28); a curious I
used in 1515 by Hüpfüff (1518 Sept. 6); large open A, with arms of France, 71 mm.
(Laienspiegel, 1518); S, a copy of Grüninger α, also used by Hüpfüff (ib.).

10047. 1504 July 3. Raymundus de Pennaforti: summula sacramentorum.
[RAYMOND.] 4°. P. VI. 31. 45; SK. 6. Types 1–4.

10048. 1505 Feb. 20. WIMPHELING: adulescentia. 4°. P. VI. 32. 55; SK. 10.
Types 1, 2; cuts; a.

10049. 1505 March 5. WIMPHELING: de integritate. 4°. P. VI. 32. 56; SK. 12.
Types 1, 2.

10050. 1506. Ringmann: der Text des Passions. [BIBLE.] F°. W. 373; SK. 24.
Types 5, 6; cuts.

10051. 1506 Oct. 22. WIMPHELING: de integritate. 4°. P. VI. 35. 73; SK. 19.
Types 1, 7.

10052. 1506 Dec. 22, 1507 Jan. 31. Ioh. Fr. Picus: opera uaria. [PICO.] F°. P.
VI. 35. 74 and 37. 92; SK. 20, 28. Types 7, 8 [caps.]; gk. i.

10053. 1507 June [25?] GVLIELMVS Aruernus: de collationibus beneficiorum, etc.
4°. P. VI. 37. 93; SK. 30; H. 8322. Type 7; αΔ.

10054. 1507 July 16. HENRICVS de Hassia: speculum animae. 4°. P. VI. 38. 97;
SK. 31. Types 1, 7.

10055. 1507 Oct. 21. MANDEVILLE: Reisen. F°. DA. 596; W. 408. Types 3ᴮ,
5ᴮ; cuts; Y; Δ. [Perhaps by Hüpfüff.]

10056. 1507 Dec. 5. Ficinus: de religione christiana. [FICINO.] 4°. P. VI. 37. 94;
SK. 33. Types 1, 7, 8 [caps.]; b.

10057. 1507. Ringmann: passio domini nostri. [BIBLE.] F°. P. VI. 38. 100?
(Not in SK.) Types 1, 4, 7; cuts.

10058. 1507. Ringmann: passio domini nostri. [BIBLE.] F°. (Not in SK.) Types
4, 7, 8 [caps.]; cuts.

10059. 1508 Jan. 13. Gregorius Nazianzenus: libelli decem. [GREGORY.] P. VI.
41. 120; SK. 36. Types 1, 7; b.

10060. 1508 Feb. 18. OTTO von Passau: die xxiv. Alten. F°. DA. 601c; W. 430;
SK. 38. Types 3ᴮ, 5ᴮ; cuts; Y; β.

1508 Aug. 20. Manipulus curatorum. Hagenau, H. Gran for Knoblouch.
See no. 11638.

1508 Sept. 20. Wimpheling: adulescentia. Hagenau, H. Gran for Knoblouch. See no. 11639.

10061. 1508. CATO: disticha, lat.-germ. 4°. W. 431; SK. 49. Types 1, 2, 6, 8; α.

10062. 1508. Aesopus moralisatus cum bono commento. [AESOP.] 4°. Types 3ᴮ,8, 13.

10063. 1508. Ringmann: passio domini nostri. [BIBLE.] F°. P.VI.42.128; SK. 40. Types 1, 4, 7; cuts.

10064. 1508. Psalterium, lat.-germ. [BIBLE.] 4°. P.VI.41.118; W.456; SK.41. Types 1, 2, 3ᴮ, 6; cut; Y; βſ.

10065. 1508. HENRICVS de Hassia; secreta sacerdotum. 4°. P.VI.41.126; SK. 43. Types 1, 9.

10066. 1508. WIMPHELING: elegantiarum medulla. 4°. P. VI. 41. 121; SK. 52. Types 1, 9; ſ.

10067. 1508. NICOLAVS de Blony: tractatus sacerdotalis de sacramentis. 4°. P. VI. 41. 123; SK. 47. Types 1, 10.

10068. 1509 a. Feb. 2. HORTVLVS animae. 8°. P.VI.45.160; SK.55. Types 2, 3ᴮ; cuts, diagr.; αδΔ.

1509 Feb. 23. Summa angelica. Hagenau, H. Gran for Knoblouch. See no. 11640.

1509 Aug. 18. Heldenbuch. Hagenau, H. Gran for Knoblouch. See no. 11643.

10069. 1509. CATO: disticha, lat.-germ. 4°. W.481; SK.64. Types 1,5,11; Δ.

10070. 1509. Ringmann: Text des Passions. [BIBLE.] F°. DA.631; SK. 60. Types 2ᶜ, 5ᶜ; cuts; βſ.

10070A. 1509. Joh. SCHOTT: Spiegel christlicher Wallfahrt. 4°. W. 512; SK.62. Types 3ᴮ, 5ᶜ; cuts; b.

10071. [1509?] Hieronymus de Villa Vitis: panis quotidianus de sanctis. 4°. Types 1, 2 (with h of 2ᶜ), 11; ſ. [First quire of no. 11642.]

10072. n.d. [c. 1509.] GVLIELMVS de Gouda: expositio mysteriorum missae. 4°. P. VI. 128.893; H. *7829; SK. 46. Types 1, 2, 12; Δ.

10073. 1510 Feb. 3. Liber de contemptu mundi; Facetus; Parabolae Alani. [CON-TEMPTVS.] 4°. P. VI. 48. 183; SK. 65. Types 1, 7, 12, 13.

10074. 1510 Mar. 5. Matthaeus Vindocinensis: liber Tobiae. [BIBLE.] 4°. P. VI. 49. 187; SK. 68. Types 1, 7, 12, 13.

10075. 1510 Mar. 18. Floretus. [BERNARD.] 4°. P. VI. 48. 185; SK. 69. Types 1, 7, 12, 13; β.

10076. 1510. Vergili bucolica. [VIRGILIVS.] 4°. P.VI.48.182; SK.71. Types 1, 7, 8, 13.

10077. 1511 Mar. 14. Joh. GEILER: das Buch Granatapfel. F°. DA. 688; SK. 74. Types 5ᶜ, 12; cuts; β. [Print Room: in library, sig. f–m only.]

1511 June 16. Wimpheling: adulescentia. Flach for Knoblouch. See no. 10143.

10078. 1511. SYMMACHVS: epistulae familiares. 4°. Type 7.

1512 Jan.–May. Thomas Aquinas: summa. Hagenau, H. Gran for Knoblouch. See nos. 11650–11652, 11654.

10079. 1512 Aug. 31. MAILLARD: sermones dominicales. 4°. Types 1,2,4,7,14; cut.

10080. 1513 Jan. 24. GEILER: nauicula siue speculum fatuorum. 4°. P. VI. 59. 278; SK. 80. Types 1, 2ᴮ, 9ᴮ, 11, 12; Δ.

10081. 1513 Mar. 31. Sequentiae et hymni. [LIT.] 4°. P. VI. 59. 280, 279; SK. 82. Types 1, 2ᴮ, 4, 7, 11; B; ſeΔ.

10082. 1513 May 13. Der Stadt WORMS Reformation. F°. DA. 753. Types 3ᴮ, 5ᶜ, 9; cuts; β.

1513 Aug. 31. Summa angelica. Beck for Rinmann and Knoblouch.
See no. 10302.

1513 Sept. 1. Poggius: opera. Schott for Knoblouch. See no. 10272.

10083. 1513. WIMPHELING: elegantiae maiores. 4°. P. VI. 59. 281; SK. 85.
Types 1, 7, 13; ꝫH.

10084. 1513. IVVENALIS et Persius. 4°. P. IX. 361. 282b; SK. 86. Type 7; ꝫH.

10085. 1514 June 1. Gerson: operum pars prima; repertorium. [CHARLIER.]
F°. P. VI. 64. 320; SK. 87 (part). Types 1, 2^B, 7, 8, 12; CD; ꝫΔ

10086. 1514 Sept. 5. Ioh. de BVRGO; pupilla oculi. [For P. Götz.] 4°. P. VI. 65.
321; SK. 90. Types 1, 12, 15, 16; ꝫ.

10087. 1514 Oct. 2. MAILLARD: sermones de sanctis. 4°. P. IX. 364. 321b; SK.
91. Types 1, 2^B, 4, 7, 12; X^1.

1515 June 29. WIMPHELING: adulescentia. 4°. P. VI. 72. 374; SK. 94.
See below, no. 10338.

10088. n. d. [a. 1515 Aug. 5.] NACHTIGALL: musicae institutiones. 4°. P. VI. 72.
376; SK. 100. Types 7, gk. ij; X^{aa}; H. [Woodcut music.]

10089. n. d. [a. 1515 Aug. 5.] NACHTIGALL: senarii graecanici quingenti. 4°.
P. VI. 72. 375; SK. 101. Types 7, gk. ij; X^{ab}; ꝫH.

10090. 1515 Aug. 28. MARTIALIS: epigrammata. 4°. P. VI. 71. 369; SK. 99.
Types 7, gk. ij; X^{ab}; ꝫH.

10091. 1515 Sept. 1. Ἰσοκράτους παραίνεσις πρὸς Δημόνικον, etc., gr. et lat. [ISO-
CRATES.] 4°. P. VI. 71. 370; SK. 102. Types 7, gk. ij; ꝫH.

10092. n. d. [c. 1515.] Ἡσιόδου ἔργα καὶ ἡμέραι, gr. et lat. [HESIOD.] 4°. P. VI. 72.
377; SK. 103. Types 7, gk. ij; ꝫH.

10093. 1515 Nov. 19. MICHAEL Vratislauiensis: introductorium dialecticae.
[For Urban Kaim of Buda.] 4°. P. VI. 72. 372; SK. 105. Types 4,
11–13; cut, diagr.; ꝫΔ.

10094. 1515 Nov. Ioh. Iou. PONTANVS: amorum libri duo. 4°. P. VI. 72. 371;
SK. 104. Types 7, 13; ꝫH.

10095. 1516 Feb. 26. TROVAMALA: summa rosella. F°. P. VI. 77. 421; SK.
109. Types 1, 7, 9^B, 12, 16, gk. ij; C; ꝫH.

10096. 1516 Apr. 16. RAMPEGOLLIS: aurea biblia. 8°. P. VI. 79. 435; SK. 111.
Types 1, 2^B, 4, 9, 11; cut; H.

10097. 1516 Apr. 28. Laur. CORVINVS: hortulus elegantiarum. 4°. P. VI. 77.
423; SK. 113. Types 1, 7, 9, 12; ꝫHΔ.

10098. 1516 June 6. Burlaeus: uitae philosophorum. 4°. P. VI. 77. 425; SK.
115. Types, 1, 2^B, 9^B, 11, 12; ꝫ. [Frag.; ff. 1–8 only.]

10099. 1516 July 28. Gregoriana super nouum testamentum. [GREGORY.] 4°.
P. VI. 78. 428; SK. 119. Types 1, 9, 11–13; ꝫH.

10100. 1516 Aug. 25. Ioh. TRITHEIM: sermones. [For Joh. Haselberger.] F°. P.
VI. 78. 432; SK. 120. Types 1, 2^B, 8, 11; ꝫH.

10101. 1516 Dec. 3. Ἐρωτήματα τοῦ Χρυσολωρᾶ. [CHRYSOLORAS.] 4°. P. VI.
78. 430; SK. 123. Types 7, 13, gk. ij; X^{ab}.

10102. 1516. Ioh. ADELPHVS: die türkische Chronik. F°. W. 991; SK. 126.
Types 1, 5^D, 12; cuts; Y; H.

10103. 1516. ALBERTVS Magnus: das Buch der Versammlung. 4°. DA. 851;
SK. 131. Types 3^C, 5^D, 12; cut; ꝫH.

10104. 1516. BARTHEMA: ritterliche und lobwürdige Reise. 4°. DA. 853; SK.
132. Types 1, 3^C, 5^D, 12; cuts; ꝫH.

10105. 1516. BÜCHLEIN von Complexion der Menschen. 4°. W. 988 ; SK. 127.
Types 1, 5^D, 12 ; cut ; ʒH.

10106. 1516. MURNER : der Schelmen Zunft. 4°. DA. 878 ; S. 133. Types
3^C, 5^D, 12 ; cuts ; Y.

1516. Richardus de S. Victore : de duodecim patriarchis. 8°. P. VI. 78.
434 ; SK. 128. See no. 10325.

1516. Wimpheling : elegantiae maiores. 4°. SK. 130. See no. 10326.

1517 [a. 1516 Dec. 1]. Nider : formicarius. Schott for Knoblouch &
Götz. See no. 10282.

10106A. n.d. [c. 1516-17.] Erhart LURCKER : Historie von einem Ritter Thorelle
genannt. 4°. DA. 99c. Types 1, 5^D, 12, 18; cuts; XY.

1517 March 1. Ioh. de Burgo : pupilla oculi. Schott for Knoblouch
& Götz. See no. 10283.

10107. [a. 1517 March 1.] Kaiserlicher Majestät Einreitung zu Brüssel.
[MAXIMILIAN.] 4°. W. 1047. Types 1, 3^C, 5^D, 12 ; cut ; ʒ.

10108. 1517 March 29. Ex Luciano quaedam iam recens traducta. [LUCIAN.]
4°. P. VI. 83. 473 ; SK. 139. Types 7, (17), gk. ij ; X^{ab}.

10109. 1517 March 29. NACHTIGALL : progymnasmata graecanicae litera-
turae. 4°. P. VI. 83. 474 ; SK. 138. Types 7, (17), gk. ij ; X^{ab}.

10110. [a. 1517 March 31.] Ulr. KRAFFT : der geistliche Streit. [For Joh.
Haselberger.] 4°. DA. 869 ; SKer. 2. Types 16, 18 ; cut ; F ; ʒH.

10111. 1517 Apr. 1. Martinus MYLLIUS : passio Christi, germ. [For Joh. Haselberger.] 4°. DA. 870. Types 1, 7, 18 ; cut ; H.

10112. 1517. PERSIVS. 4°. P. VI. 83. 475 ; SK. 145. Type 7 ; ʒH. [By Prüss?]

10113. 1517. Platina : de honesta uoluptate. [SACCHI.] 4°. Types 7, (17), gk. ij ; ʒ.

10114. 1517 Sept. 1. Iac. de Voragine : der Heiligen Leben. [LEGENDA AVREA.]
F°. DA. 873b ; SK. 141. Types 1, 12, 16, 18 ; cuts ; CDY ; ʒHΔ.
[Partly by Beck and Schott.]

10115 a. 1518 Jan. 23. Baptista Mantuanus : parthenice prima. [SPAGNUOLI.]
4°. P. VI. 87. 506; SK. 151. Types as b, c, d. (Sig. A–L.)

b. 1518 Feb. 5. id. : parthenice secunda. P. VI. 87. 507 ; SK. 152. Types
as a, c, d. (Sig. aa–hh.)

c. 1518 a. Feb. 24. id. : parthenice tertia. P. VI. 87. 508 ; SK. 154. Types
as a, b, d. (Sig. Aa–Hh.)

d. 1518 March 15. id. : de calamitatibus mundi. P. VI. 87. 509 ; SK. 157.
Types 4, 7, (17), 19 ; H. (Sig. AA–LL.)

10116. [n. b. 1518 Feb. 5.] Seb. BRANT : naenia in Turcorum niceteria. 4°. P. IX.
369. 531b ; SS. 41. Types 7, 8, (17), 19.

1518 Feb. 19. Petrus de Crescentiis. Schott for Knoblouch & Götz.
See no. 10286.

10117. 1518 March 12. Seb. BRANT : vom Anfang und Wesen der Stadt Jerusalem. F°. DA. 912 ; W. 1096 ; SK. 156. Types 3^C, 12, 18 ; cuts ;
X^{3}Y ; ʒHθ.

1518 May 31. IOANNES Gallensis : summa collationum. [With P. Götz.]
4°. P. VI. 87. 510 ; SK. 158. See no. 11673.

10118. 1518 Sept. 6. MURNER : Narrenbeschwörung. 4°. DA. 922 ; SK. 161.
Types 3^C, 12, 18 ; cuts ; Y ; Δ.

10119. 1518 Oct. 7. Ioh. de BVRGO : pupilla oculi. [For P. Götz.] 4°. P. VI.
88. 516 ; SK. 162. Types 1, 2^B, 12 ; ʒHΔ.

1518 Dec. 8. Ioh. Glogouiensis: introductorium in sphaeram Ioannis
de SACRO BOSCO. 4°. P.VI.88. 513; SK. 165. See no. 11675.

1518 Dec. 30. TORRENTINVS: elucidarius. 4°. See no. 11676.

1518. Murner: chartiludium. Prüss for Knoblouch. P. VI. 87. 504.
See no. 10328.

10120. 1518. SERMONES thesauri noui quadragesimales. F°. Types 1,9, 12, 20;
C; ƺ.

10121. 1518. Ulr. TENGLER: der neue Laienspiegel. F°. DA. 904. Types 3ᶜ,
4, 7, 12, (17), 18, 21 (others in diagr.); cuts, diagr.; Y; ᵣƺнΔ.

10122. 1519 Jan. 5. Heinr. GESSLER: Formulare und teutsch Rhetorica. F°.
DA. 934; S.171. Types 3ᶜ, 12, 18; cut; ƺΔ. [See also no.10343A.]

10123. 1519 March 15. Sequentiae et hymni. 4°. P. VI. 92. 558; SK. 174
(imp.). Types 1, 2ᴮ, 4, 8, 11, 20; B²; eƺ.

1519 Apr. Calpurnius et Nemesianus. Anshelm for Knoblouch. See
no. 11699.

1519 Apr. Brassicanus: Πᾶν, Omnis. Anshelm for Knoblouch. See no.
11700.

10124. 1519 Sept. 16. Theologia teutsch. [GERMAN THEOLOGY.] 4°. DA. 932;
SK. 178. Types 3ᶜ,12,18; X⁴; ƺнθ.

1519. Luther: die sieben Busspsalmen. [BIBLE.] 4°. DA. 926c; SK.
183. See no.10335.

10125. 1519. Mich. SCHRICK: von den ausgebrannten Wassern. 4°. W. 1266;
SK. 182. Types 3ᶜ,18; cut.

10126. 1519. Joh. WIDMANN: Regimen wie man sich in pestilentischem Luft
halten soll. 4°. DA. 942; W. 1300; SK. 189. Types 3ᶜ, 18; X⁵; ƺ.
[By Flach, types 10, 12 ?]

10127. 1520 Feb. 23. SVRGANT: manuale curatorum. 4°. P.VI. 93. 562; SK.
194. Types 1,2ᴮ,12; cut; E; ƺθ.

10128. 1520 Apr. 24. Merc. VIPERA: de diuino et uero numine apologeticon.
4°. P.IX. 371. 562b; SK. 209. Types 7, 19; E; δн.

10129. 1520 May 29. Merc. VIPERA: de disciplinarum uirtutumque laudibus
opusculum. 4°. Types 7,(17),19; E; ƺ.

10130. 1520 Aug. 1. Theologia teutsch. [GERMAN THEOLOGY.] 4°. DA. 970;
SK. 197. Types 3ᶜ,12,18; F; ƺн.

10131. [a. 1520 Aug. 10.] Andr. BODENSTEIN: von Vermögen des Ablasses.
4°. DA. 988d. Types 3ᶜ,18; E; н.

10132. 1520 Sept. LVCANVS: Pharsalia. 8°. P.VI. 93.563; SK.198. Type 22.

10133. [a. 1520 Sept.11.] Ulr.von HUTTEN: die verdeutschte Klage an Herzog Friedrich zu Sachsen. 4°. DA.985b; B. xxxi. Baα. Types 3ᶜ, 18.

10134. n.d. [1520 ?] HUTTEN: Klage und Vormahnung gegen dem Gewalt des
Papstes. 4°. W. 1417; B. xxxiv. 2. Types 3ᶜ,12,18; нΔ.

xxvi. JOHANN SCHOTT, first press, continued.

TYPES. Types 1 (schwabacher with A, C, H, L, N as Knoblouch 5ᶜ, but single hyphen only;
used only at Freiburg after 1500; 97-98 mm. Cf. Kistler 4); 2 (square church text with rounded
caps., very like Hüpfüff 1 or Knoblouch 3ᴮ; used only at Freiburg after 1500); 4 (small
german roman; hyphen double in 1500, mixt in 1503, single in 1504; cf. Knoblouch 13);

for these see part i. [Type 5 of part i. is the same as 3, which = Prüss sen. 15.]—Type 5,
text roman, with double hyphen; 98–99 mm.; cf. Knoblouch 8.—First greek type, like
Knoblouch i.

Type *1, see fig. 55; 2, see fig. 19; 3, see fig. 16; 4, see fig. 11; 5, see fig. 3.
DEVICES. a, EBM. II. 3. b, EBM. II. 2.

10135a. n. d. Baptista Mantuanus: duarum parthenicum libri (a–Ll).
    b. n. d. id. contra poetas impudice loquentes (8 leaves).
    c. 1501 Aug. 28, 1502 Mar. 15. id. opus calamitatum, etc. (AA–XX; a.)
    [SPAGNUOLI.] 4°. P. VI. 27.8; SS. 6, 7. Types 4, 5, gk. i; ab.

xxix. MARTIN FLACH THE YOUNGER.

The two great gaps in the younger Flach's work, the first from Oct. 1503 to March 1507, the
second from Sept. 1513 to Oct. 1519, have not yet been explained.

TYPES. Type 1, large round = xvi. (Flach the elder) 1; new (round) d first on 26 Jan.
1501; in 1509 a new v is used. Short letters nearly 6 mm. Cf. Hüpfuff 8.—Type 2 = xvi.
2; small text, single hyphen, curly-tailed h, ¶; 74 mm.—Type 3 = xvi. 5; text, with open V,
single hyphen; ¶ (not before 1502); 81 mm. Facs. Muther 236, 237. 3ᴮ, with double
hyphen and w.f. V and h. In this form it seems = Knoblouch 2.—Type 4, middle roman,
like Knoblouch 7; double hyphen; 86 mm. Used 1511 Aug. 20.—Type 5, square canon
type, like Prüss sen. 4; short letters 10 mm.—Type 6, text schwabacher, with fraktur forms of
b, d, g, h, l, &c., like Grüninger 5 or Prüss sen. 12; curly D, like the S reversed; long double
hyphen; thick ¶; 93 mm.—Type 7, large round, smaller than 1; short letters 5 mm. Cf.
Knoblouch 1.—Type 8, text schwabacher without fraktur forms; D like Kistler 1; thick ¶;
92 mm.—Type 9, another type very like 8 but slightly smaller face; thin ¶; L differs, the other
capitals are almost the same; 94–95 mm.—Type 10, church text like Quentell 10 or Prüss sen.
13.—Type 11, small schwabacher like Knoblouch 6; thin ¶; 77 mm.—Type 12, fourth text
schwabacher, the same as Knoblouch 18; double hyphen, ⁋; 92–3 mm.

Type *1, see fig. 63¹; 2, see fig. 45 (h differs); *3, see fig. 38; 4, see fig. 8; 5, see fig. 15;
6, see fig. 54; 7, see fig. 24; 8, 9, see fig. 55; 10, see fig. 18; *11, see fig. 63²; 12, see fig. 53.

BORDER. A, quarto, used also by Knoblouch (F; 1520), and Kerner (1517); at sides,
boys with instruments of the passion; vernicle at top, cannon at base. The rest are X borders.

DEVICES. a, EBM. vi. 1; occurs in some copies (not B.M.) of no. 10136.—b, EBM. vi.
3 [1511 Feb. 2]; Muther 237.—c, EBM. vi. 2 [1519].

INITIALS. These are for the most part rather strays than regular sets, and are here
arranged more by size than by unity of design.—α, white Maiblumen, 28–30 mm.—β, Maiblumen
style, 22 mm.—ɼ, like β, but 17 mm.—δ, dotted ground, mostly floral, Strassburg style; 22–
25 mm.; cf. Knoblouch ƹ, &c.—ε, like δ, but 17–19 mm.; cf. Knoblouch н, &c.

10136. 1501 Jan. 8. Aegidius [COLONNA] de Roma: castigatorium in corrupto-
    rium librorum S. Thomae de Aquino. F°. P. VI. 27. 10; SF. 1. Types 1, 2.
10137. 1501 Jan. 26. Raym. de SABUNDE: theologia naturalis. F°. P. VI. 26.3;
    SF. 2. Types 1, 3.
10138. 1501 Aug. 29. MARSILIVS de Ingen: questiones super libros sententia-
    rum. F°. P. VI. 26. 1; SF. 3. Types 1, 2.
10139. 1502 Feb. 27. Gerson: operum quarta pars. [CHARLIER.] F°. P. VI. 28.
    13; SF. 7. (H.*7622.) Types 1, 3; cut.
10140. 1503. Nic. de Blony: TRACTATVS sacerdotalis de sacramentis. 4°. SF. 11.
    Types 1, 3.
10141. 1503 Oct. 6. HEROLT: sermones discipuli. F°. SF. 10. Types 1, 3.

10142. 1509 [a. Dec. 3]. MVRNER: de augustiniana et hieronymiana reforma-
    tione poetarum. 4°. P. VI. 45. 161; SS. 11. Types 1, 4, 5; Δ.

10143. 1511 June 16. WIMPHELING: adulescentia. [For J. Knoblouch.] 4°. P. VI.
51. 209; SF. 24. Types 3ᴮ, 7.

10144. 1512 Aug. 21. Wolfg. WINTPERGER: Tractat der Badenfahrt. 4°. DA.
733; W. 751; SF. 26. Types 1, 6; cut; αΔ.

10145. 1512. Ioh. TOLLAT: margarita medicinae. 4°. DA. 727; SF. 29. Types
1, 6; ab; β.

10146. 1512. Wenc. BRACK: uocabularius rerum. 4°. P. VI. 55. 243; SF. 27.
Types 1, 3ᴮ, 5; a.

10147. 1513 Jan. 25. Gul. CAOURSIN: Historie von Rhodis. F°. DA. 759; SF.
32. Types 1, 5, 8; cuts; Y; a.

10148. 1513 Mar. 6. Euch. ROESSLIN: der schwangern Frauen und Hebammen
Rosengarten. 4°. DA. 755; SF. 34. Types 1, 8, 9, 10; cuts; X.

10149. 1513 Mar. 12. Ioh. ADELPHVS: die türckische Chronik. F°. DA. 760; SF.
36. Types 1, 5, 8; cuts; a; α.

10150. 1513. MVNDINVS: anatomia. 4°. P. VI. 78. 273; SF. 38. Types 1, 3ᴮ, 11; cut,
diagr.: αβгΔ.

1519. Widmann, DA. 982. Knoblouch, but perhaps by Flach; types
10, 12; X. See no. 10126.

10151. n. d. [c. 1519–20.] Tyman FELMAN: an den grossmächtigsten Fürsten
Karolum eine Supplication. 4°. W. 1182. Types 10, 12; cut.

10152. [a. 1520 June 23.] LUTHER: an den christlichen Adel deutscher Nation.
4°. W. 1498. Types 5, 10, 12; δε. [Title wanting.]

10153. 1520 July 18. PLINIVS: panegyricus, germanice. F°. DA. 1000; SF. 41.
Types 5, 10, 11, 12; cuts; XY; b; δεΔ.

10154. [a. 1520 Sept. 28.] Ulr. v. HUTTEN: eine Klagschrift. 4°. W. 1422; B.
xxxi. Bbα. Types 10, 12; δ.

10155. 1520. LUTHER: Sermon von dem Wucher. 4°. W. 1587; SF. 43. Types
10, 12; cut; b.

10156. 1520. ERASMUS: Paraclesis teutsch. 4°. W. 1359. Types 5, 10, 12; cut; Y; δ.

10157. 1520. LUTHER: eine kurze Form das Paternoster zu verstehen. 4°. SF.
52. Types 10, 12; A; δε.

10158. 1520. LUTHER: Sermon von dem Sacrament der Taufe. 4°. SF. 49.
Types 10, 12; X; Δ.

10159. n. d. [1520.] LUTHER: Sermon von dem Sacrament der Busse. 4°. W. 1575;
SF. 48. Types 10, 12; X.

10160. n. d. [1520.] LUTHER: Sermon von dem Bann. 4°. W. 1546; SF. 44. Types
10, 12; X; δ.

10161. n. d. [a. 1520?] Ein neues LIED von den falschen Predigern. 8°. W. 1486.
Type 12.

[For other books in types 10, 12 without name of printer see Knoblouch (types 3, 18).]

xxx. JOHANN WÄHINGER.

TYPES. Type 1, large church text like Prüss sen. 15.—Type 2, small schwabacher, like Flach jun. 11 or Knoblouch 6.

Type 1, see fig. 16 ; 2, see fig. 63ª.

INITIALS. White Maiblumen of three sizes : α, 28 mm. ; β, 20–22 mm. ; Γ, 16–18 mm.

10162. 1503 Feb. 6. HORTVLVS animae. 16°. SW.2. Types 1,2 ; cuts; αβΓ.

xxxi. WILHELM SCHAFFENER, third press.

TYPES. Type 1, latin text gothic like Quentell 7, as in 1498, with the same thick ¶ and w.f. L ; 81 mm. See Burger 44.—Type 2, large round type ; some of the caps. are like Grüninger 17.—Type 3, narrow square church text = Basel vij. 2 ; Burger 58, middle type. Short letters 5 mm. Cf. G. Stuchs 11.

Type 1, see fig. 37 ; 2, see fig. 28.

10163. 1508 Mar. 15. Geo. MORGENSTERN; sermones contra omnem mundi
        peruersum statum. 4°. P.IX.357.142b; SSf. 2. Types 1,3.
10164. 1513 March 10. MORGENSTERN: sermones. 4°. P.VI. 64. 315; SSf. 4.
        Types 1, 2.

xxxij. MATTHIAS SCHÜRER.

TYPES. Type 1, middle roman of the usual sort ; double hyphen, Q and Qu; ę and æ; thin ¶. In 1508 Q and ę only, and short sloping comma ; the round comma comes in Jan. 1509. 92 mm.—Type 2, large round gothic like Knoblouch 1 or Schott 9. Short letters 5 mm.—Type 3, text gothic with open V like Knoblouch 2, Flach jun. 3 ; single hyphen, small lopsided F ; ¶ thin till July 1510 ; afterwards a thick one is used. 80–81 mm.—Type 4, small roman like Knoblouch 13 or Schott 4 ; single hyphen till Dec. 1513 ; double from Jan. 1515 ; perhaps the fount was recast in 1514 ; 76–77 mm.—Type 5, roman slightly larger than 4 and more italian ; based on Aldus type 8; very like Joh. Schöffer 18, Anshelm 11, &c. Double hyphen; ę and æ: Qu in 1509, Q in 1510; later both are used; 76–77 mm.—Type 6, text schwabacher = Knoblouch 5ª, with thick ¶; 94–95 mm.—Type 7, square canon type = Knoblouch 12.—Type 8, german text roman with double hyphen, like Knoblouch 8, Schott 5 ; 100 mm. In Jan. 1517 a recast appears (cf. Schott 5*) on a larger body, 108 mm. ; ę and æ; Q only; double hyphen, round comma.—Type 9, square church type like Quentell 10, Knoblouch 3.—Type 10, larger text gothic, apparently imported from Italy (Venezia); round h, single hyphen, 90 mm.—Type 11, small gothic, also venetian ; resembles Hamman 5 ; tailed h, single hyphen, 70 mm.—Type 12, very large roman capitals (14 mm.) as Knoblouch 17, Schott 13 or Prüss jun. 8. Almost always used only for initials.—Type 13, smaller roman capitals (8 mm.) like Joh. Schöffer 15, Prüss jun. 11 ; not thin-faced as Ratdolt 21, Knoblouch 19 or Schott 14.—Type 14, large round type with some pointed letters ; perhaps the same as Schott 9*; short letters, 5 mm.—Type 15, second german text, like 6, but distinctive H (continuous line) and L (two, both have rounded top; the taller seems broken) ; long comma ; 95 mm. Weller 1474 and 1478 have this type for their text, but are certainly later than 1520. Schmidt, Morhard 14 is in the same types.—The Greek types are somewhat complex. The first (gk. i) is rude and straggling.—i* (Aug. 1510) appears to be a recast of i on smaller and narrower body.—ij is more sloping than i and has accents usually ; it is cast on a larger body than i* and is used with types 1 or 8, i* with 4 or 5.—iij is like Froben's second greek, and has accents, but few ligatures ; very small caps. ; used with types 1 or 8.—iij* the same, recast on smaller body (used with 4 or 5), with many ligatures and some new letters.—iv (later replaced by iij*) like iij, but on smaller body, and may be recognised by its α, δ, σ.

Type 1, see fig. 8 ; 2, see fig. 24 ; 3, see fig. 38 ; *4, see fig. 11 ; *5, see fig. 9 ; 6, see fig. 55 ; 7, see fig. 15 ; 8, see fig. 3 ; 9, see fig. 18 ; 13, see fig. 1 ; *15, see fig. 56.

BORDERS. A, quarto, openwork architectural, signed by Urs Graf; double eagle at foot. A¹, first state, with ornamental work above architrave ; in A² this has been cut away.—B, folio border dedicated to Maximilian by Beatus Rhenanus ; first used May 1512.—C, quarto, an imitation of Froben's Fool and Satyr border ; EBM. XIII. 6, but usually without the inserted initials. A close

copy of this was used, perhaps by Prüss, in 1517; see no.10265–6.—D, four-piece quarto; four
prophets at top; two fathers of the church on each side; at foot boys holding blank escutcheon.
Afterwards used by Laz. Schürer.—E, used in the Valerius Maximus of June 1518 (afterwards by
Laz. Schürer); like D, but in one piece, and the portraits are those of classical sages. Cf. no. 10607.
—Of X-borders (besides D) one is used constantly with little variation; it is here called X^1;
the right side piece is different in some books (X^{1a}) from others (X^{1b}). X^2 is used in June 1516
and in 1520 (X^{2a}); the pieces are copied from some of Froben's. In 1517 three pieces of it are
used with one piece from D (X^{2b}). X^3 (August 1518) is remarkable; the top piece represents a
king in procession (white ground, not dark as the Knoblouch-Flach block); the sides are renascence
pilasters with boys; the base represents Silenus asleep with boys playing over him.

DEVICES. a, EBM. XII. 1; b, EBM. XII. 2; c, EBM. XII. 3; d (1515–16), EBM.
XII. 4; e, EBM. XIII. 5 (cf. Laz. Schürer); q, device of Leonardus and Lucas Alantsee of
Wien, EBM. XIII. 7.

INITIALS. All are of Strassburg style. α, 18–19 mm.; β, 25 mm.; but an A and M,
perhaps others, occur, which are 23 mm. only.—γ, 12 mm. only. α and β are a good deal mixt
and perhaps hardly to be called sets. The Δ initials are the E from Schott β; a V from
Knoblouch γ, both used in June 1510; Q, 48 mm., identical with that of Prüss ζ (May 1511);
an I with two griffins (June and Aug. 1518); a calligraphic I, 88 mm. (Oct. 1520), and an A,
35 mm., used May 1512, Feb. 1513, Feb. 1517, and Dec. 1520.

10165. 1508 July 7.   Lupoldus de EGLOFFSTEIN: de iuribus et translatione
imperii. 4°. P.VI. 42. 134; SSr. 3. Type 1.

10166. 1508 Dec. GEILER: fragmenta passionis Christi. 4°. P.VI. 43. 137; SSr.
7. Types 2, 3; cut.

10167. 1509 Jan. 17. Lud. BIGI opuscula christiana. 4°. P.VI. 46. 162; SSr.
11. Type 1.

10168. 1509 Feb. ANDRELINVS: de moralibus et intellectualibus uirtutibus. 4°.
P.VI. 46. 163; SSr. 14. Type 1.

10169. 1509 Mar. EPHRAIM: sermones. 4°. P.VI. 46. 164; SSr. 15. Types 2, 3.

10170. 1509 July 8. Georgius Trapezuntius: dialectica. [GEORGE.] 4°. P.VI.
47. 175; SSr. 19. Types 1, 4; diagr.

10171. 1509 July. GREGORIVS Tifernas: opuscula. 4°. P.VI. 46. 168; SSr. 21.
Type 1; a.

10172. 1509 Aug. RAMPEGOLLIS: biblia aurea. 4°. P.VI. 47. 171; SSr. 24.
Types 2, 3.

10173. 1509 Dec.   Geo. de GEMMYNGEN: annotatiuncula pro confessoribus.
4°. P.VI. 48. 177; SSr. 26. Types 1, 2, 5.

10174. 1510 Feb. Polydorus VERGILIVS: prouerbiorum libellus. 4°. P.VI. 49.
194; SSr. 30. Types 1, 5, gk. i; a.

10175. 1510 Mar. Ioh. Ant. MODESTVS: carmen ad Maximilianum. 4°. P.VI.
50. 196; SSr. 33. Type 1.

10176. 1510 May. Gerson: sermo de passione domini. [CHARLIER.] 4°. P.VI.
51. 204. Types 2, 3; cut.

10177. [a. 1510 May 15.] GEILER: nauicula fatuorum. 4°. P.VI. 50. 202; SSr.
44. Types 1, 2, 3; cuts.

10178. 1510 June 20. Baptista Mantuanus: de fortuna Marchionis Mantuae.
[SPAGNUOLI.] 4°. P.VI. 50. 198; SSr. 36. Type 1.

10179. 1510 June 22. GEILER: der Seelen Paradies. F°. DA. 669; SSr. 37. Types
6, 7; cut; Δ.

10180. 1510 July. ERASMVS: collectanea adagiorum. 4°. P.VI. 50. 199; SSr. 40.
Type 4, gk. i.

                F

10181. 1510 July 29. GEILER: sermones de oratione dominica. 4°. P.VI. 50.
200; SSr. 39. Types 2, 3.

10182. 1510 Aug. 27. Baptista Mantuanus: Georgius. [SPAGNUOLI.] 4°. P.VI.
51. 208; SSr. 41. Types 4, 8, gk. i*.

10183. [a. 1510 Nov. 18.] Baptista Mantuanus: de patientia. [SPAGNUOLI.] 4°.
P.VI. 50. 201; SSr. 42. Types 4, 8, gk. i.

10184. n.d.[c. 1510?] Ein LOOSBUCH aus der Karten gemacht. 4°. Type 3; cuts.

10185. n.d.[c. 1510?] GEILER: das irrige Schaf (Sieben Tractätlein). 4°. DA.
670; SSr. 43. Types 2, 6, 9; cuts.

10186. 15[11] Mar. 21. Cornelius Nepos: uitae imperatorum. [AEMILIVS
PROBVS.] 4°. P.VI. 36. 83; SSr. 51. Type 1.

10187. 1511 May 12. PAVLVS Aegineta: praecepta salubria. 4°. P.VI. 53. 224;
SSr. 53. Type 1; Δ.

10188. 1511 Aug. 13. GIRALDVS: syntagma de musis. 4°. P.VI. 53. 227; SSr.
54. Types 1, 4, gk. i*; cuts.

10189. 1511 [a. 13] Aug. ERASMVS : moriae encomium. 4°. P.VI. 53. 225; SSr.
56. Types 1, 4, 5, gk. ij.

10190. 1511 Aug. Ioh. Franc. Picus: hymni heroici tres. [PICO.] F°. P.VI. 53.
226; SSr. 55. Types 1, 4, 8, gk. i*.

10191. 1511 Nov. GEILER: fragmenta passionis Christi. 4°. P.VI. 53. 228; SSr.
59. Types 2, 3, 10.

10192. 1511 Nov. Barth. ZAMBERTVS: comoedia Dolotechne. 4°. P.VI. 53. 230;
SSr. 60. Types 1, 5.

10193. 1511. BERNO: libellus de officio missae. 4°. P.VI. 54. 238; SSr. 62. Types
1, 4, gk. i*.

10194. 1511. Elisius CALENTIVS: Croacus, de bello ranarum. 4°. P. VI. 54. 235;
SSr. 67. Type 1.

10195. 1511. Collenucius: apologi quattuor. [COLLENUCCIO.] 4°. P.VI. 54. 233;
SSr. 63. Type 8.

10196. 1512 May. GEILER: nauicula paenitentiae. 4°. P.VI. 56. 251; SSr. 73.
Types 2, 5, 10, 11; Δ.

10197. 1512 June. ERASMVS: collectanea adagiorum. 4°. P.VI. 56. 253; SSr. 75.
Types 1, 4, gk. i*.

10198. 1512 July. CLICHTOVEVS: dogma moralium philosophorum. 4°. P.VI.
56. 254; SSr. 76. Types 1, 2, 4, 5.

10199. 1512 July. GIRALDVS: syntagma de musis. 4°. P. VI. 56. 256; SSr. 77.
Types 1, 4, gk. ij.

10200. 1512 Aug. Ioh. BRASSICANVS: grammaticae institutiones. 4°. P.VI. 57.
261; SSr. 83. Types 1, 2, 4, 5, gk. i*.

10201. 1512 Aug. Hadr. CASTELLANVS: uenatio. 4°. P. VI. 57. 260; SSr. 81.
Type 1.

10202. 1512 Aug. Ant. MANCINELLVS: epigrammata. 4°. [Cf. P.VI. 57. 259 &
SSr. 80.] Type 5.

10203. 1512 Sept. 1. Andr. GVARNA: bellum grammaticale. 4°. SSr. 84. Types
1, 4.

10204. 1512 Oct. ERASMVS: moriae encomium. 4°. P. VI. 57. 262; SSr. 85.
Types 1, 4, gk. ij.

10205. 1512 Dec. Ioh. DESPAVTERIVS: ars uersificatoria. 4°. P.VI. 57. 266; SSr.
89. Types 1, 2, 4, 5, gk. i*.

10206. 1512. Elisius CALENTIVS: Croacus. 4°. P.VI. 58. 269; SSr. 91. Types 1, 2.

10207. 1513 Jan. [17]. ERASMVS: de duplici copia. 4°. P.VI. 61. 289; SSr. 94. Types 1, 2, 5, gk. i*; b.

10208. 1513 Feb. GEILER: peregrinus. 4°. P.VI. 61. 290; SSr. 96. Types 1–4, 10; Δ.

10209. 1513 Feb. Pierius Valerianus: de honoribus episcopo Gurcensi habitis epistula. 4°. P.VI. 63. 307; SSr. 95. Type 1; b. [Ff. 11–14 only.]

10210. 1513 Mar. Iac. MONTANVS: odae spirituales. 4°. P.VI. 61. 291; SSr. 97. Types 1, 2, 5; b.

10211. 1513 Apr. Platinus PLATVS: de carcere. 4°. P.IX. 361. 291c. Types 1, 5.

10212. 1513 May. Henr. BEBEL: de institutione puerorum. 4°. P.VI. 61. 293; SSr. 102. Types 1, 4, gk. i*, ij.

10213. 1513 May. Conr. CELTES: odarum libri. [For L. & L. Alantsee.] 4°. P. VI. 61. 294; SSr. 99. Types 1, 4; cut; A¹.

10214. 1513 Aug. Politiani et aliorum epistulae. [AMBROGINI.] 4°. P.VI. 62. 296; SSr. 108. Types 1, gk. iij; b.

10215. 1513 Aug. Henr. BEBEL: commentaria epistularum conficiendarum. 4°. P.VI. 62. 298; SSr. 109. Types 1, 2, 4, 5, gk. i*, iij; b.

10216. 1513 Oct. MANCINELLVS: de parentum cura. 4°. P.IX. 362. 299b. Types 1, 2, 4, 5; b. [Wants Epigrammata.]

10217. 1513 Dec. ANDRELINVS: ecloga moralissima; hecatodistichon. 4°. SSr. 117. Type 1.

10218. 1513 Dec. Georgius Trapezuntius: dialectica. [GEORGE.] 4°. P.VI. 62. 302; SSr. 115. Types 1, 4; diagr.

10218A. 1513. Die wälsche Gattung. [ITALIAN RACE.] 4°. DA. 761; SSr. 123. Type 6; cuts.

10219. 1514 Feb. Germanus BRIXIVS: chordigerae nauis conflagratio. 4°. P. IX. 364. 329b; SSr. 126. Types 1, gk. iij; b; αβ.

10220. 1514 Feb. PLINIVS: epistulae. [For L. & L. Alantsee.] 4°. P.VI. 66. 328; SSr. 325. Type 5, gk. iij; β.

10221. 1514 Aug. BEBEL: opuscula noua. 4°. P.VI. 67. 336; SSr. 138. Types 1, 5, gk. iij; cut; αβ.

10222. 1514 Nov. ERASMVS: moriae encomium. 4°. P.VI. 68. 338; SSr. 143. Types 1, 5, gk. iij; X¹ᵃ; αβ.

10223. 1514 Dec. ERASMVS: de duplici copia. 4°. SSr. 145(1). Types 1, 5, gk. iv; αβ. [Wants Parabolae.]

10224. 1515 Jan. ALBERTVS magnus: de natura locorum. [For L. & L. Alantsee.] 4°. P.VI. 73. 389; SSr. 150. Types 1, 4; X¹ᵇ; q; αβ.

10225. 1515 June. STATIVS: Achilleis. 4°. P.VI. 74. 397; SSr. 157. Types 1, 2, 5; bc; αβ.

10226. 1515 July. Ioh. DESPAVTERIVS: syntaxis. 4°. P.VI. 74. 399; SSr. 162. Types 1, 2, 4, gk. iij; X¹ᵇ; αβſ.

10227. 1515 Aug. 24. BEBEL; triumphus Veneris. 4°. P.VI. 76. 414; SSr. 163. Types 1, 2, 4, gk. iij, iv; cut; αſ.

10228. 1515 Oct. Elementale introductorium in declinationes graecas. [GREEK DECLENSIONS.] 4°. P.VI. 75. 401; SSr. 166. Types 1, 2, 4, gk. iij.

10229. 1515 Nov. Lilius: de octo orationis partium constructione. [LILY.] 4°. P.VI. 75. 405; SSr. 169. Types 1, 4, gk. iij; C; αβſ.

STRASS-
BURG.
xxxij. Matt.
Schürer.

10230. 1515 Dec. 4. GEILER: sermones de oratione dominica. 4°. P.VI.76.418;
SSr. 170. Types 2, 3, 10.

10231. 1516 Feb. Ric. BARTHOLINVS: de bello norico. [For L. & L. Alantsee.]
4°. P.VI. 80. 446; SSr.181. Types 1, 4, gk. iij; D; q; α.

10232. 1516 Feb. ERASMVS: de duplici copia. 4°. P.VI. 80. 443; SSr. 180 (1).
Types 1, 5, (12), gk. iv; C; αβ. [Wants Parabolae.]

10233. 1516 Feb. HORATIVS: carmina. 4°. P.VI. 80. 444; SSr. 182. Types 1,
2; C; αγ.

10234. 1516 Mar. PHILOSTRATVS: de uitis sophistarum. 4°. P.VI. 80. 447; SSr.
183. Types 1, 4 [caps.], gk. iij; X¹ᵃ; e; αβ.

10235. [a. 1516 March 26.] Gerardus GELDENHAVRIVS: pompa exequiarum His-
paniarum regis Ferdinandi. 4°. Types 5, 13; α.

10236. 1516 Apr. Andr. GVARNA: bellum grammaticale. 4°. P. VI. 80. 449;
SSr. 185. Types 1, 4, (12), gk. iij.

10237. 1516 June. Aesopus: fabulae. [AESOP.] 4°. P.VI. 81. 452. Types 1, 5
[caps.], (12), gk. iij; C.

10238. 1516 June. ERASMVS: lucubrationes. 4°. P.VI.81. 453. Types 1, 5, (12),
gk. iij; DX²ᵃ; β.

10239. 1516 July. Plutarchus: de placitis philosophorum. [PLUTARCH.] 4°. P.
VI. 81. 456; SSr. 191. Types 1, (12); X¹ᵇ; β.

10240. 1516 July. VALERIVS MAXIMVS. 4°. P.VI.81.455; SSr. 190. Types 1, 4,
5, (12); A²; e; β.

10241. [a. 1516 July 31.] Vlr. de HVTTEN: epistula ad Maximilianum Italiae
fictitia. 4°. P. IX. 386. 276d; B. xi. 1. Types 1, 4 [caps.], 12, gk.
iij; X¹ᵇ.

10242. 1516 Aug. APVLEIVS: floridorum libri iv. 4°. P.VI. 81. 457; SSr. 193.
Types 1, 4 [caps.], 5, (12), gk. iij; X¹ᵇ; β.

10243. 1516 Sept. NILVS: sententiae morales. 4°. P.VI.82. 463; SSr. 194, 204.
Types 1, 4; X¹ᵇ.

10244. 1516 Oct. ERASMVS: de duplici copia. 4°. P.XI. 363. 471; SSr. 195.
Types 1, 4 [caps.], 5, (12), gk. iv; C; β.

10245. n. d. [c. 1516.] Polydorus VERGILIVS: de inuentoribus rerum. 4°. P. VI.
129. 897; SSr. 175. Types 1, 2, 5, gk. iv; X¹ᵇ; αγ.

10246. 1517 Jan. PALAEPHATVS: de non credendis historicis. 4°. P.VI. 86. 495;
SSr. 206. Types 4, 8*, (12), gk. iij, iv; X¹ᵇ.

10247. 1517 Feb. HORATIVS: carmina. 4°. P. VI. 86. 496; SSr. 209. Types 1,
2, 4 [caps.], (12); C.

10248. 1517 Feb. GEILER: nauicula paenitentiae. 4°. P.VI. 84. 485; SSr. 210.
Types 2, 4, 10, 11, (12), gk. iij; Δ.

10249. 1517 March. SVETONIVS: liber illustrium uirorum. 4°. P.VI. 85. 487;
SSr. 212. Types 1, 2, 4, (12), gk. iv; β.

10250. 1517 Aug. Laur. VALLA: elegantiae. 4°. P.VI. 85. 491; SSr. 216, 225.
Types 1, 4, 5, (12), 13, gk. iij, iv; X²ᵇ.

10251. [n. b. 1518 Jan.] Luciani Piscator. [LUCIAN.] 4°. P. IX. 118. 119. Types 1,
4, (12), 13, gk. iij; X¹ᵇ.

10252. 1518 June. Quintus CVRTIVS: historia Alexandri magni. F°. P.VI. 89.
520; SSr. 231. Types 1, 4, 8*, (12), 13, gk. iij; B; βΔ.

10253. 1518 Aug. Baptista Mantuanus: fasti. [SPAGNUOLI.] 4°. P.VI. 89. 522;
SSr. 233. Types 1, 4 [caps.], (12), 13; cut; X³; βΔ.

10254. 1519 Feb. LVTHER: resolutiones disputationum, etc. 4°. Types 1, 4, 5, 8*, 11, (12), 13, gk. iij ; αβ.

10255. 1519 March. ERASMVS: collectanea adagiorum. 4°. P. VI. 92. 552; SSr. 250. Types 1, 4, (12), 13, gk. iij*; X^{ib}.

10256. 1519 Aug. Aesopi et aliorum fabulae. [AESOP.—With Laz. Schürer.] 4°. P. VI. 92. 551; SSr. 249. Types 1, 4, (12), 13; X^{ib}; e; αβ.

10257. 1520 Jan. HORATIVS: epodon liber, carmen saeculare, epistulae. 4°. P. VI. 94. 573. Types 1, (12), 13.

10258. n.d.[c. 1520.] Vlr. de HVTTEN: Οὖτις, Nemo. 4°. B. xv. 2. Types 4 [caps.], 8*, (12), gk. iij*; cut; β.

10259. 1520 June 18. ERASMVS: Der Krieg ist lustig den Unerfahrenen. 4°. W. 466. Types 4 [caps.], 13–15; A²; β.

10260. [a. 1520 June 24.] LUTHER: drei Büchlein zuletzt ausgegangen. 4°. W. 1509. Types 14, 15; X^{aa}; β.

10261. 1520 Oct. LUTHER: mancherlei Büchlein und Tractätlein. 4°. DA. 974gggg. Types 9, 11, 14, 15; X^{aa}; αβΔ.

10262. 1520 Dec. 20. Kaiser Sigmunds Reformatoin. [SIGISMUND.] 4°. DA. 981. Types 14, 15; X^{aa}; αΔ.

10263. n.d. [1520–21?] Ulr. von Hutten: Gesprächbüchlein neu KARSTHANS. 4°. (Cf. W. 1794.) B. xli. 1. Types 11, 14, 15. [2ª, l. 1 of text: ... Däck dir. ‖]

10264. n.d. [1520–21?] Ulr. von Hutten: Gesprächbüchlein neu KARSTHANS. 4°. W. 1794? Types 11, 14, 15. [... Danck dir ‖]

COUNTERFEIT EDITIONS.

[Perhaps by Prüss jun.—Type 1 = Prüss jun. 2, with similar ¶, curved at foot. (Cf. Schürer 1.)—Type 2 = Prüss 8 or Schürer 12.—Greek type as Prüss, not as Schürer.—Border A, a close copy of Schürer C.—Initials (α) imitated from Schürer Γ (12 mm.) ; these occur only on B 1, 2, 7, 8 of the undated Aesop.]

10265. n. d. [c. 1516?] Aesopi et aliorum fabulae. [AESOP.] 4°. Types 1, 2; A; α.

10266. 1517 March. Aesopi et aliorum fabulae. [AESOP.] 4°. P. VI. 85. 486 ; SSr. 213? Types 1, 2, gk.; A.

xxxiij. JOHANN SCHOTT, third press.

TYPES. Type 4*, a recast of 4 (see press 26), with round comma and single hyphen; 77 mm. ; first used in 1519.—Type 5*, a recast of 5 (text roman; see Freiburg press 3) with Q separate ; double hyphen and round comma ; 110 mm.—Type 7, middle roman, as Knoblouch 7, &c. ; double hyphen ; 87 mm.—Type 8, text gothic, like Knoblouch 2, but some caps. (M, V) are from a fount like Grüninger 20 ; short double hyphen ; 83 mm. ; facs., EBM. III.— Type 9, large round like Knoblouch 1. Facs. Butsch I. 67. 9⁶, the same type germanised; the new letters, d, pointed h and f, &c., are from a smaller fount like Grüninger 17 (after 1506).— Type 10, square canon type like Knoblouch 12. Facs. Butsch I. 67.—Type 11, small text, like Knoblouch 9. Round h, double hyphen ; 71 mm.—Type 12, remarkable text schwabacher, which differs from Köbel's type 8 only in its h, the tail of which curves in and out again ; 95–96 mm. See also Heumann 4.—Type 13, very large caps. as Knoblouch 17 ; 14 mm.—Type 14, smaller caps., 7–8 mm. ; thin, like Knoblouch 19.—Type 15, italic, with roman capitals; not like Knoblouch 22.—Second greek, in the style of Froben's or Knoblouch's ; but being designed to range with type 5* it is larger-faced, bolder, and less contracted.

45

Type 4*, see fig. 11; *5*, see fig. 3; 7, see fig. 8; 8, see fig. 38 (and 34); 9, see fig. 24; 10, see fig. 15; 11, see fig. 45; *12, see fig. 57; 14, see fig. 2; 15, see fig, 12.

BORDERS.   A, folio, as B, except size; imperial eagle and label at foot.   Facs. Butsch I. 67.   In Nov. 1510 printed in black and brown from two blocks (in chiaroscuro).   Used in a second state by Beck in 1513 (his B).——B. like A, but quarto, the same as Knoblouch B; used 1510 Nov. 17.   Butsch I. 86.   Bª; see Knoblouch B².——C, octavo, stripy ground, printed in chiaroscuro; at sides weapons; at foot two boys wrestling before two umpires.——D, large folio; the judgment of Paris.——The Y piece of 1510 is a hare on a white ground, like one used by Froben; those of 1515 are very curious, black and narrow, without edge-lines.

DEVICES.   e (1512), EBM. III. 6a; f (1516), EBM. III. 7; g is the device used at S. Dié (1507) by G. and N. Lud.

INITIALS.   α, black grounded, 28–30 mm.; largely = Knoblouch Γ, but a good deal mixt; a P and E with diced ground are distinctive; some letters are thinner than others; of A there are both thick and thin forms.   Some (L, R, S, and the P, E, just mentioned) have no medial line, or if it is found, it is on one side.   The usual I is that of xiv. H; but there is a second (1518 Feb.) agreeing with the diced P and E.——β, part of the historiated set to which the Nativity used by Beck and the Annunciation and Death of O. L. used by Knoblouch (ε) belong: A (55 mm.), David harping; C (54 mm.), procession with Corpus Domini; E (55 mm.), Adoration of Magi (also used by Schürer); S (57 mm.), procession with candles.——Γ, same set as Knoblouch β; shaded letters, 46–50 mm.; an I (49 mm.) is of different design, unshaded, and a larger version of that of α.——δ, two letters, G and Q, used in Ptolemy of 1520; G, 46 mm., white letter, boy with astronomical globe; Q, 40 mm., black letter, Sagittarius.   The only Δ initial of note is a S, black letter on a white ground representing Moses receiving the law; no edge line; first used 1516 Aug. 30.

10267.   1510 Aug. 10.   Iac. PORCIA comes Purliliarum: de liberorum educatione. 4°. P. VI. 49. 190; SS. 13. Type 7; Y.

10268.   1510 Nov. 5.   Nicolaus Panormitanus: lectura super libris decretalium. F°. P. VI. 49. 191; SS. 16. Types 7, 8, 9, 10; A; α. [Print Room.]

10269.   1511 Feb. 3.   Ioh. LVPVS: de libertate ecclesiastica. 4°. P. VI. 52. 220; SS. 18. Types 8, 9; C.

10270.   1511 March 6.   Marsilius Ficinus: de triplici uita. [FICINO.] 4°. P. VI. 52. 221; SS. 19. Types 8, 9.

10271.   1513 March 12–15.   PTOLEMAEVS: geographia. F°. P. VI. 60. 283; SS. 21. Types 5*, 7, 8, 10, gk. ij; diagr., maps.

10272.   1513 Sept. 1.   Poggius: operum partes ij. [BRACCIOLINI.—For J. Knoblouch.] F°. P. VI. 61. 285; SS. 22. Types 5*, 7; cut; βΓ.

10273.   1513.   Ioh. Franc. Picus: de expellendis Venere et Cupidine, etc. [PICO.] 4°. P. VI. 61. 287; SS. 23. Type 5*.

10274.   1513.   WIMPHELING: castigationes locorum in canticis ecclesiasticis deprauatorum. 4°. P. VI. 61. 286; SS. 24. Type 5*.

10275.   1514 March 24.   Wendel. HOCK: mentagra. 4°. P. VI. 65. 324; SS. 27. Types 5*, 9.

10276.   1515.   NACHTIGALL: collectanea sacrosancta. 4°. P. VI. 73. 387; SS. 32. Types 5*, gk. ij; Y.

10277.   1515.   Λουκιανοῦ θεῶν διάλογοι, gr. & lat. [LUCIAN.] 4°. P. VI. 73. 385; SS. 31. Types 5*, gk. ij; Y; αΔ.

10278.   1516 Feb. 26.   Surgant: manuale curatorum. [For P. Götz.] 4°. P. VI. 79. 436; SS. 35; W. 1019. Types 8, 9, 12; cut; B²; f; α. [Print Room.]

10279.   1516 Aug. 30.   NICOLAVS de Dinkelsbühl: tractatus uarii. F°. P. VI. 79. 437; SS. 36. Types 5*, 8, 9, 10; αΓΔ.

10280.   1516. Ioh. LINTHOLZ: arbores consanguinitatis, affinitatis, etc. F°. Types 5*, 8, 9; cuts; f; αΓ.

10281. n. d. [c. 1516.] BONIFACIVS ord. min.: defensorium elucidatiuum obseruantiae regularis. 4°. P. IX. 167. 50. Types 8, 9; cut; Δ.

10282. 1517 [a. 1516 Dec. 1]. Ioh. NIDER: formicarius. [For Knoblouch & Götz.]
4°. P. VI. 84. 481; SS. 39. Types 8–11; α.

10283. 1517 March 1. Ioh. de BVRGO: pupilla oculi. [For Knoblouch & Götz.]
4°. P. VI. 84. 482; SS. 38. Types 9, 10, 11 (= Kn. 1, 9, 12).

10284. n. d. [c. 1517.] Nic. MENGIN: venediger Chronica. 4°. W. 514. Types
9^B, 12; g.

10285. 1517 [a. Aug. 22]. Hans von GERSDORFF: Buch der Wundarznei. F°.
DA. 882; SS. 40. Types 9^B, 12; cuts; Y; αгΔ.
1517 Sept. 1. Der Heiligen Leben. Types 9^B, 12; cuts; α. (Sig. mm
1–6, nn 1, 6 only.) See no. 10114.

10286. 1518 Feb. 19. Petr. de CRESCENTIIS: vom Nutz der Dinge die in Äckern
gebaut werden. [For Knoblouch & Götz.] F°. DA. 908; W. 1103;
SS. 42. Types 9^B, 12; cuts; Y; αΔ.

10287. [a. 1519 June 28.] Oratio legationis Francisci regis Franciae ad electores
imperii. [FRANCE.] 4°. P. IX. 370. 544b; SS. 47. Types 4*, 5*; cut.

10288. 1519 [a. July 15]. Hier. GEBWEILER: libertas Germaniae. 4°. P. VI. 91.
542; SS. 52. Types 4*, 5*; cut; α.

10289. 1520. PTOLEMAEVS: geographia. F°. P. VI. 94. 572; SS. 54. Types 5*,
13, 14, gk. ij; cuts, diagr.; D; αδ.

10290. [a. 1520 July 15.] Leo x.: bulla contra errores Lutheri cum annota-
tionibus Hutteni. [ROME.] 4°. P. IX. 124. 166; B. xxxii. 1. Types 4*,
5*, 14.

10291. [a. 1520 Sept. 28.] HVTTEN: conquestiones (a–f). 4°. P. IX. 456. 1; B.
xxxi. 4. Types 4* [caps.], 5*, 14.

10292. [a. 1520 Sept. 28.] HVTTEN: conquestiones (a–e). 4°. B. xxxi. 1. Type 5*.

10293. n. d. [1520?] Ulr. v. HUTTEN: Anzeige wie die Päpste sich allwegen
gegen den deutschen Kaisern gehalten haben. 4°. W. 1406; SS. 57;
B. xxxv. 1. Types 9^B, 12, (13), 15; B².

10294. n. d. [1520?] Vlr. de HVTTEN: exclamatio in incendium lutheranum.
4°. SS. 56; B. xxxiii A3. Types 4*, 5*, (13, 14).

10295. n. d. [1520?] Ulr. von HUTTEN: Gedicht von einem Tyrannen. 4°. W.
1118; B. xiia. Type 12; cut.

10296. n. d. [1520?] Ulr. von HUTTEN: Klage und Vormahnung gegen dem Gewalt des Papsts. 4°. W. 1416; B. xxxiv. 1. Types 4*, 5* [caps.], 9^B, 12,
(13); cut; α.

10297. n. d. [1520?] LVTHER: de captiuitate babylonica ecclesiae. 4°. SS. 55.
Types 4*, 13, 14; cuts.

10298. n. d. [1520?] LUTHER: von der babylonischen Gefängnis der Kirchen.
4°. W. 1536; SS. 55a. Types 4* [caps.], 9^B, 12; cuts; α.

10299. [a. 1520 Dec. 25.] Matth. GNIDIVS: defensio Christianorum de cruce. 4°.
P. VII. 91. 184. Types 5*, 9, (13), 15; g.

STRASS-
BURG.
xxxiij. Joh.
Schott.

xxxiv. REINHARD BECK, first press.

TYPES. Type 1 = xiv. (Prüss sen.) 13.—Type 2 = xiv. 19 ; large text schwabacher like Joh.
Otmar 17 ; small ℂ.—Type 3 = xiv. 17.—Type 4 = xiv. 4. For continuation see Baden and
press 35 below.

BORDER. A, quarto ; described in SB. no. 1.

INITIALS. α, Maiblumen, partly the same as xiv. ε.—β, Maiblumen, like ſ, but not the
same ; 30 mm.—ſ, Maiblumen, the same as xiv. δ ; 27 mm.—Δ is the T for the Canon which
the elder Prüss used.

10300. 1511 Sept. 12. Missale Bremense. [LIT.—For Caspar de Mellerstadt.]
F°. Types 1–4 ; cut ; αβſΔ. [Wants cut.]

xxxv. REINHARD BECK, from Baden, third press.

TYPES. Types 1–4, see press 34.—Type 5 (small roman as xiv. 16) see Baden.—Type 6 =
xiv. 15.—Type 7 = xiv. 14, with ℂ.—Type 8, small text, like xiv. 11, but perhaps new ; 72 mm.
Cf. Knoblouch 9ᴮ.—Type 9 = xiv. 20 ; 87 mm.—Type 10, large latin text = Knoblouch 11.—
Type 11, large round type, different from 14. Cf. Knoblouch 1.—Type 12, text roman ; cf. xiv.
18 ; but this is 108 mm.—Type 13, text schwabacher = xiv. 12, with a different (latin) B and E,
and double hyphen ; in the books of 1519–20 the h is variable (no. 10318 has a new one), and
there are two forms of H. The L is also a new one.—Type 14, middle large round = xiv. 7.—
Type 15, latin text = xiv. 8.—Type 16, small = xiv. 10.—Greek type.

Type 11, see fig. 24. For types 1–9, 12, 13, 15, 16, see the references given in press xiv.

BORDERS. A, see press 34 ; in the Alexandreis of 1513 it is printed in chiaroscuro (red
and black) from two blocks.—B, folio, stripy ground, like A but simpler ; owl at top, imperial
eagle at foot. This is a later state of Schott A.—Cc, border-device, EBM. XIV. 1, used in the
Gemma gemmarum of 1514–15 ; but in 1520 (or later) it was in the possession of Melchior Ramminger at Augsburg ; the Gründlicher Unterschied by Chr. Hitz, 1526, mentioned in EBM. is
also in Rammiger's type, but in this case the monogram has been cut out from the border. Cf.
SB. 34, probably also by Rammiger.—D, folio, inner edge of top rounded ; boys hold a blank
shield at foot. Cf. Knoblouch D.—E = Prüss jun. A.—An X border, almost identical in the various
books where it is found ; only the position of the parts varies. That of no. 10309 (X²) is different.

DEVICES. a (EBM. XV. 2), see Baden.—b, EBM. XIV. 3.—c, see border C.

INITIALS. α–ſ, see press 34.—δ, see Baden.—ε = xiv. ſ ; one letter only found.—ʒ, french
style, 30–32 mm.—н, french style, 26–27 mm.—θ, Strassburg style, 16–17 mm. ; each letter has
an inner bounding line.—ι, like θ, but 12–13 mm. only.—κ, = xiv. α, much worn.—λ, calligraphic,
29 mm. = xiv. β.—м, french, 23 mm.—ν, like θ, with similar inner lines, but somewhat smaller ;
15 mm.—ξ, also like θ, but letters thicker, and all white ; 16 mm. The odd (Δ) initials include a
stripy P with the Nativity, 56 mm. (Aug. 1513 ; part of the set Schott β ; cf. Knoblouch ε) ; R of
xij. β? and G of xij.ʒ? (1513 Dec.) ; D from xiv. ε (1515) ; and a calligraphic W, 18 mm. (1519 July).

10301. 1512 Mar. 18. HENRICVS de Hagenoia : de uita et moribus episcoporum. 4°.
P. VI. 58. 271 ; SB. 5. Types 1, 5, 6, 7 ; cut ; a ; ε.

10302. 1513 Aug. 31. ANGELVS de Clauasio : summa angelica. [For J. Rinmann
and J. Knoblouch.] F°. P. VI. 63. 313 ; SB. 7. Types 1, 4, 6, 8–11 ; B ;
b ; ʒнΔ.

10303. 1513 [a. Dec. 25]. GVALTHERVS : Alexandreis. 4°. P. IX. 363. 313c ; SB. 11.
Types 1, 5, 7, 12 ; A ; нΔ.

10304. 1513–14. TORRENTINVS : elucidarius carminum et historiarum. 4°. P. VI.
69. 350 ; SB. 14. Types 1, 6, 7, 8, 13, gk. ; A ; ʒθ.

10305. 1514 [a. Feb. 15]. GRESEMVNDVS : carmen de historia uiolatae crucis. 4°.
P. VI. 68. 347 ; SB. 15. Types 5, 6, 7 ; cut ; ʒнθ.

10306. 1514. Iac. Faber : introductio in physicam paraphrasim. [LEFÈVRE.] 4°.
P. VI. 68. 348 ; SB. 17. Types 5, 6, 7 ; A ; diagr. ; ʒθ.

10307. 1515 June 16. Aeneas Syluius: Germania. [PIUS ij.] 4°. P.VI. 75.410; SB.21. Types 2,5,6,7,12; X; b; δϩηθι.

10308. 1515. Psalterium dauidicum, cantica et hymni. [BIBLE.] 4°. Types 1,4,6, 12; X²; κΔ.

·10309. [a. 1516 June 25.] HENRICVS de Hassia: contra disceptationes fratrum mendicantium. 4°. P.VI. 82.470; SB.23. Types 1,2,7,8,12,14; cut; X; ηθι.

1517 Sept. 1. Der Heiligen Leben. [Knoblouch; sig. a 1ᵃ, a 2, 7, 8 by Beck?] Types 1,2,6,13; D; H. See no. 10114.

10310. 1517. HORTVS sanitatis. F°. P. IX. 115. 99. Types 1, 4, 7 [caps.], 8,9, 10,14,15,16; cuts; D; ϩηθιλ.

10311. 1518. Hier. CINGVLARIVS: synonymorum collectanea. 4°. P.VI.90. 529; SB.28. Types 1,2,6,8,12; X; μ.

10312. 1519 [a. Mar. 15]. HAYMO: expositio super epistulas Pauli. F°. P.VI. 92.553; SB.29. Types 1,4,6,7,12,15; B; δηθιμνξ.

10313. [a. 1519 July 3.] Verschreibung und Verwilligung Karls v. gegen dem Reich. [GERMANY.] 4°. DA. 948b. Types 1,13; cut; ημ.

10314. [a. 1519 July 3.] Die Verschreibung und Verwilligung . . . [GERMANY.] 4°. W. 1287. Types 1, 6, 13; cuts; ηΔ.

10315. [a. 1519 July 29.] Franz von SICKINGEN: Erforderung an und wider Provincial, Prioren und Conventen Prediger Ordens. 4°. W. 1268. Types 1,13; cuts; H.

10316. n. d. [1520?] Luther: von der Freiheit eines christen Menschen. [CHRISTIAN MAN.] 4°. W. 1527. Types 1,13; E.

10317. n. d. [1520?] KARSTHANS. 4°. W. 1433. Types 4,13; cut; βθ.

10318. n.d. [1520?] Das teutsche Requiem der verbrannten Bullen. [GERMAN REQUIEM.] 4°. W. 1543. Types 1,13; β.

10319. n. d. [1520–21?] Lux GEMIGGER: Lob des Luther. 4°. W.2073. Type 13.

xxxvi. JOHANN PRÜSS THE YOUNGER.

TYPES. Type 1 = xiv. (Prüss sen.) 13.—Type 2 = xiv. 14. In 1520 this type has a single hyphen.—Type 3 = xiv. 16.—Type 4 = xiv. 12.—Type 5 = xiv. 7 (medium large round, mixt capitals).—Type 6 = xiv. 11.—Type 7, latin text gothic = xiv. 8?—Type 8, very large roman caps., 14 mm.; cf. Knoblouch 17, M. Schürer 12, &c.—Type 9 = xiv. 17.—Type 10 = xiv. 15.—Type 11, large roman caps., 8–9 mm.; the same as M. Schürer 13.—Greek type, different from that of xiv., less regular; forms in it from a fount like Knoblouch's second greek from the beginning; these at last are the majority.

Types 1–4, 6, 9, 10; see references given under press xiv. Type 5, see Burger 77, larger type; 7, see fig. 37; 11, see fig. 1.

BORDERS. A, quarto, dark stripy ground; boys playing at foot. Used later, as it seems, by Beck (E).—B, also quarto, light stripy ground; at foot lions holding a shield.—An X border used in nos. 10322 and 10323 without change. No. 10332 has X borders to every page.

INITIALS. α, Strassburg style, dotted ground, 25–26 mm.; cf. Knoblouch ζ, Schürer β, &c. —β, similar initials, 18 mm.; cf. Knoblouch H, Schürer α, &c.

10320. 1513. Ioh. BRASSICANVS: grammaticae institutiones. 4°. P.IX.361.277b; SPb. 3 (1512). Types 1–3, gk.; α.

10321. 1513. Steph. HOEST: modus praedicandi. 4°. P.VI. 58. 274; SPb. 5. Types 1–4; α.

G

10322. 1513. Franc. Philelphus: epistulae breuiores. [FILELFO.] 4°. P.VI. 59.
275; SPb. 7. Types 1, 2, 3; X.

10323. 1515 Mar. 23. Ioh. ALTENSTAIG: uocabularius. 4°. P.VI. 69. 357; SPb.
10. Types 2, 3, 5, 6, gk.; X; αβ.

10324. 1515. Ioh. Cochlaeus: grammatica. [DOBNECK.] 4°. P.VI. 70. 359; SPb.
14; W. 892. Types 2, 3, gk.; A; αβ.

10325. 1516. RICARDVS de S. Victore; de duodecim patriarchis. 8°. P.VI. 78.
434; SK. 128. Types 2, 5, 6, 10; β. [Knoblouch.]

10326. 1516. WIMPHELING: elegantiae maiores. 4°. SK. 130. Types 2, 3, 5, 10;
A; α. [Knoblouch.]

n. d. [c. 1516–7.] Aesopi fabulae. 4°. Types 2, 8. [Schürer counterfeit,
probably by Prüss; see no. 10265.]

10327. [a. 1517 Feb. 28.] Ad Leonem x. Maximiliani Caesaris responsio.
[MAXIMILIAN.] 4°. P. IX. 116. 109. Types 2, 8.

1517 March. Aesopi fabulae. 4°. Types 2, 8, gk. [Schürer counterfeit,
probably by Prüss: see no. 10266.]

1517. Persius. 4°. P.VI. 83. 475; SK. 145. [Knoblouch, but perhaps
by Prüss; type 2; αβ.] See no. 10112.

10328. 1518. MVRNER: chartiludium institutae. [For Joh. Knoblouch.] 4°. P.VI.
87. 504; SPb. 15. Types 3, 5–9, 10; cuts.

10329. 1519 May. ERASMVS: paraclesis. 8°. P.VI. 92. 557. Types 2, 3, 11, gk.; α.

10330. 1519. NILVS: sententiae morales. 8°. P.VI. 92. 556. Types 3, (8), 11.

10331. n. d. [c. 1519.] Iulius; dialogus uiri cuiuspiam eruditissimi. [JULIUS ij.]
8°. Types 3, 11; α.

10332. 1520 Aug. SVETONIVS: uitae Caesarum. 4°. P. VI. 93. 561; SPb. 22.
Types 2, 3 [caps.], 11, gk.; BX; α.

10333. n. d. Ratbüchlein. Wolchem an kürtzweill thet zerrinden... [KURZWEIL.]
4°. W. 1260. Types 1, 4?; cut.

xxxvij. WILHELM SCHAFFENER, from Lahr, fifth press.

[The only book of Schaffener after his return to Strassburg is the edition of Morgenstern's
Sermones dated 31 Aug. 1515; P. VI. 76. 413; Schmidt 6.]

xxxviij. CONRAD KERNER.

The relation of Kerner and Knoblouch is perplexing. The first of the two books (both of 1517)
bearing Kerner's name is printed in a quite distinctive type (type 1). This is found elsewhere
only in one book professing to be printed by (durch) Knoblouch, where it is associated with one
other non-Knoblouch fount (type 3) and two founts (2 and 4) common to many Strassburg printers.
On the other hand the second book with Kerner's name (Die Arch Noe, 1517; Schmidt 3) is printed,
if Schmidt is to be trusted, in two founts otherwise connected only with Knoblouch (and Flach),
and has a border used by Knoblouch and Flach. As the companion volume (Der geistliche
Streit) has no printer's name, and it does not seem justifiable to assign all books printed in these
types to Kerner, it is here placed among Knoblouch's books.

TYPES. Type 1, fine and distinctive schwabacher, with thin saw-edge C; 94–95 mm. This
is the only type which can be attributed with certainty to Kerner.—Type 2, canon = Knoblouch 12.
—Type 3, large round = Grüninger 17 (not a Knoblouch type).—Type 4, small schwabacher as
Knoblouch 6, Flach 11, Wähinger 2; with C; 75 mm.

Type 2, see fig. 15; 3, see fig. 28; 4, see fig. 63°.

BORDER. A = Knoblouch F, according to Schmidt; cf. Flach jun. A.

INITIALS. A Strassburg style D, very like a letter of Knoblouch н, but seemingly not identical; called α.

10334. 1517. Joh. von Paltz: die himmlische Fundgrube. 4°. DA. 867; W. 1041; SKer. 1. Type 1. [Ff. 17–24 only.]
    [a. 1517 Mar. 31.] Ulr. Krafft: der geistliche Streit. SKer. 2. See no. 10110.

10335. 1519. Luther: die sieben Busspsalmen. [BIBLE.] 4°. DA.926c; SK.183. Types 1–4; cut; α. [Knoblouch.]

STRASS-
BURG.
xxxviij.
Conr.
Kerner.

xxxix. ULRICH MORHARD, first press.

The book described by Schmidt as no. 1, with the date Jan. MD.IXX, belongs to 1521, not to 1519, as is shown by a copy in B.M. with corrected date.

TYPES. Type 1, middle roman, in which the M is noticeable; the middle point comes down to the line-level. Double hyphen; 93 mm.—Type 2, roman caps. as M. Schürer 13; 8 mm. Some similar but smaller caps. are used as initials.

Type 1, see fig. 8; 2, see fig. 1.

BORDER. A, a close copy of a border of Froben (Butsch I. 41), Holbein's name and Froben's device being omitted.

INITIALS. α, shaded ground, with figures; 30 mm.—β, Strassburg style, 24–25 mm., like M. Schürer β.

10336. 1520 Sept. Quattuor euangelia ab Erasmo recognita. [BIBLE.] 4°. P.VI. 94. 578; SM. 2. Types 1, 2; A; αβ.

WITHOUT PRINTER'S NAME.

WITHOUT NAME OF PLACE OR PRINTER.

Type 1, small latin text gothic, very like Hüpfüff 6, but has double hyphen as 6ᴮ, and the face is slightly different; it has both round and square C, but the former is not quite the same as Hüpfüff's; the capitals are mixt, but the added ones are not the same as in the other Strassburg types of this class. 71 mm.

Type 2, large round, larger than Knoblouch 1; short letters nearly 6 mm. Like Flach jun. 1, but distinguishable by the a. Type 3, latin text gothic of Kesler-Richel style, with some duplicate caps. from a Furter-Hochfeder fount; large face, very small double hyphen; 83 mm. Type 3 bis, middle german roman, very like Hüpfüff 10; ę and æ, double hyphen, no paragraph mark; comma like Hüpfüff; 86 mm.

Type 4, text schwabacher, very like Prüss jun. 4 (sen. 12), but the comma, which is short, slopes the normal way, and H is like Knoblouch 5ᶜ [1509]; tall L as Prüss; 95 mm.—Initial α, calligraphic, as Prüss sen. β.

Type 5, very like 4, but normal H, long comma; long double hyphen as 4; differs from Prüss jun. 4 in comma and hyphen only; 95 mm. Initial as last.

Type 6, text schwabacher = M. Schürer 15, except D, which is differently sloped; but in a book dated 1521 March 15 both sorts of D are used. The date of no. 10343 is however difficult to reconcile with Schürer.—Initials; calligraphic W, 61 mm., Z, 31 mm.

Type 7 = Knoblouch 5ᶜ, but the date does not agree. Type 8, broad church text; short letters 5 mm.—Initial; Strassburg style, quite new, dotted ground, 24 mm. Not Knoblouch ⸮.—These types are found only on leaves 2 and 3 of no. 10122. Perhaps they come from the edition of 1511.

Type 1, see fig. 45; 2, see fig. 63¹; 3, see fig. 42; 3 bis, see fig. 8; 4, see fig. 54 (for D), 55 (for H); 5, see fig. 54; 6, see fig. 56; 7, see fig. 55.

10337. n. d. [c. 1505?] MATTHAEVS ord. praed.: tractatus super nauiculam beatae Vrsulae. 4°. Type 1; cut.

10338. 1515 June 29. WIMPHELING: adulescentia. [By, i.e. for Knoblouch.] 4°. P.VI. 72. 374; SK. 94. Types 2, 3.

10339. n. d. Rich. de MONTECRVCIS: confutatio Alcorani. 4°. P. IX. 170. 85. Types 2, 3 bis.

10340. [a. 1515 Sept. 28.] Mandat gegen Deutsche im französischen Dienst. (d: Innsbruck.) [GERMANY.] open F°. W. 925. Type 4; α.

10341. [a. 1516 Jan. 16.] Mandat gegen alle welche König Franz Hülfe leisten. (d: Augsburg.) [GERMANY.] open F°. W. 1012. Type 4; α.

10342. [a. 1518 July 19.] Verbot die Reben vor Herbst zu verkaufen. [STRASS-BURG.] F°. W. 1157. Type 5; α. [One leaf.]

10343. [a. 1518 Nov. 4.] Mandat die Büchsen betreffend. (d: Augsburg, 28. vii. 18; Strassburg, 4. xi.) [GERMANY.] open F°. W. 1143 + 1144. Type 6; Δ. [By M. Schürer?]

1519 Jan. 5. Gessler: Formulare. Ff. 2, 3 in types 7, 8; Δ. See no. 10122.

III. BAMBERG.

3 (c) Johann Pfeil.

---

iij. JOH. PFEIL.

TYPES. Types 10 (square church, larger) and 11 (smaller), see part i; facs. Druckschriften 25; both types are on the same body; 195 mm.—Type 13, large text, like Koberger 16, G. Stuchs 7; type 14, smaller than 13, like Koberger 15, G. Stuchs 8; both on same body; 110 mm. Facs. Woolley Phot. 20. These types are first used in 1495.—Type 18, rounded canon, as Joh. Stuchs 7, Joh. Otmar 26, &c.—Type 19, round church text, like Weissenburger 4 or Gutknecht 4; double hyphen; type 20, smaller, like Gutknecht 5 without the german sorts; lowercase like 13, but the caps. are those of 19; hyphens like 19, not as 13. Both types are on the same body; 149 mm.—Type 21, narrow church text = G. Stuchs 5; type 22, smaller ditto = G. Stuchs 6; both types are on the same body; 169 mm. See Burger 35.—Type 23, thick bold square canon, seemingly modelled on type 8 (Burger 105, right half) but not the same; E differs notably. Short letters 10 mm. Not a Nürnberg type.—Type 24, latin text gothic = G. Stuchs 12, but note the ⁋; 87 mm.—Type 25, small text schwabacher, like G. Stuchs 18; double hyphen, short comma, ⁋; 87 mm. The connexion with Nürnberg so marked before 1500 is thus fully kept up.

INITIALS. α, 49–50 mm., for service-books, with pictures of the events commemorated; e.g. L (Leuaui) = David; G (Gaudeamus) = crowning of Our Lady; and so on.

10344. 1501 Dec. 14. Breuiarium Babenbergense. [LIT.] F°. Types 13,14; cut.

10345. 1506 Feb. 3. Speciale missarum secundum chorum Babenbergensem. [LIT.] F°. P.VI.172.1. Types 18–20; cuts; α. [A fourth type in sigs.]

10346. 1507 Dec. 20. Missale Babenbergense. [LIT.] F°. P.VI. 172.2. Types 19, 21–23; cuts; α.

10347. 1509 Aug. 31. Statuta synodalia. [BAMBERG.] F°. P.VI. 172. 3. Types 21,24; cut.

10348. [n. b. 1511.] Die Legende und das Leben Kaiser Heinrichs. [HENRY ij.] 4°. DA. 690. Types 19, 25; cuts.

10349. 1518 Apr. 30. Missale Ratisponense. [LIT.] F°. P. IX. 388. 4c. Types 10,11,18,19,21,23; cuts. [On vellum.]

IV. KÖLN.

---

i. ULRICH ZEL.

Zel's material passed into the hands of Lorenz Bornemann (1507) and later belonged to Theod. Tzwivel (1514); both were printers at Münster in Westphalen. Zel died after August 1507. See Merlo-Zaretzky, Ulrich Zell (1900).

TYPES. Types 5 (latin text gothic with open V; single hyphen; at this time mixt with caps. from types 3 and 4); 7 (canon, like Quentell 9); 10 (church text, very like Joh. Schöffer 5, Arnt of Aachen 1); see part i.—Type 11, dutch text, like Bumgart 6.

Type 5, see fig. 38; 7, see fig. 15; 10, 11, see type register.

10350. [1502 b. May 28.] Raym. Peraudi: literae indulgentiarum. [ROME.] obl. Types 4, 7, 10, 11. [On vellum.]

xxiij. LUDWIG, OF RENCHEN.

At least two books by Ludwig are dated later than 1500. One is the Aureum reminiscendi memorandique opusculum of 1501 Dec. 10; the other is Weller suppl. i. no. 340, dated 1505 Aug. 28. The address given is the same in both books: in noua platea in rota; zom rait in der newer gassen. No. 1274 (part i) doubtless belongs to this period.

TYPES. Type 1 (larger church; cf. M. of Werden 6), 2 (smaller church), 4 (text schwabacher, here mixt with caps. from type 8, which is like Bumgart 6); see part i.

10351. n.d. Ioh. SCHIPHOWER de Meppis: tractatus de beata Maria Magdalena. 4°. Types 1, 2, 4; cuts; Y.

TYPES. Types 5 (small text, as revived in 1499; 72 mm.; tailed h, broad and narrow; on and after 1508 Jan. 24 a third, quasi-schwabacher form is found; single hyphen, but a double one is also used in and after July 1503; caps. of type 13 are first used in the Petrus Rauennas of 1506, and are always found afterwards in increasing numbers; cf. Prüss sen. 11); 6 (small type, 63 mm.; tailed h alone before 1510 May 31; on and after that date round h is also found; very large double hyphen; cf. Prüss sen. 10); 7 (latin text gothic, single hyphen, round h; 80 mm.; cf. Prüss sen. 8); 9 (square canon of Strassburg style, short letters 9 mm.; cf. Prüss sen. 4); 10 (church type like Prüss sen. 13; double hyphen); 12 (text roman like Prüss sen. 18; double hyphen; very small us; a new W in Nov. 1520; 95 mm.); 13 (small roman, like Grüninger 23 [or Prüss sen. 16, but double hyphen]; 72 mm.). For these see part i.—Type 14, smaller church type, apparently a reduction of type 10, but some caps. seem those of Koelhoff sen. 14 (Burger pl. 16). Cf. Heinrich of Neuss 2.—Type 15, small german, Kirchheim style, very like Burngart 5, but the hyphen is mixt, and a w.f. h is much used; the few w.f. caps. are also different, being mostly from type 7; 80 mm. This is the text type of the Spegel der Sielen, Peter Quentell, 1520. —Greek type.

Types 5, see fig. 45 (not h); 6, see fig. 46; 7, see fig. 37; 9, see fig. 15; 10, see fig. 18; 12, see fig. 3; 13, see fig. 11; 14, see fig. 20; 15, see fig. 64.

INITIALS. α, a copy of Grüninger β (Heitz 2), 24–25 mm. The A is last found whole in Feb. 1505; after 1510 it is still more broken.—β, a copy of Grüninger δ, 15–16 mm.—Γ, a copy of Grüninger Γ; only two letters found; 17 mm. The Δ initials are few and for the most part (marked *) recur constantly: *S copied from the Wagner set, with a square draught round it, 40 mm. (cf. Burngart α); V, saint writing at desk, letter black, 42–43 mm.; *Q, a fool's head, black ground, 30 mm.; Q, black ground, 3-flowered plant, 37 mm.; P, of similar style, 38 mm.; *a calligraphic letter used for C or T indifferently, or reversed, once for D.—Cut c of part i is used in no. 10354, 10361, 10376, 10381, 10397, 10409, 10413, 10414, 10425.

(a) Heinrich Quentell.

1501 Jan. 8. LAVACRVM: conscientiae. 4°. P. VI. 347. 1. Martin of Werden for Quentell; see no. 10499.

10352. 1501 May 15. IACOBVS Magdalius Gaudensis: aerarium poetarum. 4°. P. VI. 348. 3. Types 9, 10, 12, 13.

10353. 1501 July 16. Pet. DORLANDVS: uiola animae. 4°. P. VI. 348. 4. Types 5, 9, 10, 12.

10354. 1501. Bernardus: floretus. [BERNARD.] 4°. P. VI. 349. 16. Types 6, 7, 9, 10; cut.

10355. 1501. Nic. WOLLICK: opus aureum musicae. 4°. P. VI. 348. 9. Types 5, 9, 10, 12; diagr. [Woodcut music. Wants leaf 7.]

10356. 1501. Ioh. de SACRO BOSCO: opus sphaericum. 4°. P. VI. 349. 11. Types 5, 9, 10; cuts, diagr.

10357. 1501. Ioh. de LAPIDE: resolutorium dubiorum. 4°. P. VI. 349. 14. Types 6, 7, 9, 10.

10358. 1501 Aug. 31. THOMAS Aquinas: de ueritate catholicae fidei. F°. P. VI. 349. 12. Types 5, 9, 10; Δ.

(b) Sons of H. Quentell.

10359. 1501. Ioh. HVSWIRT: enchiridion nouus algorismi. 4°. P. VI. 349. 10. Types 6, 7, 9, 10, 12.

10360. 1502 Jan. 28. FORMVLARE instrumentorum. 4°. P. VI. 351. 33. Types 6, 7, 9, 10.

10361. 1502 March 21. THEOBALDVS: physiologus. 4°. Types 6, 7, 9, 10; cut; Δ.

10362. 1502 April 15. ALANVS: doctrinale altum. 4°. P. VI. 350. 23. Types 6, 7, 9, 10.

10363. 1502 April 30. ARMANDVS de Bellouisu: declaratio difficilium terminorum. 4°. Types 6, 7, 9, 10; Δ.

10364. 1502 Aug. 27. ALBERTVS Magnus: mariale. 4°. P. VI. 350. 21. Types 5, 9, 10; Δ.

10365. 1502 Oct. 20. BOETHIVS: de consolatione philosophiae. 4°. P. VI. 350. 22. Types 6, 7, 9, 10, 12.

10366. 1502. Ioh. HVSWIRT: enchiridion nouus algorismi. 4°. Types 6,7,9,10,12.

10367. 1502 Dec. 1. RVTGERVS Sicamber : dialogus de syllabarum quantitate. 4°. P. VI. 350. 25. Types 9, 10, 12, 13.

10368. 1502, 17 kal. Ian. IACOBVS Magdalius Gaudensis: aerarium poetarum. 4°. P. VI. 350. 30. Types 9, 10, 12, 13.

10369. 1503 Feb. 3. IACOBVS Magdalius Gaudensis: stichologia. 4°. P.VI.351. 37. Types 9, 10, 12, 13; Δ.

10370. 1503 mid March. EPITOME siue compendium theologicae ueritatis. 4°. P. VI. 352. 39, XI. 393. 46c. Types 6, 9, 10, 12, 14; αβ.

10371. 1503 March 29. ALBERTVS Magnus: opus tripartitum. F°. P. VI. 352. 41. Types 5, 7, 9, 10, 12, 14, gk.; woodcut hand; αβг.

10372. 1503 Apr. 12. HENRICVS de Gorinchem: tractatus consultatorii. 4°. P. VI. 352. 40. Types 5, 6, 7, 9, 10, 12, 14; αβΔ.

10373. 1503. Vergili bucolica. [VIRGILIVS.] 4°. P.IX.419.42b. Types 9,10,12,13; α.

10374. (1503.) IACOBVS Magdalius Gaudensis: aerarium poetarum. 4°. Types 9, 10, 12, 13, gk.; α.

10375. 1503 July? Ioh. de SACRO BOSCO: opus sphaericum. 4°. P. VI. 352. 43. Types 5, 6, 9, 10; cut, diagr.; α.

10376. 1503, 9 kal. Ian. Auctoritates Aristotelis. [ARISTOTLE.] 4°. Types 7, 9, 10; cut.

10377. 1504 end Jan. Nicasius de VOERDA: arborum trium lectura. 4°. Types 5, 6, 9, 10, 12; diagr.; αβ.

10378. 1504 end May. FORMVLARE instrumentorum. 4°. P. VI. 354. 65. Types 6, 7, 9, 10; αг.

10379. 1504 mid Aug. Textus sequentiarum cum interpretatione. [LIT.] 4°. P. VI. 354. 61. Types 5, 6, 9, 10; αΔ.

10380. 1504 mid Aug. Expositio hymnorum. [LIT.] 4°. P.VI. 354. 62. Types 5, 6, 9, 10; α.

10381. 1504 mid Sept. MAGNVS de Magdeburg: expositio Donati. 4°. Types 5, 9, 10; cut; α.

10382. 1504 Oct. 9. Ioh. MVRMELIVS: opuscula duo. 4°. Types 5, 6,9,10, 12; α.

10383. 1504. Ioh. HVSWIRT : enchiridion nouus algorismi. 4°. Types 5,6,9, 10, 12; α.

10384. 1504. Ioh. de LAPIDE: resolutorium dubiorum. 4°. P. XI. 393. 67b. Types 6, 7, 9, 10.

10385. 1504. Nic. WOLLICK: aureum musices opusculum. 4°. P. VI. 354. 67. Types 5, 9, 10, 12; diagr. [Woodcut music.]

10386. 1505 end Jan. Ioh. de SACRO BOSCO: opus sphaericum. 4°. P.VI.355.72. Types 5, 9, 10; cuts, diagr.; α.

10387. 1505 end Feb. Nicasius de VOERDA: arborum trium lectura. 4°. P. VI. 356. 81. Types 5, 6, 9, 10, 12; diagr.; αβ.

10388. 1505. Theod. TZWIVEL: opuscula duo de numerorum praxi. 4°. Types 5, 6, 9, 10, 12; α.

10389. 1505 March 27. Geo. SIBVTVS: ars memoratiua. 4°. P. VI. 355. 73. Types 5, 9, 10, 12, 13; α.

10390. 1505 [a. June 20]. Aurelius Victor: de uiris illustribus. [PLINIVS.] 4°. P. VI. 356. 83. Types, 5, 9, 10, 13.

10391. 1505 Aug. 23. NICOLAVS de Lyra: praeceptorium. 4°. P. VI. 356. 88. Types 5, 6, 9, 10, 12; α.

10392. 1505. Bernardus: speculum diuini amoris. [BERNARD.] 4°. P. IX. 420. 88b. Types 9, 10, 13; α.

10393. 1505. In Hieronymi epistulam ad Niciam Ioh. Murmelii commentarioli duo. [JEROME.] 4°. P. VI. 356. 78. Types 5, 6, 7, 9, 10, 12; α.

10394. 1505. IACOBVS Magdalius Gaudensis: passio magistralis. 4°. P. VI. 355. 76. Types 6, 7, 9, 10; αΔ.

10395. 1505. Nic. WOLLICK: opus aureum musicae. 4°. Types 5, 9, 10, 12; diagr. [Woodcut music.]

10396. n.d. [c. 1505.] SENECA: epistulae ad Lucilium, 4°. P. IX. 193. 338. Types 5, 9, 10, 12; α.

10397. n.d. [c. 1505.] Gul. ZENDERS de Werdt: lilium grammaticae. 4°. Types 6, 7, 9, 10, 12; cut; α.

10398. n. d. [c. 1505–6.] COMPVTVS nouus adiecto commentariolo. 4°. Types 5, 6, 9, 10; βΔ.

10399. 1506 mid Feb. Nicasius de VOERDA: lectura arborum trium. 4°. P. VI. 359. 112. Types 5, 6, 9, 10, 12, 14; diagr.; α.

10400. 1506 a. beg. March. Raymundi summula. [RAYMOND.] 4°. P. VI. 358. 103. Types 5, 6, 7, 9, 10; Δ.

10401. 1506 mid May. Textus sequentiarum cum interpretatione. [LIT.] 4°. P. XI. 394. 108b. Types 5, 6, 7, 9, 10; αΔ.

10402. 1506 end May. Expositio hymnorum. [LIT.] 4°. P. VI. 359. 111. Types 5, 6, 9, 10; α.

10403. 1506 mid June. CORDIALE seu quattuor nouissima. 4°. P. VI. 359. 113. Types 5, 9, 10.

10404. 1506 mid June. Ioh. de LAPIDE: resolutorium dubiorum. 4°. P. VI. 359. 109. Types 5, 6, 7, 9, 10.

10405. 1506 Aug. 7. Georgius SIBVTVS: ars memoratiua. 4°. P. VI. 358. 104. Types 5, 9, 10, 12, 13; α.

10406. 1506. IACOBVS Magdalius Gaudensis; textus passionis dominicae. 4°. P. VI. 358. 100. Types 5, 6, 7, 9, 10, 12, 13, 14, gk.; αΔ. [Woodcut hebrew.]

10407. 1506. IACOBVS Magdalius Gaudensis: passio magistralis. 4°. P. VI. 358. 99. Types 6, 7, 9, 10; αΔ.

10408. 1506. EPITOME alias compendium theologicae ueritatis. 4°. P. VI. 357. 98. Types 6, 7, 9, 10, 12; α.

10409. 1506. Aristotelis problemata. [ARISTOTLE.] 4°. Types 6, 7, 9, 10, 12, 14; cut; α.

10410. 1506. LAVACRVM conscientiae. 4°. P. VI. 359. 107. Types 6, 7, 9, 10; α.

10411. 1506. Petrus Rauennas: aurea opuscula. [TOMMAI.] 4°. P. VI. 358. 105. Types 5, 6, 9, 10, 12, 13; αΔ. [Wants sig. A–F.]

10412. 1507. Historia undecim milium uirginum. [N., Frater.] 4°. Types 5, 9, 10, 13; α.

10413. 1507. Expositio Donati secundum uiam doctoris sancti. [DONATVS.] 4°.
P. VI. 361. 126. Types 5, 9, 10; cut.

10414. 1507. Ioh. VERSOR: super octo partes orationis Donati commentum. 4°.
Types 5, 6, 9, 10, 14; cut; α.

10415. 1508 Jan. 24. Ioh. de SACRO BOSCO: opus sphaericum. 4°. Types 5, 9,
10; cuts, diagr.; α.

10416. 1508 end June. Summula Raymundi. [RAYMOND.] 4°. P. VI. 363. 147.
Types 5, 6, 7, 9, 10; Δ.

10417. 1508 June 30. IACOBVS Magdalius Gaudensis: correctorium bibliae. 4°.
P. VI. 363. 148, 149. Types 5, 6, 9, 10, 12, gk.; αΔ. [1300 copies
printed.]

10418. 1508 Aug. 11. IACOBVS Magdalius Gaudensis: passio magistralis. 4°.
P. VI. 364. 151. Types 6, 7, 9, 10; Δ.

10419. 1508 end Oct. Nicasius de VOERDA: arborum trium lectura. 4°. P. VI.
363. 150. Types 5, 6, 9, 10, 12; diagr.; α.

10420. 1508. DIRECTORIVM concubinariorum. 4°. P. VI. 365. 166. Types 5, 9,
10, 12; αΔ.

10421. 1508. Ioh. MVRMELIVS: elegiae morales. 4°. P. IX. 110. 34. Types 5,
9, 10, 12; α.

10422. 1508. SENECA: de quattuor uirtutibus. 4°. P. VI. 363. 146. Types 5, 6,
9, 10; α.

10423. 1508. Nic. WOLLICK: opus aureum musicae. 4°. P. VI. 364. 155. Types
5, 9, 10, 12; diagr. [Woodcut music.]

10424. 1508 prid. kal. Ian. Petrus Rauennas: aurea opuscula. [TOMMAI.] 4°.
P. VI. 364. 153. Types 5, 9, 10, 12; αΔ.

10425. n. d. [c. 1508?] Elegantiarum uiginti praecepta. [ELEGANTIAE.] 4°.
(Part i. no. 1453.) Types 5, 9, 10; cut; α.

10426. n.d.[c. 1508.] IACOBVS Hochstratus: defensorium fratrum mendicantium.
4°. P. VI. 362. 139 note. Types 5, 6, 10, 14; α.

10427. n. d. [c. 1508–9?] Herm. Buschius: de psalterio B.V.M. [BUSCHE.] 4°.
Types 5, 6, 7, 9, 10, 12; α.

10428. 1509 Oct. 9. STIMVLVS beneficiatorum. 4°. P. VI. 366. 171. Types 5,
9, 10; αΔ. [Wants sig. B.]

10429. 1509 Oct. 23. PVRGATORIVM detractorum. 4°. P. VI. 367. 179. Types
5, 6, 9, 10, 12; αΔ.

10430. 1509 Oct. 31. Sequentiae et hymni cum uocabulorum interpretatione.
[LIT.] 4°. Types 5, 6, 9, 10; Δ.

10431. 1509. DIRECTORIVM concubinariorum. 4°. P. VI. 366. 175. Types 5, 9,
10, 12; α.

10432. n. d. [c. 1509–10?] Victor von CARBEN: wie er zum christlichen Glauben
gekommen ist. 4°. Types 9, 10, 15; cuts; αΔ.

10433. 1510 May 1. Baptista Mantuanus: bucolica siue adulescentia. [SPAG-
NUOLI.] 4°. P. VI. 369. 200. Types 5, 6, 9, 10; α.

10434. 1510 May 31. Baptista Mantuanus: parthenice secunda. [SPAGNUOLI.]
4°. P. VI. 369. 196. Types 5, 6, 9, 10; αΔ.

10435. 1510 May 27. IVVENALIS: saturae. 4°. P. XI. 396. 214b. Types 5, 9,
10, gk.; α.

10436. 1510 Dec. 3. Ioh. MVRMELIVS: de magistri et discipulorum officiis epigrammata. 4°. P. VI. 371. 212. Types 5, 9, 10; α.

10437. n.d.[c. 1510?] Ioh.Ant.CAMPANVS: uita Thomae Aquinatis. 4°. Types
5, 9, 10, 12, 13; α. [Wants leaves 7–10.]

10438. n. d. [c. 1510?] Collationes Salomonis et Marcolphi. [SOLOMON.] 4°.
H. *14250. Types 5, 7, 9, 10; βΔ.

10439. 1511. IACOBVS Hochstratus: protectorium principum Alemaniae de
maleficis non sepeliendis. 4°. P. VI. 371. 220. Types 5,6, 9, 10; α.

10440. 1512 Aug. 28. Arnoldus de Tungris: refutatio articulorum Reuchlini
de iudaico fauore. [REUCHLIN.] 4°. P.VI.372.221. Types 5,6,9,10; α.

10441. [a. 1512 Sept.6.] Kaiserliches Mandat. [GERMANY.] obl. W.719. Type
15. [For an addendum see no. 10573.]

10442. 1512 Oct. 7. THOMAS Aquinas: prima secundae. F°. P. VI. 372. 223.
Types 5, 6, 9, 10, 12, 14; αΔ.

10443. 1514 Apr. Historia trium regum. [MAGI.] 4°. P. VI. 373. 236. Types
5, 9, 10, 12; αΔ.

10444. 1514. Ioh. PFEFFERKORN: Sturm über und wider die Juden. 4°. DA.
779. Types 9, 10, 15; cut; α.

10445. 1515 Apr. Ant.TVNICIVS: monosticha. 4°. P. VI. 375. 246; W. suppl. i.
126. Types 5, 6, 9, 10; α.

10446. 1515 June. IACOBVS Magdalius Gaudensis: orationes super infirmos di-
cendae. 4°. P. VI. 375. 247. Types 5, 9, 10; cut; α.

10447. 1515 [a. Aug. 6]. Ant. MANCINELLVS: uersilogus. 4°. P. VI. 375. 248.
Types 5, 6, 9, 10; α.

10448. 1515. Ioh.CINCINNIVS: uita diui Ludgeri. 4°. Types 5, 6, 9, 10, 12; α.

10449. n. d. [c. 1515?] ANDRELINVS: ex amorum libris uersus selecti. 4°. Types
5, 9, 10; α.

10450. 1516 [a. Lent]. BERNARDVS de Lutzenburgo: sermones de symbolica
colluctatione uitiorum et uirtutum. 4°. P.VI. 376.259. Types 5, 9, 10,
12; cuts; α.

10451. 1516 May. Raym. Lullus: ianua artis. [LULL.] Types 5, 9, 10, 12.

10452. 1516 July 10. Bern. LAVINHETA: de incarnatione uerbi. 4°. P. VI. 376.
258. Types 5, 9, 10, 12; cut; α.

10453. 1516. Iac. Faber Stapulensis: opus nouum astronomicum. [LEFEVRE.]
4°. P. IX. 427. 267d. Types 5, 6, 9, 10; cut, diagr.; α.

10454. [1517 b. May 28.] Ioh. Ang. Arcimboldus: literae indulgentiarum.
[ROME.] obl. Types 12, 14; cut. [On vellum.]

10455. [1517.] Ioh. Ang. Arcimboldus: literae indulgentiarum. [ROME.] obl.
Types 5, 6; cut. [On vellum.]

10456. 1517 June. Historia trium regum. [MAGI.] 4°. P. VI. 377. 268. Types
5, 9, 10, 12; αΔ.

10457. 1517. Planetisches Werk. [INHALT.] 4°. W. 1069. Types 5, 6, 9, 10.

10458. 1517. Thesaurus animae ex reuelationibus beatae Birgittae collectus.
[BRIDGET.] 16°. Types 6, 10, 12.

10459. 1518 Feb. IACOBVS Hochstratus: apologia contra dialogum Georgio
Benigno ascriptum in causa Ioannis Reuchlin. 4°. P. VI. 380. 302.
Types 5, 9, 10, 12, 13 [caps.]; αΔ.

10460a. 1518. Ortuinus Gratius: LAMENTATIONES obscurorum uirorum (A–C).
4°. P. VI. 381. 305. Types 5, 9, 10, 12, gk.; cut.

  b. 1518 March 11. id. epistula apologetica (a, b). [GRATIVS.] 4°. P. VI.
379. 288. Types 5, 12; α.

10461 1518 Apr BERNARDVS de Lùtzenburgo moralis expositio literae pytha-
       goricae 4°. P VI 379. 286 Types 5, 6, 10, 12, gk , diagr.
10462 1518 Aug Ortuinus GRATIVS lamentationes obscurorum uirorum,
       epistula apologetica P. VI. 381 305b Types 5, 9, 10, 12, gk ; cut, α
10463. 1518 Ioh MVRMELIVS· scoparius 4° P VI. 379 287 Types 5,9,10,12, α
10464. 1518. Herm Buschius in Ioannis Murmelii obitum carmen. [BUSCHE]
       4° P. VI. 381. 308 Types 5, 9, 10, 12, α
10465 1518 Oct 1, 1519 IACOBVS Hochstratus apologia secunda. 4°. P. VI.
       382 311 Types 5, 9, 10, 12, α
10466 1519 Apr IACOBVS Hochstratus destructio cabalae 4° P. VI 381.
       310 Types 5, 9, 10, 12, α.
10467 1519 Septem psalmi paenitentiales cum argumentis Iacobi Fabri.
       [BIBLE.] 4°. Types 5, 9, 10, cut, α.

<h2 style="text-align:center">(c) Peter Quentell [1520 March].</h2>

10468 1520 Nov Tho RADINVS TODISCHVS ad principes Germaniae aduer-
       sus Lutherum 4°. P VI 383 324 Types 5, 9, 10, 12.

xxviij. JOHANN KOELHOFF, THE YOUNGER

No books by the younger Koelhoff dated after 1500 seem to be recorded except three described by Reichling, no 168 of 1501 June 24, no 167, also of 1501, and no 172, dated 1502
Jan 17   See also Ennen, pp x–xi, he seems to have turned to the cattle trade

xxix. HERMANN BUMGART

TYPES   Types 1 (small, like Quentell 6, but single hyphen, tailed h, thin ℭ usually, ¶
rarer and late, 63 mm), 3 (large round as Landen 1, Grüninger 17), 5 (small german, like
J Schoffer 10, Hupfüff 3, &c, see Burger 96, text, many caps added from type 10, single hyphen,
81 mm , cf Quentell 15), 6 (dutch text as Eckert 2 (MT 85b), facs KBM 19, cf Zel 11;
often with caps of 7), 7 (text schwabacher, like Landen 3), 8 (church type as Mart. of Werden 7,
the same caps , facs KBM 20, larger type), 9 (like 6 but larger, as MT 80d), for these see
part 1 —Type 10, latin text, mostly like Koelhoff sen 17, but mixt caps , some from 5, strange V,
round h (mixt in the Bonaventura of c 1515), single hyphen , ¶ with turned-back foot, 82 mm
Cf Heinr of Neuss 3, and Pafraet 4 (MT 64e2)
   Type 1, see fig 46 (h differs), 3, see fig 28, *5, see fig 64, 7, see fig 54, 8, see fig 19.
   CUT   A woodcut (teacher and scholars) of remarkable style is used in no 10471, 10472
   DEVICES   a (before 1500), KBM 18 —b, KBM 16 —c, KBM 17 —d, KBM. 19   (KBM
20 is not a device)
   INITIALS   α, the same set as the S (copied from Wagner's initials) used by Quentell, D
and O —In 1503 a canon T with crucifixion, white ground, 51 mm   One calligraphic W, 30 mm

10469 [a 1501 Aug 5] Copia articulorum conclusorum inter legatum et con-
       uentum imperii Nurmbergae [ROME] F° Types 3, 6
10470 n d [c 1501?] Verstand Kurfurst Hermanns mit der Stadt Koln [HER-
       MANN iv] Double bs Types 6, 8, Δ.
10471. 1502. DOMINVS cuius partis orationis sit, etc 4°. Types 1,3,5,6,7,8,10,
       cut, b, α
10472 1502. POETA salutaris. 4° Types 1,3,5,6,10, cut, b.
10473. 1503 Raym Peraudi legenda decem milium martyrum [PERAULT] 4°.
       P VI 353. 54. Types 6,8, cuts, Y, Δ

10474. [n. b. 1503 Aug. 31.] Epistola de morte Alexandri pp.vi. [ALEXANDER.]   KÖLN.
       obl. Type 6.   xxix. Herm.
10475. n. d. [c. 1503?] Testamentum Henrici HAICH (d: 4 Iul. 1452), germ. F°. Bumgart.
       Types 6, 9, 10.
10476. n.d. [c. 1505?] Imitatio Christi, germ. [JESUS.] 8°. (Cf. W. 4071.) Types
       5, 6, 10; cut.
10477. n. d. [c. 1508?] IACOBVS Hochstratus: iustificatorium principum Al-
       maniae. 4°. P.VI. 368. 189? Types 1, 2, 6, 7, 10.
10478. 1509. Psalter latijn vñ duytsch myt der glosen. [BIBLE.] 4°. P.VI. 369.
       193 = DA. 630b. Types 5, 6, 7, 8, 10; cuts; Y; c.
10479. n.d. [1509.] Henricus de Bynsfelt: de expositione reliquiarum in mona-
       sterio Indensi. F°. Types 7, 8; cut. [One leaf.]
10480. 1513. Gertrudis diuae uirginis officium. [LIT.] 4°. Types 1, 5, 6, 8, 9, 10;
       cuts.
10481. 1513. Thomas a Kempis: hortulus rosarum, etc. 8°. Types 5, 6, 8, 9; Y.
10482. n.d. [c. 1515?] BONAVENTVRA: epistel vñ lere mit xxv puntgere vur alle
       die ghene dy geistlichen leeuen willen in christo. 8°. Types 5, 6, 10;
       cut. [Sig. a–k.]
10483. n.d. [c. 1515?] Dry Rosenkrentzs ... [MARY.] 8°. W. 109. Types 6, 7; cut.
       [Sig. L.]

xxx. JOHANN [OF] LANDEN.

No dated book of Landen is recorded for the years 1502–1505.

TYPES. Types 1 (large round, like Grüninger 17 ; cf. Bumgart 1); 2, small, like Quentell 6,
but round h ; double hyphen, smaller than that of Quentell ; 66 mm. (Quentell 63 mm.) ; ¶ at this
period, ⅃ in 1496); 3 (text schwabacher, thick long single hyphen, thin ⅃, 94 mm.; cf. Bumgart 7);
4 (latin text, like Knoblouch 14, strange capitals ; ⅃ and ¶ with the perpendicular turned back at
foot as in Bumgart 10; 78 mm.; cf. Corn. of Zierikzee 6); for these see part i.—Type 5, large round,
style of Froschauer 6 or Schönsperger jun. 2 ; tailed h ; larger than type 1.—Type 6, small black
angular latin text, like Koberger 5, or still more, Münster, Joh. Limburg 1 or Magdeburg v. 7 ;
round h, double hyphen, 78 mm.—Type 7, roman capitals, 8 mm. high ; cf. J. Schöffer 15, &c. ;
not thin as Ratdolt 21, &c.

Type 1, see fig. 28; 2, see fig. 46; 3, see fig. 54; 4, see fig. 39; 5, see fig. 27; 7, see fig. 1.

CUT. A cut almost identical with no. 2 of Mart. of Werden, but not the same block, is used
in no. 10484, 10486–8, 10493–4. The three cuts figured in KBM. 13–15 are not devices.

(a) Infra sedecim domos.

10484. 1506. Ioh. de LAPIDE: resolutorium dubiorum. 8°. P. IX. 421. 118b.
       Types 1, 2, 4; cut.
10485. [a. 1506 May 30.] Melchior SCHAVPECHIVS: computus uulgaris. 4°. P.VI.
       360. 119. Types 1, 3, 4; cut.
10486. 1506 Nov. 11. Bern. LAVRENTIVS: casus in quibus iudex saecularis potest
       manus in clericos imponere, etc. 8°. P.VI. 360. 118. Types 1, 2, 4; cut.
10487. 1507 Feb. 1. Gesta proxime per portugalenses in India, etc. [PORTUGUESE.]
       4°. P.VI. 362. 137. Types 1, 2; cuts; Y.

10488. 1507 July 10. Ioh. Cochlaeus: musica. [DOBNECK.] 4°. P.VI. 362. 136.
       Types 1, 4; cut; Y. [Woodcut music.—No address.]
10489. n. d. [c. 1507?] Ioh. SACRANVS: errores atrocissimorum ruthenorum. 4°.
       Types 1, 4; cut.

(b) In platea S. Gereonis in domo facultatis artium
rubea porta nominata

10490 1508 Feb 14. Joh. PFEFFERKORN der Juden Beicht 4°. W 455 Types 1, 3, cuts.

10491 1508 PFEFFERKORN de iudaica confessione 4°. P.IX 423.165b. Types 1,3; cuts

10492. [n b.1508] PFEFFERKORN der ioeden bicht 4°. DA. 612 = W 454 Types 1,3; cuts, Y.

10493. 1508 May 8 IACOBVS Hochstratus defensio scholastica principum Almaniae. 4°. P.VI. 365. 165. Types 1,2, cut, Y.

10494. n d [c 1509–10] De fraternitate septem gaudiorum B. M. V. [MARY] 8°. Types 1,2,3, cuts; Y. [Woodcut music]

10495. 1510 June 20. Victor von CARBEN Tractat von der unbefleckten Jungfrauschaft Mariae 4° (Cf W 382.) Types 2,3,5, cuts, Y

10496. n.d. Victor de CARBEN propugnaculum fidei christianae. 4°. P.VI. 438. 833. Types 5,6, cut, diagr, Y.

10497. [n b. 1515.] VSVARDVS martyrologium. 8°. P VI 375 253, H. 16109. Types 5, 6; cut (metal).

10498. n d Vita diui Brunonis [BRVNO] 8°. Types 5,6,7; cuts

xxxi. MARTIN OF WERDEN.

TYPES Types 1 (text = Guldenschaff 1, double hyphen), 2 (large = Guldenschaff or Quentell 2, double hyphen), 3 (text like Quentell 7, single hyphen, large us, ¶ like Quentell, sloping comma in 1501 only, a wrong-fount h, found only from 1508 to 1510, 80 mm), 4 (small, like Quentell 6, but single hyphen, in Jan 1501 round and tailed h mixt, afterwards tailed only, ¶ rather thick, with short stem, 63 mm), for these see part 1 —Type 5, square canon = Quentell 9 —Type 6, large church = Ludwig of Renchen 1 (Burger 69, col 1) —Type 7, church type, like Quentell 10, but with different caps, like Hupfuff 1, Joh Schott 2 or Knoblouch 3ᴮ, cf Burger 43, col 1, the larger type, single hyphen This type replaces 2 —Type 8, text schwabacher, exactly like Joh Schott 12, cf Kobel 8

Type 3, see fig 37, 4, see fig 46, 5, see fig 15, *7, see fig 19, 8, see fig 57

CUTS Three cuts are characteristic of Martin's books, the same cut is often found three or four times in a single book No 1, used in no 10499, 10507, 10518–20, 10525–7, 10529, 10531, is of a master at his desk, facing the reader, four pupils, prominent lock to desk No 2 is of the Holy Family, shaded, the child stepping across This is found in no 10501, 10502, 10503A, 10505, 10506, 10508–11, 10514, 10517, 10523, 10530 No 3 is like 2, but without shading, and the child is seated, and stretching across Used in no 10510–14, 10516, 10517, 10523 A cut of the arms of Köln, used only in Aug 1510 (no 10528) is reproduced as a device in KBM no 21

INITIALS Very few In 1503 a canon T with crucifix, 45 mm, an initial H (apparently based on Quentell α), 28 mm (1508–9), C, G, calligraphic, 28–29 mm (1509 Feb)

(a) Retro minores, without Martin's name.

10499. 1501 Jan. 8. LAVACRVM conscientiae [For H Quentell] 4°. P.VI. 347 1 Types 1–5, cut.

10500. 1501 March 18 NICOLAVS de Lyra praeceptorium. 8° P VI. 349. 19 Types 1–5, cuts.

10501 1501 July 31. Imitatio Christi. [JESVS] 8° Types 1–4; cut.

10502. 1501 Aug. 11, 26. FVNDAMENTVM aeternae felicitatis, Lotharius de miseria condicionis humanae. 8°. P. XI. 392 19b, c. Types 1–4, cut.

10503. [a. 1502 Jan. 13.] Vita S. Albani. [ALBAN.] 4°. Types 1–3.

10503A. 1502 Jan. 31. BONAVENTVRA: stimulus diuini amoris. 8°. P.VI. 351. 34.
Types 1–4; cut.

10504. 1503. Missale itinerantium. [LIT.] 8°. P. XI. 393. 89(2). Types 1–5; Δ.
[Sig. a, f–k, but no break in text.]

10505. 1503 Oct. 5. Imitatio Christi. [JESUS.] 8°. P.VI. 352. 47. Types 1–4; cut.

10506. 1504 Jan. 3. Hugo FOLIETINVS: tractatus de claustro animae. 8°. P.VI.
354. 69. Types 1–5; cut.

(b) Prope domum consulatus in uico Burgensi uulgo
die Burgerstraes: with the printer's name.

10507. 1505. Sequentiae et hymni per totum annum. [LIT.] 4°. Types 1, 3, 6.

10508. 1506 end Sept. FVNDAMENTVM aeternae felicitatis; Lotharius, de miseria
condicionis humanae. 8°. Types 1–4; cut.

10509. n.d. [c. 1506?] Lectiones super euangelia ferialia per quadragesimam in
ecclesia maiori Coloniensi. [LIT.] 8°. Type 4; cut; Y.

10510. 1507 Feb. 8. Imitatio Christi. [JESUS.] 8°. P.VI. 361. 130. Types 1, 2,
4; cuts.

10511. 1507. Vinetum S. Annae. [ANNE.] 8°. Types 1, 2, 4; cuts.

10512. 1507 Dec. 1. Ioh. ANNIVS: glossa super Apocalypsim. 8°. P.VI. 361.
132. Types 1–4; cut.

10513. 1507 Dec. 22. Augustinus: manuale de aspiratione hominis ad deum,
etc. 8°. P.VI. 361. 131. Types 1,2,4; cut.

10514. n. d. [c. 1507.] Casus papales episcopales et abbatiales. [PAPAL CASES.]
8°. P.VI. 439. 848? Types 2,3; cuts.

10515. [a. 1508 Jan. 5.] PFEFFERKORN: speculum adhortationis iudaicae ad Chri-
stum. 4°. P. I. 324. 365 (assigned to 1500). Types 2,3,4; cut.

10516. 1508 June 21. THOMAS Aquinas: confessionale. 8°. P.VI. 364. 162. Types
1, 2, 4; cut.

10517. 1508. Psalterium. [BIBLE.] 8°. Types 1–4, 6; cuts.

10518. 1508. Laur. CORVINVS: compendiosa carminum structura. 4°. P.VI. 363.
161. Types 1–4,6; cut.

10519. 1508 Dec. 20. ALEXANDER Gallus: doctrinalis pars prima. 4°. P.IX. 423.
162b; R. 218 (1). Types 1–4; cut; Δ.

10520. 1509 Feb. 1. ALEXANDER Gallus: doctrinalis pars secunda. 4°. P.IX. 424.
179b; R. 218(2). Types 1–4; cut; Δ.

10521. n. d. [c. 1508–9.] Historia undecim milium uirginum. [N., Frater.] 4°.
P. VI. 440. 853. Types 2–4; cut.

10522. 1509 June 25. FORMVLA uiuendi sacerdotum. 8°. P.VI. 367. 184. Types
2–4; cut.

10523. 1509. IOANNES de Tambaco: consolatio theologiae. 8°. P.VI. 167. 180.
Types 1–4; cuts.

10524. 1509 Nóv. 10. CVRA clericalis. 8°. P.VI. 367. 183. Types 1, 3, 4, 7.

10525. 1510 Jan. 30. BERNARDVS de Lutzenburgo: compilatio in recommenda-
tionem beati Ioseph. 4°. P.VI. 370. 204. Types 3, 4, 7; cut.

10526. [a. 1510 Feb. 17.] IACOBVS Hochstratus: tractatus magistralis contra
quaerentes auxilium a maleficis. 4°. P.VI. 370. 205. Types 1, 3, 4, 7; cut.

10527. 1510 a. Apr. 4. Theoph. BONA Brixianus. de uita solitaria et ciuili carmen. 4° Types 1,3,7, cut
10528. 1510 Aug. 27 BARTHOLOMAEVS Coloniensis· epistula mythologica 4° P.XI 396 203b Types 3, 7, cut.
10529 1510 POETA salutaris 4° Types 3,4,7, cut
10530. n d. [c 1510] REFRIGERIVM animae peccatricis. 8°. Types 1,3,7, cuts
10531 n d. [c. 1510] Bernardus de Lutzenburgo· expositio in symbolum Athanasii [ATHANASIANCREED.]4°.P IX 184 235. Types1,3,4,7, cut.
10532. n.d.[c. 1510?] Baptista Mantuanus. sententiosa dicta [SPAGNUOLI.] 4°. Types 1,3,7.
10533 1514 Sept 1. CLAVDIANVS. de raptu Proserpinae 4° Types 1,3,4,7.
10534 1514[a. Sept 27] Ant TVNICIVS. monosticha. 4°. P.VI. 374. 240, W. suppl. i. 114. Types 1,3,4,7
10535 [1514] Nov 20 Catonis disticha et alia opuscula ab Erasmo recognita. [ERASMVS.] 4°. Types 1,3,4,7
10536 1515 Feb 14 Macarius MVTIVS de triumpho Christi 4° P.VI 375 251 Types 1,3,4,7
10537. [a 1515 Aug. 6.] Ant. MANCINELLVS. uersilogus 4°. P.IX. 184. 238. Types 1,3,4,7.
10538. 1516. Grammaticarum institutionum ENCHIRIDION 4°. P.VI.376.262. Types 1,3,7,8

xxxij. CORNELIS, OF ZIERIKZEE.

ADDRESS   Apud praedicatores

TYPES   Types 1 (large round, venetian, like Torresanus 15 or Sorg 6), 2 (text latin with open V, as Flach 3, from 1503 to 1507 so much mixt with 6 that the two are often indistinguishable from Sept.1507, when 6 disappears, type 2 is purer again, round h normal, but a tailed h sometimes found after 1504, ℭ and two sorts with turned back tail), 3 (large text, Hamman style), 5 (small, like Quentell 6, h mixt, the tailed form very small, ℭ and ¶, short double hyphen, 63 mm), for these see part 1—Type 6, text like Landen 4, in a pure state has wider h than 2, larger us, different que, double hyphen almost horizontal, distinctive s (final), but as a rule is almost indistinguishable from 2—Type 7, large round as Bumgart 3, Landen 1, rarely used—Type 8, also rare, canon type like Quentell 9—Type 9, roman of commentary size, Capcasa style, but Qu with prominent curve, small &, ℭ with turned-back tail, double hyphen, 82 mm

Type *1, see fig 26, 2, see fig 38, 5, see fig. 46, 6, see fig 39, 7, see fig 28, 8, see fig. 15.

DEVICE   None, KBM 12 not being a device (first used 1508 March 17)

10539. 1501 March 25   PETRVS Cracouiensis   computus ecclesiasticus et astronomicus 4°. Types 1,2,3
10540 1503. EVAGATORIVM Modus praedicandi, etc. 8°. P XI 393. 50 (1) Types 1,2,5,6,7; cuts; Y, Δ
10541. 1503 Sept 4 Henricus Suso HOROLOGIVM aeternae sapientiae. 8°. Types 1,2,5,6,7. [Wants first leaf.]
10542. 1503 Dec 2 Aug [de CAMPELLIS] de Leonissa sermones (ed. 3ª). 8°. P VI 353. 51. Types 1,2,5,6, Δ
10543. 1504 March 23 Herolt de eruditione christifidelium [DISCIPVLVS] 4°. Types 1,2,3,5,8, cuts, Y.
10544 1505 March 6. RAMPEGOLLIS· biblia aurea 8° P.VI. 357. 95 Types 1,2,5,6, cuts.
10544A.1505 Herm.TORRENTINVS uocabularius poeticus. 4° Types1,2,3,5,cuts

10545.   NIDER: consolatorium timoratae conscientiae. 8°. Types
        1,5,6; cut. [Colophon torn.]
10546. n. d. [c. 1506–7.] Cyrillus: speculum sapientiae. [CYRIL.] 8°. P.VI. 439.
        845. Types 1,3,5,6; cuts.
10547 a. n. d. MODVS legendi abbreuiaturas. Types 1,2?,3,5,9.
       b. n. d. Bartolus: tractatus iudiciorum, etc. Types 1,2,5,6?,9; cuts.
       c. n. d. Ars notariatus. Types 1,3,5.
       d. n. d. Ioh. Andreae: summa super 2° decretalium. Types 1,5,6?; Y.
       e. n. d. Rubricae siue tituli iuris canonici et ciuilis. Types 1,2,3,5.
       f. n. d. Ioh. Andreae: summa super 4° decretalium. Types 1,2,5; cuts; Y.
       g. 1507 May 12. Flores legum. P.VI. 362. 134. Types 1,2,5; Y. 8°.
10548. 1507 Sept. 1. Regimen sanitatis salernitanum. [ACAD.] 4°. P.VI. 362.
        135. Types 1,2,5; cut.
10549. 1507 Oct. 30. Oliu. Maillardus: sermones de sanctis. [MAILLARD.] 4°.
        Types 1,2,3,5; cuts.
10550. 1508 March 17. MENSA philosophica. 4°. P.VI. 365. 163. Types 1,2,
        3,(8); cuts.
10551. 1508 Apr. 6. Mich. Scotus: physiognomia. [SCOTT.] 4°. P.VI. 365.
        164. Types 1,2; cut.
10552. n. d. [c. 1508–9.] Georgius de Hungaria: de ritu et moribus turcorum.
        [TURKS.] 4°. Types 1,2,3; Y; Δ.
10553. 1509 March 12. Herolt: de eruditione christifidelium. [DISCIPVLVS.]
        4°. P.VI. 367. 186. Types 1,2,3,5,9; cuts; Y.
10554. 1509 Sept. 4. Henricus Suso: HOROLOGIVM aeternae sapientiae. 8°.
        P.VI. 368. 187. Types 1,2,5,9; cuts. [Sept. 4 copied from 1503.]
10555. n. d. [c. 1509?] QVAESTIONES naturales philosophorum. 4°. P.VI. 439.
        846. Types 1,2,3; cut.

10556. 1514 Jan. 17. Plutarchus: de tuenda bona ualetudine. [PLUTARCH.] 4°.
        Type 9.
10557. 1515 March 18. ERASMVS: de constructione octo partium orationis. 4°.
        P.VI. 375. 254. Type 9.
10558. n. d. OVIDIVS: de tribus puellis, de nuncio sagaci, etc. 4°. Types 5,9.

xxxiij. RULOFF SPOT.

For the little that is known of Spot and his connexion with Zel see Merlo-Zaretzky, Ulrich Zell,
p. 20, and KBM. p. 34–5.

TYPES.   Type 1, Zel's type 2 germanised: double hyphen (rare); remarkable ℂ.—Type 2,
text schwabacher with fraktur forms: single hyphen, short comma, ¶; like Landen 3 or Bumgart
7; 98 mm.—Type 3, church text, probably like Mart. of Werden 7 or Bumgart 8.

10559. 1501. DIETRICH v. Münster: Spyegel offt hantboichelgyn der christen
        mynschen. 8°. Types 1,2,3; cuts.

xxxiv. JOHANN HELMAN.

I find no trace of this printer, unless he be the Johann von Solingen mentioned in 1501 (Ennen
p. xxv.), save in the Passie Ons Heren described by Weller 4072 (suppl. i.).

The earliest dated book of Heinrich of Neuss seems to be Weller suppl 1 no 37, if this be correct The date 1500 of Hain 12866 is due to an obvious misreading of the colophon in no 10561, M cccc ix Mensis Februarii A book by Pfefferkorn of 1500 is of course impossible Heinrich seems to have acquired some of the younger Koelhoff's materials, e g types 2 and 3, and the cut KBM 6, he seems also to have had some relations with Landen, as two of Landen's metal cuts were in Heinrich's hands in 1509, and a cut of Our Lady in the same book (no 10560) was used later (with some alterations to the labels) by Landen, but before the alterations by Quentell also

TYPES Type 1, square canon like Quentell 9, rough and badly justified —Type 2, small church type, the same as Koelhoff sen 14 (Burger 16, Primum metrum), cf Gutschaiff 1, J Otmar 23 —Type 3, text latin, very like Bumgart 10 (similar V), but double hyphen, and caps of Heinrich's type 5 mixt in it instead of those of Bumgart's type 5, round h, ℂ with turned-back tail, 80 n m — Type 4, small type, lowercase like Quentell 6, but caps quite distinctive, single hyphen, tailed h, ¶, 63 mm —Type 5, text schwabacher like Landen 3, similar ℂ —Type 6, small roman in the style of Quentell 13, but a singular M, cf Cervicornus 2. hyphen seems to be double, but prints blurred, round comma, ¶, 76 mm —Type 7, roman caps, 8 mm, very rough, especially the M —Hebrew type with vowel-points

Type 1, see fig 15, 2, see fig 20, *4, see fig 47, 5, see fig 54, 6, see fig 11, 7, see fig 1

BORDER A, a copy of one of Froben's (BBZ 30), the device is replaced by a rabbit See KBM 133 It was used in 1518 by Elisabeth the widow of Martin von Werden, and in 1520 by Cervicornus Two cuts containing the arms of Koln are also found, one is like KBM 12, the other is KBM 6

INITIALS The only one used at this period is the S (copied from the Wagner set) used earlier by Quentell, by Heinrich in 1514

10560. 1509 [a Feb 8] Victor de CARBEN: opus de erroribus iudaeorum 4°
P VI 368 190 Types 1–4; cuts

10561. 1509 [a 20] Feb Ioh. PFEFFERKORN de pascha iudaeorum. 4°. P VI
368 191. (H. 12866) Types 1, 2, 3, hb., cut.

10562 1509 March Ioh PFEFFERKORN hostis iudaeorum 4°. P. VI 369 192
Types 1, 2, 3, 5, hb.

10563a. n d. [1509] BARTHOLOMAEVS de Vsingen· interpretatio Donati minoris
(A–E) 4° Types 1–5, cut.

b 1509 Mar. 30 id. regulae congruitatis (a–e) 4° Types 1–5, cuts.

10564. 1510 March 8 Ioh PFEFFERKORN in laudem Maximiliani (de libris iudaeorum) 4° P VI 370 211. Types 1, 2, 3, 5, hb., cut.

10565 1510 Gerson modus uiuendi christifidelium [CHARLIER] 4°. Types
1, 2, 3, cuts

10566 1511. Henr. Institoris malleus maleficarum. [SPRENGER.] 8° P VI.
371. 219 Types (1), 4. [Imp]

10567 n d. Historia undecim milium uirginum [N, Frater] 4°. P VI 440
857 Types 2, 3, 4; cuts

10568 n d HENRICVS de Hassia speculum animae. 4°. Part i, no. 1465; H.
8401. Types 1–4

10569 n d. Problemata Aristotelis [ARISTOTLE] 4°. Types 1–4; cuts.

10570. 1514. Nic SIMONIS: exercitium signorum sacerdotalium, seu ars memoratiua sacerdotum. 8°. P. VI. 374 243 Types 2, 3, 4, Δ.

10571 [1519] Jan ERASMVS· familiarium colloquiorum formulae. 4°. Types 6,
7, A

xxxvi. HERMANN GUTSCHAIFF.

ADDRESS. In der Schmierstrasse. This same address was afterwards (after 1520?) that of Anton Kaiser (W. 644).

TYPES. Type 1, small church type, as Koelhoff sen. 14, Quentell 14, Heinrich of Neuss 2.—Type 2, text schwabacher, like Landen 3; single hyphen and ℭ.—Type 3, large round type, seemingly like Cornelis of Zierikzee 1.

Type 1, see fig. 20; 2, see fig. 54; 3, see fig. 26.

10572. [n.b. 1511.] Ioh. PFEFFERKORN: Brantspiegel. 4°. [Not W. 731?] Types 1, 2, 3.

10573. [a. 1512 Sept. 6.] Maximilian: Anhang zum kaiserlichen Mandate (no. 10441). [GERMANY.] F°. W. 719. Type 2; Δ.

10574. 1515 Sept. EMANVEL rex Portugaliae: epistula de uictoriis in India. 4°. Types 1, 2; cuts.

xxxvij. ARNT, OF AACHEN.

For the book dated 1514 see DA. 785b = W. suppl. i. 103. There is no other dated book of Arnt before 1519.

TYPES. Type 1, broad church type with mixt caps., almost identical with Joh. Schöffer 5 or Zel 10: double hyphen.—Type 2, text schwabacher like Landen 3, &c.; single hyphen, large ¶, short comma.

DEVICE. a. A cut of the Holy Family bears a shield with trade mark, the same as that in KBM. 73 (ascribed to Cervicornus).

INITIALS. α, French (Paris) style, black or dotted ground; 19 mm.—β, like α, but 28–29 mm.

10575. n. d. [a. 1513 Feb. 20.] Euch. ROESSLIN: der schwangeren Frauen Rosengarten. 4°. [W. 733?] Types 1, 2; cuts; X; Δ.

10576. 1519 March 22. Nic. SIMONIS: Historie und Leben von S. Anna. 4°. W. 1192. Types 1, 2; cuts; X; a; α.

10577. 1519. Ioh. de SACRO BOSCO: sphaera materialis geteutscht. 4°. DA. 967b = W. 1270. Types 1, 2; cuts, diagr.; X; β.

xxxviij. JOHANN GYMNICUS.

The extent to which Gymnicus was actually a printer himself at this period is uncertain. For the book of 1516 bearing his name see P. VI. 376. 263. That of 1517 containing his device is clearly stated to be printed by Cervicornus, and another book (P. VI. 377. 273) was printed for him by Cornelis of Zierikzee. The two books here entered differ typographically from those of other Köln printers.

TYPES. Type 1, middle roman, like Cervicornus 1 or Heil 3; ȩ and æ; two hyphens, both single; ℭ with turned-back tail, as Nic. Kaiser; 88 mm.—Type 2, small roman, not like other Köln types, but in face very like Lotter sen. 16; round comma, two hyphens, both single; ¶; 67 mm.—Type 3, roman caps. 10 mm. high.—Type 4, smaller roman caps., 5½ mm.—Type 5, middle roman, seemingly not type 1; double hyphen.—Type 6, very small french gothic, like Wolf and Kerver 14; æ and ȩ from 7; tailed h; double hyphen, round comma. Where 20 ll. measure 63 mm. the type seems to be leaded.—Type 7, very small roman, 63 mm.; curious & and ¶; double hyphen; in Qu the tail of Q is nearly straight.—Greek type like Cervicornus.

Types 1, 5, see fig. 8; 2, see fig. 9.

DEVICE. a, KBM. 91, at top.

INITIALS. α, 17–19 mm., at least partly = Kaiser β.—β, 18 mm., white on white; seemingly copied from Italian letters.—γ, 13–14 mm., white.—δ, 23 mm., white.—ε, 18 mm., striped ground.—ζ, 17–18 mm., dotted ground.—Also (1520) an I, 30 mm., arabesque pattern on black ground.

I 2

1517 Dec. Erasmus: uita Hieronymi. Printed by Cervicornus. See no. 10582.

10578. [n. b. 1518.] Hieronymus: epistulae tres ab Erasmo recognitae. [JE-ROME.] 4°. P. XI. 398. 306b. Types 1, 2, gk.; cut; Y; a; α.

10579. 1520. Henr. Institoris: malleus maleficarum. [SPRENGER.] 8°. P.VI. 384. 329. Types 2–7; β-ʒΔ.

xxxix. EUCHARIUS CERVICORNUS.

TYPES. Type 1, middle roman; M has a low point like Math. Schürer 1, but single hyphen; ¶; 87–88 mm.—Type 2, small roman with abnormal M, as Heinr. of Neuss 6 and Elisabeth 2; single hyphen, round comma, ¶; 71 mm.—Type 3, roman caps. 8 mm., of the thicker variety. —Type 4, german text roman; Qu; single hyphen; 107 mm.—Type 5, like 2, except M, which is more like Froben's or Heil 1, but has the middle point lower. Capitals only, cast on the body of 4.—Type 6, small gothic, like Quentell 6, but single hyphen, and a tailed h of unusual form. —Greek type, very like Froben's second fount; the same small caps.; 109 mm.—Hebrew type. Type 1, see fig. 8; 2, 5, see fig. 11; 3, see fig. 1; 4, see fig. 3; 6, see fig. 46 (h differs).

BORDERS. Quarto border-device Aa; at top one shield with Köln arms, another with mark and initials of the printer; greek motto; at foot device of καιρός standing on a horizontal wheel. —B, quarto; black renascence pilasters; face at top, arms of Köln with supporters at foot; faces in the pedestals of the columns.—C, quarto; at top Magi, at sides SS. Bruno and Barbara, five shields at foot.—D, quarto, previously used by Elisabeth (1518) and Heinr. of Neuss (his A; 1519).

DEVICES. a, see border A.—b, figure of καιρός detached, standing on a vertical wheel.— c is the device a of Gymnicus.

INITIALS. α, black ground, 37–39 mm. (V is 33 mm.), very like a set used by Adam Petri. —β, like α, but 24–25 (P is 21) mm.—Γ, similar, but 14–16 mm. only.—δ, black ground, very like Froben H; 45–46 mm.

10580. [a. 1517 June 5.] IOSEPHVS : περὶ αὐτοκράτορος λογισμοῦ, latine. 4°. P.VI. 377. 272? Type 1, gk., hb.; cuts; αβΓ.

10581. 1517 Aug. 7. Aldus MANVTIVS: de literis graecis et diphthongis. 4°. P. VI. 378. 279. Types 1, 2, gk., hb.; Aa; b.

10582. 1517 Dec. ERASMVS: uita Hieronymi. [For Gymnicus.] 4°. Types 1, 2, gk.; cut; Y; c; α. [Titlepage facs. KBM. 91.]

10583. n.d. [c. 1517.] ERASMVS: querela pacis. 4°. Types 1, 2, gk.; αβ.

10584. 1518 May. Epistulae trium illustrium uirorum ad Hermannum comi-tem Nuenarium. [NUENARE.] 4°. P.VI. 379. 291. Types 1, 2, gk.; cut; Γ.

10585. 1518 June 1. Iac. MONTANVS: uita S. Pauli apostoli. 4°. Types 1, 2; cut; αβ.

10586. 1519 May. PLAVTVS: aulularia. 4°. Types 1, 2, 3; cut.

10587. 1519 [a. Aug. 14]. ERASMVS: enchiridion militis christiani. 4°. P.VI. 382. 317. Types 1, 2, 3, gk.; BXY; αδ.

10588. n.d. [c. 1519.] Aldus MANVTIVS: institutiones grammaticae. 4°. Types 1, 2, 3, gk.; βΓ.

10589. [a. 1520 March 17.] Ioh. CAESARIVS: apologia in mala consulentes; dia-lectica. 4°. Types 1, 3, gk.; cuts; αΓδ.

10590. [a. 1520 May 12.] Probatissimorum ecclesiae doctorum sententiae. [ECCLESIA.] 4°. Types 3, 4, 5, 6, gk.; C; δ.

10591. 1520. ERASMVS: antibarbara. 4°. P.VI. 384. 331. Types 1, 3, 4, 5; D; αδ.

10592. 1520 Dec. SOLINVS: polyhistor. [With Hero Fuchs.] 4°. Types 1–5; D; αβ.

xl. NICOLAUS AND CONRAD KAISER.

ADDRESS. In uico qui dicitur uenter felis, uulgo Katzenbuch.

TYPES. Type 1, middle roman; single hyphen, round comma smaller than that of Cervicornus, but the whole fount very like Cervicornus 1 (similar M) except ℂ, which has the tail turned back (not used by Cervicornus before 1520); 88–89 mm.—Type 2, large roman capitals, 8 mm., rather rough.—Greek type like Cervicornus.

Type 1, see fig. 8; 2, see fig. 1.

BORDER. A, one-piece, quarto; portraits of latin writers, arms of Köln at foot; cf. the border of no. 10608, M. Schürer E, Laz. Schürer B.—The border-pieces (Y) of 1520 are those of Cervicornus.

DEVICE. a, see KBM. 31.

INITIALS. α, 36 mm. = Cervicornus α.—β, 17–18 mm., like Cervicornus Γ, but a different size.—Γ, small calligraphic, 15 mm.—δ = Cervicornus β.

(a) Nicolaus Kaiser.

10593. 1518 Apr. 12. Herm. BVSCHIVS: uallumhumanitatis. [BUSCHE.] 4°. P.VI. 380. 294. Type 1; a; αβΓΔ.

10594. 1518 Apr. 30. Ioh. Picus: epistulae. [PICO.] 4°. P.VI. 381. 307. Type 1, gk.; a; αβΓ.

10595. 1518 May 20. ERASMVS: declamationes duae. 4°. P.VI. 380. 295. Type 1; a; αβ.

(b) Conrad Kaiser.

10596. 1518 Dec. 9. Herm. Buschius: dictata quaedam utilissima. [BIBLE.] 4°. Type 1, gk.; a; αΔ.

10597. 1519 June. EVRIPIDES: Hecuba, Iphigenia in Aulide, lat. per Erasmum. 4°. P.VI. 382. 318. Types 1, 2; AY; δΔ.

xli. JOHANN HEIL, OR SOTER.

TYPES. Type 1, small roman, like Quentell 13 (M normal, not as Cervicornus 2 or 5), double hyphen; ę; the W is noticeable.—Type 2, text roman, of german style, like Quentell 12; double hyphen; ę only; & is not quite straight; W like that of 1; 104 mm.—Type 3, middle roman, like Cervicornus 1 (same M) but rather spiky; odd us; double hyphen; 92 mm.—Type 4, very large roman caps., 15 mm.—Type 5, roman caps., 8 mm., like Landen 7.—Type 6, italic, like J. Schöffer 21 or Knoblouch 22; double hyphen, horizontal.—Greek type, tall and narrow, not like Cervicornus; caps. to match.—Hebrew (hb.), rather small, with vowel points.—Ethiopic type (eth.).

Type 1, see fig. 11; 2, see fig. 3; 3, see fig. 8; 5, see fig. 1; 6, see fig. 13.

BORDER. A, folio, interlaced ornament; copied from that of the Psalterium quincuplex, Genova, 1516.

10598. 1518 June 11. Psalterium in quattuor linguis exaratum. [BIBLE.] F°. P. VI. 379. 293. Type 1, gk., hb., eth.; A; Δ.

10599. 1519 Apr.–Sept. Alb. KRANTZ: Wandalia. F°. P.VI. 382. 321. Types 1, 2; A.

10600. 1520 May. Alb. KRANTZ: Saxonia. F°. P.VI. 383. 328. Types 2, 3, 4; A.

10601. [a. 1520 May 12.] Probatissimorum ecclesiae doctorum sententiae. [ECCLESIA.] 4°. Types 4, 5, 6; Δ.

xlij. ELISABETH, WIDOW.

ADDRESS. In platea ciuica.

TYPES. Type 1, middle roman = Cervicornus 1 ; single hyphen, round comma.—Type 2, small roman = Cervicornus 2 or Heinrich of Neuss 6 ; single hyphen and round comma.—Type 3, roman caps., 8 mm. = Cervicornus 3.—Greek type as Cervicornus. The cuts and one initial (of set α) are also his.

BORDER. A, the copy of a border of Froben, used in 1519 by Heinrich of Neuss (his A) and in 1520 by Cervicornus (his D).

10602. 1518 Oct. 8. Cyprianus: de contemnenda morte. 4°. P.XI.398.297b. Types 1,2,3; cut; Δ.

10603. 1518 Nov. Herm. Buschius: decimationum plautinarum quintana secunda. [BUSCHE.] 4°. P.VI. 380. 297. Types 1–3, gk.; cut; A.

xliij. SERVATIUS CRUFTANUS.

ADDRESS. Up Marcellen straissen.

TYPES. Type 1, text schwabacher, rough ; three kinds of D, one from a type like Bumgart 6 ; ¶ and ₡ with tail turned back, both too small ; h of fraktur form, and a w.f. h of curious appearance ; a second I from a fount like Pafraet 1 (MT. 64 a) ; double hyphen and short comma ; 96–97 mm.—Type 2, square church text, like Quentell 10.—Type 3, square canon, like Quentell 9. Type 1, see fig. 54; 2, see fig. 18; 3, see fig. 15.

INITIALS. Two D and an A from the set of gospel scenes, Grüninger λ ; 101 mm. Also odd initials ; the occurrence in the Sent Barbaren Passi of an I with a wormhole in it which is used much less worn and with no wormhole in a book which was written in April 1520 (no. 10608), shows that this and the Arent Bosman are later than 1520.

10604. n.d. Berufung des Kölner Rats wider die Türken. [COLOGNE.] obl. Types 1,2; Δ.

10605. n.d. [a.1520.] Sent Barbaren passi. [BARBARA.] 4°. Types 1, 2, 3; cut; αΔ.

10606. n.d. [a.1520.] Van Arnt Buschmann. [BOSMAN.] 4°. Types 1, 2, 3; cut; αΔ.

WITHOUT PRINTER'S NAME.

1501. Bernardi floretus	10354.
1503. Peraudi: legenda decem milium martyrum	10473.
1508. Directorium concubinariorum	10420.
1510 June 20. Victor von Carben: von der Jungfrauschaft Mariae	10495.
1511. Iac. Hochstratus: protectorium principum	10439.
1514. Pfefferkorn: Sturm über und wider die Juden	10444.
1514. Nic. Simonis: exercitium signorum sacerdotalium	10570.
1517. Planetisches Werk	10457.
1518 Feb. Iac. Hochstratus; apologia contra dialogum	10459.
1518 June 11. Psalterium tetraglottum	10598.
1518 Aug. Gratius: lamentationes obscurorum uirorum	10462.
1520. Erasmus: antibarbara	10591.
n.d. Ioh. Andreae: summa super quarto decretalium	10547f.

Type 1, middle roman; a few caps. only.—Type 2, latin text gothic, perhaps like Cornelis of Zierikzee 2, but two lines only, with no characteristic letter or hyphen; wrong-fount M.—Type 3, small, almost identical with Heinrich of Neuss 4, but has mixt hyphen, and æ, ę from a roman fount; 64 mm.—Border A, all in one piece with a cut; the bottom piece is separate, but fits in its place.

Type 4, roman capitals, 8 mm., thick.   Cf. Heil 5, Cervicornus 3.—Type 5, middle german roman, double hyphen, ¶, ę and æ, round comma; 88 mm.   No us; else like Heil 1.—Type 6, small german roman, like Quentell 13; single hyphen, ę; except for hyphen very like Heil 3; 76 mm.—Border B, a copy of Laz. Schürer B, but in one piece: AMRROSIVS for AMBROSIVS. Cf. also Kaiser A.—Initials.   α, Strassburg style, coarse dotted ground, with figures, 25 mm. The I is used, much more worn, in the books by S. Kruffter, no. 10605–6.

Types 1, 5, see fig. 8; 2, see fig. 38?; 3, see fig. 47; 4, see fig. 1; 6, see fig. 11.

10607. n.d.[1517?] Epistulae obscurorum uirorum ad Ortuinum Gratium. [GRATIVS.] 4°. P.IX. 174. 126. Types 1–3; A. [Impressus romanae curiae.]

10608. [a. 1520 Apr. 7.] Aug. ALVELD: libellus quo ostendere conatur diuino iure institutum esse ut totius ecclesiae caput romanus sit pontifex. 4°. Types 4–6; B; α. [Wants all after G6.]

VI. AUGSBURG.

---

xiij. JOHANN SCHÖNSPERGER THE ELDER, FIRST PRESS, CONTINUED.

It is often difficult in the books of reference to distinguish the work of the elder and the younger Schönsperger; but at present there seem to be no known productions of the elder to bridge the gap between 1505 and 1514; see below, press 31.

TYPES. Types 4 (square church text), 5 (square canon), 6 (large text schwabacher; 104 mm.), 7 (large round), 8 (latin text like G. Stuchs 13) and 9 (smaller text schwabacher; 88 mm.); see part i. Type 4 is like J. Otmar 21, 5 like J. Otmar 22, 6 like J. Otmar 17, 9 like J. Otmar 18 or Öglin 3 (cf. also no. 10949).

Type 4, see fig. 19; 5, see fig. 15; 7, see fig. 24; 8, see fig. 43; 9, see fig. 60.

INITIALS. α, maiblumen, 36–37 mm.—β, black ground, arabesque design, 17–18 mm.—Γ, outline letters in quasi-rustic style; 17–18 mm.—Δ, a W in a style resembling that of Grüninger α–δ; 15 mm. α and β were both used by Schönsperger as early as 1491.

10609. 1501 March 11. Eyke von Repgow: Sachsenspiegel. [SAXONY.] F°. DA. 516. Types 4–8; cut; αβΔ.
10610. [n.b. 1504.] Hans GERN: Lied von der böhmischen Schlacht. F°. W. 279. Type 9.
10611. [n.b. 1505.] Der königliche Vertrag…[ALBERT IV.] 4°. DA. 560. Types 4, 9; cut; β.
10612. [a. 1505 Aug. 28.] Expurgatio rectoris et concilii gymnasii Ingolstadiensis pro Georgio Zingel. [ACAD.] 4°. P. VII. 126. 3. Types 6, 9; cut.
10613. n.d. [c. 1505.] Von der neugefunden Region. [VESPUCCI.] 4°. Types 4, 9; cut.

TYPES. Types 3 (text schwabacher, double hyphen, distinctive D and H, narrow ℂ; 90 mm.); 4 (smaller rounded church text, like Ratdolt 9, with tailed h; short letters 4 mm.); 5 (small text like Knoblouch 9, Schott 11; round h, no hyphen, 74 mm.); for these see part i.—Type 6, larger bold round type with remarkable capitals, like Schönsperger jun. 2; h slightly tailed; short letters 5 mm. full. This type is not found before 1503, and therefore nos. 1852–1859 must belong to this period.

Type 4, see fig. 32¹; 5, see fig. 45; 6, see fig. 27.

BORDERS. A, quarto, white ground; a bird in the lower left corner. A copy of this border was used by Hans of Erfurt; see below, press xxxiii.—B, quarto, black ground.

10614. 1501. De laude et utilitate studii. [LAVS.] 4°. P.IX. 378. 6b. Type 3; cut.

10615. 1501. REGVLAE grammaticales antiquorum. 4°. P.VI. 131. 3. Types 3, 4, 5; cut.

10616. 1502. Aurea scholarium pharetra. [SCHOLARES.] 4°. P.VI. 131. 8. Types 4, 5; cut.

10617. [a. 1502 June 26.] Iac. LOCHER: spectaculum more tragico effigiatum. 4°. P. VII. 126. 2. Type 3; cuts.

10618. 1503. HENRICVS de Hassia: secreta sacerdotum. 4°. P.VI. 132. 16. Types 3, 5, 6.

10619. 1503. Gerson: de cognitione peccatorum. [CHARLIER.] 4°. P.VI. 133. 17. Types 3, 4.

10620. 1503 Dec. 8. Imperatoris Friderici tertii desponsatio et coronatio. [FREDERICK.—For Joh. Wacker.] 4°. P.VI. 133. 18. Types 3, 6.

10621. [a. 1504 Nov. 2.] Vermerkt den Vertrag zwischen Herzog Ruprecht und Herzog Georgs gelassener Landschaft…[RUPERT.] 4°. W. 302. Types 3, 6; cut.

10622. n.d. [c. 1504–5.] Hans Schneider: ein neues GEDICHT von dem Krieg. 4°. Types 3, 6.

10623. 1505. Geo. MORGENSTERN: sermones. 4°. P.VI. 134. 28. Types 3, 5, 6.

10624. [1505.] Paulus OLEARIVS: de fide concubinarum in sacerdotes, etc. 4°. P.VI. 134. 29, 30. Types 3, 6; cut. [Wants sig. a, d, e.]

10625. 1506. Paulus OLEARIVS: de fide concubinarum in sacerdotes, etc. 4°. Types 3, 6; cut.

10626. 1506. Joh. von PALTZ: die himmlische Fundgrube. 4°. W. 353. Types 3, 6; cut.

10627. 1507. ANDREAS de Escobar; modus confitendi, etc. 4°. P.VI. 136. 39. Types 3, 6.

10628. [n.b. 1507.] Wimpheling: AVISAMENTVM de concubinariis non absoluendis. 4°. P.VI. 362. 138? Types 3, 6; cut.

10629. [n.b. 1507.] Vermerkt der römischen königlichen Majestät Reichstag zu Konstanz. [GERMANY.] 4°. W. 420; DA. 583? Types 3, 6.

10630. 1510. Teutsch Kalender mit Figuren. [EPH.] 4°. DA. 686. Types 3, 6; cuts.

10631. 1513. ANDREAS de Escobar: modus confitendi. 4°. P.VI. 141. 64. Types 3, 6.

10631A. 1514. Passion zu teutsch. [BIBLE.] 8°. DA. 769. Types 3, 6; cuts.

10632. [n.a. 1514.] Der Wächter an der Zinnen lag…[WAECHTER.] F°. W. 95. Types 3, 6.

10633. [a. 1514 Mar. 6.] Ioh. LANTZPERGER: oratiuncula de uita et honestate clericorum. 4°. Types 3, 5, 6.

10634. 1519. ANDREAS de Escobar: modus confitendi. 4°. P. XI. 367. 134
Types 3,6; A.

10635. 1519. Gerson: de cognitione peccatorum. [CHARLIER.] 4°. P.VI. 152.
134. Types 3, 6; A.

10636. n.d. HENRICVS de Vrimaria: passio domini explanata. 4°. Types 5,6; B.

10637. [a. 1519 June 29.] LUTHER: Sermon geprediget zu Leipzig. 4°. DA.
932 ff. Types 3, 6; A.

10638. n.d. [1520?] LUTHER: kurze Unterweisung wie man beichten soll. 4°.
W. 1246. Types 3, 6; B.

10639. n.d. [1520?] LUTHER: eine kurze Form das Pater noster zu verstehen.
4°. W. 1521. Types 3, 6; B.

xviij. ERHARD RATDOLT.

TYPES. (TS. refers to Burger pl. 5.) Type 4, round italian small text, wrong fount h (straight
pointed tail), single hyphen; 76 mm. (TS. 7).—Type 7, large text gothic (TS. 5), also venetian;
single hyphen; 92 mm. on its own body, but when used with 13 in service-books it is cast on that
body, or leaded. In 1520 it is used with 22 in the same way, and has its hyphen.—Type 8, middle
roman (not german) with round h; 91 mm. (TS. 12.) Cf. Joh. Otmar 20.—Type 9, middle large,
with curly-tailed h; 129 mm., short letters 4 mm.; single hyphen (TS. 3 and at end: WP. 60,
larger type.).—Type 10, small italian gothic (TS. 9); round h at first, later one like that of 4; single
hyphen; 65 mm., but when used with 15 in service-books it is cast on that body or leaded.—Type 11,
rounded canon (TS. 1); h like that of 4, single hyphen; short letters 7 mm.—Type 12, large,
rounded but angular, venetian (TS. 2); short letters 5 mm.—Type 13, smaller rounded church
text (TS. 4); at this time usually with mixed capitals; in this state it was miscalled 19 in part i.
On its own body 113 mm., but often in service-books on that of 9 (or leaded); see WP. 60, smaller
type, for the latter, and 61 for the former.—Type 15, small text italian gothic (TS. 8), between 4 and
10; 69 mm. Round h at first, later one like types 4, 11.—Type 20, smaller than 13 and rougher,
106 mm. (not in TS.); occurs in these books only in a germanised form as 20ᴮ, with pointed f and
long s; h of 20ᴮ as 4, 11, of 20 curly-tailed; single hyphen. All these are fifteenth century founts.
—Type 21, roman capitals, 8 mm., thin: the prototype of all the capitals of this sort used.—Type 22,
large text, resembling Öglin 11, Miller 6, Grim 2, Stöckel 8; double hyphen, round h, ℭ; 107 mm.
Types *9, *13, see fig. 32; *21, see fig. 2; 22, see fig. 35.

DEVICES. a (Redgrave pl. 10) smaller (112 × 80 mm.); b, larger (139 × 104 mm.) device of
an astronomical male figure on a shield with crest on helm and mantling; printed in red and black.
—c, similar shield without crest, &c.; 59 × 54 mm.

INITIALS. These are so complex that they are sorted here rather by size than in sets.—α, white
letters on black ground, arabesque ornament; size varies from 30–37 × 26–29 mm.—β, like α, but
larger, 49 mm. Some letters have a white shield in the middle.—Γ, calligraphic versals, 26 mm.—
δ, pictures of saints, later style, white ground; one A and four B are used; 37–38 mm.—ε, shaded
floral, 27 mm.—ζ, like δ, but 56 mm. B (David) and F (Peter and Paul) only.—H, curious heavy
calligraphic; 45 mm. D, S only.—θ, exaggerated renascence, white ground and no straight outer
line; 45 mm.; ACDEG in 1520. ι, smaller calligraphic, 25–26 mm.; DLM only.—The odd
(Δ) initials include: a Canon T, 89 mm. (1502 March–1510 March); another, 80 mm. (1504
April); A, like β, with a shield in it, but 63 mm. (1502 March–1510 March); P of branches, like
the Calendar set of 1476 (33 mm.; 1520), and a few others.

10640. 1501. Index siue directorium Constantiense. [LIT.] 4°. P.VI. 130. 1.
Types 4, 7, 12; cut; a; α.

10641. 1502 March 10. Missale Frisingense. [LIT.] F°. P. XI. 367. 7b. Types
9, 11, 12, 13, music; cuts, diagr.; b; βΔ.

10642. 1504 April 24. Missale Constantiense. [LIT.] F°. P.VI. 133. 21. Types
7, 9, 12, 13, music; cuts, diagr.; b; βΔ.

10643. 1504 Oct. 12. Breuiarium Augustense, pars aestiualis. [LIT.] 8°. P.VI.
133. 20. Types 4, 10, 15; cut; a; α.

10644. 1505 Jan. 5. Missale Patauiense. [LIT.] F°. Types 9, 11, 12, 13, music; cuts, diagr.; b; β_rΔ.

10645. 1505 Sept. 24. Conr. PEVTINGER: romanae uetustatis fragmenta in Augusta. F°. P.VI.134.26. Types 8, 21.

10646. 1506 Aug. 1. Statuta dioecesana Augustensia. [AUGSBURG.] F°. P.VI. 1 5.34. Types 4, 7, 12; cut; c.

10647. 1507 Apr. 26. Diurnale Frisingense. [LIT.] 16°. P.VI.136.38. Types 4, 15; cut; c; α. [Wants most of pars aestiualis.]

10648. [a. 1507 Nov. 4.] Statuta aliis statutis synodalibus adiungenda. [AUGSBURG.] F°. P.XI.367.34 (2). Types 7, 12, 20ᴮ; cut; Δ.

10649. [a. 1508 Dec. 4.] Brief des Augsburger Rats an Kaiser Maximilian. [AUGSBURG.] bs. W.471. Type 4; Δ. [On vellum.]

10650. 1509. Breuiarium Constantiense. [LIT.] 8°. P.VI.138.49. Types 4, 10, 15; cut, diagr.; a; α.

10651. 1510 March 27. Missale Augustense. [LIT.] F°. P.VI.138.51. Types 9, 11, 12, 13, music; cuts, diagr.; b; βΔ.

10652. 1510 July 18. Obsequiale Ratisponense. [LIT.] 4°. Types 7, 11, 12, 13, music; αβe.

Georg Ratdolt.

10653. 1515 Nov. 20. Breuiarium Ratisponense. [LIT.] 8°. P.VI.142.77. Types 4, 10, 13, 15; cut, diagr.; δeΔ.

10654. 1520. Breuiarium Curiense, pars aestiualis. [LIT.] F°. Types 4, 7, 12, 22; cuts, diagr.; αϡнθιΔ.

xxiij. LUCAS ZEISSENMAIR.

TYPES. Types 1 (=Schönsperger sen. 4); 2 (Schönsperger sen. 6); see part i.

INITIALS. α, large Maiblumen, 41–2 mm.—β, large, fine, but rather florid initials in the style of Joh. Zainer's; also 41–2 mm.—The Δ initials are two; a D, 38 mm., four flowers on a black ground; and a S, 29 mm. arabesque pattern on a black ground.

10655. 1501 Nov. 18. STEPHAN Lanzkranna: die Himmelstrasse. F°. DA.510. Type 2; cut; αΔ.

10656. 1502 Apr. 21. Herzog Gottfried wie er wider die Türken gestritten hat. [GODFREY.] 4°. DA.530b. Type 2; cut; αβΔ.

10657. 1502 Dec. 9. Alanus de RVPE: Von unser lieben Frauen Psalter. 4°. DA.525b; W.240. Types 1, 2; cuts; α.

[For continuation see Wessobrunn.]

xxiv. JOHANN OTMAR, third press.

ADDRESS (1511 Apr.) : suis in aedibus ex transuerso sacelli sanctae Vrsulae intra riuos Lici.

TYPES. Type 14, large round; cf. Öglin 4. Facs. Butsch I. pl. 18.—Type 15, small latin text gothic, like Grim 8; slightly kerned; cf. Koberger 17, Lotter 1, Weissenburger 7, &c.; 70–71 mm.—Type 16, as 15, but slightly larger; 75 mm.—Type 17, large text schwabacher, as Schönsperger sen. 6, but 108 mm.; saw-edge ℂ.—Type 18, small text schwabacher, exactly as Öglin 3; cf. Schönsperger sen. 9; 89 mm.—Type 19, text roman=Öglin 1; in 1509 with long double hyphen: in 1511 and later with ę; 106 mm.—Type 20, Ratdolt's second roman, type 8, brought by him from Venezia; 91 mm.—Type 21=Schönsperger sen. 4; square church type, 152 mm.; short letters 5 mm.—Type 22, square canon type, short letters 9–10 mm. Cf. Schönsperger sen. 5.—Type 23, small church type like Koelhoff sen. 14; short letters under 4 mm.—Type 24, round schwabacher text like Miller 7 ; 90 mm.—Type 25, smaller roman=Öglin 2.—Type 26, rounded canon type, like Öglin 6 ; roundels in some letters ; short letters 8 mm.—Type 27, larger latin text gothic ; two lines of it only are found in these books ; but cf. Silv. Otmar 9.—First greek type (one word only); second, smaller type, also very little used.

Type 14, see fig. 24; 15, 16, see fig. 40; *17, see fig. 52; 18, see fig. 60; 21, see fig. 19; 22, see fig. 15; 23, see fig. 20; 24, see fig. 53; 25, see fig. 10; 26, see fig. 23.

BORDER. A, folio border, specially designed for Geiler's Nauis paenitentiae.—A four piece folio border (X) is used in 1515.

INITIALS. α, large black ground arabesque, 50 × 42 mm.—β, large calligraphic, 41 mm. In 1515 an E and I, 38–39 mm.

10658. 1502. Pelbartus de Themeswar: stellarium coronae B.M.V. [MARY.—For J. Schönsperger the younger.] F°. P.VI. 132. 12. Types 14, 15; cut.

10659. 1502 Dec. 8. Theod. RYSICHEVS: oratio in laudem s. Iuonis. [For Joh. Rinmann.] F°. P. VI. 132. 13. Types 14, 16; cuts.

10660. 1503 Dec. 24. Auszug Kaiser Friedrichs gen Rom. [FREDERICK III.— For J. Rinmann & J. Wacker.] 4°. DA. 542. Types 17, 18.

10661. 1504 Aug. 6. Ambr. ALANTSEE: foedus christianum. [For J. Rinmann.] 4°. P. VI. 133. 24. Types 14, 16.

10662. 1504. Mundus nouus. [VESPUCCI.] 4°. P. VI. 133. 22. Types 14, 16.

10663. 1505. Patriarchatus, archiepiscopatus, episcopatus. [CATHOLIC CHURCH.] 4°. P. VI. 135. 32. Types 14, 16.

10664. 1505. Ioh. FABER de Werdea: prouerbia. [With E. Öglin, for Jobst Birlin.] 4°. P. VI. 134. 31. Types 14, 16, 19.

10665. 1505. Conr. CELTES: rhapsodia laudes et uictoria de Boemannis. 4°. P. VI. 135. 33. Types 19, 20, gk. i; cuts.

10666. 1507 Feb. 12. Biblia germanica. [BIBLE.—For J. Rinmann.] F°. DA. 575. Types 14, 17; cuts; α. [Vol. 2 only.]

10667. 15[0]7. Libellus de fraternitate rosarii et psalterii B.M.V. [MARY.] 4°. P. VI. 136. 40. Types 16, 17; cut.

10668. 1508 Jan. 15. Tractatus gloriosissimae uirginis Mariae qualiter festa celebranda sint ostendens. [MARY.] 4°. P. IX. 110. 33. Types 16, 17, 21.

10669. 1508 Mar. 18. Von Zucht der Kinder nach Lehre Plutarchi. [PLUTARCH.] 4°. Types 17, 21; cuts; α.

10670. 1508 (May–June). Joh. TAULER: Sermones deutsch. [For J. Rinmann.] F°. DA. 602. Types 17, 21–24; cut; α.

10671. 1508. Joh. GEILER: Predigten deutsch. F°. DA. 603. Types 21–24; cuts; α.

10672. [a 1508 Sept. 11.] Erklärung der Landsfreiheit des Herzogthums Baiern. [BAVARIA.] F°. DA. 615; W. 993. Types 17, 21; cut; Δ.

10673. 1508 Dec. 13. Eyke von REPGOW: Remissorium mit dem Weichbilde... [For J. Rinmann.] F°. W. 459. Types 17, 21, 22; αβ.

10674. [a. 1509 June 17.] Julius ij: Bull wider die Venediger (27. iv. 1509). F°. W. 480. Types 17, 21, 24; cut; Δ.

10675. 1509 Nov. 29. Ulrich TENGLER: Laienspiegel. [For J. Rinmann.] F°. DA. 645. Types 16, 17, 19, 21; cuts.

10676. 1510 May 12. Lud. HELIANVS: oratio de bello suscipiendo. 4°. P. VI. 138. 52. Types 19, 25.

10677. 1510 May 31. STEPHAN Lanzkranna: die Himmelstrasse. [For J. Rin- mann.] F°. DA. 671. Types 17, 21, 26; cut.

10678a. 1510. GEILER: das Buch Granatapfel (A–M).
   b. 1510. id.: die geistliche Spinnerin (a–f).
   c. 1510 Aug. 10. id.: geistliche Bedeutung des Häsleins im Pfeffer.
   d. 1510 Sept. 14. id.: die sieben Hauptsünden. [For Georg Diemar.] F°.
      DA. 667. Types 21, 23, 24, 26; cuts; α.
10679. 1510. Geiler: Predigten deutsch. [For J. Rinmann.] F°. DA. 667b.
      Types 23, 24, 26; cuts; α. [Print Room.]
10680. n. d. [c. 1510.] Hector Schöffler: von zweierlei Menschen Sterben. bs.
      Types 18, 23, 26; cuts. [Print Room.]
10681. n. d. [c. 1510.] Figura Christi ad pestilentiam fugandam. bs. Types 14,
      17, 26; cut. [Print Room.]
10682. 1511 Mar. 25. Ioh. PINCIANVS: carmina. 4°. P. VI. 139. 56. Type 19; cuts.
10683. 1511 Apr. 11. Vbertinus PVSCVLVS: Simonidos libri duo. 4°. P. VI. 139.
      57. Type 19; cuts.
10684. 1511 Apr. 12. Victor von CARBEN: Tractat von der unbefleckten Jung-
      frauschaft Mariae. [For G. Diemar.] 4°. DA. 687b; W. 634. Types
      16, 18, 21; cut.
10685. 1511 May 31. BONAVENTVRA: der Psalter Mariae. [For Sixtus Schregel.]
      16°. DA. 687. Types 17, 18, 21; cuts.
10686. 1511 June 18. TENGLER: der neue Laienspiegel. [For J. Rinmann.] F°.
      DA. 698. Types 16, 17, 19, 21, 26; cuts; α.
10687. 1511 (Sept. 8–15). GEILER: nauicula paenitentiae. [For G. Diemar.] F°.
      P. VI. 139. 58. Types 15, 17, 21, 26; cuts.
10688. 1511 Sept. 20. Alb. von EYBE: der Spiegel der Sitten. [For J. Rinmann.]
      F°. DA. 689. Types 16, 17, 19, 21, 26; cut; α.
10689. 1512 June 20. HENRICVS Suso: der Seusse. [For J. Rinmann.] F°. DA.
      710. Types 17, 18, 21, 26, cuts; α.
10690. 1512 July 31. Ioh. PINCIANVS: uirtus et uoluptas, etc. 4°. P. VI. 140. 61.
      Types 15, 19; cuts.
10691. 1512 Dec. 24. TENGLER: der neue Laienspiegel. [For J. Rinmann.] F°.
      DA. 723. Types 15, 17–19, 21, 26; cuts; α.
10692. 1513 Dec. 24. Eckius: orationes quattuor. [JOHANN.] 4°. P. VI. 141.
      65. Types 16, 18, 19, 25, gk. ij.
10693. 1514 Mar. (1–7.) GEILER: das Schiff der Penitenz. [For G. Diemar.] F°.
      DA. 774; W. 830. Types 14, 17, 19, 24, 26, 27; cut; A.
10694. 1515. Historie und Legende Katharine von Senis. [CATHARINE.—For
      J. Rinmann.] F°. DA. 810b; Types 14, 17; cuts; X; β.
10695. n. d. Epistula cuiusdam puellae romanae. 4°. P. IX. 385. 267d; H.*6620.
      Type 19.

10696. n. d. Cursus beatae Mariae uirginis, etc. [LIT.] 4°. Types 14, 17? cuts.
      [Or by the elder Schönsperger? Imperfect.]

xxv. ERHARD ÖGLIN.

TYPES. Type 1, italian text roman, dotted i, long double hyphens (none before 1508 Feb.),
Qu; 106 mm. Cf. J. Otmar 19.—Type 2, italian commentary roman, Capcasa style; single
hyphens (none before 1508 May); 82 mm. Cf. J. Otmar 25. Facs. of 1 and 2: Butsch I. 19.—
Type 3, small text schwabacher, E like Schönsperger sen. 9; single hyphen (in 1512 double),
wide C. A broken Q is often used for O, generally upside down; a w.f. I is sometimes found;
88 mm. Cf. also J. Otmar 18.—Type 4, large round type; short letters 5 mm. Cf. Joh. Otmar 14,

Schönsperger sen. 7.—Type 5, middle large, very round ; short letters 4 mm. ; like Nadler 1.   Cf. Grim 13.—Type 6, rounded canon ; not the same as Miller 5, but slightly shorter and broader, as J. Otmar 26 ; some of the caps. have roundels in them ; short letters 8 mm.—Type 7, second small text schwabacher, with normal E, double hyphen, long comma ; in 1514 has a thin ℭ mixt with a thick one with serrated edge.   In no. 10723 the E and ℭ of 3 are used in 7, and the hyphens are mixt.   No. 10721 and 10722 have a different hyphen altogether.—Type 8, second text roman, german style, very like Miller 2 ; short double hyphen ; 109 mm.—Type 9, smaller round church text (short letters 4 mm.), narrower than 5 ; like Weissenburger 4 or Meurl 2, but has some additional caps.   Cf. Miller 11.—Type 10, larger round church text, very like Meurl 1 ; short letters 5½ mm. Cf. Miller 10.—Type 11, large text latin, like Miller 6 or Grim 2.—Square hebrew (hb. i.) ; a larger rabbinic fount (hb. ij.) is used for majuscules.

Type 2, see fig. 10 ; *3, see fig. 60 ; 4, see fig. 24 ; 5, see fig. 29 ; 6, see fig. 23 ; 7, see fig. 59 ; 8, see fig. 3 ; 9, see fig. 31 ; 10, see fig. 30 ; 11, see fig. 35.

BORDER.   A = Grim C, q. v.

DEVICE.   a, black ground, E O and fleur de lis, 85 × 69 mm.

INITIALS.   α, black ground, arabesque design, like Schönsperger sen. β ; 21–23 mm.—β, larger calligraphic, 37 mm.—γ, smaller calligraphic, 25 mm.—δ, larger than α, but like them ; 27 mm.

1505. Ioh. Faber de Werdea: prouerbia. With Joh. Otmar. See no. 10664.

10697. 1506. PRVDENTIVS: psychomachia. 4°. P. VI. 135. 35. Types 1, 2.

10698. [n. b. 1506.] Fünf andächtiger Gesetze neue Gedichte. obl. W. suppl. i. 358. Types 3, 4; cut; Y. [Print Room.]

10699. 1507 Apr. GVNTHERVS Cisterciensis: Ligurinus. F°. P. VI. 136. 41. Types 1, 2; α.

10700. 1507 Aug. 22. Pet. TRITONIVS: harmoniae super carmina Horatii. 4°. Types 1, 2, 4, music; a.

10701. 1507. Pet. TRITONIVS: melopoiae. [For Joh. Rinmann.] F°. P. VI. 137. 42. Types 1, 2, music; cuts.

10702. 1507. Heinr. GESSLER: Formulare und deutsche Rhetorica. [For Joh. Widmann.] 4°. DA. 589. Types 3, 4; cut; βγ.

10703. 1508 Feb. 11. Conr. REITTERIVS: mortilogus. [With G. Nadler.] 4°. P. VI. 137. 44. Types 1, 2; cut.

10704. 1508 May 22. Ioh. STAMLER: dialogus de diuersarum gentium sectis. [With G. Nadler.] F°. P. VI. 137. 46. Types 1, 2; cut.

10705. 1508. Imitatio Christi, germ. [JESVS.—With G. Nadler, for J. Widmann.] 8°. DA. 601e; W. 441. Types 3, 4; cut; Δ.

10706. [a. 1509 Jan. 3.] Joh. PFEFFERKORN: der Juden Feind. 4°. DA. 640. Types 3, 4, hb. i; cut.

10707. [a. 1509 Jan. 3.] Joh. PFEFFERKORN: Vortrag wie die Juden Ostern hal- ten. 4°. DA. 637. Types 3, 4, hb. i; cut.

10708. 1510. Joh. PFEFFERKORN: wider die Bücher der Juden. 4°. DA. 674. Types 3, 5, hb. i; cut.

10709. [n. b. 1510.] Der kaiserliche Reichstag zu Augsburg anno 1510. [GER- MANY.] 4°. W. 528. Types 3, 5; cut.

10710. 1512 July 19. Gesangbuch; Tenor. [GERMAN SONGS.] obl. 4°. W. 692. Types 3, 6, music; a; α.

10711. [a. 1512 July 20.] Ein Kind im Dorfe Ertingen geboren. F°. W. suppl. i. 78. Types 5, 7; cut. [One leaf; Print Room.]

10712. [a. 1512 Aug. 26.] Aufsatzung und Ordnung auf dem Reichstag zu Köln. [GERMANY.] F°. DA. 719. Types 5, 6; cut.

10713. [a.1513 Aug.] Neue Gezeitigung aus dem Heere vor Terebona. [GER-
MANY.] 4°. W.765. Types 5,7; cut.
10714. [a.1513 Sept.] Abdruck eines lateinischen Sendbriefs von der eroberten
Stadt Malacha. [EMANUEL.] 4°. DA. 758. Types 5,6,7; cut; α.
10715. 1514 May. Ioh. BOESCHENSTAIN: elementale introductorium in literas
hebraeas. 4°. P.VI. 142.70. Types 7,8,hb.i,ij; a; α.
10716. 1514. Ioh. BOESCHENSTAIN: ein neu geordnet Rechenbüchlein. 4°. DA.
800 (2). Types 5,7,9,10; cut; αβ.
10717. 1514. Iac. KOEBEL: ein neu geordnet Rechenbüchlein auf den Linien. 4°.
DA. 800(1). Types 7,9,10,11; cut, diagr.; αβδ.
10718. [a. 1515 July.] Neue Zeitung wie Kaiserliche Majestät zu Wien einge-
ritten ist. [MAXIMILIAN.] 4°. W.966. Types 5,7; cut.
10719. 1516 March 12. Introductio quaedam utilissima siue uocabularius quattuor linguarum. [DICT.] 4°. P.VI. 147.97; DA. 861. Types 4,7; A; a.
10720. (1520–21.) Seb. Neythardt: Kalender auf das Jahr 1521. [EPH.] bs.
Types 2,5,7; cut.

10721. n. d. [1520.] LUTHER: Appellation an ein christliches freies Concilium.
4°. DA. 974yy. Types 5,7?
10722. n. d. [1520?] Poggius: wie Hieronymus von Prag gebrannt worden ist.
[BRACCIOLINI.] 4°. W.1970. Types 5,7 [as last]?
10723. n. d. LVCIFER: epistula ad regentes ecclesiasticos, etc. 4°. Types 5,7? α.

APPENDIX.

Types 5, 6, 7, 9, 10, as above.   Type 7 has the thinner ℭ only.—Type 12, small schwabacher,
like Miller 9.—Type 13, large text schwabacher, like J. Otmar 17.—Type 14, text schwabacher,
like Miller 7.—Border A; initials α, β, as above. The border is used again in DA. 1888 (1523).
Type 12, see fig. 63; 13, see fig. 52; 14, see fig. 53.

10724. [n. b. 1515.] Chronica von viel namhaftigen Geschichten bis auf 1515.
[HUNGARY.] 4°. W.889 or 890? Types 5,6,7,10; β.
10725. [n. b. 1516.] Chronica…bis auf 1516. [HUNGARY.] 4°. Not W. 990?
Types 5, 6, 7, 10; β.
10726. [n.b. 1520.] OECOLAMPADIVS: Urteil und Meinung. 4°. W.1913. Types
7,9,14; A.
10727. [a.1520 Oct 25.] Römischer Königlicher Maiestät Krönung zu Aachen.
[CHARLES V.] W.1448. Types 5,6,7,10; cut.
10728. n. d. [1520?] KARSTHANS. 4°. W.1439. Types 6,7; cut; α.
10729. n.d. [1520?] LUTHER: Unterrichtung warum des Papsts und seiner Jün-
ger Bücher gebrannt sind. 4°. W. 1593. Types 5,6,7,9,10,12,13,14.
10730. n.d. [1520?] KLAGE etlicher Stände. 4°. W.1101. Types 5,7,10,12,13; A.
10731. n.d. [1520?] Was Nutz von ALMOSEN kommt… 4°. W.1308. Type 7;
cut; Y; β.

xxvi. JOHANN SCHÖNSPERGER THE YOUNGER.

ADDRESS.   Am Weinmarkt (in no. 10741, 10744).

TYPES.   Type 1, large bold round type, different from the ordinary types of this class, but
like Froschauer 6; double hyphen; Muther pl. 174-5. Cf. Konstanz, Schäffler 2.—Type 2, text
schwabacher; 89 mm. Muther pl. 172, 174-5. The E is characteristic; but in no. 10745 the
E is different. Cf. Konstanz, Schäffler 1.—Type 3, latin text gothic, like Joh. Otmar 15 or 16.
—Type 4, small latin gothic, probably=xiij. 11; like Gran 9, &c.; double hyphen, round h;
66-67 mm.—Type 5, middle large type, like Öglin 5 or Nadler 1.

Type *1, see fig. 27; 2, see fig. 53; 3, see fig. 40; 4, see fig. 46; 5, see fig. 29.

BORDERS.   A–E, five octavo borders used as frames to the smaller cuts in no. 10738; see Muther 172–175.

1502. Stellarium coronae B.V.M.   Joh. Otmar for Schönsperger; see no. 10658.

10732. 1510 Nov. 8. Ich bin genant der freygedanck. [FREYDANK.] F°. W. 547. Types 1,2; cuts.

10733. 1510 Dec. 20. Die Weissagung von zukünftiger Betrübnis. [BRIDGET.] 4°. DA. 685c; W. suppl. i. 54. Types 1,2; cuts.

10734. 1511. HENRICVS de Hassia: secreta sacerdotum. 4°. P.VI. 139.54. Types 1,3,4.

10735. 1512 Jan. 22. Büchlein von Complexion der Menschen. [BUECHLEIN.] 4°. DA. 734; W. suppl. i. 77. Types 1,2; cut.

10736. 1514. Narrenschiff vom BUNDSCHUH. 4°. W. 813. Types 1,2,4.

10737. [a. 1514 Oct. 5.] Kaiserliche Verordnung eines Landtags in Landshut am 30. Okt. 1514. (d: Innsbruck.) obl. Type 2; Δ. [Three editions, cropt; Print Room.]

10738. 1515. Wolfgang von MANN: Das Leiden Jesu Christi. 4°. DA. 804. Types 1,2,4; cuts; A–E, X.

10739. n. d. Von dem ehelichen Stande eine schöne Lehre. [STAND.] 4°. W. 768. Types 1,2; cuts.

10740. n. d. Pamph. GENGENBACH: die Prophezeiungen Methodii und Nolhardi. 4°. W. 1051. Types 1,2; cut.

10741. 1518. Die zehn ALTER dieser Welt. 4°. DA. 921. Types 1,2; cuts.

10742. n. d. Das ist jetzt der gemeine und neue GEBRAUCH. 4°. (Not W. 27–29.) Types 1,2; cut.

10743. n. d. Der FRAUEN Spiegel. 4°. W. 1388. Types 1,2; cut.

10744. n. d. [c. or a. 1520.] Von dem ehelichen Stande. [STAND.] 4°. W. 1369. Types 2,5; cut.

10745. n. d. [c. 1520.] Das ist jetzt der gemeine und neue GEBRAUCH. 4°. W. 28. Types 1,2; cut.

xxvij. JOHANN SITTICH.

Panzer DA. 567b gives the date 1506 as that of an edition of Proles; but this seems to be an error due to the resemblance between MDVI and MDXI.

TYPES.   Type 1, rough text schwabacher, like (but different from) Hans of Erfurt 2; D like S reversed; single hyphen, also used as comma; 91 mm.—Type 2, smaller rounded church text, like Miller 11 or Grim 3.—Type 3, small text schwabacher, like Öglin 7 or Miller 8; 89 mm. Type 1, see fig. 54; 2, see fig. 31; 3, see fig. 59.

10746. 1511. Andr. PROLES: eine innige Lehre wie man sich halten soll bei der Taufe. 4°. DA. 691. Types 1,2; cut; Y.

10747. 1512 Aug. 14. Ioh. Regiomontanus: Kalendarius teutsch. [EPH.] 4°. DA. 739. Types 2,3; cuts, diagr.; X; Δ.

10748. n. d. ARNALDVS de Villa noua: von Bereitung und Brauchung der Weine. 4°. DA. 731. Types 2,3; cut.

10749. [1512–3.] Georg Tanstetter: Kalender auf 1513. bs. Types 2?3. [Fragment.]

10750. [1513–4.] Georg Tanstetter: Kalender auf 1514. [EPH.] bs. Types 2?3. [Fragment.]

TYPES.   Type 1, text roman = xxiv. 19 ; ę and saw-edge ℂ ; large round comma from c. 1518.
Facs. Butsch I. 23, 24.—Type 2, small roman = xxiv. 25 ; at first with single hyphen, low us ;
82 mm.—Type 3, rounded canon = xxiv. 26.   Facs. Butsch I. 23, 24, 30.—Type 4, small latin
text gothic = xxiv. 15.—Type 5, text schwabacher = xxiv. 24.   Facs. Muther 186–189.—Type 6,
large roman capitals, like Ratdolt 21 or Miller 1 ; 8 mm.—Type 7, large round = xxiv. 14.   Facs.
Butsch I. 23, 24, 30.—Type 8, very small gothic ; A like that of G. Leeu, type 3 (MT. 79d 2) ;
59–60 mm.   Cf. Gran 15.—Type 9, latin text gothic (probably = xxiv. 27), like G. Stuchs 12 ; 85 mm.
—Type 10, large text schwabacher = xxiv. 17.—Type 11, smaller text schwabacher = xxiv. 18.—
Type 12, very large roman caps., like Grim 4 ; 13 mm.—Type 13, latin small text gothic, venetian
style ; 75 mm.

Types 2–5, 7, 9–11 ; see references under press xxiv.   Type 6, see fig. 2.

BORDERS.   All are quarto borders except B.   Two borders (X) made up of four pieces are
found.   A, black ground ; cornucopiae at sides ; signed D. H. (cf. F.).   Facs. Butsch I. 24.—
B, folio, also signed D. H., in the style of A ; Miller G is a copy.   Facs. Butsch I. 23.   Cf. also
Grüninger E.—C, architectural ; round pillars and a flat cornice.—D, flamboyant, black ground ;
top and bottom wider than sides ; cut into four pieces before being used by Otmar.   Facs.
Butsch I. 30.—E, elaborate architectural, scallop-shell arch ; satyr at foot.—F, a copy of A,
but no cornucopiae or signature.   Facs. Butsch I. 26.—G, shaped like E, but ground white ; a sill
for insertion of date in upper part ; boys round the columns ; demivieillard at base.—H, boys
riding various animals, &c.—I, Adam and Eve.—K, six saints and the evangelist symbols ; not
found with Otmar's name before 1521.   Cf. a folio border used by Adam Petri.

INITIALS.   α, calligraphic, 37 mm.—β, large, black ground, very like, if not the same as
Joh. Otmar α.   Δ initials include many sizes of rough roman caps. from 25 mm. to 12 mm.

10751. 1513. Ioh. PINCIANVS: epitome grammaticae. 4°. P.VI. 141.68; W.
795. Types 1–5; cut.

10752. 1513. Iac. LOCHER: poematia. 4°. P.VI. 141. 66. Types 1, 2, 5.

10753. 1515 July 24. XENOCRATES: de morte. 4°. P.VI.143.78. Types 1,6; X; α.

10754. 1516 Jan. 26. Ioh. PINCIANVS: promptuarium uocabulorum. 4°. P.VI.
145.89. Types 1, 3, 4, 7, 8, 9, gk.; A.

10755. 1516 Feb. 1. Sassenspegel mit velen nyen addicien. [SAXONY.—For
J. Rinmann.] F°. DA. 842. Types 1, 3, 4, 7, 10, 11; cut; B; α.

10756. 1516 Oct. 4. Leben und Wunderwerke SS. Ulrichs, Simprechts und
Afrae. [ULRIC.] 4°. DA. 838. Types 5, 7; cuts; C; α.

10757. 1516. Laur. CORVINVS: hortulus elegantiarum. 4°. P.VI.145.91. Types
1, 2, 4, 7; A.

10758. [1517b. Apr. 15.] Albertus archiepisc. Mogunt.: literae indulgentiarum
[Tetzel]. [ROME.] obl. Types 4, 7, 10. [On vellum.]

10759. 1517 Apr. 25. Sachsenspiegel. [SAXONY.—For J. Rinmann.] F°. DA.
877. Types 3,4,7,9–11; cut; B; α.

10760. 1517. Alb. von EYBE: ob einem sei zu nehmen ein ehliches Weib. [For
J. Rinmann.] 4°. DA. 876. Types 1, 3,5, 7, 9; cuts; α.

10761. 1517. Henr. GRIENINGERIVS: epitome de generibus nominum. 4°. Types
1–4, 10.

10762. [a. 1517 Sept. 23.] Eckius: oratio funebris Henrici episc. August.
[JOHANN.] 4°. P.VI. 147. 99. Types 1, 7; cuts.

10763. 1518 Jan. 27, Feb. 12. Biblia germanica. [BIBLE.—For J. Rinmann.] F°.
DA. 888. Types 3, 7, 10; cuts; B; β. [Vol. 2 only.]

10764. 1518 May 29. Gabr. BIEL: der übertrefflichste Weg zu der Seligkeit. 4°.
DA. 895b. Types 3, 5, 7; cut; X; α.

10765. 1518 Sept. 7. LUTHER: Auslegung des 109. Psalms. [BIBLE.] 4°. DA.896f.
Types 5, 7, 8; A.

10766. 1518 Sept. 23. Eine deutsche Theologia. 4°. Types 3,5,7; D; α. [Fragment.]

10767. 1518 Oct. 30. Joh. Haselberger: die Stände des H. R. Reichs. [HASELBERG.—For J. Haselberger.] 4°. DA. 915. Types 2, 3, 5, 9; cut.

10768. 1518 Nov. 16. LUTHER: Predigt von der würdigen Bereitung zu dem Sacrament. 4°. DA. 896s. Types 3, 5, 7, 10; E; α.

10769. 1518 Nov. 20. Hans von LEONRODT: Himmelwagen. 4°. DA. 901. Types 5, 7; cuts; A; α.

10770. 1518. Ric. BARTHOLINVS: de conuentu Augustensi. 4°. P.VI. 149.111. Types 1, 2, 7; D.

10771. (1518.) LVTHER: sermo de uirtute excommunicationis. 4°. P. IX. 381. 109b. Types 1, 3; C; Δ.

10772. 1518. Ex probatissimis auctoribus uocabula. [AVCTORES.] 4°. W. 1159. Types 1, 7, 8, 9; F ; α.

10773. 1519 Jan. 13. Luther: SERMO de digna praeparatione ad eucharistiam. 4°. P. IX. 381. 136b. Types 3, 7, 9; α.

10774. 1519 April. Vlr. de HVTTEN: Febris. 4°. P. IX. 120. 141; B. xxi. 5 (note). Types 1, 12; Δ.

10775. 1519 June 10. Chr. ODOFRANCVS; de Ratisbona et Iudaeorum proscriptione. [For J. Wagner, Regensburg.] 4°. P.VI. 152. 136. Types 1,2,8,12.

10776. 1519 June 22. LUTHER: Sermon von dem ehlichen Stande. 4.° DA. 932u. Types 3, 5, 7.

10777. 1519 July 30. Franc. Philelphus: epistulae breuiores. [FILELFO.] 4.° P.VI. 152. 137. Types 1–4, 7, 9; G.

10778. [a. 1519 Aug. 15.] LVTHER: epistula de disputatione sua, etc. 4°. P.VII. 212. 737. Types 1, 4, 7, 12.

10779. 1519 Oct. 12. Hier. EMSER: opuscula. P.VI. 152. 138. Types 1, 12.

10780. [a. 1519 Nov. 30.] Abschied des gemeinen Bundsversammlungstags. [SUABIAN CONFEDERATION.] F°. Type 10.

10781. 1519. LUTHER: Unterricht auf etliche Artikel. 4°. DA. 932ll. Types 1, 3, 5, 7; A.

10782. 1520 Feb. 13. LUTHER: Sermon von dem Sacrament des Leichnams Christi. 4°. DA. 973nn. Types 5, 7; cut.

10783. 1520 Mar. Ioh. GVSSVBELIVS: oratio. 4°. P.VI. 157.171. Types 1,12; G; Δ.

10784. 1520 May 4. LUTHER: Sermon von dem Sacrament der Taufe. 4°. DA. 973bbb. Types 5, 7; A.

10785. 1520 May 7. LUTHER: die zehn Gebote mit einer kurzen Auslegung. 4°. DA. 974k. Types 5, 7; A.

10786. 1520 May 9. LUTHER: Predigt von der würdigen Bereitung zu dem Sacrament. 4°. DA. 973p. Types 3, 5, 7; G; α.

10787. 1520 May 19. LVTHER: decem praeceptorum compendiosa explanatio. 4°. P.VI. 157. 172. Types 1, 2, 7; H.

10788. 1520 May 26. LVTHER: confitendi ratio. 4°. P.VI. 157. 173. Types 1,2; H.

10789. 1520 June 23. LUTHER: der zehn Gebote eine nützliche Erklärung. 4°. DA. 974s. Types 3, 5, 7, 8; cut; G: α.

10790. 1520 June 27. Luther: eine kurze Form der zehn Gebote, etc. [L., D.M.] 4°. DA. 974q. Types 5, 7; H.

10791. 1520 July 13. LUTHER: Auslegung des Vaterunser. 4°. DA. 973e. Types 3, 5, 7; G.

10792. 1520 Aug. 21. LUTHER: Sermon von dem neuen Testamente. 4°. DA.
974bbbb. Types 5, 7; I.

10793. 1520 Sept 26. Theologia teutsch. [GERMAN THEOLOGY.] 4°. DA.971.
Types 5, 7; I; α.

10794. 1520 Oct. 2. LUTHER: Sermon von dem ehlichen Stande. 4°. DA.973s.
Types 3, 5, 7.

10795. 1520. LUTHER: Sermon von dem Sacrament der Busse. 4°. W. 1571.
Types 5, 7; A.

10796. 1520. LUTHER: Predigt von zweierlei Gerechtigkeit. 4°. DA. 974z.
Types 5, 7; A.

10797. 1520. LUTHER: Sermon von dem Bann. 4°. DA. 974f. Types 3, 5, 7; D.

10798. 1520. Laz. Spengler: Schutzrede und christliche Antwort. [N.] 4°. W.
1635. Types 3, 5, 7; G.

10799. 1520. LUTHER: kurze Unterweisung wie man beichten soll. 4°. W. 1598.
Types 3, 5, 7; G.

10800. 1520. LUTHER : tröstliches Büchlein in aller Widerwärtigkeit eines
christgläubigen Menschen. 4°. DA. 974ll. Types 5, 7; cut; G.

10801. 1520. LUTHER: tröstliches Büchlein. 4°. DA.974kk. Types 5, 7; G.

10802. 1520. LUTHER: Sermon von dem neuen Testamente. 4°. DA. 974cccc.
Types 5, 7; I.

10803. 1520. LUTHER: Sermon von dem Wucher. 4°. DA.973x. Types 5, 7; cut.

10804. 1520. LVTHER: tessaradecas consolatoria. 4°. P.VI. 158. 174. Types
3, 7, 9, 13.

10805. n.d.[a.1520 May 8.] LUTHER: Büchlein von der Beichte. 4°. DA.973kk.
Types 5, 7; K.

10806. n.d.[1520.] LUTHER: von der babylonischen Gefängnis der Kirchen. 4°.
DA. 974ooo. Types 5, 7; cut.

10807. n.d.[1520.] Von Tegkendorff das geschicht…[TECKENDORF.] 4°. W.
35. Types 5, 7, 10; cut.

10808. n.d.[1520.] LUTHER: Sermon von dem Sacrament der Taufe. 4°. W.
1580. Types 5, 7; A.

10809. n.d.[1520.] LUTHER: Sermon von dem Gebet und Prozession in der
Kreuzwoche. 4°. W. 1567. Types 5, 7; A.

10810. n.d.[1520.] LUTHER: Sermon von dem Gebet … 4°. W. 1566. Types
5, 7; A.

10811. n.d. LVTHER: sermo de paenitentia. 4°. P.IX. 385.267c. Types 1, 3, 7; D.

10812. n.d.[1520?] LUTHER: Erklärung etlicher Artikel. 4°. DA. 973qq.
Types 5, 7; D.

10813. n.d. ERASMVS: familiarium colloquiorum formulae. 4°. Types 1, 2, 12; F.

10814. n.d.[1520?] LUTHER: Sermon von dem Sacrament der Busse. 4°. W.
1574. Types 5, 7; F.

10815. n.d.[1520?] LUTHER: Sermon von der Bereitung zum Sterben. 4°. W.
1555. Types 3, 5, 7; cut.

10816. n.d.[1520?] LUTHER: Sermon von der Bereitung zum Sterben. 4°. W.
1554. Types 3, 5, 7; cut.

10817. n.d. LUTHER: Sermon von der Betrachtung des heiligen Leidens Christi.
4°. W. 1234. Types 3, 5, 7; cut.

10818. n.d. LUTHER: Sermon von der Betrachtung des heiligen Leidens Christi.
4°. W. 1233. Types 3, 5, 7; cut.

AUGS-
BURG.
xxviij. Silv.
Otmar.

83

L 2

10819. n.d. LUTHER: von dem Papsttum zu Rom. 4°. DA.974hhh. Types 3, 5, 7.
10820. n.d. LUTHER: von dem Papsttum zu Rom. 4°. Types 3, 5, 7.
10821. n.d. LVTHER: resolutio lutheriana super propositione sua decimatertia.
4°. Types 1, 4, 12.
10822. n.d. [a. 1519 Aug. 13.] Hier. EMSER: epistula de disputatione lipsicensi.
4°. P. VII. 212. 737. Types 1, 7, 8, 9, 12, 13; cut.

xxix. JOHANN MILLER.

TYPES. Type 1, large roman caps., thin-faced; A has a horizontal bar at the top; 8 mm.
Cf. Ratdolt 21, S. Otmar 6.—Type 2, text roman, german style, like Öglin 8 or Grim 7; double
hyphen, two sorts of thin ℭ, one with saw-edge; 108 mm.—Type 3, middle german roman;
double hyphen, ℭ; 88 mm. Cf. Grim 5.—Type 3ᵇ, the same type germanised.—Type 4, small
roman, german style, small face; double hyphen; 74 mm.—Type 5, rounded canon, like Grim 9;
not like J. Otmar 26 or Öglin 6; short letters 8½ mm.—Type 6, large text gothic, kerned; round h,
double hyphen; 104 mm. Cf. Grim 2, Öglin 11.—Type 7, text schwabacher, like Joh. Otmar 24;
curious ¶; 88 mm.—Type 8, small text schwabacher, like Öglin 7; has ℭ from 3 and ¶
from 7; 88 mm.—Type 9, small schwabacher, like Öglin (appendix) 12, Hölzel 5, Anshelm 2,
&c., but has some w.f. caps.; 74 mm.—Type 10, larger round church text, like Meurl 1, Öglin 10;
short letters 5½ mm.—Type 11, smaller round church text, like Öglin 9 or Weissenburger 4;
short letters 4 mm. Cf. Grim 3.—Type 12, latin text gothic, like Lotter sen. 1, J. Otmar 15,
Grim 8, &c.; 74 mm.—Type 13, roman caps. larger than 1; 10 mm. Cf. Anshelm 14, Grim 11.
—Greek type, cast on different bodies.—Square hebrew type.

Type 1, see fig. 2; 2, see fig. 3; 3, see fig. 8; 4, see fig. 11; 5, see fig. 23; *6, see fig. 35;
7, see fig. 53; 8, see fig. 59; 9, see fig. 63ᵃ; 10, see fig. 30; 11, see fig. 31; 12, see fig. 40.

BORDERS. Miller used at first title-woodcuts with sills to insert type (see e.g. Butsch I. 20–22),
and afterwards made-up borders (X).—A, one-piece quarto; at foot imperial eagle supported by
griffins.—B, one-piece quarto; at foot are winged monsters holding a basket.—C, quarto, three
sides in one piece, signed HS (monogram); the fourth piece is separate and contains the arms
of the see of Plock.—D, one-piece quarto; boys riding to left.—E, one-piece quarto, architectural;
boys with drum fife and horn at foot; at top engaged pediment and sill for date.—F, one-
piece quarto, renascence ornament; on right is a roman soldier holding a bident.—G, folio, a copy
of Silv. Otmar B. By the same hand (D. Hopper) is the combined border and cut to no.
10829A (Butsch I. 21).—H, smaller quarto (150 × 103 mm.), very ugly renascence ornament,
white ground; at foot two nondescript animals facing across a double cornucopia from which
a dragon issues.

DEVICES. a, black ground, I M and trade mark, 58 × 36 mm.—b, an escutcheon, party per
fess sable and or; a miller (half-length) holding on his head half a grindstone; 55 × 52 mm.—
c, an escutcheon like b, surmounted by a helm with mantling and the same bearing as crest;
outer line all round; 100 × 74 mm.

INITIALS. α, black ground, flowers or fruit, freely designed; 33 mm.—β, like α, but 19 mm.
only.—γ, plain roman capitals, 20 mm.—Δ initials: I, black ground, shaded letter, arabesques;
16½ mm. (1514 Apr. 4); A, with twisted floral ornament, 29 mm. (no. 10831); N, black ground,
13 mm. (1516 May 2); I, dotted black ground, two tassels, 25 mm. (1517 Aug. 18); I, M, black
ground, 24–25 mm. (no. 10845), &c.

10823. 1514 Apr. 4. Paulus RICIVS: in apostolorum symbolum dialogus. 4°. P.
VI. 142. 73. Types 1–4; cut; a; Δ.
10824. 1514 Nov. Eckius: Chrysopassus. [JOHANN.] F°. P. VI. 142. 71. Types
1–4; cut; b; α.
10825b. 1514 Dec. 9. Paulus RICIVS: sal foederis [A–F]. 4°. P. VI. 142. 72.
Types 1–4; cut; αβ.
   a. 1515 Jan. 8. id.: de DC et XIII mosaicae sanctionis edictis [a–f]. 4°. P.
VI. 143. 79. Types 1–6; cut; αβ.

10825d. 1515 c. Jan. 25. id. : de nouem doctrinarum ordinibus [AA–CC]. 4°. AUGS-
      Types 1–4, 6; b; αβ. BURG.
    c. 1515. id.: in cabalistarum eruditionem isagogae [aa–dd]. 4°. Types
      1–4, 6; αβ.

10826. 1515 Mar. 21. IORNANDES: de rebus gothorum, etc. F°. P. VI. 143. 81.
      Types 1, 2, 4; cut; c; αβ.
10827. 1515 Apr. 28. Ioh. FOENISECA: opera. 4°. P. VI. 143. 82. Type 4, hb.;
      diagr.
10828. 1515 May 11. Eckius: de uera paschae celebratione. [JOHANN.] 4°. P.
      VI. 144. 83. Types 1–4; X; α.
10829. 1515 June 16. BARTHEMA: die ritterliche und lobwürdige Reise … 4°.
      DA. 820. Types 5–7; cuts; β.
10829A. 1515 Oct. 23. Chronicon abbatis Vrspergensis. [CONRADVS.] F°. P.
      VI. 144. 84. Types 1–4; border-cut; c; αβ.
10830. 1515 Dec. 14. Ioh. BOEMVS Aubanus: liber heroicus de musicae laudi-
      bus, etc. 4°. P. VII. 144. 87. Types 2–4; X; αβ.
10831. (1515–16.) Kalender auf das Jahr 1516. bs. Types 8, 10; cuts; Δ. [Print
      Room ; fragment.]
10832. 1516 May 2. Hauerius: instituendorum puerorum ratio. [HAUER.] 4°. P.
      VI. 145. 93. Types 1–6, 8, 9 ; cut ; αβΔ.
10833. 1516 May. Eckius: in summulas Petri Hispani explanatio. [JOHN XXI.]
      F°. P. VI. 145. 92. Types 2–6, 10–12, gk.; cut, diagr. ; β.
10834. 1516 May 21. Ioh. [THURNMAIER] Auentinus: musicae rudimenta.
      4°. P. VI. 146. 94. Types 1–3 ; cuts, diagr.; a ; β. [Woodcut
      music.]
10835. 1516 June 9. Paulus RICIVS: portae lucis. 4°. P. VI. 144. 95. Types 1–4,
      hb. ; cut, diagr.; b; αβ.
10836. 1516 June 10, 1516 Nov. 7, 1517 Apr. 27. Aristoteles: dialectica, etc.
      (Organon.) [ARISTOTLE.] F°. P. VI. 146. 96; 148. 106. Types 2–6, 10,
      11, gk. ; cut, diagr.; ſ. [Imperfect at end.]
10837. 1517 Jan. 27. Eckius: disputatio Viennae habita. [JOHANN.] 4°. P. VI.
      147. 102. Types 2–4, 10, gk. ; A.
10838. 1517 Feb. 12. Eckius: elementarius dialecticae. [JOHANN.] 4°. P. VI.
      148. 103. Types 3–6, 10, 11, gk. ; diagr.; B; ſ.
10839. 1517 Mar. 2. Iac. LOCHER: papyrotheca. 4°. P. VI. 148. 105. Types 1–6,
      10, 11; X; ſ.
      1517 Apr. 27. See 1516 June 10 (no. 10836).
10840. 1517 Aug. 18. Hauerius: instituendorum puerorum ratio. [HAUER.] 4°.
      W. 4082. Types 1–6, 8, 9, gk. ; cut; αβΔ.
10841. 1518 Apr. 9. ALANVS de Insulis: summa paenitentionalis. 8°. P. VI.
      149. 113. Types 5, 6, 11, 12; cuts.
10842. 1518 July 1. Ioh. Regiomontanus: Kalendarius teutsch. [EPH.] 4°. DA.
      925. Types 3*, 6–8, 10, 11 ; cuts, diagr.; X; α.
10843. [a. 1518 Aug. 31.] Erasmus VITELLIVS: oratio in conuentu Augustensi.
      4°. P. VI. 149. 114. Types 1–4; C; αβ.
10844. 1518 Sept. 24. BERENGARIVS: liber de euentibus rerum. 4°. P. VI. 149.
      115. Types 5, 6, 10–12; D.
10844A. 1518 Dec. 26. Eckius: elementarius dialecticae. [JOHANN.] 4°. P. VI.
      149. 112. Types 3–6, 10, gk.; cuts, diagr.; ſ.

10845. [1518.] Leo x.: consultationes pro expeditione contra Turcam (1517 Nov. 12). [ROME.] 4°. P.IX. 118. 117. Types 1,3; Δ.

10845A. 1519 Jan. 2. Vlr. de Hutten: exhortatorium Maximiliani contra uenetos, etc. 4°. P.VI.152.139; B.xx.1. Types 1,2,3,gk.; cuts; E; αβ. [Print Room.]

10846. 1519 Jan. 8. Iohannis Capistrani uita et sermones. [JOHN.] 4°. P.VI. 153. 140. Types 1–4,6,10–12; cut; β.

10847. 1519 Feb. 19. Vrbanus RHEGIVS: de dignitate sacerdotum. 4°. P.VI. 153. 141. Types 1–6,13.

10848. 1519 July 20. Ioh. Alex. BRASSICANVS: Caesar. 4°. P. IX. 381. 142b. Types 1,2,4,13; F; г.

10849. 1519 Aug. 4. BRASSICANVS: in Carolum romanorum regem dialogus. 4°. P.VI. 153. 143. Types 1–4,13; E; α.

10850. [a. 1519 Oct. 19.] Eckius: ad criminatricem Lutheri offensionem responsio. [JOHANN.] 4°. P.IX. 120.137. Types 1,3,5,6,10,11; β.

10851. [a. 1519 Oct. 28.] Hier. EMSER: epistula de disputatione Lipsica. 4°. Types 1–4,10,13; β.

10852. [a. 1519 Nov. 13.] Eckius: defensio aduersus inuectiones Ricianas. [JOHANN.] 4°. P.IX. 120. 139. Types 3–6,10,11; β.

10853. [1519.] Joh.RUBIUS: ein neues Büchlein von der Disputation zu Leipzig gehalten. 4°. DA. 954. Types 5–7,9–11; D.

10854. 1520 June 15. Ioh. KVEFFNER: congratulatio cessantis interregni. 4°. Types 1–4; cut; β.

10855. 1520 Aug. 8. Ioh. FABRI: declamationes de humanae uitae miseria. F°. P.VI. 158. 177. Types 1,2,4,10,13,gk.; G; c.

10856. n. d. [c. 1520.] Testamenta duodecim patriarcharum. [PATRIARCHS.] 4°. Types 3,5,6, 10–12; H; Δ.

xxx. GEORG NADLER.

ADDRESS. Beim Barfüsser Thor.

TYPES. Type 1 = Öglin 5, but the D is usually different; short letters 4 mm.—Type 2, small text schwabacher, as Öglin 7; thin ℭ; 88 mm.
Type *1, see fig. 29; 2, see fig. 59.

BORDERS. All Nadler's borders are X-borders, but all the blocks, of which some eight are used, are in the same style. One of the cuts in no. 10862 is used in Feb. 1508 by Öglin and Nadler on sig. c5ᵇ of no. 10703.

INITIALS. The only one found in these books is a calligraphic letter of Öglin's set β (38 mm.) in no. 10867.

1508 Feb. 11. Reitterius: mortilogus. With Öglin. See no. 10703.
1508 May 22. Stamler: dialogus. With Öglin. See no. 10704.
1508. Imitatio Christi, germ. With Öglin. See no. 10705.

10857. [a. 1519 June 29.] LUTHER: Sermon geprediget zu Leipzig. 4°. DA. 932gg. Types 1,2.

10858. n.d. [1519?] Juan de ANGLIARA: die Schiffung mit dem Lande der goldenen Insel. 4°. W.1265. Types 1,2; X.

10859. 1520. LUTHER: Predigt von dem ehelichen Stande. 4°. DA.973t. Types 1,2; cut; X.

10860. 1520. LUTHER: Sermon von dem Bann. 4°. DA. 974g. Types 1,2; cut; X.

10861. 1520. LUTHER: Sermon von dem Wucher. 4°. DA. 973y. Types 1,2; cut.

10862. 1520. LUTHER: Sermon von der Bereitung zum Sterben. 4°. DA. 973cc. Types 1,2; cuts.

10863. 1520. LUTHER: eine Freiheit des Sermons päpstlichen Ablass und Gnade belangend. 4°. DA. 973n. Types 1,2; X.

10864. 1520. LUTHER: Sermon von dem Ablass und Gnade. 4°. DA. 973i. Types 1,2.

10865. n. d. [1520?] LUTHER: Sermon von der Betrachtung des heiligen Leidens Christi. 4°. Not W. 1236? Types 1,2; cut; X.

10866. n.d. [1520.] LUTHER: warum des Papsts Bücher verbrannt sind. 4°. DA. 974ddd. Types 1,2. [Title cut in wood.]

10867. n. d. [1520.] LUTHER: von dem Papsttum zu Rom. 4°. DA. 974ggg. Types 1,2; Δ. [l. 1 of title woodcut.]

10868. n. d. [1520.] LUTHER: ein Sendbrief an den Papst Leo x. 4°. DA. 974qqq bis. Types 1,2.

10869. n.d. [1520.] LUTHER: Appellation oder Berufung an ein Concilium. 4°. DA. 974uu. Types 1,2.

10870. n.d. [1520 Nov.–Dec.] Ulr. von HUTTEN: Klage über den Luterischen Brand zu Mainz. 4°. W. 1787; B. xxxiiib. 3. Types 1,2.

xxxi. JOHANN SCHÖNSPERGER THE ELDER, second press.

Without an inspection of the books containing the name of Schönsperger without the addition of Elder or Younger, it is impossible to say if any of those dated 1510–1513 belong to the elder; but it seems probable that they are all to be ascribed to the younger.

TYPES. Type 12, largest Frakturschrift, short letters 8 mm.; facs. Druckschriften 1.

10871. 1514. Liber horarum ad usum Maximiliani Imp. [LIT.] F°. P. IX. 380. 69b. Type 12. [On vellum.]

xxxij. SIGISMUND GRIM AND MARCUS WIRSUNG.

TYPES. Type 1, small text schwabacher, like Öglin 7; double hyphen, thin small ¶, not often used; 87 mm.—Type 2, large text gothic, as Miller 6; with ℭ.—Type 3, smaller round church text, as Miller 11, except F; short letters 4½ mm.—Type 4, roman caps., 13 mm. Facs. Butsch I. 27, 28. Often used for initials.—Type 5, middle roman, not normal or like Miller 3; double hyphen, M with low point; two sorts of ¶; 87 mm. Facs. Butsch I. 28.—Type 6, small german roman, single hyphen (rarely double), ¶ in some books; 75 mm. Cf. Miller 4.—Type 7, text german roman; ę, ℭ, M with point lower than in Miller 2, short double hyphen, very small us; 108 mm. Facs. Butsch I. 27.—Type 8, latin text gothic, as Lotter sen. 1, Miller 12, J. Otmar 15; 76 mm.—Type 9, rounded canon, like Miller 5; short letters 8 mm. (e, m, n are slightly more; v is 9 mm.).—Type 10, roman caps. 5½–6 mm.—Type 11, roman caps., like Miller 13, Anshelm 14; 10 mm.—Type 12, first fraktur type; 95 mm.—Type 13, small church text, the height of 3, but slightly wider and rounder; like Öglin 5, Nadler 1, but better justified. —Type 14, second fraktur, mainly a recast of 12 with changes and additions, including flourishes in the style of Theuerdank; 106 mm.—Type 15, large round type with tailed h; broader than 3; short letters 5 mm.—Greek type, which ranges in its face with 6, but is also used with 5 and 7. —Hebrew types; i. square, ij. rabbinic; cf. those of Öglin.

Type 1, see fig. 59; 2, see fig. 35; 3, see fig. 31; 5, see fig. 8; 6, see fig. 11; 7, see fig. 3; 8, see fig. 40; 9, see fig. 23; 13, see fig. 29; 14, see fig. 66; 15, see fig. 27.

BORDERS. A–E, G–I are quarto, and all are one-piece borders. A, sea-horses; facs. Butsch I. 28.—B¹, broad architectural, with a pendent wreath, and the date MDXVIII. In B² the

wreath and date are cut out and the block patched. A copy of this border was used by
Ramminger.—C, smaller architectural, round pillars; the same as Öglin A.—D, renascence
arabesque and scallop-shell; facs. Butsch I. 27.—E, satyrs chained.—F, a folio border; facs.
Butsch I. 29.—G, H, two extravagant borders designed for use together.—I, square, no outer
bounding line, curious rough style; cf. BBZ. 48a.—K–R, eight (or more) octavo borders used
in the Deuotissimae meditationes de uita Christi, 1520; facs. Muther 170–171.

DEVICE. a, the arms of the two printers side by side; 124 × 125 mm.

INITIALS. α, black ground, floral; 18–19 mm.—β, large rustics, 43 mm.—γ, middle rustics,
20 mm.—δ, small rustics, 12 mm.—ε, larger calligraphic, 36 mm.—ζ, smaller calligraphic, 23 mm.
—The Hebrew books have plain 14 mm. initials.

10872. [a. 1518 Apr. 4.] FRANCISCUS Abt von Werd: Anzeigung der Blutschweissung des Dorns von der Krone Christi. 4°. Types 1,2; A; α.

10873. 1518 June. Aristotelis physica. [ARISTOTLE.] F°. P.VI. 150. 118. Types
3–6. gk.; βγδ.

10874. 1518 July 1. Raym. Lullius: de secretis naturae. [LULL.] 4°. P.VI. 151.
129. Types 2,4,6; A; βδ.

10875. 1518 July 9. MOSES ben Maimon: de regimine sanitatis. 4°. P.VI. 151.
130. Types 2,4,6; A; βγδ.

10876. 1518 July 13. Eckius: de materia iuramenti. [JOHANN.] 4°. P.VI. 149.
116. Types 4,5,7, gk.; cut; γδ.

10877. [a. 1518 Aug. 1.] Iac. Mennel: de inclito actu ecclesiastico Augustae
celebrato. [GERMANS.] 4°. P.VI. 152. 133. Types 2,8; cuts.

10878. [a. 1518 Aug. 1.] MENNEL: von der ehrlichen geistlichen Geschichte zu
Augsburg begangen. 4°. W. 1145. Types 1,2; cut.

10879. 1518 Aug. 4. Matthias de Miechow: de duabus Sarmatiis. [MACIEJ.] 4°.
P.VI. 151. 131. Types 2,4,8; A; α.

10880. 1518 Aug. 14. Eckius: defensio contra Andreae Bodenstein inuectiones. [JOHANN.] 4°. P.VI. 151. 128. Types 4,5; A; γ.

10881. 1518 Aug. Ioh. [THVRNMAIER] Auentinus: imperatoris Henrici iv. uita.
4°. P.VI. 150. 119. Types 1,2,4,5; A; αγδ.

10882. 1518 Sept. 17. Vlricus de HVTTEN: aula. 4°. P.VI. 150. 120; B. xvii. 1.
Type 5, gk.; B¹; βγ.

10883. 1518 Sept. 20. Ric. BARTHOLINVS: oratio de expeditione contra Turcas.
4°. P.VI. 150. 122. Types 4,5; B¹; βγ.

10884. 1518 Sept. 26. FICINVS: de epidemiae morbo. 4°. P.VI. 150. 121. Types
4,5; cut; βγδ.

10885. 1518 [a. Oct. 13]. Vlr. de HVTTEN: ad principes Germaniae exhortatio.
4°. P.VI. 149. 117; B. xix. 1. Types 4,5; A; γδ.

10886. 1518 Nov. 4. Joh. ENGEL: Tractat von der Pestilenz. 4°. DA. 910d.
Types 1,2,9; cut.

10887. 1518 Nov. 6. Vlr. de HVTTEN: epistula de uita sua ad Bilibaldum Pirkheimer. 4°. P.VI. 151. 123; B. xviii. 1. Types 4,5, gk.; A; γ.

10888. 1518 Nov. 13. Marx WIRSUNG: wann das löbliche Ritterspiel erdacht
ist. 4°. W. 1158 (not DA. 914). Types 1,2,9; cut; α.

10889. 1518 Dec. 14. Chr. BARZIZIVS: introductorium in medicinam. 4°. P.VI.
151. 127. Types 2,8; A; α.

10890. 1518. Matthias de Miechow: Tractat von beiden Sarmatien. [MACIEJ.]
4°. DA. 916. Types 1,2; C; α.

10891. 1518. Reisen Lud. Vartomans. 4°. DA. 917. Types 1, 2; cuts; C.
[Print Room, imp.]

10892. n. d. [c. 1518–9.] Siluester [MAZZOLINI] de Prierio: dialogus de potestate papae. 4°. P.IX. 190. 304? Types 2, 4, 8; A; α.
10893. 1519 Mar. 2. Paulus RICIVS: de anima caeli. 4°. P.VI. 154. 146. Types
2,4,7,8; D.
10894. 1519 Mar. 4. ERASMVS: hymnus in laudem S. Annae. 4°. P. VI. 154.
147. Types (4), 7, 8; D.
10895. 1519 Mar. 19. GREGORIVS Nazianzenus: de amandis pauperibus. 4°. P.VI.
154. 148. Types (4), 6, 7, gk.; D.
10896. 1519 Mar. 24. Alsaharauius: liber theoriae necnon practicae. [KHALAF.]
F°. P.VI. 154. 149. Types 3–7; cut; βɼ.
10897. 1519 Mar. 26. Vlr. de HVTTEN: aula. 4°. P. VI. 154. 150; B. xvii. 4.
Types 5, 6, 7, gk.; D; βɼ.
10898. [a. 1519 Mar. 27.] Eckius: ad P. Ricium de anima caeli responsio.
[JOHANN.] 4°. (P. VI. 155. 153 ?) Types 4–7, gk.; E.
10899a. 1519 Apr. 7. P. RICIVS: talmudica commentariola. 4°. P.VI. 154. 151.
Types 4, 5, 7; E.
    b. 1519 Apr. 13. id.: de anima caeli aduersus Eckium examinatio. 4°. P.
VI. 154. 152. Types 4, 5, 7; D.
    c. 1519 Apr. 15. id.: lepida in psalmum Beatus uir meditatio. 4°.
Types 4, 5, 7; D; βɼ.
10900. 1519 May 18. Aristoteles: de caelo, etc. [ARISTOTLE.] F°. P. VI. 155.
156. Types 2, 3, 4, 6, 7; cuts, diagr.; a; βɼ.
10901. 1519 May 22. GREGORIVS Nazianzenus: sermones. [GREGORY.] 4°. P.
VI. 155. 155. Types 4, 6, 7; A; a; βɼ.
10902. 1519 May 30. Phil. CALLIMACHVS: historia de rege Vladislao. 4°. P.
VI. 155. 157. Types 4–7; B¹ ; a; βɼ.
10903. [a. 1519 June 14.] Werbung der Botschaften . . . [SPAIN.] 4°. W. 1296.
Types 1, 2, 3, 9; E; ε.
10904. [a. 1519 June 14.] Werbung der Botschaften . . . [CHARLES V.] 4°. W.
1291. Types 1, 2, 3, 9; D; ε.
10905. 1519 June 28. Oratio oratorum Francisci regis Gallorum. [FRANCE.] 4°.
P. VI. 156. 164. Types 4, 7; E; ɼ.
10906a. 1519 July 26. Ioh. FABER: oratio funebris in depositione Maximiliani
[a–h]. 4°. P. VI. 155. 160. Types 4, 6, 7; cuts; β.
    b. 1519 Aug. 6. Ioh. SAVROMANNVS: oratio post obitum Maximiliani [aa–
ee]. 4°. (P. IX. 381. 160b.) Types 4, 6, 7; A; β.
    c. 1519. Pet. AEGIDIVS: threnodia [Aa–Cc]. 4°. Types (4), 6, 7; E; a; δ.
10907. 1519 Sept. 13. LVTHER: resolutiones lutherianae. 4°. P. VI. 157. 169.
Type 7, gk. ; D; β.
10908. 1519 Sept. 20. AGATHIVS: de bello gothorum. 4°. P.VI. 156. 165. Types
4–7; B¹; β.
10909. [a. 1519 Nov. 30.] MAXIMILIANVS Transiluanus: legatio ad Carolum v.
4°. P. IX. 120. 142. Types (4), 5, 6, 10; cut.
10910. 1519. Paulus Ricius: in psalmum i. commentariolum. [BIBLE.] P. VI.
156. 161. Types 2, 4, 7. 8; D; α. [Sig. Aa; part of no. 10899?]
10911. 1519. Karl von Gottes Gnaden . . . (Portrait engraved by Jost de
Necker.) F°. W. suppl. i. 151. Type 1. [One leaf; Print Room.]
10912. [1519.] P. RICIVS: apologetica ad eckiana responsa narratio. 4°. P. IX.
191. 321. Types 6, 7, 10; A; ɼ.

10913. [n. b. 1520 Feb.] MELANCHTHON: de theologia Pauli declamatiuncula.
4°. Types 4–7, 10; βδ.

10914. 1520 Mar. 16. Aristoteles: de anima, etc. [ARISTOTLE.] F°. P. VI. 158.
180. Types 2, 4–7, 10, 11, 13; cuts; β.

10915. 1520 Mar. 29. Werbung … an Karl erwählten Römischen König. [GER-
MANY.] 4°. W. 1655; DA. 995. Type 12; cut; ꝛ.

10916. 1520 May. MOSES ben Ioseph Kimchi: rudimenta hebraica. 4°. P. VI.
158. 182. Types 7, 13, hb. i.

10917. 1520. Septem psalmi paenitentiales, heb. lat. germ. [BIBLE.] 4°. P. VI.
159. 186. Types 1, (4), 5, 6, 7, 9, 13; hb. i, ij.

10918. 1520 July. Ioh. BOEMVS Aubanus: repertorium de omnium gentium
ritibus. F°. P. VI. 158. 183. Types 4–7, 10, 13; F; βɼ.

10919. 1520. Gregorius Thaumaturgus: metaphrasis in Ecclesiastem. [GRE-
GORY.] 4°. P. VI. 159. 190. Types 6, 7, 10, gk.; E; ɼ.

10920. 1520. ERASMVS: epistula de Luthero ad praesulem Moguntinum. 4°. P.
IX. 123. 159. Types 4, 5, 7, 10, 11; B².

10921. 1520. Chrysostomus: von Wiederbringung des Sünders. [JOHN.] 4°.
W. 1346; DA. 978b. Types 2, 7, 9, 12, 15; B²; ꝛ.

10922. n.d. [1520.] Das teutsche Requiem über die verbrannte Bulle. [GERMAN
REQUIEM.] 4°. DA. 974fff. Types 1, 2.

10923. 1520. Ric. SBROLIVS: elegia in Caroli Caesaris in Germaniam reditum.
4°. P. VI. 160. 191. Types (4), 6, 7, 10, gk.; cut.

10924. [a. 1520 Oct. 25.] Römischer königlicher Maiestät Krönung. [CHARLES.]
4°. W. 1447. Types 1, 14; cut; ꝛ.

10925. [a. 1520 Oct. 25.] Römischer und Hispanischer Maiestät Einreiten und
Krönung. [CHARLES.] 4°. DA. 995d. Types 1, 14; cut.

10925A. 1520 Dec. 20. Hübsche Tragedia von Calisto und Melibea. [CELES-
TINA.] 4°. DA. 1003. Type 14; cuts; GH; ɼ.

10926. 1520 Dec. Aug. NIPHVS: de falsa diluuii prognosticatione. 4°. P. VI. 159.
185. Types 4, 6, 7, 10.

10927. [1520.] Andr. BODENSTEIN: Missive von der allerhöchsten Tugend Ge-
lassenheit. 4°. DA. 1099 (cf. W. 1345). Types 1, 2, 6, 13; ꝛ.

10928. n.d. [1520.] OECOLAMPADIVS: Sermon vom Vers im Magnificat; Exultauit.
4°. W. 1612. Types 1, 2; I; ꝛ.

10929. n. d. [1520.] Ulr. von HUTTEN: Anzeigung wie allwegen sich die Päpste
gegen den Kaisern gehalten haben. 4°. W. 1407; B. xxxv. 3. Types
1,12; ꝛ.

10930. n. d. [1520?] Casp. SCHATZGER: scrutinium diuinae scripturae. 4°.
Types 4–7, 10; Y; β.

xxxiij. HANS, OF ERFURT.

TYPES. Type 1, large round type, like J. Otmar 14, Öglin 4.—Type 2, rough text schwabacher,
like Schaur (xxi) type 2; 89 mm. Cf. Sittich 1.
Type 1, see fig. 24; 2, see fig. 54 (H differs).

BORDER. A, a close copy of Froschauer A.

10931. 1518. Der drei GLAUBEN die frömmsten und bösesten Männer und Frauen.
4°. DA. 902. Types 1, 2; cuts.

10932. [n. b. 1518 Oct.] Ric. BARTHOLINVS: de conuentu augustensi concinna AUGS-
BURG.
    descriptio. 4°. Types 1, 2; X; Δ.

10933. 1519 Nov. 11. Ric. SBROLIVS: moduli aliquot. 4°. P. VI. 157. 167. Types
    1, 2.

10934. n.d. Sebast. de ROTENHAN: prisci aliquot Germaniae populi. 4°. Types
    1, 2.

10935. n. d. [1520.] Sendbrief an Pfarrer von Hohensinn Luthers Lehre be-
    treffend. [LUTHER.] 4°. W. 1332. Types 1, 2.

10936. n. d. [1520.] LUTHER: von den neuen eckischen Bullen und Lügen. 4°.
    DA. 974qq. Types 1, 2; A.

10937. n.d. [1520.] LUTHER: von des christlichen Standes Besserung. 4°. Types
    1, 2; A.

[For continuation see Worms.]

xxxiv. JOHANN SCHÖNSPERGER, THE ELDER, from Nürnberg, fourth press.

TYPES. Type 12, see press 31 above; types 13, 14, see Nürnberg press 30.—Type 15, latin text; one letter used for the signature bij in no. 10938.—Type 16, small text schwabacher, like 9, but much compressed by kerning; 75 mm.

BORDERS. A–Q, sixteen one-piece octavo white borders, with flowers and insects.—R, used round Burgkmair's cuts in no. 10941, but not designed by him.

INITIALS. Flourished initials in no. 10939; one calligraphic initial, 28 mm., in no. 10940.

10938. n.d. [c. 1518.] Der Gilgengart einer jeglichen christlichen Seele. [CHRIS-
    TIAN SOUL.] 8°. (Not DA. 37; cf. 972 [1520]) Types 12–16; cuts;
    A–Q. [Sig. b1 wanting.]

10939. 1519. Melchior PFINTZING: Theuerdank (ed. tertia). F°. DA. 958b.
    Types 13, 14.

10940. 1519. Eine wahrhaftige Historie von dem Kaiser Friedrich dem Ersten.
    [FREDERICK.] 4°. DA. 945. Types 13, 14, 16; cut.

10941. [n. b. 1519.] Helden die durch Frauen verleitet sind (Salomon, Samson,
    Aristoteles [David]). F°. Type 14; cuts; R. [Four single leaves;
    David has no text.—Print Room.]

xxxv. MELCHIOR RAMMINGER.

There appears to be no dated book by Ramminger earlier than 1521 (Weller 1687 [types 2, 3, and another], 1772), but it seems probable that the books here given belong to the year 1520.

TYPES. Type 1, rounded canon, like J. Otmar 26, &c.; short letters 8 mm.—Type 2, middle large, with curly-tailed h, as Ratdolt 9.—Type 3, text schwabacher, sorts usually a good deal mixt; lombardic capitals in no. 10942.—Type 4, large text gothic, archaistic, not like Grim 2; some caps. like Ulm iij. 4.—Type 5, square canon type, like J. Otmar 22; short letters 9½ mm. Type 1, see fig. 23; 2, see fig. 32¹; 3, see fig. 53; 5, see fig. 15.

BORDERS. All are quarto. A, architectural; shields of empire and papacy; single line at top of arch.—B, a copy of Grim B, with wreath but no date.—C, R. Beck's border-device Cc (see Strassburg press 35); in 1526 the monogram has been erased.—D, architectural; flat arch, and flat pilasters; shield-shaped sill at foot; there is a large crack near this.

INITIALS. α, narrow calligraphic, 28–29 mm.—β, wide calligraphic, 24–26 mm.

91

10942. n.d. Luther: ohne Ablass von Rom kann man doch selig werden. [ROME.]
4°. W. 1125. Types 1,2,3; cuts; α. [Shorter text; 4 leaves.]

10943. n.d. Luther: ohne Ablass von Rom ... [ROME.] 4°. W. 1126. Types 1,
2, 3; cut; α. [Longer text; 6 leaves.]

10944. n. d. Das teutsche Requiem über die verbrannte Bulle. [GERMAN RE-
QUIEM.] 4°. W. 1542. Types 2,3,4; A; β.

10945. n.d. [a. 1520 Feb. 20.] Den grossmächtigsten Fürsten und Herrn Herrn
Lucifer, samt ganzer höllischer Versammlung ... [LEO X.] 4°. Types
1,2,4,5; B; αβ.

10946. n.d. KARSTHANS mit vier Personen. 4°. DA. 1005b; W. 1438. Types
2,3,4,5; cut; αβ. [Imperfect.]

10947. n.d. [n.b. 1520.] LUTHER: an den Christlichen Adel deutscher Nation.
4°. DA. 974y. Types 2,3,5; C; β.

10947A. n.d. [1520?] Ermahnung an kaiserliche Maiestät. [CHARLES V.] 4°. W.
1320. Types 2, 3; cut; Y; α.

10948. n. d. [a. 1520?] Von den Almosen. [CHRISTIANS.] 4°. W. 1311. Type 3;
DY; β.

WITHOUT PRINTER'S NAME.

WITHOUT NAME OF PLACE OR PRINTER.

Type 1 = Schönsperger sen. 4.—Type 2 differs from his 9 only in the ℂ and the absence of
a comma, but is 86 mm. (Schönsperger 88 mm.).
Type 3, normal small text schwabacher with very short comma ; possibly Öglin 7 ; 88–89 mm.
—Calligraphic A, 47 mm.

Type 4, rounded canon, like Miller 5 (not as Otmar-Öglin).—Type 5, smaller church text =
Miller 11. Cf. 10.—Type 6, small text schwabacher, apparently normal; double hyphen;
88 mm.—Type 7, larger church text = Miller 10.—Type 8, large text of northern style, not
unlike Gothan 5, except the M; cf. also Lotter sen. 6, but the V is different.—Type 9, smaller
text, also of northern style, like Magdeburg v. 7; double hyphen; 74 mm.

Type 10 = Miller 11; F not as Grim 3. Cf. 5.—Type 11 = Grim 1 (same hyphen and comma),
but ¶ differs, being taller.

Type 12, large round, like Öglin 4, S. Otmar 7.—Type 13, commentary italian roman, Capcasa
style, but opener than usual; high us, round comma, double hyphen, ę; 90–91 mm.—Initial E,
almost of Strassburg style; 13 mm.

Type 14, large roman caps., very like M. Schürer 12; 15 mm.—Type 15, roman caps. 8 mm.;
thick.—Type 16, commentary roman, Capcasa style, but not type 13; very short single hyphen,
low us (cf. S. Otmar 2), sloping comma, ℂ both small and large; 88–89 mm. Very like
Joh. Winterburger 12. In no. 10955 type 16 has no comma or ℂ.

Type 17, middle roman, very like Grim 5 in all forms, though the face is shorter and broader;
but it has ℂ not ¶, and is 92 mm. instead of 87.—Border A, architectural, round pillars; engaged
pediment at top; the bottom piece is loose, but was not so originally.—Initials: calligraphic C,
G, 37 mm., like Öglin β. L, Strassburg style, dotted ground, 25 mm.; apparently of the same set
as the I, M used by Miller in no. 10845.

Type 18, large round, seemingly S. Otmar 7, with E from a square fount.—Type 19, large text
schwabacher with double hyphen (Otmar 10 has single hyphen); 112 mm. Many lombardic
capitals.

Type 1, see fig. 19; 2, see fig. 60; 3, 6, 11, see fig. 59; 4, see fig. 23; 5, 10, see fig. 14² and 31;
7, see fig. 30; 8, see fig. 51¹; 12, 18, see fig. 24; *13, 16, see fig. 10; 15, see fig. 1; 17, see fig. 8; 19,
see fig. 52.

10949. (1500–1501.) Joh. STABIUS: practica teutsch auf das Jahr 1501. 4°. DA.
521. Types 1, 2; cut.

10950. [a. 1512 Oct. 14.] Ordnung des Bundes in Schwaben wegen Reiterei,
Absagung, Räuberei und Beschädigung. (d: Augsburg.) [SUABIAN
CONFEDERACY.] open F°. Type 3; Δ.

10951. 1513. Ioh. THVRNMAIER Auentinus: grammatica noua. 4°. Types 4–9.

10952. [1518.] LUTHER: eine Freiheit des Sermons Päpstlichen Ablass und
Gnade belangend. 4°. DA. 896n. Types 10, 11; cut.

10953. [a. 1519 July.] Disputatio inter Eckium et Lutherum habita. [JOHANN
von Eck.] 4°. Types 12, 13; Δ.

10954. n.d. [1520.] LVTHER: de captiuitate babylonica ecclesiae. 4°. P. IX. 183.
232. Types 14–16; cuts.

10955. n.d. Epistula diui Hulderichi de cleri caelibatu. [ULRIC.] 4°. (Not P. IX.
101. 333.) Types 15, 16; X.

10956. [a. 1520 July 15.] Leo x.; bulla contra errores Lutheri. Cum mandato
episcopi Augustensis. [ROME.] 4°. Type 17; A; Δ.

10957. [a. 1520 July 15.] Idem opus cum mandato episcopi Eistettensis. [Except
leaf 1ᵃ–2ᵃ, the same as no. 10956.]

10957A. Hans FUCHS: ein schönes Lied von dem Leben unsers lieben Herrn.
8°. Types 18, 19.

VII. NÜRNBERG.

---

ij. ANTON KOBERGER.

The date 1511 printed in the Sermones Dormi secure, no. 10961, is impossible, the last book of Koberger's printing being dated 1504 June 17 (P. XI. 469. 27b). It has the first leaf blank, which makes an early date probable. It may be that M. cccc. xj is an error for M. cccc. xcj, or even for M. ccccc. ij; the former is the earliest possible year for type 19; the latter seems late for a book without titlepage.

TYPES. Types 11 (large round type, with german lowercase, very open; caps. like Basel v. 4. Short letters 5 mm.); 14 (middle large, like Ratdolt 9; round h); 19 (small text, as Hüpfüff 9; round h, single hyphen, ℭ; 74 mm.); 20 (small type in the french style like Basel v. 19; round h, single hyphen; 63 mm.); 25 (large text, like Grüninger 20, double hyphen as 26; 82 mm.); for these see part i.—Type 26, small text schwabacher=Hochfeder 9; very thin ℭ; double hyphen, short and upright; short sloping comma; 88 mm. Cf. G. Stuchs 18.

Type 14, see fig. 32'; *19, see fig. 44; 20, cf. TP. XVII. 4; *25, see fig. 34; 26, see fig. 59.

10958. 1501 March 24. Biblia Latina. [BIBLE.] F°. P. VII. 439. 1. Types 14,
    20, 25; cut.

10959. 1502 July 12. Das Buch der himmlischen Offenbarung der heiligen
    Birgitte. [BRIDGET.] F°. DA. 523. Types 11, 26; cuts.

10960. 1502. HEROLT: sermones de tempore et de sanctis. F°. P.VII. 441. 13.
    Types 14, 19.

10961. 1511 Nov. 24. SERMONES dormi secure de sanctis. F°. (Cf. Hain 15977.)
    Types 14, 19. [See above.]

xi. GEORG STUCHS, first press, continued.

TYPES. Type 5 (narrow church text, 170 mm., short letters 5 mm.; cf. Lotter sen. 2, Pfeil 21, &c.); 6 (smaller face than 5, short letters 4 mm., same body; cf. Hölzel 3, Weissenburger 2); 7 (large text, as Koberger 16; single hyphen, 107 mm. Cf. Pfeil 13); 8 (smaller face than 7, same body; as Koberger 15, Pfeil 14); 10 (larger square church text, like Prüsssen. 15; double hyphen, 205 mm., short letters 6½ mm. Cf. W. Huber 6); 11 (smaller face than 10, same body: cf. Kollicker 2; the P and I are similar, but the face differs; short letters barely 5 mm.); 12 (latin text like Hüpfüff 7, Hochfeder 1, &c.; cf. J. Stuchs 9, Ambr. Huber 2, Wolfg. Huber 5; double hyphen, 84 mm.); 13 (small text latin; cf. Pfeil 16, Hölzel 11; round h, double hyphen, 72 mm.); 15 (square canon, Nürnberg style, short letters 11 mm.; cf. Kollicker 4, and Hölzel 7, xxi. 2, Weissenburger 6, J. Stuchs 4, Peypus 5, Gutknecht 3); 16 (round church text, 140 mm., short letters 4 mm.; the D is distinctive; in 1508 (besides a V and M from type 6) it has also a Ratdolt D (as Gutknecht 1), but never the D of Hölzel 2; the V is always square, as Hölzel or Gutknecht. Cf. Joh. Stuchs 2); 17 (smaller face than 16, same body; short letters 3 mm.; very like Ratdolt 13; cf. J. Stuchs 3); for all these see part i.—Type 18, small text schwabacher like Grim 1, Miller 8, &c.; 89 mm.; short comma, double hyphen, slightly different from that of Hölzel 4; thin ¶. Cf. Koberger 26, Hochfeder 9, J. Stuchs 1.—Type 19, italian text roman, rather small-faced of its size; double hyphen, which generally prints like a single one; tall thin ℭ; us small and rather low; S sticks up; T has the left side of the top broken away: 98–99 mm. Cf. Hölzel 8, J. Stuchs 5.

Type *5, see fig. 21; 6, see fig. 22; 7, 8, see fig. 33; 10, see fig. 16; 12, see fig. 36; *13, see fig. 43; 15, 16, see fig. 14; 17, see fig. 32*; 18, see fig. 59; 19, see fig. 4.

INITIALS. α, large, black ground, acanthus ornament; 41 mm.—β, narrow, black ground; some letters (which are white) have figures of beasts in them, others leaf ornaments: I and S have the ground semé with quatrefoils; 30–32 mm.—ᴦ, letters in black, filled with ornament; no square outline; 26 mm.—Δ, in 1502, an initial A with a dragon (15th cent. style); 25 mm.; in 1503–5 a canon T (sacrifice of Isaac), white ground, 79 mm.; in Oct. 1508 a large E, letter black, maiblumen style, edge scolloped, 71 mm.; and a Q, not unlike β, but the ground white; in 1511 and 1513 a new canon T, 59 mm.

10962. [a. 1502 May 20.] Mandat des Nürnberger Rats das Vieh von Brun betreffend. [NUREMBERG.] F°. Types 6, 12; Δ. [One leaf.]

10963. 1502 Dec. 22. Breuiarium Pragense. [LIT.] F°. Types 7, 8, 15, 16, 17; cut; α.

10964. 1503 Dec. 15. Missale Magdeburgense. [LIT.] F°. Types 10, 11, 15; cut; αβᴦΔ.

10965. 1505 May 15. Missale Salzburgense. [LIT.—For J. Rinmann.] F°. Types 7, 15, 16, 17, music; cuts; αΔ.

10966. [c. 1505-6.] Den rechten Weg aus zu fahren von Lissabon gen Calicut … [LISBON.] 4°. W. 304. Types 16, 18; cut, diagr.

[For continuation see below, press 26.]

xvi. HIERONYMUS HÖLZEL.

TYPES. Types 1 (latin text gothic, short comma, double hyphen, thin ¶, N like Kesler; 80 mm.); 2 (rounded smaller church text, like G. Stuchs 16, but D is different; V is the same square form); 3 (=G. Stuchs 6); for these see part i.—Type 4, small text schwabacher like G. Stuchs 18; in 1501 small ℭ; in and after 1512 thick ¶; otherwise distinguishable only by a slight difference in the hyphen.—Type 5, small schwabacher like Miller 9, Anshelm 2, &c.; about 71–72 mm.—Type 6, rounded canon type like Miller 5, J. Stuchs 7, &c., short letters 8 mm.—Type 7, square canon = G. Stuchs 15.—Type 8, roman = G. Stuchs 19, with the same broken T (as early as 1504; cf. type 13), ç, and a different ℭ. Flat dots to i in 1504, stroke to j, i with stroke rare; in 1511 both dot and stroke to i.—Type 9, small latin gothic, french style, like Koberger 20; round h, curious thin ¶; double hyphen, no comma; 60–61 mm.—Type 10, larger church text; in 1517 has ¶ with curly tail; 169 mm., short letters 5 mm. Very like Miller 10; cf. Schleiffer 1, Meurl 1.—Type 11 = G. Stuchs 13.—Type 12, like G. Stuchs 7 or Koberger 16, large latin text gothic, 110 mm. Used in the Apocalypse

of 1511, which is without Hölzel's name, but the Dürer books of 1511 must all be by one printer.—
Type 13, smaller roman, Capcasa style, like Öglin 2 or J. Otmar 25; broken T as type 8; comma
rather long, double hyphen; thick ¶; 86 mm. Cf. J. Stuchs 6.—Type 14, small text latin, as J. Stuchs
10, Knoblouch 20, Lotter 14; curly h, double hyphen, thick ¶; 68 mm.—Type 15, smaller church
text, like 2, but body as 10; different M, V; cf. Weissenburger 4.—A single greek word is found in
1513; in Sept. 1504 blanks are left, or the word is cut on wood and placed in the margin.

Type *1, see fig. 42; *2, see fig. 14²; *3, see fig. 22; *4, see fig. 59; 5, see fig. 63ᵛ; *6, see fig. 23;
*7, see fig. 14¹; *8, see fig. 4; 9, cf. TP. XVII. 4; *10, see fig. 30; 11, see fig. 43; 12, see fig. 33ᵛ;
13, see fig. 10; *14, see fig. 48; 15, see fig. 31.

INITIALS. α. A set of initials, historiated, of seven different sizes, was made specially for the
Missale Eystettense of 1517, and is used nowhere else. (1) 75–76 mm., T of Canon; A of Ad te
leuaui. (2) 67 mm., narrow; E P R. (3) 58–59 mm.; D G S¹ Sᵃ. (4) 50–51 mm.; B C D T V. (5) 41–42
mm.; G M R S¹ Sᵃ. (6) 30–31 mm.; M, and ten P for the prefaces. (7) 24–25 mm.; D E.—The
Δ initials, with two exceptions, are calligraphic letters of various sizes.

10967. [a. 1501 Jan. 26.] Spiritualium personarum feminei sexus facta. [LUCY.]
    4°. P. IX. 176. 147. Types 1, 2; cut.

10968. [a. 1501 Jan. 26.] Wunderbärliche Geschichten von geistlichen Weibs-
    personen. 4°. W. 187. Types 2, 4; cut.

10969. 1501 May 15. Conr. CELTES: ludus Dianae. 4°. P. VII. 439. 3; H.*10317.
    Types 1, 2; cut. [Woodcut music.]

10970. 1503. CATO: carmen de moribus, lat.-germ. 4°. P. VII. 442. 24; DA.
    542 b. Types 1, 2, 4, 5; cuts.

10971. 1503 Aug. 3. Geo. MORGENSTERN: sermones. 4°. P. VII. 442. 22. Types
    1, 2, 6; cut.

10972. [a. 1503 Nov. 29.] Kaiserliches Mandat wider Hainz Baum (d: Augs-
    burg). Fᵒ. Types 2, 4; Δ. [One leaf.]

10973. 1503 Dec. 22. Canon missae cum expositione eiusdem. [LIT.] 4°. P. XI.
    469. 24b. Types 1, 2, 3, 7; cut.

10974a. [a. 1504 Apr. 13.] Kaiserliches Mandat wider Pfalzgraf Philipp (an das
    Reich). [GERMANV.] Fᵒ. Types 2, 4; Δ.

    b. [a. 1504 Apr. 13.] Dasselbe Mandat (an die österreichischen Staaten).
    Fᵒ. W. 287. Types 2, 4; Δ. [On one sheet with 10974a.]

10975. [a. 1504 May 3.] Copei der Absagung wider Herzog Albrecht und
    Herzog Wolfgang. Fᵒ. (Not W. 307, 308.) Types 2, 4. [On back of
    no. 10977.]

10976. 1504 Sept. 16. Iod. BADIVS: de epistulis componendis compendium.
    [For J. Rinmann.] 4°. P. VII. 443. 27. Types 1, 8, 9.

10977. [a. 1504 Oct. 22.] Kaiserliche Acht wider Georg von Rosenberg. [GER-
    MANY.] Fᵒ. Types 2, 4; Δ. [One leaf; on back is no. 10975.]

10978. n. d. [c. 1504.] Paenitentionarius, lat.-germ. [POENITENTIONARIVS.] 4°.
    Types 1, 2, 5, 7, 8.

10979. 1505 March 11. ORDO constructionum. 4°. Types 1, 2, 7; cuts.

10980. 1505 May 19. Es tu SCHOLARIS? 4°. Types 1, 2, 6; cuts.

10981. 1505 June 24. Paulus NIAVIS: latinum idioma pro paruulis. 4°. Types 1,
    2, 6; cuts.

10982. [a. 1505 May.] Von der neu gefundenen Region … [VESPUCCI.] 4°. W.
    337. Types 3, 4; cut, diagr.

10983. 1506 Dec. 23. Ioh. ANDREAE: lectura super arboribus consanguinitatis
    et affinitatis. 4°. P. VII. 443. 29. Types 1, 2, 6, 7; cuts, diagr.

10984. 1507 Apr. 20. Alb. TROTTVS: de horis canonicis. 4°. P. VII. 444. 33.
    Types 1, 2, 6, 7, 9.

10985. [a. 1507 Apr. 29.] Das Einreiten des Königs von Frankreich in Genua.
    [LOUIS XII.] 4°. W. 384. Types 2, 4; cut.

10986. 1507 May 4. Canon missae una cum expositione eiusdem. [LIT.] 4°.
    P. VII. 444. 34. Types 1, 2, 3, 7; Δ.

10987. 1507 June 2. HENRICVS de Hassia: secreta sacerdotum. 4°. P. VII. 444.
    36. Types 1, 2, 6.

10988. 1507 June 10. HVGO de S. Charo: expositio missae. 4°. P. VII. 444. 37.
    Types 1, 2, 6, 7.

10989. 1507 June 16. INFORMATIONES et cautelae presbyteris obseruandae. 4°.
    P. VII. 444. 38. Types 1, 2, 6.

10990. 1507 July 9. SENECA: de quattuor uirtutibus. 4°. P. VII. 444. 39. Types
    1, 2, 5, 7, 8, 9.

10991. 1507 Sept. 24. Missale itinerantium. [LIT.] 4°. P. VII. 445. 40. Types
    1, 3, 7, 10, 11; cut; Δ.

10992. 1507 Nov. 12. Wimpheling: AVISAMENTVM de concubinariis non absol-
    uendis. 4°. P. VII. 445. 41. Types 1, 2, 3, 7, 8, 9; cut.

10993. 1508 Apr. 21. ANDREAS de Escobar: modus confitendi, etc. 4°. P. VII.
    446. 51. Types 1, 2, 9.

10994. 1508. Vocabula pro iuuenibus, lat.-germ. 4°. W. 467. Types 1, 2, 6, 9.

10995. n. d. [c. 1508?] Conr. Celtes & Seb. Schreyer: carmina in laudem S.
    Sebaldi [ed. 2ª]. F°. Types 6, 8; cut; Δ. [One leaf; Print Room.]

10996. [1510.] Die sieben Tageszeiten . . . obl. Types 2, 4; cut [by Dürer,
    dated 1510. One leaf; Print Room].

10997. [1510.] Wer recht bescheiden will werden . . . obl. Types 2, 4; cut [by
    Dürer, dated 1510. One leaf; Print Room].

10998. n. d. [c. 1510?] Ex-libris Christophori Scheurli. F°. Types 1, 2; cut.
    [One leaf; Print Room.]

10999. [a. 1510 Dec. 19.] Mandat des Nürnberger Rats Georg und Hans von
    Geissling betreffend. [NUREMBERG.] bs. DA. 683; W. 626. Type 4; Δ.

11000. 1511. CHELIDONIVS: epitome in diuae parthenices Mariae historiam
    cum figuris Alb. Dureri. F°. P. VII. 450. 77. Type 8; cuts.

11001. 1511. CHELIDONIVS: passio domini nostri cum figuris Alb. Dureri. F°.
    P. IX. 544. 75b. Types 2, 7, 8; cuts.

11002. 1511. Apocalypsis cum figuris Alb. Dureri. F°. P. VII. 450. 76. Type
    12; cuts. [Print Room.]

11003. 1511. CHELIDONIVS: passio Christi ab Alb. Durero effigiata. 4°. P. VII.
    450. 75. Types 2, 8; cuts.

11004. 1511 Dec. 16. Apologia sacrae scripturae. [BIBLE.] 4°. P. VII. 449. 72.
    Types 1, 2, 5, 9; cuts.

11005. 1512 Apr. 7. BONAVENTURA: die Legende des heiligen Vaters Francisci.
    [For Caspar Rosentaler of Schwaz.] 4°. DA. 717. Types 2, 4; cuts.

11006. 1512 May 22. STATVTA synodalia et prouincialia Gnesnensia, etc. [For
    Franc. Klosse of Breslau.] 4°. Types 1, 2; cut.

11007. 1512 June 25. ORDO constructionum. 4°. Types 1, 2. [Wants title.]

11008. [a. 1512 Nov. 25.] Ausschreien der Bündnis zwischen Julio ij. und dem
    Kaiser. [STATES OF THE CHURCH.] 4°. W. 672. Types 2, 4; cut.

11009. [a. 1512 Dec. 18.] Missgeburt zu Spalt geboren. F°. Type 4; cut.
    [One leaf; Print Room.]

11010a. n. d. [c. 1512.] S. Laurentius. F°.
    b.   Christus mortuus. F°. Types 4, 8; cuts. [Two single
        leaves; Print Room.]
11011. 1513 [a. Aug. 8]. Gilbertus NICOLAI: tractatus de confraternitate de de-
        cem Aue Maria. 4°. P. IX. 545. 92b. Types 1, 6, 9, 13, gk.; cuts; Y.
11012. [a. 1513 Aug. 16.] Neue Gezeitung aus dem Heere vor Terebona. [GER-
        MANY.] 4°. (Not W. 764, 765.) Types 2, 4.
11013. 1514 May 19. HVGO de S. Charo: expositio missae. 4°. P. IX. 545.
        105b. Types 1, 2, 6; cut.
11014. 1514 June 8. Alb. TROTTVS: de horis canonicis. 4°. P. VII. 454. 106.
        Types 1, 2, 6, 14; cut.
11015. 1516 Feb. 5. Cyprianus BENETI: De sacrosancto eucharistiae sacra-
        mento. 4°. P. VII. 457. 123. Types 2, 13, 14.
        1516 May 25. Informationes et cautelae. See Collio di Val Trompia.
11016. 1517 July 16. Missale Eystettense. [LIT.] F°. P. VII. 458. 130. Types
        3, 6, 10, 15; cuts; α.
11017. 1517. LVTHER: theses lxxxxv. bs. P. IX. 70. 27. Types 1, 14.
11018. [a. 1517 Oct. 1.] Leo x.: Brief das Spital zum Heiligen Geist in Nürn-
        berg betreffend. bs. W. 1036. Types 2, 4, 7.
11019. (1518–19.) Kalender auf das Jahr 1519. [EPH.] bs. Types 3, 4 ? cuts.
        [Fragment.]
11020. [n. b. 1519.] Wie die neue Kapelle in Regensburg erstlich aufkommen
        ist. [MARY.] 4°. W. 1303. Types 1, 2, 4; cut.
11021. 1520 May 19. IACOBVS de Clusa: confessionale compendiosum. 4°. P.
        VII. 461. 154. Types 1, 6, 10, 14, 15; cut.
11022. [n. b. 1520.] An Karolum gemeine Klage vom Adel ... [CHARLES V.] 4°.
        DA. 995h; W. 1348? Types 1, 2, 4; cut.

xvij. AMBROSIUS HUBER.

For other books of Ambr. Huber dated 1501, see P. VII. 440. 7, W. 192, 193; the last of his recorded is of 1503, P. IX. 542. 26b.

TYPES. Type 1, small narrow church like G. Stuchs 6 ; short letters 4 mm.—Type 2, latin text
gothic like G. Stuchs 12 (Furter-Hochfeder style); double hyphen, ¶; 82 mm. Cf. Wolfg. Huber
5.—Type 3, small text italian, like Ratdolt 15 (no. 8 on his type-sheet).

Type 1, see fig. 22; 2, see fig. 36.

11023. 1501. CRATES: epistulae. 4°. P. VII. 440. 6. Types 1, 2, 3; cut.

xix. BALTHASAR SCHLEIFFER.

TYPES. Type 1, larger rounded church text, like but not the same as Hölzel 10. Cf. Meurl 1.—
Type 2, latin text gothic like Weissenburger 7, but has caps. from Koberger 17 mixt in it; 83 mm.
Cf. Meurl 4.—Type 3, small latin gothic, very like Ratdolt 10; called characteresueneti; 60 mm.

Type 1, see fig. 30; 2, see fig. 40.

11024. 1501 Apr. 7. Reinhardus de LAVDENBVRG: passio domini nostri. 4°. P.
        VII. 440. 9. Types 1, 2, 3; cut.
11025. 1501 Apr. 15. Theod. RYSICHEVS: oratio in funere Margaretae ducissae.
        [For Joh. Muscatell, Ingolstadt.] 4°. P. VII. 440. 8. Types 1, 2, 3; cut.

xx. JOHANN MEURL.

Address: An dem Ponerperg.

TYPES. Type 1=Schleiffer 1.—Type 2, body as 1, face like Weissenburger 4. Cf. Hölzel 15.—
Type 3, rounded canon type like Hölzel 6.—Type 4=Schleiffer 2.

Type 1, see fig. 30; 2, see fig. 31; 3, see fig. 23; 4, see fig. 40.

INITIAL. Δ is a Canon T, 75 mm.

11026. 1501 Aug. 27. Missale romanum. [LIT.] F°. Types 1, 2, 3, cut; Δ.
[Wants ff. 1–7.]

11027. 1502. Ioh. KVNHOFER: confessionale. 4°. P IX. 542.18b. Types 1, 4.
[Two copies with different imprint.]

xxi. PRINTER FOR THE SODALITAS CELTICA.

Though there is no direct clue to this printer's name, it is a noteworthy fact that all his types but
one were at a later date in the possession of Peypus. But see also the addenda, p. 15–16.

TYPES. Type 1, text roman of italian style resembling Hölzel 8, but distinguished by the T,
large us, and single hyphen; short comma, flat-topt 3: 102 mm. Cf. Weissenburger 1, Peypus 3
(hyphen and comma different); also J. Otmar 19, Öglin 1.—Type 2, square canon, as G. Stuchs 15;
cf. Peypus 5.—Type 3, large, like Weissenburger 4 (q. v.); cf. Peypus 1.—Type 4, small text schwabacher, like G. Stuchs 18, Hölzel 4, &c.; double hyphen, short comma; ¶ of middle size; 89 mm.
Cf. Peypus 2.—Type 5, smaller roman, remarkable for its &; small open us; no hyphen; 78 mm.
Cf. Peypus 4 (recast).—Type 6, rounded canon type, as Hölzel 6.—Greek type (woodcut letters
used in 1501) in 1502, most remarkable.

Type 1, see fig. 4; 2, see fig. 14¹; 3, see fig. 31; 4, see fig. 59; 6, see fig. 23.

DEVICES. a, AP on a white ground.—b, the same on a black ground.

11028. 1501. Opera Hrosvitae a Conrado Celte inuenta. [ROSWITHA.] F°. P.
VII. 439. 5. Type 1; cuts; a.

11029. 1502 Apr. 5. CELTES: libri amorum et alia opuscula. 4°. P. VII.441.17.
Types 1, gk.; cuts; b.

11030. 1505 Oct. 9. Ulr. Pinder: der beschlossene Garten des Rosenkranzes
Mariae. [MARY.] F°. DA. 554. Types 2, 3, 4; cuts; Y.

11031. 1507 Aug. 30. Vlr. PINDER: speculum passionis Iesu Christi. F°. P. VII.
446. 48. Types 1, 2, 5; cuts; Y.

11032. 1509 Aug. 30. Vlr. PINDER: speculum patientiae, etc. 4°. P. VII. 448.
61. Types 1, 5, 6; cuts.

11033a. 1510. Vlr. PINDER: speculum intellectuale (A–O). Types 1, 2, 5, 6;
cuts, diagr.

  b. [1510.] id. compendium de bona ualetudinis cura (Aa–Dd). Types
1, 2, 5; cut.

  c. [1510.] id. speculum phlebotomiae, etc. (a–i.) Types 1, 2, 5; cut. F°.
P. IX. 543. 70b.

11034. n.d. [c. 1510–12?] Sankt Ursula Brüderschaft zu Braunau. bs. Types 3,
4; cut. [Print Room.]

xxij. GEORG SCHENCK.

TYPES. Type 1, narrow smaller church type like G. Stuchs 6; cf. Ambr. Huber 1, Hölzel 3,
Weissenburger 2.—Type 2, small text schwabacher, which differs from G. Stuchs 18 and the other
types of this class (except Weissenburger 3) in having a wide C (as Creusner 4), a round instead of

square E, and single hyphen for double. Small ℭ as that of Hölzel 4 in 1501; 88 mm.—Type 3, square canon, as G. Stuchs 15; cf. Weissenburger 6.

Type 1, see fig. 22; 2, see fig. 61; 3, see fig. 14.

11035. 1502 Sept. 21. Iac. SCHONHEINTZ: apologia astrologiae. 4°. P.VII.441. 16. Types 1, 2, 3; diagr.

11036. 1502 Oct. 8. Kunst des Notariats. [ARS.] 4°. DA. 527. Types 1, 2.

xxiij. JOH. WEISSENBURGER.

TYPES. Type 1 = xxi. 1; text roman with short comma, large us and flat 3; 102 mm.—Type 2 = xxij. 1.—Type 3 = xxij. 2.—Type 4, middle large, very like Miller 11 or Hölzel 15; the l. c. is like G. Stuchs 16, but the caps. differ, especially M, S, V; D like Hölzel 2; V differs from that of Joh. Stuchs 2 in the position of the diagonal lines. Cf. also xxi. 3, Peypus 1. Facs. Muther 214b.— Type 5, second small text schwabacher, as G. Stuchs 18, Hölzel 4; normal C, E, but the C of 3 is found in it (out of register) till July 1510. Double hyphen like that of G. Stuchs 18 in the Dialogus Philosophiae of 1509 only; elsewhere it has a much steeper slope; this is distinctive. Long comma after July 1510; ℭ and ¶, both thin: 89 mm.—Type 5 bis, square canon, larger and heavier than 6; the a is quite distinctive; short letters 11 mm. In one book (no. 11055) the two founts are mixt.— Type 6, square canon, like G. Stuchs 15, &c.; cf. xxij. 3. Facs. Muther 214b.—Type 7, latin text gothic, like Joh. Otmar 15, Koberger 17, Lotter sen. 1, &c.; double hyphen, long comma, thick ¶; 82 mm. Cf. Peypus 6. Facs. Muther 214b.—Greek type (that of press 21?) in 1505; but cut on wood in Dec. 1506.

Type 1, see fig. 4; 2, see fig. 22; *3, see fig. 61; *4, see fig. 31²; 5, see fig. 59; *5 bis, see fig. 31¹; 6, see fig. 14¹; *7, see fig. 40.

DEVICES. a, large, black ground; mark and initials only. 115 × 89 mm.—b, black shield with initials, supported by two amoretti. 53 × 93 mm. The cut with the symbols of the Evangelists, not a device, though used almost as one, is found in no. 11054, 11060, 11061, 11071.

INITIALS. α, in the style of Grüninger α–δ; 23–24 mm.—Δ, in 1512, a white A of venetian style, 39 mm.

11037. (1502-3.) Ioh. STABIVS: prognosticon ad annos M.D.iii. et iiii. 4°. Type 1; cut.

11038. 1503 July 24. Sermo de conceptione B.V. Mariae. [MARY.—With Nic. Fleischmann.] 4°. P.VI. 442. 25. Types 2, 3; cut; α.

11039. 1503 Aug. 4. Rob. GROSSETESTE: de physicis lineis angulis figuris. 4°. P.VII. 442. 23. Type 1; cut.

11040. 1503. Bern. de HARDERWICK: quaestio de crucibus omnibusque Christi armis inuentis. 4°. P.VII. 442. 26. Types 2, 3.

11041. 1504 Apr. 3. Messahalah de scientia motus orbis. [MA SHA ALLAH.] 4°. P.VII. 443. 28. Type 1; cuts, diagr.

11042. [c. 1504.] Die böhmische Schlacht. (Holzschnitt mit Gedicht.) bs. (Not W. 297 or suppl. i. 22.) Types 3, 4; cuts. [Imp.; on back of no. 11181.]

11043. [n. b. 1505.] Iac. Lilienstein: tractatus contra WALDENSES. 4°. P.IX.108. 12. Types 3, 4.

11044. 1506. ANDREAS de Escobar: modus confitendi, etc. 4°. P.IX. 542. 30b. Types 3, 4.

11045. 1506 Dec. 6. Iac. LOCHER: opuscula. 4°. P.VII. 444. 32. Types 1, 3, 4; cuts; a.

11046. n. d. [c. 1506-7?] Von der unchristlichen Handlung so der König von Portugal... geübt hat. [EMANUEL.] 4°. Types 3, 4; cuts.

11047. n. d. [c. 1506-7?] Den rechten Weg aus zu fahren von Lissabon gen Calicut. [LISBON.] 4°. W. 305. Types 3, 4; cuts.

11048. 1507. Gesta proxime per portugalenses in India...[EMANUEL.] 4°. P.VII. 445. 43. Types 3, 4; cut.

11049. (1507–8?) Aderlasstafel Lipsensis magistri Conradi Norici. [EPH.] bs. W. 392. Types 3, 4; cut. [Cropt.]

11050. 1508 Feb. 16. Laur. CORVINVS: Latinum idioma. 4°. Types 3, 4.

11051. 1509. Dialogus philosophiae de ritu omni uerborum uenustate editus. [PHILOSOPHIA.] 4°. P.VII. 446. 57. Types 4, 5.

11052. [a. 1509 Oct. 9.] Henr. RYBISCH: disceptatio an uxor sit ducenda. 4°. P.VII. 448. 60 ? Types 4, 5, 5bis.

11053. 1510 June 18. De continentia sacerdotum. [PRIESTS.] 4°. P.VII. 448. 64. Types 4, 5, 5bis, cut.

11054. 1510. Helias Capreolus: de confirmatione christianae fidei. 4°. P.VII. 448. 66. Types 4, 5, 5bis; cut.

11055. 1510 July 29. MARIANVS de urbe Senarum: repetitio super materia irregularitatis. 4°. P.VII. 448. 65. Types 4, 5, 5bis & 6 mixt; a.

11056. n. d. [c. 1510–11.] Liber uagatorum. Der Bettlerorden. [VAGATORES.] 4°. Types 4, 5, 6; cut. [12 leaves.]

11057. n. d. [c. 1510–11.] ARS moriendi ex uariis sententiis collecta. 4°. P.IX. 550. 342e. Types 4, 6, 7; cuts; X.

11058. [a. 1512 Jan. 23.] Pomponius MELA: cosmographia. 4°. P.VII. 451. 86. Types 4, 6, 7; cut.

11059. 1512 Feb. 18. LENTVLVS: epistula ad romanos de Christo. 4°. P.VII. 450. 79. Types 4, 5, 6; a.

11060. 1512 March 1, MANVALE parochialium sacerdotum. 4°. P.VII. 450. 80. Types 4, 6, 7; cut; a.

11061. 1512 March 26. Honorius: ELVCIDARIVS. 4°. P.VII. 450. 81. Types 4, 6, 7; cut.

11062. 1512 [a. May 3]. Ioh. Adelphus: wahrhaftige Sage oder Rede von dem Rock Christi. [JESUS.] 4°. DA. 715. Types 4, 5, 6; cut; b; a.

11063. 1512 July 9. Walafridus STRABO: hortulus. 4°. P.VII. 451. 83. Types 4, 6, 7; cut; b.

11064. 1512. ARS moriendi. 4°. P.VII. 451. 85. Types 4, 6, 7; cuts; X.

11065a. 1512. Iulius ij.: bulla intimationis generalis concilii (A, B). [18. vii. 1511.] Types 4, 6, 7; cut.

    b. id.: bulla monitorii apostolici contra tres cardinales (C). [28. vii. 1511.] Types 4, 6, 7; cut.

    c. Oratio Angeli anachoritae pro Concilio (D). [8. ix. 1511.] Types 4, 6, 7; cut.

    d. Oratio Maximi Coruini Parthenopei (E). [3. viii. 1511.] Types 4, 6, 7; cut; a.

    e. Iulius ij.; breue de priuatione cardinalium (F). [24. x. 1511.] Types 4, 6, 7; cut.

    f. Cursii panegyris de foedere ... (G). [31. x. 1511.] Types 4, 6, 7; cut; Δ.

    g. Conuocatio generalis concilii ex parte principum (Aa). [23. v. 1511.] P.VII. 452. 90. Types 4, 6, 7; a. [ROME.] 4°. P.IX. 544. 90b.

11066. n. d. [c. 1512?] DECISIO quaestionis de audientia missae. 4°. Types 4, 6, 7; cuts; Y.

11067. 1513 Jan. 14. Ioh. THVRNMAIER: grammatica. 4°. P.VII. 452. 93. Types 4, 6, 7; cut; b.

11068. 1513 Jan. 20. Chr. SCHEVRL: utilitates missae, etc. 4°. P. VII. 453. 94.
Types 4, 6, 7; b.
11069. 1513 Apr. 9. TITELBÜCHLEIN. 4°. W. 803. Types 4, 5, 6; b.
11070. 1513 Apr. 14. GEORGIVS Peurbachius: institutiones in arithmeticam. 4°.
P. VII. 453. 95. Types 4, 6, 7.
11071. 1513 Apr. 18. CVRA pastoralis. 4°. P. IX. 545. 95b. Types 4, 6, 7; cut; α.
11072.· 1513. Simon de QVERCV: opusculum musicae. 4°. P. VII. 454. 101. Types
4, 6, 7; cuts, diagr.; b; α. [Woodcut music.]

[For continuation see Landshut.]

xxiv. HIERONYMUS HUBER.

Hier. Huber printed in 1504 only. For his first dated book see W. 294c.

xxv. WOLFGANG HUBER.

Wolfgang Huber seems to have been printing from 1505 May (DA. 561b), presumably in continuation of press xxiv., till 1514 (W. 840).

TYPES. Type 1, small text schwabacher like G. Stuchs 18, Hölzel 4, &c.; double hyphen, short comma, ¶. 88 mm.—Type 2, middle large round; lowercase like Öglin 5, rounder than type 3 or G. Stuchs 16, Hölzel 2, &c.; capitals partly as Ratdolt 9, others (E, M, R, V, &c.) differ; round h. Short letters 4 mm.—Type 3 = Weissenburger 4.—Type 4, square canon like G. Stuchs 15, &c.— Type 5, latin text gothic like, but not the same as G. Stuchs 12; 80 mm.—Type 6, larger square church text, like G. Stuchs 10 or Prüss sen. 15.—Type 7, smaller narrow church text, like G. Stuchs 6, Hölzel 3 or Weissenburger 2.

Type 1, see fig. 59; 3, see fig. 31²; 4, see fig. 14¹; 5, see fig. 36; 5, see fig. 16; 7, see fig. 22.

INITIALS. In 1510, a Canon T on black ground; 33 mm.

11073. 1509. VERSEHUNG Leib Seele Ehre und Gut. 4°. DA. 635e. Types 1, 2.
11074. [a. 1509 June 26.] Rede der Botschafter der Venediger an Kaiser Maximilian. [VENICE.] 4°. W. 509; DA. 656. Types 1, 2, 3.
11075. [a. 1509 June.] Historie der vier Ketzer Predigerordens. [MARY.] 4°.
DA. 642 (2). Types 1, 2, 4; cuts.
11076. [a. 1509 June.] Ioh. VETTER: de quattuor heresiarchis ordinis praedicatorum. 4°. P. IX. 110. 38. Types 2, 4, 5; cut.
11077. (1510 Aug. 22.) Missale itinerantium. [LIT.] 4°. Types 1, 4–7; cuts; Δ.
[No colophon.]
11078. n. d. [c. 1510.] CATO: codicillus de doctrinis moralibus, lat.-germ. 4°.
Types 2, 5.

xxvi. GEORG STUCHS, third press.

The migration of Stuchs to Schneeberg, whether on account of plague, or a special summons to print the Missals of Havelberg and Kammin, was only temporary. After his return to Nürnberg he continued printing as late as 1518 July 24 (P. IX. 470. 140b).

For types &c. see press 11 above.

11079. 1508. Missale Pragense. [LIT.] F°. Types 15, 16, 17, music; cut; αβ.
[Wants last leaf.]
11080. [a. 1508 July 24.] Abschrift eines Sendbriefs König Emanuels an den Papst. [EMANUEL.] 4°. W. 426. Types 16, 18; cut.

11081. 1508 Sept. 20. Aloysius de CADAMOSTO: neue unbekannte Lande. F°.
    DA. 625. Types 16, 18; cut, diagr.

11082. 1508 Oct. 26. GRÜNBECK: speculum naturalis caelestis propheticae uisi-
    onis. F°. P. VII. 446. 49. Type 19; cuts; Y; βΔ.

11083. 1508 Oct. 27. GRÜNBECK: Spiegel der natürlichen, himmlischen und
    prophetischen Sehungen. F°. DA. 608. Types 16, 18; cuts; Y.

11084. 1511 Dec. 14. Missale Hildesemense. [LIT.] F°. Types 5, 6, 15, music;
    cut; αΔ.

11085. 1513 June 18. Missale Mindense. [LIT.] F°. P. XI. 469. 91b. Types 5,
    6, 15, music; cut; αΔ.

xxvij. ADAM DYON.

Books of Dyon at Nürnberg are dated 1509 (W. 501) to 1512 May 28 (W. 682). This last book
was printed for a Breslau stationer, Anton Minzenberg, but Dyon's own press at Breslau appears
to date only from 1519.

TYPES. Type 1, like Weissenburger 4, but the hyphen and W differ.—Type 2, large text
schwabacher like Weissenburger (Landshut) 9, but single hyphen; 107 mm.

11086. n. d. Von dem neuen Propheten in Persia Sophey genannt. [ISMAII I.]
    4°. Types 1, 2; cuts.

xxviij. JOHANN STUCHS.

For the first book of J. Stuchs, printed in 1509, see P. IX. 542. 26b.

TYPES. Type 1=G. Stuchs 18, with thick ¶; small text schwabacher: comma rather long in
1510; short (as Gutknecht) or absent in other books containing this fount; these are all without
printer's name, but appear to be too early for Gutknecht.—Type 2, smaller rounded church text=
G. Stuchs 16, with (in 1510) the second (Ratdolt) D only, as Gutknecht 1; in the undated Turrecre-
mata (an exceptional book) and one of the Rosenkranz broadsides it has a D like that of Hölzel
2: the V differs from that of G. Stuchs; it is the same as that of Gutknecht 1, and like that of Weissenburger 4 in general shape.—Type 3=G. Stuchs 17; 122 mm.—Type 4=G. Stuchs 15.—Type
5=G. Stuchs 19.—Type 6=Hölzel 13, smaller roman. Round comma first after March 1518.—
Type 7, rounded canon, like Hölzel 6.—Type 8, small schwabacher, not like Hölzel 5, but like a reduction of type 1; thick ¶, caps. mixt.—Type 9=G. Stuchs 12, with single hyphen and other variations; ¶, not thick. 82 mm.—Type 10=Hölzel 14. Greek (no accents) with type 6 in 1520.

Type 1, see fig. 59; 2, see fig. 14²; 3, see fig. 32²; 4, see fig. 14¹; 5, see fig. 4; 7, see fig. 23; *9, see
fig. 36; 10, see fig. 48.

BORDER. A, four-piece quarto; renascence pillars; at foot Our Lady, SS. John Ev. and Lau-
rence.

DEVICE. Trade mark and H S on black ground; 56 × 44 mm.

INITIALS. α, white on black or dotted ground, very plain; 19–21 mm.—β, similar, 38 mm.—
Γ, black ground; figures, or ornaments; 21–22 mm.—δ, like Γ, but larger; 31–33 mm.—ε, similar
style, 12–14 mm.—ζ, white letter and ornament on ground with light horizontal shading; F S only;
20 mm.—н, floral ornament, dark shaded ground, diagonal (F, V, horizontal); 13 mm.—Δ initials;
(1514 Apr. 29) P, a schoolmaster with two pupils; 44 mm. (1516 June 17) G, in style of Γ or δ,
but 27 mm. (1517 July 17) P, similar style (a satyr); 39 mm. (1520) O, black letter on white
ground; 13 mm.

11087. 1510. BEICHTSPIEGEL der Sünder. 4°. DA. 666. Types 1–4; cuts.

11088. [a. 1512 Feb. 24.] Das Einnehmen der Stadt BRESCIA. 4°. W. 697. Types
    1, 2; cut.

11089. 1512. Ioh. Cochlaeus: tetrachordum musicae. [DOBNECK.] 4°. Types 3,
    5, 6, 7; diagr. [Woodcut music.]

11090. (1513.) Hans SCHNEIDER: die Zwietracht und der Auflauf in der löblichen Stadt Köln. 8°. Types 1, 2.

11091. [a. 1513 June 6.] Epistula Emanuelis regis de uictoriis habitis in India. [EMANUEL.] 4°. Types 1, 2, 4; cut.

11092. [a. 1513 June 6.] Sendbrief des Königs zu Portugal … [EMANUEL.] 4°. Types 1, 2, 4; cut.

11093. (1513–14.) Georg Tanstetter: Kalender auf das Jahr 1514. [EPH.] bs. Types 1, 2; cuts; Y.

11094. 1514 Apr. 29. DONATVS minor cum expositione uulgari. 4°. Types 3, 7, 8; cut; Δ.

11095. 1514 Nov. 4. PTOLEMAEVS: geographia. F°. P. VII. 454. 104. Types 3, 6, 7; diagr.

11096. 1515 [a. Apr. 5]. Ioh. SCHÖNER: terrae totius descriptio. 4°. P. VII. 455. 112. Types 3, 6, 7, 8; cuts, diagr; αβ.

11097. 1515. Joh. ROTA: das Leben und Gewohnheit des Sophi. 4°. DA. 822. Types 1, 2, 4.

11098. n.d. [c. 1515 ?] TVRRECREMATA: tractatus de efficacia aquae benedictae. 4°. H. *15743; P. VII. 486. 340. Types 2, 9; cut; a.

11099. n.d. [c. 1515–16?] Die löbliche Brüderschaft des himmlischen Rosenkranzes. bs. Types 2, 4; cut. [Print Room.]

11100. n. d. [c. 1515–16?] Gegenwurf christliches Gebetes des himmlischen Rosenkranzes. bs. Type 3; cut. [Print Room.]

11101. 1516 June 17. GEORGIVS Peurbachius: quadratum geometricum. F°. P. VII. 457. 122. Types 3, 6, 7; cut, diagr.; Δ.

11102. 1517 July 17. Ioh. SCHÖNER: globi astronomici canones. 4°. P. VII. 458. 128. Types 3, 6, 7; cut, engr.; ΓδΔ.

11103. 1518. Appendices Io. Schöneri in opusculum globi astriferi. 4°. P. VII. 459. 138. Types 3, 6; engr.; Γ.

11104. 1518 March 19. Ioh. THVRNMAIER: historia et antiquitates Otingae Boio rum. 4°. P. VII. 459. 137. Types 2, 6; cut; Γ.

11105. [a. 1518 July 20.] Heinr. SCHREIBER: ein neues künstliches Buch. [For Lucas Alantsee.] 8°. W. 1114. Types 1, 2, 3, 6, 8; cuts, diagr.; a; δ.

11106. [a. 1519 Jan. 1.] ERASMVS: familiarium colloquiorum formulae. 4°. Types 3, 4, 6; A; Γε.

11107. 1520 March 7. Ioh. HEROLT: sermones. [For Joh. Koberger.] F°. P. IX. 547. 153b. Types 3, 10…; ΓδεʒH. [Title wanting.]

11108. 1520. Franc. Mataratius: de componendis uersibus. 4°. P. VII. 461. 153. Types 3, 6, gk.; A; δεHΔ.

xxix. FRIEDRICH PEYPUS.

For Peypus see also above, press 21.—His first dated book, 1512 Nov. 12, is cited by Panzer VII. 452. 88. In July 1515 his address is given as: prope capellam diuae uirginis; i.e. on the east side of the market place.

TYPES. Type 1=xxi. 3; cf. Weissenburger 4, Miller 10. Large C from 1517 Jan. Facs. Muther 214a.—Type 2=xxi. 4; short comma; medium ¶, and C as Hölzel 4 (before 1512) at first; later thin ¶; thick in 1519; thin again in 1520. Facs. Muther 214a.—Type 3=xxi. 1, but double hyphen and small round comma; the ʒ is rarely found; large thick ¶ and C in 1515: on 24 July 1515 (and in the undated Morbachus) a w.f. ę is found.—Type 4=xxi. 5, recast; 74 mm. instead of 78; double hyphen, very thick ¶, open us, short comma.—Type 5=xxi. 2; cf. Weissenburger 6, &c.

Facs. Muther 214a.—Type 6, latin text gothic, like Weissenburger 7; double hyphen, small ℭ, 76 mm.—Type 7, small latin text, strongly Lyonnese; 73 mm. Facs. Muther 206, 207.—Greek type, different from other Nürnberg founts. The large capitals which occur in several books appear to be woodcut rather than cast type.

Type 1, see fig. 31²; 2, see fig. 59; 3, see fig. 4; 5, see fig. 14¹; 6, see fig. 40.

BORDERS. A, one-piece quarto, architectural; at top two dolphins tail to tail.—Ba, one-piece quarto border-device, the original (according to Butsch) of Froben's Fool and Satyr border. Facs. Butsch I. 32.—C, one-piece quarto, quasi-architectural; S. Peter and a female saint at sides; two shields at top, one that of the empire; two blank shields at foot.—D, folio, four-piece: apocalypse at top, baptism of Christ at foot; facs. Butsch I. 34.—Ec, quarto four-piece border-device; flat arch at top.

DEVICES.   a, see border B.—b, white ground, a tree, with FP; 75 × 57 mm.—c, see border E.

INITIALS.   α, Lyonnese (?) style, black ground, mostly floral; 18–19 mm.—β, like α, 11–12 mm.—ɼ, like α, β, but 8–9 mm. only.—δ, black grounded, figures of boys, &c. like the Basel initials; 40 (C only) to 46 mm.—ε, german historiated, 29–30 mm.; C (used as O), D, I only in these books.

11109. [a. 1512 Nov. 8.] Epistel von den Ehrerbietungen dem Hochwürdigen von Gurk beschehen. [VALERIANO BOLZANI.] 4°. DA.725b. Types 1, 2; A.

11110. [a. 1512 Nov. 10.] Bulla tertiae et quartae sessionis habitae in concilio Lateranensi. [ROME.] 4°. Types 1, 3, large caps.; cut.

11111. 1513 June 30. Plutarchus: de his qui tarde a numine corrumpuntur. 4°. P. VII. 453. 99. Type 3; Ba.

11112. [a. 1513 Oct. 7.] Verzeichnis wie sich die Schlacht zwischen den Deutschen und Venedigern begeben hat. [GERMANS.] 4°. (Not W. 804,805.) Types 1, 2; cut.

11113. 1515 Jan. 26. Plutarchus: de uitanda usura. [PLUTARCH.] 4°. P. VII. 457. 119. Type 3; Ba.

11114. 1515 Feb. 11. Burchardus de Horneck: compendium theologiae excerptum e libris sententiarum. [PETRUS Lombardus.] 4°. P. VII. 456. 115. Types 1, 3, 4; A.

11115. 1515 March. Lucianus: de ratione historiae conscribendae. [LUCIAN.] 4°. P. VII. 456. 118. Types 1, 3, 4; Ba.

11116. 1515 July 24. Chr. SCHEVRL: uita domini Antonii Kressen. 4°. P. VII. 456. 116. Types 1, 3; A; b.

11117. 1515 Dec. 7. Leonh. REYNMANN: Natiuität-Kalender. 4°. DA. 829. Types 1, 2; cut, diagr.

11118. [a. 4 kal. Jan. 1516.] NILVS: sententiae morales. 4°. P. VII. 457. 125. Types 1, 3, 4, large caps.; Ba.

11119. n.d. [c. 1515 ?] BEROALDVS: de die dominicae passionis carmen. 4°. P. IX. 550. 342b. Types 1, 3; A.

11120. n.d. [c. 1515–16.] Epistulae obscurorum uirorum. [GRATIVS.] 4°. P. IX. 173. 124. Types 3, 4. [In Venetia impressum in impressoria Aldi Minutii.]

11121. 1517 Jan. 19. Joh. von STAUPITZ: Büchlein von der endlichen Vollziehung ewiger Vorsehung. 4°. DA. 873. Types 1, 2, 3, 5; cut.

11122. 1517 Feb. 6. Ioh. de STAVPITZ: de executione aeternae praedestinationis. 4°. P. VII. 459. 136. Types 1, 3, 5, 6; cut; αβ.

11123. 1517 July 15. Plutarchus de exilio. [PLUTARCH.] 4°. P. VII. 458. 131. Type 3, large caps.; C; b; α.

11124. 1517 Oct. 2. Luciani Piscator. [LUCIAN.] 4°. P. VII. 459. 133. Types 3, 6, gk.; Ba; b; α. [Wants leaf 6.]

11125. 1517 Nov. 15. Reuelationes S. Brigittae. [BRIDGET.—For J. Koberger.] F°. P. VII. 459. 134. Types 1, 5, 6; cuts; D; αβ.

11126. 1518. Ioh. WILDENAUER Egranus: contra calumniatores suos apologia. 4°. P. IX. 119. 128. Type 3, gk.; cuts; X; α.

11127. 1518 Oct. 8. RICARDVS de S. Victore: de trinitate libri vi. 8°. P. VII. 460. 143. Types 1, 6; cut; b; αβ.

11128. 1518 Nov. 13. CLAVDIANVS: de raptu Proserpinae. 4°. P. VII. 460. 141. Types 1, 3, 4, 5, gk.; b; αβ.

11129. 1518 Dec. 12. HORTVLVS animae. [For J. Koberger.] 8°. P. VII. 460. 142. Types 1, 7; cuts; X; αɼΔ.

11130. 1519 March 29. Hortulus animae. [For J. Koberger.] 8°. P. VII. 461. 148. Types 1, 7; cuts; X; αɼΔ. [Print Room; wants last leaf.]

11131. 1519 May 13. BARTHOLOMAEVS Anglicus: de proprietatibus rerum. [For J. Koberger.] F°. P. VII. 461. 149. Types 1, 3, 5, 6; D; αβδε.

11132. 1519 Oct. 11. Vlr. PINDER: speculum passionis Christi. [For Georg Glockendon.] F°. Types 1, 3, 4, 5, 6; cuts; βε.

11133. 1519 Nov. [a. 21.] Sixt KOLBENSCHLAG: ein nutzbarliches Regiment wider die Pestilenz. 4°. DA. 941; W. 1203. Types 1, 2, 5; cut.

11134. 1520 Jan. PLINIVS: panegyricus. 4°. P. VII. 462. 157. Types 1, 3, 4, 5, 6; Ec; α.

11135. 1520 March 17. Auszug etlicher Sendbriefe von wegen einer neuge-fundenen Insel. [CHARLES V.] 4°. DA. 995i. Types 1, 2, 5; Δ.

11136. 1520 [a. March 29]. LUTHER: von den guten Werken. 4°. DA. 974ee. Types 1, 2, 3; cuts; C; b.

11137. 1520. Luther: eine kurze Form der zehn Gebote. [L., D.M.] 4°. DA. 974p. Types 1, 2, 4 [caps.]; C.

11138. 1520. LUTHER: Sermon von dem neuen Testament. 4°. DA. 974dddd. Types 1, 2, 5; cut; EcY; b.

11139. [a. 1520 Oct. 21.] Einzug Kaiser Karls zu Aachen beschehen. [CHARLES V.] 4°. DA. 995e. Types 1, 2.

11140. n. d. [1520.] ERASMVS: apologia de In principio erat sermo. 4°. Type 3, gk., and large caps; αε.

11141. n. d. [1520.] LUTHER: von dem Papsttum zu Rom. 4°. DA. 974mmm. Types 1, 2, 5; Δ.

11142. n. d. Achatius MORBACHVS: dialogus festiuus de mala medendi ratione. 4°. P. IX. 186. 262; 550. 342c. Types 1, 3, 4, 5; cut; Ec; α.

xxx. JOBST GUTKNECHT.

Books printed without name of printer in types 1–3 of Gutknecht but seemingly before 1515 are assigned to Joh. Stuchs (see no. 11088, 11091–93, 11097). For the Passau Missal of Oct. 1514 (in Trinity College, Dublin) see Weale, Bibl. Liturg. 1886, p. 121.

TYPES. Type 1, large, as Joh. Stuchs 2; same D and V.—Type 2, text schwabacher, as Hölzel 4, J. Stuchs 1, &c.; short comma; two sorts of ¶, both thin; this distinguishes the type from all others.—Type 3, square canon, as G. Stuchs 15, Hölzel 7, J. Stuchs 4, &c.—Type 4 = Weissenburger 4 or Peypus 1.—Type 5, large text latin gothic germanised; capitals, except V, nearly all those of 4; wrong-fount h, curious ⵞ; cast on body of 4, probably for use in a service-book.—Type 6, latin text like W. Huber 5; double hyphen, 81 mm.

Type 1, see fig. 14²; 2, see fig. 59; 3, see fig. 14¹; 4, see fig. 31²; 6, see fig. 36.

11143. [a. 1515 July 31.] Die Vereinigung Kaiserlicher Majestät mit den Königen von Ungarn Polen und Böhmen. [MAXIMILIAN.] 4°. (Not W. 960, 961.) Types 1, 2; cut.

11144. 1516. Ioh. de SACRO BOSCO: sphaera materialis, germ. 4°. DA. 860b. Types 1, 2, 3; cuts, diagr.

11145. [a. 1516 Nov. 24.] Brandenburgische Halsgerichts-Ordnung. [BRANDENBURG.] F°. DA. 847. Types 2, 3, 4, 5; cuts.

11146. n. d. [c. 1517?] Wie durch Gottfried von Bouillon das gelobte Land gewonnen ist. [GODFREY.] 4°. W. 1153. Types 1, 2, 3; cut.

11147. 1518 Apr. 24. Mich. SCHRICK: von allen gebrannten Wassern. 4°. DA. 909; W. suppl. i. 149. Types 1, 2, 3; cut.

11148. 1518. Laur. CORVINVS: latinum idioma. 4°. P. VII. 460. 144. Types 1, 3, 6; cut.

11149. 1518. LUTHER: Sermon von dem Ablass und Gnade. 4°. W. 1135. Types 1, 2, 3.

11150. n. d. [1518.] LUTHER: Sermon von dem Ablass und Gnade. 4°. W. 1137. Types 1, 2, 3.

11151. 1518. LUTHER: eine Freiheit des Sermons päpstlichen Ablass und Gnade belangend. 4°. Types 1, 2, 3.

11152. n. d. [1518.] LUTHER: eine Freiheit des Sermons ... 4°. W. 1131. Types 1, 2, 3.

11153. n. d. [c. 1518?] Lied vom Rock unsers lieben Herren. F°. W. suppl. i. 79. Types 1, 3. [One leaf; Print Room.]

11154. 1519. Wenceslaus LINCK: Lehre wie das Herz oder Gewissen durch die sieben Sacramenten auf das Wort Gottes gebaut wird. 4°. DA. 928. Types 1, 2, 3.

11155. 1519. Exercitium spirituale hominis christiani. [CHRISTIAN MAN.] 8°. Types 1, 2, 3; cut.

11156. 1519. Der HIMMELWAGEN. 4°. DA. 931; W. 1187. Types 1, 2, 3.

11157. [a. 1519 June 29.] LUTHER: ein Sermon am Tag Petri und Pauli. 4°. DA. 932ee. Types 1, 2, 3.

11158. n. d. [1519.] LUTHER: ein Sermon von dem hochwürdigen Sacrament des Leichnams Christi. 4°. W. 1240? Types 1, 2, 3; cut. [1ᵇ, line 3: bruderschafften; l. 5: dingk.]

11159. n. d. [1519.] LUTHER: ein Sermon von dem hochwürdigen Sacrament. 4°. Types 1, 2, 3; cut. [Bruderschafften; ding.]

11160. n. d. [1519.] LUTHER: Predigt von der würdigen Bereitung zum Sacrament. 4°. W. 1227. Types 1, 2, 3; cut.

11161. n. d. [1519.] LUTHER: Predigt von der würdigen Bereitung. 4°. Types 1, 2, 3; cut.

11162. n. d. [c. 1519–20.] LUTHER: kurze Form das Paternoster zu verstehen. 4°. W. 1523. Types 1, 2, 3.

11163. n. d. [c. 1519–20.] LUTHER: Die zehn Gebote Gottes mit einer kurzen Auslegung. 4°. W. 1532. Types 1, 2, 3.

11164. n. d. [c. 1519–20.] LUTHER: kurze Unterweisung wie man beichten soll. 4°. W. 1247. Types 1, 2, 3.

11165. 1520. Herm. KÜNIG: Die Strasse zu Sankt Jakob. 8°. DA. 979b. Types 1, 2; cut.

NÜRN-
BERG.
xxx. Jobst
Gutknecht.

11166. n.d. [1520.] Luther: kurze Form der zehn Gebote, etc. [TEN COMMAND-
MENTS.] 4°. W. 1515. Types 1, 2, 3.

11167. n.d. [1520.] LUTHER: Sermon von der Bereitung zum Sterben. 4°. W.
1551. Types 1, 2, 3.

11168. n.d. [1520.] LUTHER: Sermon von der Bereitung zum Sterben. 4°. W.
1553. Types 1, 2, 3.

11169. n.d. [1520.] LUTHER: Sermon von dem Bann. 4°. W. 1547. Types 1, 2, 3.

11170. n.d. [1520.] LUTHER: Sermon von dem Gebete und Prozession in der
Kreuzwoche. 4°. W. 1564. Types 1, 2, 3.

11171. n.d. [1520.] LUTHER: Sermon von dem Sacrament der Busse. 4°. W.
1570. Types 1, 2, 3.

11172. n.d. [1520.] LUTHER: Sermon von dem Sacrament der Taufe. 4°. W.
1578. Types 1, 2, 3.

11173. n.d. [1520.] LUTHER: Sermon von dem Sacrament der Taufe. 4°. W.
1579. Types 1, 2, 3.

11174. n.d. [1520.] LUTHER: Erklärung etlicher Artikel in seinem Sermon von
dem heiligen Sacrament. 4°. DA. 973rr. Types 1, 2, 3.

11175. n.d. [1520.] LUTHER: Sermon von dem Wucher. 4°. W. 1588. Types 1,
2, 3.

11176. [a. 1520 Oct. 25.] Krönung des allerdurchlauchtigsten Herrn Karls v.
[CHARLES V.] 4°. W. 1452. Types 1, 2, 3.

11177. n.d. In diesem Büchlein findet man wie man einem deutschen Fürsten
schreiben soll. [GERMAN PRINCE.] 8°. W. 1338. Types 1, 2; cut.

11178. n.d. Von Sibylla Weissagung und von König Salomons Weisheit.
[SIBYL.] 8°. (Not W. 1639; cf. DA. 875, note.) Types 1, 2; cut.

11179. n.d. Ein kurzweiliges LIED zu hören von dem Hausrat. 8°. Types 1, 2; cut.

11179A. n.d. [a. 1520?] Lied von einem Apfel und von dem Leiden Christi.
[JESUS.] 8°. (Not W. 55 or 1206.) Types 1, 2; cut.

xxxi. JOHANN SCHÖNSPERGER, THE ELDER, third press.

TYPES. Type 13, second frakturschrift, smaller than 12; 20 lines when unleaded measure
152 mm. Facs. Druckschriften 2, 3.—Type 14, like 13, but smaller; 10 lines measure 59 mm.
Facs. see fig. 65.—Flourished initials are used with these types.

11180. 1517. Melchior PFINTZING: der Theuerdank. F°. DA. 885. Types 13, 14.

WITHOUT PRINTER'S NAME.

1501 Apr. 7. Reinh. de Laudenburg: passio domini nostri		11024
1501. Opera Hrosuitae		11028
1502 Apr. 5. Celtes: libri amorum		11029
1503 Aug. 4. Grosseteste: de physicis lineis		11039
1503. Bern. de Harderwick: quaestio de crucibus		11040
1505 Oct. 9. Pinder: der beschlossene Garten		11030
1507 Aug. 30. id.: speculum passionis		11031
1509 Aug. 30. id.: speculum patientiae		11032
1510. id.: speculum intellectuale		11033

1511. Chelidonius-Dürer: epitome in d. Mariae historiam   11000   NÜRN-BERG. Without printer's name.
1511. id.: passio domini nostri   11001
1511. id.: passio Christi a Durero effigiata   11003
1511. Apocalypsis Dureri   11002

WITHOUT NAME OF PLACE OR PRINTER.

Type 1, large text schwabacher like Dyon 2 or Weissenburger 9; cf. type 8.—Type 2, small text schwabacher, with C, E, O, Q, T, ℂ like Landsberg 1; cf. Wagner 1; 88 mm. The prominence given to Kunigunde points to Bamberg diocese.

Type 3, rounded canon, Nürnberg style; short letters 9 mm.—Type 4, small rounded church text, like W. Huber 2 or Schobser 11 (the v differs); short letters 4 mm.—Type 5, large text, exactly like Öglin 11, Miller 6, Grim 2.—Type 6, small text schwabacher, thin ℂ, double hyphen, long comma; 88 mm.

Type 7, small text schwabacher like Joh. Stuchs 1, similar comma; but both comma and hyphen seem different, and ed. A (no. 11184) must go with ed. B (no. 11185).—Type 8, large text schwabacher like 1; with an A from a type like G. Stuchs 6 or Weissenburger 2.

Type 9 = Hölzel 3.—Type 10 = Hölzel 6.—Type 11, like Hölzel 4, with thick ¶, but the long comma and hyphen are different; 88 mm.

Type 12, large round church text like Meurl 1; short letters 5 mm.—Type 13, smaller ditto like Meurl 2: 4 mm.—Type 14, small text schwabacher, longish double hyphen, short comma, E normal; 88–89 mm.—Type 15, small roman caps.—Initial P, stripy ground; 24 mm.

Type 1, 8, see fig. 52; 2, see fig. 62; 3, 10, see fig. 23; 5, see fig. 35; 6, 7, 11, 14, see fig. 59; 9, see fig. 22; 12, see fig. 30; 13, see fig. 31².

11181. (1503–4.) Kalender auf das Jahr 1504. [EPH.] bs. Types 1, 2; cuts. [Wants top.]

11182. n.d. [c. 1505?] Hans SCHNEIDER: wie der Römische König die Fürsten des Reichs zu Augsburg und Nürnberg haben Tag geleistet. 8°. W. 1633. Type 2; cut.

11183. (1514–5.) Conradus Noricus : Practica Lipsensis auf das Jahr 1515. [TOCKLER.] 4°. Types 3–6; cut.

11184. (1515.) Albrecht Dürers Rhinoceros. open F°. Type 7; cut. [Ed. A. Print Room.]

11185. [n. b. 1515.] Albrecht Dürers Rhinoceros. open F°. Types 7, 8; cut. [Ed. B. Print Room.]

11186. n.d. [a. 1520?] Neue Zeitung allen guten Luterischen. [LUTHERANS.] 4°. W. 1665. Types 9, 10, 11.

11187. n. d. [a. 1520?] Ein Auszug etlicher Practica … [SIBYLS.] 4°. W. 1092. Types 12–15; cut; Δ.

VIII. SPEIER.

3. Peter Drach, first press, continued.
5. Conrad Hist.
6*. Hartmann Biber [not a printer? See W.245a = DA.528] 1502 Feb. 26.
7. Peter Drach, from Worms, third press...   1507.
8. Jacob Schmidt   [a. 1514 Feb. 14.]

---

iij. PETER DRACH.

TYPES.   Types 13 (text latin, like Prüss sen. 8 or Quentell 7; double and single hyphen; 81 mm.); 19 (square church text like Prüss sen. 13 or Quentell 10; 155 mm., short letters 5 mm.); 21 (square canon as Prüss sen. 4 or Quentell 9; 280 mm., short letters 9 mm.); 22 (smaller church text on the body of 19, like Prüss sen. 17 or Quentell 14; short letters 4 mm.); for these see part i. —Type 23, large text of the Strassburg-Lyonnese class; V has the diagonal lines reversed; tailed h, large thin ⸿, double hyphen; caps. mixt with those of 18; 112 mm.—Type 24, small, like Quentell 6; round h, double hyphen; 64 mm.

Type 13, see fig. 37; 19, see fig. 18; 21, see fig. 15; 22, see fig. 20; 24, see fig. 46.

DEVICE.   b (used in 1500); monogram supported by winged dragons on a black ground; 105 × 77 mm.

INITIAL.   In the Breidenbach, one R, letter black, no outer edge-line; 23 mm.

11188.   1501 Dec. 3. Bernardus: opuscula. [BERNARD.] 4°. P.VIII.296. 1. Types 13, 19, 23, 24.

11189.   1502 Sept. Missale Leodiense. [LIT.] F°. Types 19, 21, 22; cut.

11190.   1502 Nov. 24. BREYDENBACH: peregrinatio. F°. P.VIII.297.4. Types 13, 19, 23; cuts; Δ.

v. CONRAD HIST.

Weller (no. 206, 245) attributes to Hist a press at Heidelberg in 1501–1502, but erroneously.

TYPES.   Types 2 (text schwabacher; D like S reversed; double hyphen; fraktur forms of d, h; 88 mm.); 4 (large text latin of Strassburg origin; tailed h, double hyphen, caps. mixt with those of 2; 89 mm.); 5, small text like Quentell 5, or Prüss sen. 11, but at this period there is no mixture of caps.; round h, mixt hyphen, ⸿, 72 mm.); 6 (large round type, short letters 5 mm.); for these see part i.—Type 7, small, like Drach 24.

Type 2, see fig. 54; 5, see fig. 45; 6, see fig. 24; 7, see fig. 46.

INITIALS.   Those in the Calendar for 1512 are: a calligraphic I, 193 mm., and a P of open work, with the figure of an archbishop, 47 mm.

11191.   1501 [n.b. Feb. 12]. Caelius SEDVLIVS: carmen paschale. 4°. P. VIII. 297. 3. Types 5, 6.

1506 Dec. Philelphus: epistulae. For Hist by Anshelm; see no. 11757.

11192.   [n.b. 1507.] PFEFFERKORN: speculum adhortationis iudaicae. 4°. P.VI. 363. 143. Types 5, 6; cut.

11193.   1508 [a. Feb. 18]. Franc. Philelphus: conuiuiorum libri duo. [FILELFO.] 4°. P.VIII. 297. 8. Types 4, 5, 6.

11194.   1509. BRACK: uocabularius rerum. 4°. P.VIII. 298. 12; W. 519. Types 5, 6.

11195.   (1511.) Directorium ecclesiasticum pro anno 1511–12. F°. Types 5, 6; cut; Δ. [One leaf.]

11196.   (1511–12.) Deutscher Kalender auf das Jahr 1512. F°. Types 2, 6, 7; cuts. [Printed on back of no. 11195.]

11197. 1512 [a. July 15]. SOLINVS: de memorabilibus mundi. 4°. P.VIII. 298. SPEIER.
15. Types 4, 5, 6.
1514 Aug. Wimpheling: diatriba. For Hist by Gran; see no. 11662.
v. Conrad
Hist.

vij. PETER DRACH, third press.

TYPES. See press 3.—Type 26, text schwabacher, see Worms.
DEVICE. b; see press 3.
INITIALS. In no. 11199 a calligraphic I, 210 mm.; and V, 43 mm. In no. 11202 a fine I
(not calligraphic); 177 mm.

11198. 1507. Missale Moguntinum. [LIT.] F°. Types 19, 21, 22; cut; b. [Imp.]
11199. [n. b. 1507.] Die goldne Bulle, etc. [GERMANY.] F°. DA. 582. Types 19,
25; Δ. [Wants leaf 1.]
11200. 1511. Missale Halberstatense. [LIT.] F°. Types 19, 21, 22; cut.
11201. [a. 1512 June 16.] Agenda ecclesiae Spirensis. [LIT.] 4°. Types 13, 19,
21, 23, 25; cuts; b. [2 copies; one on vellum, imperfect.]
11202. [a. 1514 Dec. 21.] Erklärung Entscheid und endlicher Vertrag der
Irrungen . . . [SPIRES.] F°. Types 19, 21, 25; Δ.

viij. JACOB SCHMIDT.

TYPES. Type 1, church text like Drach 19.—Type 2, text schwabacher as Drach 26; heavy ℭ,
double hyphen; 95 mm.—Type 3, church text = F. Heumann 1.—Type 4 probably = Heumann
4, text schwabacher, much like Schott 12; E, h are similar, but other caps. differ; ¶ like that of
Hist 2 or Schöffer 7; long double hyphen; tall A, C like some Strassburg founts. 97 mm. [Type
5, small type, perhaps Heumann 3.]
Types 3–5 are used in W. 2030, ascribed by him to 1522. The Liber uagatorum may also be
later than 1520; both these contain the so-called lombardic initials used in 1509 by Heumann, but
not found in other books of Schmidt. Type 3 is also used with a normal small text schwabacher
in a Bauern Practica, getruckt zu Speir bey Anstat Nolt, certainly after 1520.
Type 1, see fig. 18; 2, see fig. 54; 4, see fig. 57; 5, see fig. 46.

11203. [a. 1514 Feb. 14.] Ioh. VIRDUNG: Auslegung über die wunderbarlichen
Zeichen . . . [For Arnold Schlick.] 4°. W. 863. Types 1, 2; cut.
11204. n.d. PRACTICA deutsch gezogen aus der Lehre und Prophezeien Sibyllae.
4°. Types 3, 4; XY.
11205. n. d. [a. 1520?] PRACTICA deutsch, etc. 4°. Types 3, 4; cut.
11206. n. d. [a. 1520?] Liber uagatorum, der Bettler Orden. [VAGATORES.] 4°.
W. 553? Types 3, 4; cut; Y.

X. ULM.

6. Johann Schäffler, third press.
7. Johann Zainer, second press.

---

vi. JOH. SCHÄFFLER.

This press seems to cease after 1501. For a book printed in that year see W. 183. It has a device at the end, woodcuts, and an initial.

vij. JOH. ZAINER.

Books by Zainer are recorded for the years 1502 (W. 246; see also W. 242) and 1503 (W. 253); but after that, with one doubtful exception which belongs to the end of 1506 (DA. 600; without name of printer), there is nothing more till 1514 (DA. 785 and W. 853); one book in 1515 (DA. 816) seems to be the last book of Zainer's printing known, apart from conjectural ascriptions such as W. 1649; but he was still alive in 1523; see Hassler, Ulms Buchdruckergeschichte, 1840, p. 94.

XIV. LÜBECK.

3. Matthaeus Brandiss, first press.
4. Stephan Arndes, third press.
5. Georg Richolf, first press.
6. Anna Richolf   1518.
7. Matthaeus Brandiss, from København, fourth press ?   1520.

---

iij. MATTH. BRANDISS.

[For Brandiss' Nicolaus de Blony of 1502, and his undated Saxo Grammaticus, with their types, see Lange, Lubecks Bogtrykkerhistorie, pp. 36–38; Bruun, Årsberetninger I. pp. 39–43; and for the two editions of a Dominican letter of confraternity ascribed to Brandiss, see Klemming, Sveriges Bibliografi, p. 80, and Lange, p. 38. In 1504 Brandiss was at Ribe.

TYPES. Type 8, small text schwabacher, single hyphen; facs. Lange, pp. 37, 38 (text).—Type 9, smaller broad church text of northern style; Lange, p. 37, line 1.—Type 10, larger broad church text; Lange, p. 38, line 1. Types 9 and 10 were used by Brandiss at København in 1510.

iv. STEPHAN ARNDES.

The address of Arndes in the Calendar for 1057 is: in der koniges strathen; but in 1509 (DA. 664c) he was: wonaftigh in der vlesckhouwer straten. He seems to have died between 1519 Aug. 14 (DA. 967c) and 1520 Aug. A book printed in 1519 by Hans Arndes is quoted by Ebert (20506, note).

TYPES. Type 5, schwabacher text as in 1494 (Burger 71, text), with slight changes. Single and double hyphen; ℂ with turned-back tail usual; the older angular form is rare, so is the long double comma. In 1520 the single hyphen is used as comma only, not as hyphen. 91 mm.— Type 7 (used in 1494) church type, very like 3 except in its smaller size and its capitals; the curly ends to the letters differentiate it from 6. Short letters about 5·8 mm.; 2 ll. = 19, 6 ll. = 56 mm. In 1520 the caps. are mixt.—Type 8, smaller church, plainer than 7, but in a similar style; short letters about 4·9 mm.

INITIALS. α, 20–23 mm.; see Burger 71.—β, black ground, seemingly copied from Ratdolt; 43 LÜBECK.
mm.   A in 1506; P in 1494; no other letters?—Γ, 38–39 mm., black ground, like Joh. Otmar;   iv. Stephan
whole set in 1494; D only in 1507.—δ, like α, but larger; 27 mm.—A large V, 55 mm., in 1520;   Arndes.
an inspired writer at work.

11207. 1506 Aug. 3. Dat boek des hyllighen Ewangelii. [BIBLE.] F°. DA. 565.
            Types 5, 7; cuts ; αβ.
11208. (1506–7.) Kalender plattdeutsch auf das Jahr 1507. [EPH.] Double bs.
            Types 5, 8; cuts. [Upper part wanting.]
11209. 1507 Aug. 14. Passionael efte dat leuent der hyllighen to dude. [LE-
            GENDA.] F°. DA. 578. Types 5, 7; cuts; Γ.

Heirs of S. Arndes [Hans Arndes?].

11210. 1520 Aug. 4. Hortus sanitatis plattdeutsch. [CUBE.] F°. Types 5, 7;
            cuts; αδΔ. [First leaf wanting.]

v. GEORG RICHOLF.

Joh. von Groten, Lübecker Practica for 1503, in plattdeutsch, is described in the Serapeum
XX. 342; and books of 1504 and 1506 are cited by Panzer (VII. 272. 1, 2).   In 1510 Richolf was
at Upsala.

vi. ANNA RICHOLF.

See P. VII. 273. 9.   The imprint, as given by Panzer, does not seem necessarily to imply
that the book was actually printed at Lübeck.   But Anna Richolf was presumably Georg
Richolf's widow, and would naturally return to Lübeck if her husband died in Sweden.

viij. MATTH. BRANDISS, fourth press?

If, as seems probable from the identity of type between the Narrenschiff of 1497 and the Dodendantz of 1520, Brandiss is the so-called lübecker Unbekannter, it is necessary to assign to him
the latter book and the Lucidarius of the same year which, after an interval of 22 years, contain
the devices of this printer.   See Seilmann in the Centralblatt für Bibliothekswesen, I. p. 22.   The
last we hear of Brandiss by name is at København in 1510–12 (Bruun, Årsberetninger I. pp. 195–6).

TYPES.   Types 6 (very curious large text vernacular; 120 mm., short letters 3 mm.), 7 (canon
type with curly letters like Arndes 3 or 7; short letters 7 mm.); for both see part i.   They are used
for the Dodendantz of 1520 (Bodleian).

DEVICES.   a, shield with three poppyheads.—b, usually found with a, a shield with trade mark
which resembles TF in monogram.

XV. BRESLAU.

<table>
<tr><td>2. Conrad Baumgarten, from Olmütz, third press …</td><td>1503 April.</td></tr>
<tr><td>3. Adam Dyon, from Nürnberg, second press</td><td>1519.</td></tr>
</table>

ij. CONR. BAUMGARTEN.

For this press see Bauch in Centralblatt für Bibliothekswesen, 1898, pp. 244–245; six books of Baumgarten at this period are known.

TYPES. Type 2, brought from Olmütz, is used at Frankfurt by Baumgarten but apparently not at Breslau.—Type 5, large round with angular lowercase, not unlike Bergmann, or Sorg 6 (Schobser 6, Cornelis of Zierikzee 1); the caps. resemble those of Ludw. von Renchen 1–3. Short letters 5½ mm.; 4 lines 36½ mm.—Type 6, like Ratdolt 13, but duplicate forms of C and O in a different style.—Type 7, latin text, almost the same as Joh. v. Amorbach 3 (see Burger 122, comment), but some caps., e.g. C, L, P, differ. Thin ℭ, double hyphen, 83 mm.—Type 8, like Ratdolt 9, round h, rather small face; short letters a little under 4 mm. 148 mm.—Type 9, large-faced text schwabacher, like no other fount except Kerner 1; the caps. are badly justified; very short comma, long double hyphen, strange paragraph mark, 91 mm.

DEVICE. c, large square; tilting-helm over shield, no label or initials. 144 × 123 mm.

INITIALS. In no. 11210A a large calligraphic S, 55 mm., signed with a Lorraine cross; in no 11211 a calligraphic A, 35 mm., with a W cut on it.

11210A. 1503. Laur. CORVINVS: hortulus elegantiarum. 4°. Bauch 3. Types 5, 6, 7; Δ.

11211. 1504 June 19. Die grosse Legende S. Hedwigis. [HEDWIG.] F°. DA. 547; Bauch 5. Types 8, 9; cuts; c; Δ.

iij. ADAM DYON.

TYPES. Type 3, square canon of Erfurt-Leipzig style, like W. Schenck 7, Knapp 1, Landsberg 7, &c.; short letters 9 mm.—Type 4, small narrow church text as G. Stuchs 6, Lotter sen. 8; cf. Burger 117, privilege. Short letters 4 mm.; 5 ll. = 34¾ mm.—Type 5, small text schwabacher, like Hölzel 4; very short sloping comma, double hyphen, thick ¶: 89 mm.

Type 3, see fig. 14B; 4, see fig. 22; 5, see fig. 59.

11212. 1519. LUTHER: Sermon von dem Ablass und Gnade. 4°. W. 465 (suppl. 2). Types 1, 2, 3; cut; X.

XVII. ROSTOCK.

<table>
<tr><td>1. Fratres uitae communis.</td><td></td></tr>
<tr><td>2. Ludwig Dietz</td><td>1505 June 7.</td></tr>
<tr><td>3. Nicolaus Marschalk (Günther Winter, of Erfurt)</td><td>1514.</td></tr>
</table>

i. FRATRES VITAE COMMVNIS.

This office was still at work in 1521; see Lisch, in the Jahrbuch des Vereins für Mecklenburgische Geschichte, vol. 4 (1839); the very bad facsimiles there given of the Schwerin Agenda of that year

show that the original types of 1476–1481 were then still in use, together with a later small text
type, no. 4 on the plate.

DEVICE.   b, Lisch I. 5.

ij. LUDWIG DIETZ.

Lisch (ubi supra) and Wiechmann-Kadow (in vol. 22 [1857] of the same Jahrbuch) describe thirty-six books or pieces from this press in 1505–1520.   The first book (1505 June 7) bears the name of Hermann Barkhusen, and that of Dietz first appears in 1509 (Lisch no. 5), but the type in that book is the same as that of 1505, and it is probable that Barkhusen, who was Stadtsekretär of Rostock, was not himself a printer, but financed Dietz.   He is not the same as the Hermann of Emden for whom the elder Prüss printed a Missale Hamburgense in Jan. 1509.

TYPES.   Type 1 (1505) latin text gothic, curly-tailed h, double hyphen; Lisch II. 1ᵃ, 1ᵇ.—Type 2, small canon type (short letters 9 mm.); strange ℭ.   Facs. in reprint of Dat nye Schip van Narragonien (1519–1892), line 1 of title.—Type 3, larger church text, spiky; facs. ib., title line 2 and overleaf. Short letters 5 mm. Not like other types.—Type 4, smaller church, in the same style as 3; caps. very curious; ℭ like that of 2.   Short letters 4 mm.—Type 5, text schwabacher, almost exactly = Joh. Schott 12; double hyphen, short comma, ℭ with turned-back tail; 92 mm.   Facs. in Dat nye Schip… (above; text) and Lisch II. 2ᵇ.—Type 6, large round gothic; Lisch II. 2ᵃ, 2ᵇ. Cf. Marschalk-Winter 4.—Type 7, church type, probably like G. Stuchs 5 or Lotter 2; Lisch IV. 3; cf. Marschalk-Winter 6.

Type 5, see fig. 57; 6, see fig. 24; 7, see fig. 18.

DEVICES.   a, larger, Lisch IV. 1ᵇ and in Dat nye Schip… —b, smaller; Lisch IV. 4.

INITIALS.   In the Vetter a calligraphic D, 40 mm. —Initials of two sizes with dotted ground in Dat nye Schip…

11213. n. d. [a. 1509.] Ioh. vetter: de ware hystori van veer ketters predyker
ordens. 4°. Types 2–5; cuts; Δ.

iij. NICOLAUS MARSCHALK AND GÜNTHER WINTER.

The name of the actual printer in aedibus Thuriis is given in the colophon to the Annales Herulorum of 1521.   No fewer than 22 pieces printed at this press from 1514 to 1520 are described by Lisch and Wiechmann-Kadow (ubi supra).

TYPES.   Type 1, larger roman = Sertorius 1; 108–9 mm.; Lisch III. 5.—Type 2, smaller roman = Sertorius 2.—Type 3, archaistic text roman, also used by Joh. Dorn at Braunschweig (on another body); remarkable Qu; large round comma; long-tailed us, which goes below the line; no hyphen? 108 mm. (Dorn 98 mm.) Facs. (so called) Lisch III. 1–2? (1515.)—Type 4, large round gothic = Dietz 6? Lisch III. 2.—Type 5, schwabacher, probably = Dietz 5; Lisch III. 4 (1517).—Type 6, square church text, probably = Dietz 7.—Greek type as Sertorius; a few accents and breathings added.

Types 1, 2, see fig. 7; 3, see fig. 5; 4, see fig. 24; 5, see fig. 57; 6, see fig. 18.

BORDERS.   A, architectural, white; rounded arch; two monsters at top.—B, black with interlaced ornament.   Both are one-piece folio.

DEVICES.   a, larger (1515), Lisch III. 3.   [b, smaller (1521), Lisch III. 5.]

INITIALS.   α, black ground, floral, 30 mm.—β, similar style, 20–21 mm.

11214. 1517 May 1. marschalk: historiae aquatilium liber VII (III). F°. P.
VIII. 281. 10. Type 3; cuts. On cancel titlepage (1520) types 1, 6; A.
11215. 1520 March 1. marschalk: historiae aquatilium libri I–II. F°. P.VIII.
281. 15. Types 1–4; cut; BY; αβ.

XX. WÜRZBURG.

1. Georg Reyser.
2. Martin Schubart.   1503 Sept. 16.

i. GEORG REYSER.

Reyser's press continued to work intermittently well into the sixteenth century. The Missale Herbipolense of 1503 Aug. 14 is recorded by Weale (Bibl. Liturg. p. 77); and in the Bodleian is an edition of the Acta et decreta in concilio Herbipolensi 1452–53, which contains the date 1512 printed in the text. It is printed in type 1. No. 2675 (see part i.) probably belongs to this same period, and, it may be, no. 2676 also.

ij. MARTIN SCHUBART.

Three books by Schubart, with dates ranging from 1503 Sept. 16 to 1504 Aug. 3, are recorded by Weller (268, 294d, 295).

XXI. ERFURT.

4. Hans Spörer, second press.
6. Wolfgang Schenck.
7. Paul, of Hachenburg.
9. Henricus Sertorius, of Blankenburg, first press   1501 Oct. 1.
10. Wolfgang Stürmer, with Johann Ru [Rhau?], first press 1506.
11. Hans Knapp   1508 Oct. 29.
12. Sebaldus Striblita   1510 Apr. 22.
13. Matthaeus Maler   1511.

iv. HANS SPÖRER.

For Spörer see an article by F. W. E. Roth in the Archiv für Geschichte des deutschen Buchhandels, XX. (1898) pp. 196–200; but his identification of Spörer with the Hans von Erfurt of Augsburg and Worms can hardly be accepted. Only two books of Spörer after 1500 are recorded: Ebert 6907 (1502) and W. 273 (1504).

vi. WOLFGANG SCHENCK.

TYPES. Type 1 (roman, unlike others; long double hyphen; ę and ¶ from Oct. 1501; 86 mm.); 2 (wider large church text, like Landsberg 5 or Thanner 2); 3 (text gothic, round, remarkable caps., long double hyphen at an acuter angle than that of 1; 86 mm.); 4 (small round type in the style of 3; double hyphen of unusual form; ¶; 64 mm.); 5 (small text schwabacher like G. Stuchs 18, Grim 1, Stöckel 6, &c. The single hyphen of 1500 is replaced by the double hyphen of type 1 in 1502; ℂ like Thanner 1, or (in 1503 only) ¶; 87 mm.); for these see part i.—Type 6 (not used before 1501) narrow large church text like G. Stuchs 5, Kachelofen 8, Lotter 2, Stöckel 5; it usually has some caps. of 2 mixt in it.—Type 7, square canon like Knapp 1; short letters 10 mm. Smaller and narrower than vij. 2. Cf. Landsberg 7.—Type 8, new small gothic, larger face than 4,

but still round; the caps. (e. g. O, Q, V) have no inner diagonals; hyphen more normal; 65 mm.
Cf. Thanner 5.—Type 9, latin large text, larger than 3, round, curious caps.; 88 mm.—Two greek
types; for the first (1500) see facs. in The Printing of Greek in the Fifteenth Century, p. 139; the
second (1501, Priscianus) is smaller but of similar style: cf. that of press 7.

ERFURT.

vi. Wolfgang
Schenck.

Type 2, see fig. 17; 5, see fig. 59; 6, see fig. 21; 7, see fig. 14B; *8, see fig. 50; 9, see fig. 41.

DEVICE. a (as in 1500), a shield bearing a handle in chief, and below three small escutcheons
on a black ground; WS; 32½ × 34 mm.

11216. 1501. Nic. MARSCHALK: orthographia. 4°. P.VI. 494. 4. Types 1, 2, gk. i; a.

11217. 1501 Aug. 18. Iodocus TRVTFETTER: summulae totius logicae. 4°. P.
VI. 493. 1. Types 1, 3, 4, 6; diagr.

11218. 1501 Oct. 27. Baptista Mantuanus: eclogae. [SPAGNUOLI.] 4°. Types 1, 6.

11219. 1502 March 15. Ioh. de PALTZ: celifodina. 4°. P.VI. 494. 7. Types 4,
5, 6; cut; a.

11220. 1503. Petrus Rauennas: aurea opuscula. [TOMMAI.] 4°. P.VI. 495. 8.
Types 5, 6, 7; a.

11221. 1504 Feb. 27. Ioh. de PALTZ: supplementum celifodinae. 4°. P.VI.
495. 9. Types 4, 5, 6, 7; cut.

11222. 1505. Ad patrem. [PATER.] 4°. Types 5, 6, 7; cut; Δ.

11223. n. d. [c. 1505.] BEROALDVS: declamatio philosophi medici oratoris. 4°.
P.IX. 166. 42. Types 1, 6, 7; gk. ij.

11224. n. d. [c. 1505.] Domin. PICOLOMINEVS: de laudibus liberalium disciplinarum oratio. 4°. Types 1, 6, 7. [Blanks for greek.]

11225. 1507. Bartholomaeus de Vsingen: exercitium de anima. [ARNOLDI.] 4°.
P.VI. 496. 15. Types 6, 7, 8, 9; diagr.

11226. n. d. [1507.] Barthol. de Vsingen: exercitium physicorum. [ARNOLDI.]
4°. P.VI. 505. 70. Types 6, 7, 8, 9.

11227. n. d. [1507.] Barthol. de Vsingen: compendium philosophiae naturalis.
[ARNOLDI.] 4°. P.VI. 504. 69. Types 6, 7, 8, 9.

vij. PAUL, OF HACHENBURG.

TYPES.   Types 2 (very large canon type, short letters 11 mm.) and 3 (text like Ratdolt 3; cf.
Burger 81/2, text; 81 mm.; ℭ in 1500, ¶ in 1501); see part i.—Type 4, roman, very like
Schenck 1, but taller face and shorter hyphen; 83 mm.—Greek type like Schenck's second fount.

DEVICE.   a, oblong, black ground; two shields, the wheel of Erfurt on one, and p h with
a trade mark on the other; 40 × 58–59 mm.

11228. 1501. BARTHOLOMAEVS Coloniensis: epistula mythologica. 4°. P. IX.
456. 6b. Types 2, 3.

11229. 1501 Aug. 9. Nic. MARSCHALK: grammatica exegetica. 4°. Type 4,
gk.; a.

ix. HENRICUS SERTORIUS, first press.

TYPES.   Type 1, large roman text, face tall and narrow, caps. rather small; bold Qu; small
us; & rather on one side; long single hyphen, also used as comma; 109 mm.   Cf. Lotter sen.
12.—Greek type like that of press 7.   In no. 11233 this type has additional quasi-Aldine letters
and some very clumsy ligatures.—Woodcut hebrew letters.

Types 1, 2, see fig. 7.

11230. 1501 Oct. 1. Laus musarum ex Hesiodi Theogonia, etc. [HESIOD.] 4°.
P.VI. 494. 6. Type 1, gk.

117

11231. 1502 Apr. 26. Nic. MARSCHALK: enchiridion poetarum. 4°. P.VI. 505. 76; IX. 457. 7b. Type 1, gk.; cuts.

11232. n. d. Aldus MANVTIVS: introductio ad literas hebraicas. 4°. Type 1, gk. [hb.]; cut; Y.

11233. n. d. Nic. Marschalk: εἰσαγωγὴ πρὸς τῶν γραμμάτων ἑλλήνων. [GREEK LANGUAGE.] 4°. Type 1, gk.; cut; Y.

[For continuation see Wittenberg.]

x. WOLFGANG STÜRMER, first press.

Only two books attest the existence of this first press of Wolfgang Stürmer, if indeed the Wolphius of 1506 and the Wolfgang of 1522 be the same person. The Eobanus Hessus dated 1506 (P. VI. 495. 14) has Stürmer's name alone; the Baptista Mantuanus of 1507 (P. VI. 496. 16) was printed by: Ioannes Ru et Wolfius Stürmer in aedibus suis ad diui Michaelis. But the address of the Stürmer of 1522 was: zum bunten Löwen bei Sankt Paul.

xi. HANS KNAPP.

Knapp seems to have been also a wood-engraver; some of the cuts in Vegetius are signed H K 1511, and a border-piece used by Schumann at Leipzig (no. 11545) also bears his initials. For his first book (1508 Oct. 29) see P.VI. 496. 18.

TYPES. Type 1, canon type like Schenck 7.—Type 2, church type, the lowercase like Schenck 6, with caps. as Schenck 2.—Type 3, small text schwabacher like Schenck 5, but has long comma; double hyphen rather long but shorter than that of Schenck. 88 mm.—Type 4, small, probably like Schenck 8.—Type 5, roman = Sertorius 1, with ę.—Type 6 = Schenck 9.—Greek type more like the first than the second of Schenck's founts.

Type 1, see fig. 14B; 2, see fig. 21 (lowercase) and 17 (caps.); 3, see fig. 59; 4, see fig. 50; 5, see fig. 7¹; 6, see fig. 41.

BORDER. Aa, quarto, four-piece border-device; at foot H K in a shield. Not used in these books. A border piece containing the monogram H K was used in 1519 by Schumann in Hegendorff's Encomium Somni (no. 11545).

DEVICE. a, see border A.

11234. 1511. VEGETIVS: vier Bücher der Ritterschaft. F°. DA. 705. Types 1–4; cuts.

11235. 1515 June 3. Euricius CORDVS: contra maledicum Thilonium Philymnum defensio. 4°. P.VI. 499. 36. Types 1, 2, 5, 6; cut.

11236. 1519. LUTHER: Unterricht auf etliche Artikel... 4°. Types 1, 2, 3.

xij. SEBALDUS STRIBLITA.

Calcographus et grammatoglypha nouus, is Striblita's description of himself in the colophon to the Columella.

TYPES. Type 1, rude and eccentric italic, with curious caps.; 93 mm.—Type 2, large roman caps., 8½ mm. high, also very curious.

11237. 1510 Apr. 22. COLVMELLA: de cultu hortorum liber xi. 4°. P.VI. 497. 23. Types 1, 2.

11238. n. d. Vlr. de HVTTEN: Nemo. 4°. B. vii. 1. Type 1; cut.

xiij. MATTHAEUS MALER.

Maler, though no book of his seems to be dated earlier than 1511 (P.VI. 497. 26), is by his types clearly the successor to Schenck. His address is given (1517–1520) as: zum schwarzen Horn vor der Krämer-Brücke (prope mercatorum pontem).

TYPES. Type 1 = Schenck 6.—Type 2 = Schenck 5 with thick ¶, and two sorts of double ERFURT.
hyphen, one as Schenck, the other of the same length but set more upright. From 1513 ę of type xiij. Mat-
3 is used in type 2; short comma in and after 1516; a few round commas in the anonymous thaeus
Eccius Dedolatus.—Type 3 = Schenck 1; mixt hyphens as type 2 above; us also mixt; ¶ as Maler.
Schenck.   Round comma first in 1519.—Type 4 = Schenck 8.—Type 5 = Schenck 9.—Type 6 =
Schenck 7.—Greek type = Schenck's second fount.
　　Type 1, see fig. 21; 2, see fig. 59; 4, see fig. 50; *5, see fig. 41; *6, see fig. 14B.
　　BORDERS. A, one-piece quarto; arms of Erfurt at top, tree trunks at sides; at foot cattle
within an osier fence: a copy of part of Beck's device a (EBM. XV. 2).—B, also one-piece
quarto, S. John the Evangelist, a copy in reverse of Knoblouch A (Butsch I. 71).—C, one-piece
quarto; black ground: at foot boys trundling a wagon.
　　DEVICE.   a, shield borne by a lion, and label with printer's name: 74 × 65 mm.

11239. 1512. Leben S. Wendels. [WENDELIN.] 4°. Types 1, 2; cut.

11240. 1513. Murmelius: uaria Tibulli Propertii Catulli carmina. [TIBVLLVS.]
　　　　4°. Types 1, 2, 3.

11241. [n. b. 1515 Sept.–Oct.] Iac. Hartlieb: de generibus ebriosorum. [GEN-
　　　　ERA.] 4°. Types 1, 2, 3; cut.

11242. n. d. [c. 1515?] Iod. WINSHEMIVS: oratio de humilitate. 4°. Type 3.

11243. 1516. Iod. WINSHEMIVS: institutiones in rite faciendam confessionem.
　　　　4°. Types 1, 3, 4, 5.

11244. 1516. Joh. von MORSSHEIM: Spiegel des Regiments in der Fürsten Höfe.
　　　　4°. W. 1021. Types 1, 4, 5; cuts; A.

11245. 1516. Von des Endkrists Leben. [ANTICHRIST.] 4°. DA. 836. Types
　　　　1, 2, 6; cuts.

11246. 1517 [a. May 31]. Euricius CORDVS: epigrammata. P.VII.499.40. Types
　　　　1, 3, 5, 6; A.

11247. 1517. Iod. TRVTFETTER: summa philosophiae naturalis. 4°. P. IX. 458.
　　　　38b. Types 1, 3, 4, 5; A.

11248. 1517. HORATIVS: epistulae. 4°. Types 3, 5, 6.

11249. 1518. Honorius: Meister Elucidarius von den wunderbaren Sachen
　　　　der Welt. [LUCIDARIUS.] 4°. W. 1107. Types 1, 2, 6; cuts; a.

11250. n. d. [c. 1518?] CANTALITIVS: christiani paenitentis elegiaca confessio.
　　　　4°. P.VI. 506. 79. Types 1, 3–6; cuts; a.

11251. 1519 [a. July 15]. Disputatio Ioannis Eckii et Andreae Carolostadii,
　　　　etc. [JOHANN.] 4°. P.VII. 211. 735. Types 1, 3–6.

11252. n. d. [c. 1519–20?] Macarius MVTIVS: de triumpho Christi. 4°. Types
　　　　3, 6, gk.; B.

11253. [a. 1520 Feb. 20.] Ioh. Fr. COTTA Lambergius (Bilibald Pirkheimer):
　　　　Eccius dedolatus. 4°. P. IX. 122. 153. Types 1, 2, 4, 6, gk.; C.

11254. 1520. THEODERICVS de Thuringia: Cronica Sankt Elisabeth zu deutsch.
　　　　4°. DA. 979 c. Types 1, 2, 6; cuts.

11255. n. d. [1520.] Ulr. von HUTTEN: Anzeigung wie allwegen sich die Päpste
　　　　gegen den Kaisern gehalten haben. 4°. W. 1408. Types 1, 2, 5.

WITHOUT PRINTER'S NAME.

XXII. REUTLINGEN.

3. Michael Greif, second press.

iij. MICHAEL GREIF.

Greif's press seems to have been intermittent at this period; see W. 243 (1502), P. XI. 499.
1 (1509), and DA. 798b (1514). The attribution to Greif of the following book is conjectural,
but the printer can hardly be other than Greif or the elder Schönsperger, and there is no trace of
the text type among the books of the latter.

TYPES. Type 5* appears to be a recast of 5 on larger body, 92 mm. (5 is 87 mm.); no w.f.
caps., different (double) hyphen; the P less usual with 5 is alone used.—Type 9, church text,
seems the same as Schönsperger sen. 4.—Type 13, large text schwabacher like Schönsperger
sen. 6.

Type 2, see fig. 19; 3, see fig. 52.

11256. [a. 1503 May 5.] Ios. GRÜNBECK: libellus de mentulagra. 4°. Types 5*,
9, 13.

XXIII. MAGDEBURG.

5. Moritz Brandiss, second press.
6. Jacob Winter   1506 Apr. 4.

v. MORITZ BRANDISS.

1501 S. Alexius' day (17 June), see DA. 501c; 1504, see P. VII. 373. 1.

vi. JACOB WINTER.

TYPES. Type 1, broad square church like Thanner 1 or Landsberg 5; double hyphen.—Type 2,
small text schwabacher like Landsberg 1; C,E are similar, but Q,T like the normal types of this
class. Short double hyphen, medium comma; 85–86 mm. In no. 11258 a ℂ too small for the
type is used.

Type 1, see fig. 17; 2, see fig. 62.

11257. 1507. Ioh. VOCHS: de pestilentia anni praesentis. 4°. P. VII. 373. 3. Types
1, 2.
11258. 1507 Nov. 20. Herm. Buschius: spicilegium, etc. [BUSCHE.] 4°. P. VII.
160. 223. Types 1, 2.

Heirs of J. Winter.

11259. 1513. Officium de compassione B.M.V. secundum ritum ecclesiae Mag-
deburgensis. [LIT.] 4°. P. VII. 373. 4. Types 1, 2; cuts.

XXIV. MEMMINGEN.

1. Albrecht Kunne.

i. ALBRECHT KUNNE.

TYPES.   Type 6, small text schwabacher.   In 1501–2 still much mixt with 5, no other E but that of 5 is found: mixt hyphen; thin ⊄ and a hand; 87 mm.   But after 1502 the letters from 5 and the single hyphen vanish, and a new E like Öglin-Schönsperger-Otmar comes in. Same thin ⊄; also §.   In 1519 the same except for a large new ⊄.—Type 7, large round, in the style of Froschauer 6; large ⊄.—Type 8, latin text gothic like Furter 1, Joh. Otmar 27, &c.; two sorts of single hyphen, thick ⊄; 79–80 mm.

Type 6, see fig. 60; 7, see fig. 27; 8, see fig. 36.

DEVICE.   a. In the cut of a preacher in no. 11263 are two shields, one with the arms of Memmingen, the other with a trade mark.

11260. 1502. Venustissima materia passionis Christi. [JESUS.] 4°. P.IX.537. 1b. Type 6[5].

11261. 1502. Gerson: de cognitione peccatorum. [CHARLIER.] 4°. P.IX. 538. (XI.465.) 1c. Type 6[5].

11262. 1502. Gerson: tractatuli; de cognitione peccatorum, etc. [CHARLIER.] 4°. Type 6[5].

11263. n. d. TRACTÄTLEIN von dem sterbenden Menschen. 4°. Types 6, 7; cuts; a; Δ.

11264. n. d. Indulgentiae et certa priuilegia ordinis S. Antonii. [ANTONY.] F°. Types 7, 8. [One leaf.]

11265. 1519. Pamph. Gengenbach: Die zehn ALTER dieser Welt. 4°. DA.959. Type 6; cuts. [Wants last leaf.]

XXVIII. LEIPZIG.

6. Martin Landsberg, of Würzburg.
8. Melchior Lotter, the elder, first press.
9. Wolfgang Stöckel, of München, first press.
10. Jakob Thanner, of Würzburg.
11. Conrad Kachelofen, third press.
12. Marcus Brandt [Brandiss? second press?].
13. Wolfgang Stöckel, from Wittenberg, third press   1504 (April).
14. Valentin Schumann   1513.
15. Conrad Baumgarten, from Frankfurt an der Oder, fifth press 1514.
16. Melchior Lotter, the elder, from Meissen, third press   1520 (a. Feb.).

---

vi. MARTIN LANDSBERG.

Landsberg's address in 1519 is given as: in der Ritterstrasse.

TYPES. Type 1 (heavy-faced small text schwabacher; O,Q,T as Peter Wagner 1; low us; ⅭⅠ (as in a calendar for 1504, probably printed at Nürnberg, no. 11181) and double hyphen, which slopes downwards instead of upwards, are also distinctive. The hyphen is very short 1501–9: rather longer 1509–16; longer still 1519–20. A b of fraktur form used for german books only in 1504 (not in 1506) is found in and after 1516 in all books; 87 mm.); 2 (heavy square church type like W. Schenck 2 or Jac. Winter 1; double hyphen); for these see part i.—Type 6, latin text like Silv. Otmar 4, Weissenburger 7, or Lotter sen. 1; 82 mm.; very few hyphens, those that occur being mixt; very short comma; Ⅽ like 1; a second H like that of Koberger 21.—Type 7 (called 6 in part i. but not used before 1511), square canon, rather thin; like W. Schenck 7 or Thanner 3, not as Lotter 3 or Schumann 1; short letters 10½ mm.—Type 8, text roman, practically identical with Lotter 12, but the comma differs; the paragraph mark, when there is any, is that of type 1; the hyphens are uniform (sometimes reversed), and Qu is alone found: 95 mm.—Greek type, rare; used in 1520.

Type *1, see fig. 62; 2, see fig. 17; 6, see fig. 58; 7, see fig. 14B; 8, see fig. 6.

BORDER. A, four-piece, quarto, black ground, including as top piece the ribbon copied from Schumann called below device d. An X-border also copied from Schumann, two pieces of which are used in 1516, is found in most of the books of 1519 before the introduction of A, and the progress of a break in the bottom piece is of much help in the arrangement of the books of 1519.

DEVICES. a, b, c are all different forms of the same device, and may be distinguished by the position of the branch from which the two shields hang. That of c is like a in position but the shape differs; b is like c in shape but in a different position.—d, the top piece of border A, black ground; an owl and smaller birds; MHAV (which might stand for Martinus Herbipolensis . . .) on a label. But as this is a copy of a border piece of Schumann (q.v.), initials and all, and occurs again later in a border of W. Stürmer at Erfurt, it can hardly be called a device of Landsberg; Landsberg's copy is 27½ × 74 mm., Schumann's piece 29 × 66½ mm., and the position of the owl is different.

11266. 1501 [a. Apr. 30]. Leon. Aretinus: de studiis et literis. [BRUNI.] 4°. P. VII. 137. 6. Types 1, 5.

11267. 1501. Aristotelis ethica. [ARISTOTLE.] F°. P. VII. 137. 8. Types 1, 5; a.

11268. 1502. ALBERTVS Magnus: summa philosophiae naturalis. F°. P. VII. 140. 32. Types 1, 5; a.

11269. 1502. Isidorus: liber soliloquiorum. [ISIDORE.] 4°. Types 1, 5; a.

LEIPZIG.
vi. Martin
Landsberg.

11270. n. d. [c. 1503.] Von wem und wie das Kloster Helfede gestiftet wurde.
4°. DA. 537c. Types 1, 5.
11271. (1503-4.) Kalender auf das Jahr 1504. [EPH.] bs. Types 1, 5. [Upper
half only.]
11272. 1504 June 27. Ioh. PECKHAM: perspectiua communis. F°. P. VII. 149.
106. Types 1, 5; diagr.; a.
11273. 1504 Aug. 22. Ioh. de PALTZ: celifodina. 4°. P. VII. 149. 112. Types 1,
5; cut; a.
11274a. [a. 1504 Oct. 21.] Sendbrief der Grafen und Herren Herzog Ruprecht
verwandten. Types 1, 5; cut.
   b. [a. 1504 Nov. 2.] Antwort der Räten königlicher Maiestät. Types 1, 5;
cut. [RUPERT.] 4°. DA. 550c.
11275. 1504. Herm. Buschius: epigrammatum liber iij. [BUSCHE.] 4°. P. VII.
148. 111. Types 1, 5; a.
11276. [a. 1505 Jan 2.] HIPPOCRATES: de aspectibus planetarum. 4°. P. VII. 153.
147. Types 1, 5; a.
11277. 1505. Andr. MEINHART: elegantiarum rudimenta. 4°. P. VII. 155. 171.
Types 1, 5.
11278. 1506. Von den neuen Inseln und Landen... [VESPUCCI.] 4°. DA. 570e.
Types 1, 5; cut; a.
11279. 1507. Homeri Ilias per Pindarum Thebanum traducta. [HOMER.] 4°.
P. VII. 158. 203. Types 1, 5; a.
11280. 1507. Geo. Sibutus: de felicitate nuptiali carmen. 4°. P. IX. 486. 208b.
Types 1, 5. [Title only.]
11281. 1508 June. Chr. SCHEVRL: libellus de laudibus Germaniae. 4°. P. VII.
161. 229. Types 1, 5.
11282. 1508. Baptista Mantuanus: parthenice prima seu mariana. [SPAGNUOLI.]
4°. Types 1, 5, 6.
11283. 1509. Lucius FENESTELLA: de romanorum magistratibus. F°. P. VII.
164. 266. Types 1, 5; a.
11284. 1509 Dec. Chr. SCHEVRL: oratio de literarum praestantia. 4°. P. VII.
164. 263. Types 1, 5; cut.
11285. 1510 [a. July 17]. Ioh. Garzo: Christophori Cananei uita. [GARZONI.]
4°. P. VII. 168. 298. Types 1, 5; b.
11286. 1510 Aug. 10. Ioh. de PALTZ: supplementum celifodinae. 4°. P. VII.
168. 300. Types 1, 5; cut; b.
11287. 1510. Henr. BEBEL: de S. Anna hymnus. 4°. Types 1, 5; cut; c.
11288. 1510. Baptista Mantuanus: parthenice catharinaria. [SPAGNUOLI.] 4°.
P. VII. 168. 301. Types 1, 5, 6.
11289. 1510. Leonardus Aretinus: comoedia Poliscene. [BRUNI.] 4°. Types
1, 5; b.
11290. [a. 1510 Oct. 9.] Bulla censurarum in singulos de consilio . . . [ROME.]
4°. Types 1, 5.
11291. 1511 Apr. 26. Ioh. de PALTZ: celifodina. 4°. P. XI. 434. 331b. Types
1, 5, 7; cut; c.
11292. [a. 1511 Dec. 18.] Max. CORVINVS: oratio sanctissimi foederis. 4°. P. VII.
171. 334. Types 1, 5, 7; c.
11293. n. d. [c. 1511.] Alithia Collenutii. [COLLENUCCIO.] 4°. [Part i. no. 2987.]
Types 1, 5, 7.

Q 2

11294. 1512. Es tu SCHOLARIS? 4°. Types 1, 5, 7; cut.

11295. 1516. Henr. STROMER: algorismus linealis. 4°. Types 1, 5, 7, 8; diagr.; X¹; c.

11296. n. d. [c. 1518–19.] LVTHER: sermo de triplici iustitia. 4°. Types 1, 5, 7; cuts; X².

11297. 1519. Eine deutsche Theologia. [GERMAN THEOLOGY.] 4°. (Not W. 1273.) Types 1, 5; cuts.

11298. n. d. [1519.] LVTHER: sermo de digna praeparatione cordis. 4°. Types 1, 5, 7; cut; X².

11299. [1519.] LVTHER: disputatio et excusatio aduersus criminationes Ioh. Eckii. 4°. P. IX. 73. 53? Types 1, 5, 7; cut; X².

11300. 1519. Luther: Auslegung des 109. Psalms. [BIBLE.] 4°. DA. 932g. Types 1, 5, 7; cuts; X².

11301. [a. 1519 March 14.] Disputatio Ioh. Eckii aduersus criminationes Lutheri. [JOHANN.] 4°. P. IX. 120. 135? Types 1, 5, 7; cut; X².

11302. [a. 1519 March 14.] Disputatio Ioh. Eckii . . . [JOHANN.] 4°. Types 1, 5, 7; Ad.

11303. [a. 1519 Apr. 26.] Andr. BODENSTEIN: conclusiones contra Eckium. 4°. P. IX. 74. 57? Types 1, 5, 7; cut; X².

11304. 1519. LUTHER: Auslegung deutsch des Vaterunser für die einfältigen Laien. 4°. DA. 932e. Types 1, 5, 7; cut; X².

11305. n. d. [1519.] LVTHER: sermo de uirtute excommunicationis. 4°. Types 1, 5, 7; cut; X².

11306. n. d. [1519?] Siluester [MAZZOLINI] de Prierio: replica ad Lutherum. 4°. Types 1, 5, 7; cut.

11307. [a. 1519 June 14.] Werbung der Botschaften . . . [CHARLES V.] 4°. W. 1292. Types 1, 5, 7; Ad.

11308. [a. 1519 July 21.] MELANCHTHON: epistula de lipsica disputatione. 4°. P. IX. 74. 58. Types 1, 5, 8 [caps.].

11309. [a. 1519 July 25.] Excusatio Eckii contra Melanchthonem. [JOHANN.] 4°. P. VII. 211. 734? Types 1, 5, 7; cuts; Ad. [Cut of S. Jerome, A1ᵇ.]

11310. [a. 1519 July 25.] Excusatio Eckii . . . [JOHANN.] 4°. Types 1, 5, 7; cuts; Ad. [Cut of Last Supper, A1ᵇ.]

11311. [a. 1519 July 31.] Ioh. CELLARIVS: de uera et constanti serie disputationis lipsicae. 4°. P. VII. 211. 729b? Types 1, 5, 7; Ad.

11312. [a. 1519 Aug. 16.] Ioh. RVBIVS: solutiones et responsa wittenbergensium doctorum. 4°. P. VII. 212. 736. Types 1, 5, 7; Ad.

11313. [a. 1520 July 4.] Aug. ALVELD: malagma optimum. 4°. P. IX. 122. 150. Types 1, 7, 8, gk.

11314. [a. 1520 Sept. 29.] Eckius: des Concilii zu Konstanz Entschuldigung. [JOHANN.] 4°. DA. 981b; W. 1353. Types 1, 7, 8.

11315. n. d. [1520?] Aug. ALVELD: sermo de confessione sacramentali. 4°. P. IX. 501. 937b. Types 1, 7, 8.

11316. n. d. [c. 1520.] Ioh. de SACRO BOSCO: sphaera mundi. 4°. P. VII. 233. 930. Types 1, 5, 7, 8; Ad; b.

TYPES. Types 1 (latin text gothic like Weissenburger 7, Landsberg 6, &c., but 72 mm. only. 1ᵍ, the same type germanised); 2 (church type, usually distinguishable from Stöckel 5 by the position of the hyphen, which is medial after 1502; but in 1501 and 1502 it is placed high like that of Stöckel: facs. Butsch I. 88); 3 (square canon, like the Nürnberg founts; thicker and squarer than Landsberg 7; short letters 11 mm.; cf. Stöckel 9); 4 (small text schwabacher like Stöckel 6, &c.; single hyphen, low us; otherwise normal; 89 mm.); 6 (large text latin, of northern style; 97 mm.); 7 (very small, like Stöckel 7; double hyphen; 60 mm.); for these see part i.—Type 8, smaller church text (Kachelofen 9), like G. Stuchs 6, Weissenburger 2, &c.—Type 9, smaller face than 1, same body; used with it in service-books.—Type 10, large text latin, much rounder than 6; with curly h, double hyphen; round comma in 1518. 5 lines = 27 mm.—Type 11, characteristic text schwabacher; 91–92 mm.; long double hyphen, upright. Cf. Thanner 6.—Type 12, roman text like Sertorius 1, tall and narrow, but 95 mm. only, and has double hyphens; round comma of odd shape; also, at first, a very short sloping comma. Qu at first; but separate Q in 1519–20. The hyphen is at first nearly horizontal (1511), then mixt with that of 11 (1512 &c.), but less and less so as time goes on. This fount is called nouae formae in 1511: uenustiores typi in Dec. 1513. Cf. Landsberg 8; Schumann 3; Thanner 7.—Type 12 bis, latin text gothic, large face but very small body; round h, double hyphen; 81 mm. In style it resembles type 1.—Type 13, first smaller roman, almost the same as Sertorius 2, but has double hyphen and larger us; Q joins more closely to the u. 80 mm.— Type 14, small text latin of French style, with curly h; exactly like Hölzel 14, J. Stuchs 10; cf. also Knoblouch 20; ℂ not as the other types (see below); 67 mm.—Type 15, large text latin, with round h, and double hyphen; very little used: 86 mm. only, being kerned.—Type 16, second small roman, on a large body; Aldine face, like M. Schürer 5, &c.; thin ℂ with overhanging top, short single hyphen, sloping comma at first, us rather large, low and heavy; separate short-tailed Q: 88 mm.— Type 17, third small roman, little used; rough and ill justified; double hyphen, ℂ, very thin sloping comma, round comma also; ę and æ, i with dot and with stroke; 75 mm.—Type 18, very small (fourth) roman, more like Quentell 13 in style than the others, but the M differs; large us, single hyphen, round comma, noteworthy &; 66 mm.—Greek type like that of Schumann or W. Schenck's second fount. A very curiously shaped paragraph-mark is characteristic of the Lotters and Schumann. One mark of this form is first used with type 7 in 1503, and others are found with 1 and 4 in and after 1507, with 15 in 1516, 11 in 1518, and 12 in 1520.

Type 1, see fig. 40; 2, see fig. 21; 3, see fig. 14; 4, see fig. 59; *6, 7, see fig. 51; 8, see fig. 22; *11, see fig. 58; *12, see fig. 6; 13, see fig. 7²; 14, see fig. 48; 16, see fig. 9; 18, see fig. 11.

BORDERS. All are one-piece quarto. A, striped ground; at foot three figures, S. Sebastian in middle; signed HS.—B, like A in general scheme, but different saints; Our Lady on left at foot; no signature.—C; at foot children singing from an open music-book; facs. Butsch I. 88.—D, musicians at sides; at foot poets drinking at the Castalian fount.—E; sign of the brazen serpent at foot, perhaps a device; cf. the younger Lotter's border C.—F, white ground; arabesques only, no figures.

DEVICE. a, monogram ML in black on a white shield borne by an old man kneeling; 100 × 85 mm.—See also border E.

INITIALS. α, white on a striped ground; 27 mm.; first used in 1518. In no. 11568 a set of very large plain caps., 29 mm., is found as initials. Several odd (Δ) initials are used; in 1503 (no. 11323) D and E, 24 mm.; letter black, no rectangular outer line: in 1510 (no. 11338) a calligraphic A; P, with the Annunciation, 57 mm., in no. 11343; in Feb. 1512 and 1514 a C, with the Last Supper, like the P of no. 11343, but 52 mm.; in no. 11348 a D, 22 mm. and C, 17 mm., of maiblumen style, and an I, 21–22 mm. with stripy ground; in no. 11386 a large E, letter black, ground in maiblumen style, 45 mm.; N with contest of boxers, 49 mm., no. 11569.

11317. 1501 May 16? Gemma uocabulorum. [DICT.] 4°. P. VII. 137. 4. Types 1–3, 8.

11318. [a. 1501 July 30.] Raym. Peraudi: epistulae pro deliberanda in Turcas expeditione. [PERAULT.] 4°. Types 2, 4.

11319. 1501. Ioh. de KITSCHER: tragicomoedia de hierosolymitana profectione. 4°. P. VII. 136. 2. Types 1, 2, 6; cut.

11320. 1501. HENRICVS de Hassia: secreta sacerdotum. 4°. Types 2, 3, 4.

11321. 1502 March 10. Viatici Misnensis pars aestiualis. [LIT.] 8°. P.VII.140. 27. Types 1, 3, 6, 7, 9; cut.

11322. 1502. SENECA: de quattuor uirtutibus. 4°. P. VII. 140. 30. Types 2, 3, 4, 6, 7.

11323. 1503 [a. Feb. 10]. Buch geistlicher Offenbarungen Mechtildis und Gertrudis. [MATILDA.] 4°. DA. 537b. Types 2, 3, 4, 6; Δ.

11324. 1503. Vergili Georgica. [VIRGILIVS.] 4°. P.VII. 143. 59. Types 2, 3, 4, 6, 7.

11325. 1504 Aug. 15. Gemma uocabulorum. [DICT.] 4°. W. suppl.i.23. Types 1, 2, 3, 7.

11326. 1504. Expositio canonis missae. [LIT.] 4°. P.VII. 148.104. Types 1–3.

11327. 1505 Feb. Hier. EMSER: dialogus de origine propinandi. 4°. P. VII. 152. 134. Types 1, 2; cut.

11328. 1505. Legenda S. Annae. [ANNE.] 4°. P.VII. 152. 143. Types 1, 2, 3.

11329. 1505. SENECA: de quattuor uirtutibus. 4°. W. 343. Types 1–4, 6, 7.

11330. 1505 ? Guillermus: postilla. [BIBLE.] 4°. P. VII. 152. 142. Types 2, 3, 6, 7; cuts. [Imperfect at end.]

11331. 1507 June 24. Chr. CVPINER: elegantissimae annotationes. F°. Types 1, 2, 3.

11332. 1507. Büchlein vom Sterben. [ARS.] 4°. W. 378. Types 1[B], 2, 3; cuts.

11333. 1507. Leon. Aretinus: comoedia Poliscene. [BRUNI.] 4°. P. IX. 485. 200b. Types 2, 3, 6.

11334. 1507. Interpretatio somniorum Danielis. [BIBLE.] 4°. Types 2, 3, 4.

11335. 1507. Legenda S. Annae. [ANNE.] P. IX. 485. 200d. Types 1, 2, 3.

11336. 1508. Hieronymus: epistulae septem. [JEROME.] 4°. P. VII. 161. 227. Types 3, 10, 11; cut.

11337. 1509. HENRICVS de Hassia: secreta sacerdotum. 4°. Types 1[B], 2, 3; cut.

11338. [a. 1510 July 17.] Heinr. von SCHLEINITZ: Brief seinen Streit mit Herzog Heinrich von Sachsen betreffend. F°. Type 11; Δ.

11339. [a. 1510 Aug. 20.] Ein zweiter Brief desselben. obl. Type 11.

11340. [a. 1510 Sept. 2.] Nachtrag zum vorhergehenden Briefe. Type 11. [Half a folio leaf.]

11341. 1510. Iac. HENRICHMANNVS: grammaticae institutiones. 4°. P.VII.167. 290. Types 1, 2, 3, 10, gk.; cut.

11342. n.d.[c.1510?] Aug. Datus: epistula amoris leuitatem improbans. [DATI.] Types 2, 3, 11.

11343. n. d.[c. 1510?] Donatus minor. [PARTES.] 4°. Types 2, 11; Δ.

11344. 1511. LIBANIVS: declamatio de uxore loquaci. 4°. P.VI. 170. 326. Types 2, 3, 12.

11345. n. d.[c. 1511?] ARATOR: actus apostolorum. 4°. H.*1550. Types 3, 12.

11346. 1512 Feb. 20. Mart. POLICHIVS: cursus logici commentariorum collectanea. F°. P.VII. 175. 371. Types 2, 3, 7, 10, 12, gk.; cut, diagr.; Δ.

11347. 1512. Laur. CORVINVS: hortulus elegantiarum. 4°. P.VII.175.373. Types 1, 2, 3, 10.

11348. 1512. HORTVLVS animae. 8°. Types 2, 3, 4, 12bis; cuts; Δ.[Wants 3 leaves.]

11349. 1512. ALANVS de Insulis: doctrinale altum. 4°. Types 2, 3, 7, 11.

11350. [a. 1512 Oct. 11.] Sächsische Ordnung wider die Landstreicher. [SAXONY.] F°. Types 2, 11.

11351. 1512 Oct. 31. Iac. Ziegler: contra Valdensium heresim libri v. [UNITED
        BRETHREN.] F°. P. VII. 175. 372. Type 12.
11352. 1512 Dec. 1. Andr. GVARNA: bellum grammaticale. 4°. P. VII. 176. 377.
        Types 2, 3, 12.
11353. 1513 Dec. Luciani dialogi. [LUCIAN.] 4°. P. VII. 179. 416. Types 2, 10,
        12, gk.
11354. [a. 1514 Jan. 1.] Helius EOBANVS Hessus: siluae duae, Prussia et amor.
        4°. Types 2, 3, 12, 13, gk.
11355. 1514 [May 31.] Mart. POLICHIVS: cursus physici collectanea. F°. Types
        2, 3, 7, 10–13; cut; Δ.
11356. 1514. Leon. Aretinus: comoedia Poliscene. [BRUNI.] 4°. P. VII. 184. 462.
        Types 2, 3, 12.
11357. 1514. LACTANTIVS: de opificio dei. 4°. P. VII. 183. 452. Types 2, 3, 12, 13.
11358. [a. 1514 Oct. 10.] HONORIVS: gemma animae. 4°. P. VII. 183. 453. Types
        1, 2, 3, 10, 12.
11359. 1515 May. Augustinus: de doctrina Christiana. [AUGUSTINE.] F°. P. VII.
        188. 499. Types 1, 2, 3, 12, gk.; cut.
11360. 1515. Ioh. de KITSCHER: uirtutis et fortunae certamen. 4°. Types 2, 3,
        8, 10, 12; a.
11361. 1515. Balth. LICHT: algorismus linealis. 4°. P. VII. 188. 500. Types 1,
        2, 3, 10; diagr.
11362. 1516. Baptista Mantuanus: parthenice tertia. [SPAGNUOLI.] 4°. P. VII.
        197. 590. Types 2, 3, 10, 12, 14; A.
11363. 1516. NILVS: sententiae morales. 4°. P. VII. 193. 547. Types 2, 3, 10,
        12, 15; B.
11364. 1516. PERSIVS: saturae. 4°. P. VII. 193. 552. Types 2, 3, 8, 12.
11365. 1517. Baptista Mantuanus: Wider die Anfechtung des Todes. [SPA-
        GNUOLI.] 4°. DA. 871. Types 2, 10, 11, 12.
11366. 1518 [a. May 30]. LVTHER: resolutiones disputationum de indulgen-
        tiarum uirtute. 4°. P. IX. 494. 640b. Types 2, 3, 10, 16; cut; α.
11367. 1518. [a. Aug. 22]. LUTHER: Auslegung des 109. Psalms. 4°. DA. 896g.
        Types 2, 3, 11, 14; B.
11368. 1518 [a. Aug. 25]. Tranq. Parth. ANDRONICVS: oratio de laudibus elo-
        quentiae. 4°. P. VII. 202. 648. Types 2, 3, 12, 16; B; a.
11369. [a. 1518 Aug. 23.] LVTHER: acta apud legatum apostolicum Augustae.
        4°. P. VI. 171. 274? Types 2, 3, 16; cut.
11370. [a. 1518 Aug. 23.] LVTHER: acta apud legatum … recognita. 4°. Types
        2, 3, 16; cut.
11371. [a. 1518 Sept. 30.] Petrus Mosellanus: paedologia. [SCHADE.] 4°. P. VII.
        205. 676. Type 12, gk.; B.
11372. 1518. LVTHER: sermo de paenitentia. 4°. Types 2, 3, 17; B; α.
11372A. n. d. [c. 1518.] Joh. Tetzel: Vorlegung wider einen Sermon von zwan-
        zig irrigen Artikeln päpstlichen Ablass und Gnade belangend. [PAPAL
        ABSOLUTION.] 4°. W. 1149. Types 2, 3, 11.
11373. n.d. [c. 1518?] LVTHER: ad dialogum Siluestri Prieratis de potestate
        papae responsio. 4°. P. IX. 101. 337. Types 2, 3, 10, 16; B; α.
11374. n.d. [c. 1518?] LVTHER: ad dialogum Siluestri Prieratis … responsio.
        4°. Types 2, 3, 10, 16; B; α.

11375. [a. 1519 Apr. 18.] Andr. BODENSTEIN: Auslegung und Läuterung etlicher heiligen Geschriften. 4°. DA. 954c. Types 2, 3, 10, 11, 14.

11376. 1519 July 27. Ioh. LANGIVS: oratio encomium theologiae disputationis
complectens. 4°. P.VII. 207. 696. Types 3, 12, 16, gk.; C.

11377. [a. 1519 Aug. 13.] Hier. EMSER: de disputatione lipsicensi. 4°. (Not P.
VII. 212. 737.) Types 2, 3, 12; cut; α.

11378. 1519 [a. Aug. 21]. Luther: Auslegung des 109. Psalms. [BIBLE.] 4°. DA.
932f. Types 2, 3, 11, 14; B.

11379. [a. 1519 Sept. 2.] Pet. SVAVENIVS: epistula ad Ioh. Cellarium. 4°. P.VII.
208. 703. Types 3, 12, 18; D; α.

11380. 1519. Andr. BODENSTEIN: epitome de impii iustificatione. 4°. P. VII.
207. 689. Types 2, 10, 16; cut.

11381. 1519. LUTHER: Sermon von der Betrachtung des heiligen Leidens
Christi. 4°. DA. 932qq. Types 2, 3, 8, 11; cut.

11382. 1519. LUTHER: Unterricht auf etliche Artikel. 4°. DA. 932kk. Types 2,
3, 11.

11383. 1519. LVTHER: resolutio super propositione decima tertia. 4°. P. VII.
206. 686. Types 3, 12, 18; D; α.

11384. 1519. LUTHER: Sermon vom Sacrament der Busse. 4°. DA. 932o. Types
2, 3, 11; D.

11385. 1519. LUTHER: kurze Unterweisung wie man beichten soll. 4°. DA.
932mm? Types 2, 3, 11.

11386. [n. b. 1519.] Luther: in epistulam Pauli ad Galatas commentarius. [BIBLE.]
4°. P. IX. 72. 47. Types 12, 18, gk.; D; αΔ.

11387. n. d. [1519?] Siluester de Prierio: replica ad Martinum Luther. [MAZZO-
LINI.] 4°. P. IX. 190. 305. Types 2, 3, 8, 12, 16.

11388. n. d. [1519?] LUTHER: Sermon von der Bereitung zum Sterben. 4°. W.
1558. Types 2, 11; A; α.

11389. n. d. [c. 1519–20?] LVTHER: contra malignum Eckii iudicium. 4°. P.IX.
101. 335. Types 12, 18; D.

11390. n. d. [c. 1519–20?] LUTHER: Auslegung deutsch des Vaterunser. 4°.
W. 1127. Types 2, 3, 8, 11; B.

[For continuation see Meissen, and press 16.]

ix. WOLFGANG STÖCKEL, first press.

Address (1514–5): in platea Grimmensi, e regione aedis diui Pauli. In 1505 (colophon to
W. 320) he calls himself Wolfgang Müller, sonst Stöcklin.

TYPES. Types 1 (latin text gothic like Flach jun. 3, Zel 5, &c.; open V, C, 82 mm.); 2 (large
round, normal; short letters 5 mm.); 3 (small text latin with round h, 73½ mm.; in 1501 and
afterwards the hyphen, which is double, differs from that of 1498; the type is not used 1502–12;
in and after 1513 it has ¶ (so also in 1501) and the T of type 6); for these see part i.—Type 5,
narrow church text like Kachelofen 8, Lotter 2, W. Schenck 6, &c.; characteristic (but also
used by Joh. Rhau) is the double hyphen set high up; in the later books it is sometimes reversed,
and is then low down.—Type 6, small text schwabacher, like Kachelofen 12, Lotter 4, W. Schenck
5, &c.; 89 mm. No paragraph-mark in 1501; C in 1503, thick ¶ in and after 1504 (C here
and there in 1520); short comma from 1503: double hyphen (none in 1501); from 1507 this
is different, being more horizontal.—Type 7, very small, like Kachelofen 10 or Lotter sen. 7; C
in 1510; 61–2 mm.—Type 8, large latin text like Miller 6 or Grim 2, 98 mm.; short comma,
short double hyphen rather low, thin C; one book of 1519 has a roman æ.—Type 9, square

canon like Lotter 3, G. Stuchs 15, &c.; not as Landsberg 7.—Greek type in 1519 like W. Schenck's
second fount.

Type 1, see fig. 38 ; 2, see fig. 24 ; 3, see fig. 45 ; 5, see fig. 21 ; 6, see fig. 59 ; 7, see fig. 51*; 8, see fig. 35 ; 9, see fig. 14¹.

BORDERS. A, four-piece quarto, very curious and ugly ; cross-hatched ground. Copied by Thanner and Schumann.——B, one-piece quarto, narrow : pillars and a flat arch ; at foot angels adoring the Christ-child behind a pavement.

DEVICES. a, like b, but smaller; cut on the folding plate in no. 11391.——b, black ground, a pickaxe set upright on a base of three steps; WS; 57 × 42 mm. ; cracked at base from 1504 ; from 1510 also at top.——c, similar to b but larger, more shading : BMS (i.e. Baccalaureus Monacensis Stöckel) ; 87½ × 63½ mm.——d, a ribbon with W on a shield : 25 × 95–6 mm.——A cut of a wodow carrying the Leipzig arms (not strictly a device) is found in no. 11450, 11455, 11461, 11478, 11484, 11485, 11493.

11391. 1501. Magnus HVNDT: anthropologium. 4°. P. VII. 138. 12. Types 3, 5, 6; cuts, diagr.; a, b.

11392. [n. b. 1501.] Ioh. Lindholz: quaestiones cum textu Thomae Aquinatis de ente et essentia. [THOMAS.] F°. Types 1, 2, 3.

11393. 1503. Laur. Coruinus: hortulus elegantiarum. 4°. P. VII. 146. 82. Types 3, 5, 6; cut.

11394. n. d. [c. 1503?] Petrus Rauennas: artificiosa memoria. [TOMMAI.] 4°. Types 5, 6.

[For continuation see Wittenberg, and press 13.]

x. JACOB THANNER.

TYPES. Type 1 (small text schwabacher, single hyphen; the remarkable paragraph mark used till 1501 is replaced in 1503 by a ¶ of medium thickness : at the same time a new us comes in, but of this both sorts are used together till 1508, when the older form disappears. The hyphen is used also as comma from April 1504; 88 mm.); 2 (wide large type like Landsberg 5 or Schenck 2 ; a large ¶ is sometimes found) ; for these see part i.—Type 3, square canon like Landsberg 7 or the Erfurt types (Schenck 7, Knapp 1) ; short letters 10 mm. ; not like Lotter 3, &c.—Type 4, narrow church (replacing 2), like Lotter 2, Schumann 2, Stöckel 5 : hyphen rather lower than in Lotter 2, higher than when reversed in Stöckel 5.—Type 5, small type, very round, extremely like W. Schenck 8, but 63 mm. ; ¶ used with it.—Type 6, large text schwabacher = Lotter 11, but the slope of the hyphen is less steep ; ¶ like that of 1.—Type 7, text roman = Lotter 12 ; the Q is from the first separate, as with Lotter in 1520 ; double hyphen, that of 6 being also found ; ç ; long sloping comma except in the Reuchlin of 1515, where a round comma is used ; 94 mm.

Type 1, see fig. 59; *2, see fig. 17; 3, see fig. 14B; 4, see fig. 21; 5, see fig. 50; 6, see fig. 58; 7, see fig. 6.

BORDER. A, four-piece quarto, a copy of Stöckel A ; the ground instead of being cross-hatched is powdered with irregular dots. Cf. one of Schumann's X borders, another copy of Stöckel A.

DEVICES. a (used before 1500) square, black ground ; i t with trademark ; 34 × 33 mm.——b, shield-shaped, dotted ground, otherwise as a ; 31 × 28 mm.

11395. 1501. Expositio Donati. [DONATVS.] 4°. P. VII. 139. 19. Types 1, 2.

11396. 1503 June 23. Greg. Breytkopff: carmen ad D. Ioannem baptistam. [JOHN.] 4°. P. VII. 147. 94. Types 1, 2.

11397. 1503 Sept. 15. OVIDIVS: amoris remedia. 4°. P. IX. 482. 100b. Types 1, 2.

11398. 1503 Oct. 9. Pet. HAEDVS: de amoris generibus. 4°. P. VII. 147. 91. Types 1, 2.

11399. 1504 Jan. 24. CICERO: rhetorica ad Herennium. F°. P. VII. 150. 116. Types 1, 2; a.

129

R

LEIPZIG.
x. Jacob
Thanner.

11400. 1504 Apr. 1. PETRARCA: remedia aduersae fortunae. 4°. P.XI.430.116b.
Types 1, 2.

11401. 1504 July 9. COMPVTVS nouus astronomiae fundamentum continens. 4°.
P. VII. 151. 129. Types 1, 2; a.

11402. 1504 July 30. BARTHOLOMAEVS Coloniensis: epistula mythologica. 4°.
P. VII. 150. 119. Types 1, 2.

11403. 1504 July 31. Homeri Ilias per Pindarum thebanum traducta. [HOMER.]
4°. Types 1, 2.

11404. 1504 Aug. 8. Hieronymi de honorandis parentibus epistula. [JEROME.]
4°. Types 1, 2; a.

11405. 1504 Aug. 9. Hieronymi de muliere septies percussa epistula. [JE-
ROME.] 4°. Types 1, 2.

11406. 1504. Greg. BREYTKOPFF: de stricta diui Hieronymi uita carmen. 4°.
P. IX. 483. 119d. Types 1, 2.

11407. 1504. Ang. Fundius: oratio nomine Senensium apud Iulium ij. [ANGELO.]
4°. P. VII. 151. 123. Types 1, 2; a.

11408. 1504. Tho. PENTZELDT: modus studendi. 4°. P. VII. 151. 125. Types
1, 2; a.

11409. n. d. [c. 1504.] HORATIVS: epistulae. 4°. H. 8912; part i, no. 3092.
Types 1, 2.

11410. 1505 Jan. 9. Hier. de VALLIBVS: iesuida. 4°. P. VII. 154. 160. Types
1, 3, 4; a.

11411. 1505 [a. June 18]. Baptista Mantuanus: in laudem Ioannis baptistae
carmen. [SPAGNUOLI.] 4°. P. XI. 431. 167b. Types 1, 3, 4; a.

11412. 1505. OVIDIVS: Oenone Paridi. 4°. Types 1, 3, 4.

11413. 1506 Jan. 16. Petrus de Aliaco: super meteorologica Aristotelis.
[AILLY.] 4°. P. VII. 157. 187. Types 1, 3, 4, 5; a.

11414. [a. 1506 Jan. 20.] Etliche der Stadt Leipzig Gesetze. [LEIPSIC.] 4°. DA.
570b (note); W. 359. Types 1, 3, 4.

11414A. 1506 [a. Feb. 6]. Bernardus Siluester: epistula de regimine domus.
[BERNARD.] 4°. P. IX. 485. 189c. Types 1, 3, 4.

11415. 1506 July 11. COMPVTVS nouus. 4°. P. VII. 157. 191. Types 1, 3, 4, 5.

11416. 1506 July 17. Pand. Collenutius: Agenoria, Alethia. [COLLENUCCIO.]
4°. P. VII. 157. 192. Types 1, 3, 4, 5.

11417. 1507 Oct. 15. Rod. AGRICOLA: Anna mater. 4°. P. IX. 487. 215d. Types
1, 3, 4.

11418. 1508 Feb. 4. Geo. DOTTANVS: carmen lysitelilogon. 4°. P. XI. 432.
241c. Types 1, 3, 4, 5.

11419. 1508. MANCINVS: de passione domini. 4°. P. VII. 162. 242. Types 1,
3, 4, 5; a.

11420. 1508. PHALARIS: epistulae. 4°. P. VII. 162. 244. Types 1, 3; a.

11421. 1509 Jan. 3. Augustinus: de essentia diuinitatis. [AUGUSTINE.] 4°.
P. VII. 166. 278. Types 1, 3, 4, 5.

11422. 1510. Bapt. Mantuanus: parthenice prima. [SPAGNUOLI.] 4°. P. VII.
170. 322(1). Types 1, 3, 4, 6; a.

11423. 1510. SALLVSTIVS: bellum Iugurthinum. F°. P. VII. 169. 316. Types
3, 4, 6.

11424. 1510 Dec. 21. Speculum reuelationum Mechtildis et Gertrudis. [MA-
TILDA.] 4°. P. VII. 169. 315. Types 1, 3, 4; a.

11425. 1511. CICERO: paradoxa. F°. P.VII. 173. 347. Types 3, 4, 6; a.   LEIPZIG.
11426. 1511. Laur. CORVINVS: latinum idioma. 4°. P.VII. 174. 356. Types   x. Jacob
    1, 3, 4, 7.   Thanner.
11427. 1512 Jan. 30. Paruulus philosophiae naturalis. [BREVTKOPFF.] F°.
    Types 3–7; a.
11428. 1512 June 1. IVVENCVS: historia euangelica. F°. Types 3–7; a.
11429. 1512. Politianus: silua cui titulus Rusticus. [AMBROGINI.] 4°. P.VII.
    178. 403. Types 3, 4, 7.
11430. 1512. Hier. de VALLIBVS: iesuida. 4°. P.VII. 178. 399. Types 3, 4, 7.
11431. 1513. BARTHOLOMAEVS Coloniensis: epistula mythologica. 4°. P.VII.
    181. 435. Types 1, 3, 4, 5, 7.
11432. 1513. Sabellicus: breuiores epistulae. [COCCIVS.] 4°. Types 1, 3, 4, 7.
11433. 1515. Ioh. SVLPICIVS: carmen de facetia mensae. 4°. Types 1, 3, 6, 7.
11434. 1515. HORATIVS: sermones. 4°. P.VII. 191. 527. Types 3, 4, 6, 7.
11435. 1515. Ioh. REVCHLIN: scenica progymnasmata. 4°. P.VII. 191. 528.
    Types 3, 4, 7. [Woodcut music.]
11436. 1516. HORATIVS: ars poetica. 4°. P.XI. 438. 566f. Types 3, 4, 5, 7.
11437. 1517. SEDVLIVS: carmen paschale. 4°. Types 3, 4, 5, 7; A.
11438. (1517–18.) Simon Eisenmann: Kalender auf das Jahr 1518. bs. Types
    1, 3, 4; cuts. [Print Room.]
11439. 1518. Luther: die sieben Busspsalmen mit deutscher Auslegung.
    [BIBLE.] 4°. DA. 888b. Types 1, 3, 4, 6; cut; b.
11440. 1519. Luther: die sieben Busspsalmen. [BIBLE.] 4°. DA. 926b. Types
    1, 3, 4, 6; cut; b.
11441. 1520. Luther: die sieben Busspsalmen. [BIBLE.] 4°. DA. 968b. Types
    1, 3, 4, 6; cut; b.

xi. CONRAD KACHELOFEN, third press.

Kachelofen's work at this period is very intermittent. In 1501 the association of 1500 with
Lotter was continued: one book of this year is recorded (P.IX. 480. 1b; cf. H. 11330), but no
other till 1509, to which year four books belong (P.VII. 163. 250–253). Next comes 1512, with
three books (P.XI. 434–5. 365b–d), and 1516, also with three (P.VII. 191. 530, W. 1001, and
the Hortulus animae).

TYPES. Types 10 (very small; cf. Lotter 7); 11 (canon, cf. Lotter 3); 12 (small text
schwabacher, single hyphen; cf. Lotter 4); see part i. Type 12 in 1516 has a paragraph mark
like that of Lotter.

DEVICE. a, a shield, dotted black ground; CK and trademark in white; 27 × 26 mm.

11442. 1516 Feb. 23. HORTVLVS animae tho dude. 8°. Types 10, 11, 12; cuts; a.

xij. MARCUS BRANDT.

The only book assigned to Marcus Brandt at this time is the Responsio in errores Simonis Pistoris
de malo franco per Martinum Pollich, P.VII. 139. 23; it is a rejoinder to the reply of Pistoris
published in 1500 (Hain *13021). An earlier book (1498) in the same controversy, also printed
by Brandt, is cited by Hain 13020; but this entry and that of Panzer probably rest on the same
doubtful authority; and the existence of this printer or his identity with Marcus Brandiss can at
present hardly be affirmed with certainty.

xiij. WOLFGANG STÖCKEL, third press.

Stöckel's work at Wittenberg seems to have been limited to the Parthenice prima of Bapt. Mantuanus and the first part of no. 11824(see quotationfrom colophon); the book was presumably finished at Leipzig.

TYPES, &c. See press 9 above.

(1504 Apr. 20. Petrus Rauennas: compendium iuris canonici. See no. 11824.)

11443. 1505 Aug.7. Baptista Mantuanus: elegiae duae.[SPAGNUOLI.]4°. P.VII. 154. 155. Types 5, 6; b.

11444. 1505. THOMAS Aquinas: de sacramento eucharistiae. 4°. P.VII.154.158. Types 5, 6.

11445. 1505. ALGORISMVS linealis. 4°. Types 5,7,8; diagr.

11446. n. d. [c. 1505.]Sabellicus: carmina de B.V.Maria.[COCCIUS.]4°. H.14062? (Part i. no. 3111.) Types 5, 6; b.

11447. 1507 July 31. Virgilius Wellendorfer: decalogium.[VIRGIL.] 4°. P.VII. 159. 210. Types 5, 6 [new hyphens], 8; cuts, diagr.

11448. 1507. ALGORISMVS de integris. 4°. P. VII. 159, 212. Types 5, 6; diagr.

11449. 1507. Lectura super titulo de regulis iuris libro vi. [ROME.] 4°. P.VII.159. 213. Types 5, 6, 8.

11450. 1507.CHILIANVS: comoedia parthenices Dorotheae passionem depingens. 4°. P. IX. 486. 214 b. Types 5, 6; cut; c.

11451. n. d. [c. 1508.] De uisitatione beatissimae uirginis Mariae carmen.[MARY.] 4°. Types 5, 6.

11452. 1509. Flauius AVIANVS: apologus adulescentulis utilissimus. 4°. P.VII. 165. 274. Types 5, 6.

11453. [a. 1509 Oct. 9.] Henr. RYBISCH: disceptatio an uxor sit ducenda. 4°. P. XI. 433. 284 d. Types 5, 6, 8.

11454. 1510 Jan. 15. Baptista Mantuanus: eclogae.[SPAGNUOLI.]4°. Types 5,6;b.

11455. 1510. Auctoritates Aristotelis et aliorum philosophorum. [BEDA.] 4°. P.VII. 167. 291. Types 5, 6, 7; cut; b.

11456. 1510. Compendiosa capitis physici declaratio. [CAPVT.] 4°. P.VII.169. 312. Types 5, 6, 8; cuts.

11457. 1511 March. Chr. SCHEVRL: de sacerdotum praestantia. [For Georg Kelner.] 4°. P. VII. 172. 342. Types 5, 6; cut. [Print Room.]

11458. 1511. Herm. Buschius: in artem Donati commentarius.[BUSCHE.] 4°. P. VII. 174. 362. Types 5, 6.

11459. 1512. GVLIELMVS Aruernus: dialogus de sacramentis. 4°. P. VII. 178. 396. Types 5, 6.

11460. 1513 [a. June 20]. Greg. BREYTKOPFF: compendium siue paruulus antiquorum. 4°. P. VII. 181. 429. Types 3, 5, 8; diagr.

11461. 1513. Barthol. de Vsingen: interpretatio Donati minoris. [DONATUS.] 4°. P. VII. 181. 431. Types 3, 5, 8, 9; cut.

11462. 1514 March 23. Hier. DVNGERSHEYM: confutatio apologetici cuiusdam. 4°. P. VII. 185. 474. Types 3, 5, 8; cuts.

11463. 1514. Hier. CINGVLARIVS: synonymorum collectanea. 4°. P. VII. 185. 469. Types 3, 5, 8, 9.

11464. 1515. CINGVLARIVS: de componendis epistulis. 4°. P. VII. 189. 507. Types 3, 5, 8, 9.

11465. 1515. CINGVLARIVS: artis grammaticae obseruationes. 4°. P. VII. 188.
506. Types 3, 5, 8, 9.
11466. 1516. Hier. Dungersheim: conclusiones in summam Thomae Aquinatis. [THOMAS.] 4°. P. VII. 194. 558. Types 3, 5, 8, 9; A.
11467a. 1516. Virg. Wellendorfer: ualelogium (A–I). Types 3, 5, 8, 9; cut; b.
  b. n.d. id.: eleutherologium (A, B). Types 3, 5, 8, 9; cut.
  c. n.d. id.: encenilogium (A–C). Types 3, 5, 8, 9, cut.
  d. n.d. id.: annotatio peregrina (A). Types 3, 5, 8; cut.
  e. 1516. id.: correctoria et repertoria (A, B). Types 3, 5, 8, 9; cut. [ISO-CRATES.] 4°. P. VII. 194. 559.
11468. 1517. Henr. de Odendorf: repetitio capituli Omnis utriusque sexus. [ROME.] 4°. P. VII. 198. 605. Types 3, 5, 8, 9; cut.
11469. 1517. CALPVRNIVS: bucolica. 4°. Types 5, 8.
11470. 1517. Alb. KRANTZ: institutiones logicae. 4°. P. VII. 198. 606. Types 3, 5, 8; cut, diagr.; A.
11471. n.d. [n. a. 1518.] Oratio haec est funebris in laudem Ioannis Cerdonis. [CERDO.] 8°. Types 3, 5, 8.
11472. 1518. QVINTILIANVS: institutionum oratoriarum liber primus. 4°. P. VII. 203. 652. Types 3, 5, 8; B.
11473. 1518. Hier. DVNGERSHEYM: historia uitae Petri de Murone, Celestini v. papae. 4°. P. IX. 117. 115; XI. 438. 650b. Types 3, 5, 8.
11474. 1518. LVTHER: sermo de uirtute excommunicationis. 4°. Types 5, 8; cut.
11475. 1518. LUTHER: Sermon von dem Ablass und Gnade. 4°. DA. 896k. Types 5, 6.
11476. 1518. Wie durch Gottfried von Bullen das gelobte Land gewonnen ist worden. [GODFREY.] 4°. DA. 918. Types 5, 6; cut.
11477. n.d. [c. 1518.] Pomp. MELA: cosmographia. 4°. P. VII. 177. 394. Types 3, 5, 8, 9; cut; B.
11478. [a. 1519 July 25.] Excusatio Eckii ad ea quae falso sibi Ph. Melanchthon adscripsit. [JOHANN.] 4°. P. VII. 211. 734. Types 5, 6; cuts.
11479. 1519. MELANCHTHON: defensio aduersus Eckium. 4°. P. VII. 208. 699. Types 5, 6, gk.
11480. [a. 1519 Aug. 11.] Petrus SVAVENIVS: apologia pro Petro Mosellano. 4°. P. VII. 208. 702. Types 5, 6, gk.; A.
11481. 1519. LUTHER: Sermon von dem Gebet und Prozession in der Kreuzwoche. 4°. Types 5, 6; cut.
11482. 1519. LUTHER: Sermon von dem ehelichen Stande. 4°. DA. 932t. Types 5, 6.
11483. 1519. Ioh. CELLARIVS: elogium Neminis Montani. 4°. P. VII. 209. 708. Types 3, 5, 6, 8, gk.
11484. 1519. NVLLVS Lipsensis respondet Nemini Wittenbergensi. 4°. P. VII. 208. 700. Types 3, 5, 6, 8, gk.; cut; d.
11485. 1519. LVTHER: resolutiones super propositionibus suis. 4°. P. VII. 209. 709. Types 3, 5, 8; cut.
11486. 1520. LUTHER: Sermon von dem Sacrament der Taufe. 4°. DA. 973zz. Types 5, 6; cut.
11487. 1520. LUTHER: Sermon von dem Sacrament der Taufe. 4°. DA. 973yy. Types 5, 6; cut.

11488. 1520. LUTHER: Sermon von dem Gebet und Prozession . . . 4°. DA. 974c. Types 5, 6; cut.

11489. 1520. LUTHER: Sermon von dem Bann. 4°. W. 1549 (suppl. i.). Types 5, 6; B.

11490. 1520. LUTHER: kurze Unterweisung wie man beichten soll. 4°. W. 1600. Types 5, 6. [Imprint at end.]

11491. 1520. LUTHER: kurze Unterweisung wie man beichten soll. 4°. Types 5, 6. [Imprint on title.]

11492. 1520. LUTHER: Sermon von der Bereitung zum Sterben. 4°. DA. 973aa. Types 5, 6; A.

11493. 1520. LUTHER: Sermon von dem Ablass und Gnade. 4°. DA. 973h. Types 5, 6; cut.

11494. 1520. LUTHER: an den christlichen Adel deutscher Nation. 4°. DA. 974u. Types 5, 6.

11495. 1520. Andr. BODENSTEIN: von geweihtem Wasser und Salz. 4°. DA. 988e. Types 5, 6.

11496. 1520. Laz. Spengler: Schutzrede und christliche Antwort ... [LUTHER.] 4°. W. 1634. Types 5, 6; B.

11497. 1520. Mich. ROSSWICK: compendiaria musicae artis editio. 4°. Types 3, 5, 8, 9; cut. [Woodcut music.]

11498. 1520. Aug. ALVELD: Sermon wider Luther. 4°. DA. 984. Types 3, 5, 6, 8. [8 ff.]

11499. n.d. [1520.] LUTHER: Antwort auf die Zettel so unter des Officials zu Stolpen Siegel ist ausgegangen. 4°. W. 1500. Types 5, 6.

11500. n.d. [1520.] LUTHER: Verklärung etlicher Artikel . . . 4°. W. suppl. i. 172. Types 5, 6. [2ª ends: oder orden.]

11501. n.d. [1520.] LUTHER: Verklärung etlicher Artikel ... 4°. Types 5, 6. [2ª ends: fryd vñ.]

11502. n.d. [a. 1520 June 23.] Aug. ALVELD: tractatus de communione sub utraque specie. 4°. P. IX. 164. 14. Types 3, 5, 6, 8; large caps. [Woodcut hebrew.]

11503. n.d. [c. 1520.] Bedenken des AGRICOLA Boius. 4°. W. 1329. Types 5, 6; B.

xiv. VALENTIN SCHUMANN.

Schumann's address is given in 1515 as: in regione equestri. Cf. that of Landsberg.

TYPES. Type 1, square canon, like Lotter 3; short letters 11 mm.—Type 2, narrow church type like Lotter 2; hyphen rather longer than Lotter's but also medial.—Type 3, text roman, exactly as Lotter 12, but short sloping comma instead of a round one; double hyphen; 92 mm.— Type 4, round latin text gothic, beautiful and distinctive; short sloping comma; double hyphen; low open us; 79 mm. 4ᴮ, the same germanised.—Type 5, middle roman like J. Schöffer 12, Knoblouch 7, M. Schürer 1, &c.; double hyphen; comma mixt in the earlier books, later the round form only; 88 mm.—Type 6, small gothic, resembling Lotter 7; double hyphen.—Type 7, very large roman capitals, for the most part used only as initials; 17 mm. high.—Type 8, small roman, very like Lotter 18, but M is normal, and the caps. are used alone on a larger body in Froben's fashion: double hyphen; 65 mm.—Type 9, new text roman, first used (noui characteres) in May 1520. Very like Schott 5*, Knoblouch 8, M. Schürer 8*, &c.; double hyphen; 109 mm. A paragraph mark, similar to that of Lotter, and used by no other printer but these two and Kachelofen, is used with types 2 (once only), 4, 5, 6, 8, 9.—Greek type, usually with accents, and on a body much larger than that of type 5; but in 1519 it was recast on the body of type 5

without accents, and both founts are used thenceforward. In one book of 1519 it is even found
with type 8. In January 1520 Schumann promises to produce a new and better greek type.—
The hebrew and music are printed from wood blocks.

Type 1, see fig. 14¹; 2, see fig. 21; 3, see fig. 6; 5, see fig. 8; 6, see fig. 51²; 8, see fig. 11; 9, see
fig. 3.

BORDERS. A, one-piece quarto, with the arms of Archbp. Albrecht of Mainz in it, leaving
but a sill for the text: at foot SS. Maurice, Martin, Stephen.—B, one-piece quarto, style of
Wechtelin, a reduced copy in reverse of Knoblouch D (=Beck D); facs. Butsch I. 70.—Cb,
one-piece octavo, musical border-device.—D, one-piece octavo, vernicle at head; at foot a harper
before a muse holding music; a dog gnawing a bone between them.—E, one-piece quarto, white,
very ugly; at sides women encircled by snakes.—F, similar to E, but at sides boys playing bagpipe
and flute: Leipzig arms at foot.—Schumann's X borders are conspicuous, the pieces most
frequently used being well designed (copied by Landsberg). One piece, with a monkey, is useful
for dating by; the left end grows gradually shorter: another, representing an owl surrounded
by other birds with a blank label, (1514) was recut in 1520 with the letters MHAV, and copied
by Landsberg. Three pieces have the arms of Leipzig; (a) also with those of Saxony, 108 × 22
mm.; (b) and (c) differ only in the ground, which is black dotted in (b), white in (c); 79 × 25
mm. Three composite borders are more definite; one, used in no. 11505A and 11523, is a copy
of Stöckel A; the second, in a remarkable style, seems to have a continuous design, but is usually
found scattered; once only, in no. 11546, complete. The third, used in no. 11545, has a figure
of Judith (IVDIT) on the right side, and at the foot a piece containing the monogram HK (Hans
Knapp?).

DEVICES. a, 53 × 44 mm., monogram VS and letters inserted in type (explained in May
1520 thus: Quid forsan prae se gestent insignia quaeris? Illa meum nomen, technima et illa
notant); these are LD 1516–1518; MVLD 1519–1520.—b, see border C.—c, a woman holding
a book, seated in a car; four persons draw her; below, the monogram. 50 × 107 mm.

INITIALS. Only odd initials are used by Schumann: a single black-grounded initial in the
Ausonius of 1515; in Nov. 1517 a C, black ground with stars and a fleur de lis, 24 mm. (a
similar A in no. 11557), and a calligraphic S (again used in 1520), 29–30 mm.; white N on plain
black ground, 31 mm. (1518): P, white ground with vine pattern, black letter, 29 mm. (1519): E,
black ground with arabesque ornament, 34 mm. (1519).

11504. 1514. BARTHOLOMAEVS Coloniensis: epistula mythologica. 4°. P. XI.
436. 486b. Types 1, 2, 3, 4; X.

11505. 1515 June 18. SALLVSTIVS: Iugurtha. 4°. P. VII. 191. 525(2). Types 1,
2, 5; X.

11505A. 1515 [a. Oct. 23]. AVSONIVS: opera. 4°. P. VII. 190. 523. Types 3, 5,
gk.; X; Δ.

11506. 1515. Q. SERENVS Sammonicus: praecepta medicinae. 4°. P. VII. 189.
515. Types 1, 2, 3, 4, gk.; X.

11507. 1515. COMPVTVS nouus ecclesiasticus. 4°. Types 1, 2, 4, 5; cut; X.

11508. 1515. Homeri Ilias per Pindarum Thebanum traducta. [HOMER.] 4°.
P. IX. 493. 522c. Types 1–5.

11509. n. d. [c. 1515.] Reliquiae cum indulgentiis monasterii S. Maximini
Treueris. [MAXIMIN.] 4°. Types 1, 4, 5; cut.

11510. n. d. [c. 1515.] Reliquiae indulgentiaeque ecclesiae S. Paulini Treueris.
[PAULINUS.] 4°. Types 2, 4, 5; cut; Y.

11511. 1516. Laur. CORVINVS: dialogus de mentis saluberrima persuasione. 4°.
P. VII. 197. 589. Types 1, 5; X. [Woodcut music.]

11512. 1516 [a. Apr. 1]. Ric. CROCVS: tabulae graecas literas discere cupientibus
utiles. 4°. P. VII. 196. 579. Types 2, 5, gk.; cut; a.

11513. 1519 May 31. Henr. STROMER: obseruationes aduersus pestilentiam.
4°. P. VII. 195. 569. Type 5; A; a.

11514. 1516. CICERO: Paradoxa. 4°. Types 1, 4, 5, gk.; X.

135

LEIPZIG.
xiv. Valentin
Schumann.

11515. 1516. Theod. GAZA: liber quartus de constructione. 4°. P. VII. 196.
577. Type 5, gk.; A; a.

11516. 1517. Leon. Aretinus: comoedia Poliscene. [BRUNI.] 4°. Types 1, 2, 5;
cut; X.

11517. 1517. Ioh. MVRMELIVS: pappa puerorum. 4°. P. VII. 201. 632. Types 1,
2, 4, 5, 6; X; a.

11518. 1517 Nov. Andr. ORNITHOPARCHVS: musicae actiuae micrologus. 4°.
Types 1, 2, 4, 5, (7); diagr.; X; a; Δ. [Woodcut music.]

11519. n.d. [c. 1517–18.] Chr. HEGENDORFF: encomium sobrietatis. 4°. P. VII.
210. 727. Types 2, 5, (7), 8 [caps.], gk.; B.

11520. 1518. LVTHER: sermo de paenitentia. 4°. P. VII. 205. 669. Types 1, 2,
5; X.

11521. 1518 Aug. Pet. Mosellanus: oratio de linguarum cognitione. [SCHADE.]
4°. P. VII. 205. 674. Types 5, 7, 8, gk.; cut. [On vellum.]

11522. [a. 1518 Aug. 13.] ISOCRATES: de bello fugiendo. 4°. P. IX. 495. 673b.
Types 5, 7, 8, gk.; cut; a. [On vellum.]

11523. 1518 [a. Sept. 17]. Vlr. de HVTTEN: aula. 4°. P. VII. 204. 666. Types
5, 7, gk.; X; Δ.

11524. 1518. Georgius RHAW: enchiridion musicae. 8°. Types 5, (7), 8, gk.;
cut; Y. [Woodcut music.]

11525. 1518. LUTHER: Sermon von dem Ablass und Gnade. 4°. W. suppl. i.
147. Types 1, 2, 4ᴮ; X.

11526. (1518.) LUTHER: eine Freiheit des Sermons päpstlichen Ablass und
Gnade belangend. 4°. DA. 896q = W. suppl. i. 146. Types 1, 2, 4ᴮ;
cut; X.

11527. [a. 1518 Aug. 23.] LVTHER: acta apud legatum apostolicum Augustae.
4°. Types 1, 2, 5; cut.

11528. [a. 1518 Aug. 24.] Vlr. de HVTTEN: Οὖτις, Nemo. 4°. P. VII. 204. 665;
B. xv. 3. Types 5, (7); cut.

11529. [a. 1518 Nov. 28.] LVTHER: appellatio ad concilium. 4°. Types 1, 2, 5, (7).

11530. n. d. [c. 1518–19.] LVTHER: sermo de digna praeparatione cordis. 4°.
Types 1, 2, 5. [No cut; 3ᵃ ends: omnes esse.]

11531. n. d. [c. 1518–19.] LVTHER: sermo de digna praeparatione cordis. 4°.
Types 1, 2, 5; cut. [3ᵃ ends: omnes eē.]

11532. n. d. [c. 1518–19.] LUTHER: Predigt von der würdigen Bereitung zum
Sacrament. 4°. W. 1223. Types 1, 2, 4ᴮ, (7); cut.

11533. n. d. [c. 1518–19?] Eine Offenbarung und Gesicht König Sigismunds.
[SIGISMUND.] 4°. (Not W. 1613–14.) Types 2, 4ᴮ; cut.

11534. 1519. Baptista Mantuanus: parthenice secunda. [SPAGNUOLI.] 4°. Types
1, 2, 5, (7), 8; X; a.

11535. 1519. WIMPHELING: elegantiae maiores. 4°. P. VII. 212. 741. Types 1,
2, 5, (7), 8, gk.; X; a.

11536. 1519. Erasmus: paraphrasis in epistulam Pauli ad Galatas. [BIBLE.] 4°.
Types 5, 7, 8 [caps.]; XY; a; Δ.

11537. 1519. LVTHER: decem praecepta wittenbergensi praedicata populo. 4°.
P. VII. 209. 713. Types 1, 2, 4, 5, 7, 8, gk.; cuts; X; a.

11538. 1519. SALLVSTIVS: Iugurtha. 4°. P. IX. 496. 729c. Types 1, 2, 5, 6, 8; X.

11539. 1519. ERASMVS: enchiridion militis christiani. 4°. Types 4, 5, 7, 8, gk.;
Y; a; Δ.

11540. 1519. Chr. HEGENDORFF: encomium ebrietatis. 4°. P. VII. 210. 726.
Types 1, 2, 4, 5, (7), 8, gk.; Cb.

11541. 1519. LUTHER: Auslegung deutsch des Vaterunser. 4°. DA. 932b.
Types 1, 2, 4[B], 8; cuts.

11542. 1519. LVTHER: sermo de uirtute excommunicationis. 4°. P. VII. 209.
714. Types 1, 2, 5, (7), 8; cut.

11543. 1519. LUTHER: Sermon von dem Wucher. 4°. DA. 932aa. Types 1,
2, 4[B]; cut; a.

11544. 1519. LVTHER: sermo de triplici iustitia. 4°. P. VII. 209. 715. Types
1, 2, 5; cut.

11545. 1519. Chr. HEGENDORFF: encomium somni. 4°. P. VII. 210. 725. Types
1, 2, 5, (7), gk. ; X.

11546. n. d. [a. 1519 July.] Joh. RUBIUS: ein neues Büchlein von der Disputation zu Leipzig gehalten. 4°. W. 1264. Types 1, 2, 4[B]; X.

11547. n. d. [a. 1519 July.] Andr. BODENSTEIN: epistula aduersus ineptam in-
uentionem Ioh. Eckii. 4°. Types 1, 2, 5, 7, 8; X; c.

11548. 1520 Jan. 27. Phil. Mich. NOVENIANVS: elementale hebraicum. 4°. P.
VII. 216. 778. Types 2, 5, (7), 8, gk.; X. [Woodcut hebrew.]

11549a. [1520.] Georg RHAW: enchiridion utriusque musicae practicae (a–m).
Types 5, 8, 9, gk. ; Cb; cuts.

    b. 1520. Enchiridion musicae mensuralis (A–N). Types 2, 5, 8, 9, gk.;
diagr.; D; a; Δ.

    c. 1520 May. Isagoge Ioannis Galliculi de compositione cantus (A–E).
Types 5, 8, 9; X; a. 8°. [Woodcut music.]

11550. 1520. LVTHER: confitendi ratio. 4°. P. VII. 215. 763. Types 1, 2, 5, 9;
cut.

11551. 1520. LUTHER: Sermon von dem Sacrament des Leichnams Christi. 4°.
DA. 973mm. Types 1, 2, 4[B], cut; a.

11552. 1520. Chr. HEGENDORFF: comoedia noua. 4°. Types 5, 9, gk.; cut; E.
[Woodcut music.]

11553. 1520. Franc. FABER: silua cui titulus Bohemia. 4°. P. VII. 216. 776.
Types 8, 9, gk.; F.

11554. (1520.) Andr. BODENSTEIN: von geweichtem Wasser und Salz. 4°. (Not
DA. 988g ?) Types 1, 2, 4[B].

11555. n. d. [1520.] LUTHER: Antwort auf die Zettel so unter des Officials zu
Stolpen Siegel ist ausgegangen. 4°. DA. 973uu ? Types 1, 2, 4[B]; X.

11556. [a. 1520 June 23.] LUTHER: an den christlichen Adel deutscher Nation.
4°. W. 1497. Types 1, 2, 4[B]; cut. [Wants leaf 1.]

11557. [a. 1520 Dec. 10.] Exustionis antichristianorum decretalium acta.
[ROME.] 4°. P. IX. 122. 149. Types 1, 2, 9, gk.; Δ.

xv. CONRAD BAUMGARTEN, fifth press.

Baumgarten's appearance at Leipzig in 1514, after an interval of five years during which
nothing is known of him, was only momentary, as besides P. VII. 187. 488 there is no record of
any book in which his name is found at this period.

xvi. MELCHIOR LOTTER, THE ELDER, third press.

TYPES, &c. See above, press 8.

11558. [a. 1520 Feb.] Petrus Mosellanus: de ratione disputandi oratio. 4°.
    Types 3, 12, 18, gk.; C; α.

11559. 1520 [n. b. March]. MELANCHTHON: compendiaria dialecticae ratio. 4°.
    P. VII. 214. 757. Types 1, 12; E.

11560. [a. 1520 Apr. 23.] Aug. ALVELD: Büchlein von dem Päpstlichen Stuhl.
    4°. DA. 985. Types 1, 2, 11; E.

11561. 1520. LVTHER: tessaradecas consolatoria. 4°. P. VII. 213. 744. Types
    1, 2, 3; B.

11562. 1520. LUTHER: ein tröstliches Büchlein. 4°. DA. 974nn; W. 1508.
    Types 2, 3, 11; B.

11563. 1520. LVTHER: sermo de praeparatione ad moriendum. 4°. P.VII.213.
    745. Types 2, 3, 12; F.

11564. 1520. LUTHER: Sermon von dem Bann. 4°. DA. 974d. Types 2,3,11; B.

11565. 1520. LUTHER: Auslegung deutsch des Vaterunser. 4°. DA. 973c.
    Types 1, 2, 3, 11; B.

11566. 1520. LVTHER: explanatio dominicae orationis. 4°. P. VII. 212. 743.
    Types 2, 3, 12; F.

11567. 1520. Aug. ALVELD: super sede apostolica. 4°. P. VII. 213. 746. Types
    1, 2, 3, 12. [Wants sig. I⁴.]

11568. 1520 [a. Sept. 17]. Heinr. STROMER: epistulae duae de statu reipublicae
    christianae. 4°. P. VII. 213. 747. Types 2, 3, 12.

11569. [a. 1520 Dec. 24.] Ioh. CELLARIVS: iudicium de Luthero. P. IX. 497.
    787b. Types 2, 3, 12, gk.; Δ.

[Anonymous Lotter books of 1520, other than those given here, are to be found under Wittenberg.]

WITHOUT PRINTER'S NAME.

TYPES. Type 1, middle roman like Schumann 5, but single hyphen.—Type 2, small roman,
very like Lotter 17, but not identical: straight M, large us, double hyphen, ℂ; 73-74 mm.—
Initial D used for Q; dotted (?) ground; 16 mm.

1501. Aristotelis ethica	11267.
1503 [a. Feb. 10]. Buch geistlicher Offenbarungen	11323.
1505. Meinhart: elegantiarum rudimenta	11277.
1511. Buschius: in Donatum commentarius	11458.
1519. Eine deutsche Theologia	11297.
1519. Luther: Auslegung des 109. Psalms	11300.

11570. 1519 Oct. Ioh. BRIARDVS: quaestio quodlibetica contra dispensationes.
    4°. Types 1, 2; Δ.

WITHOUT NAME OF PLACE OR PRINTER.

Type 1, curious roman, very large and somewhat narrow face; long double hyphen, round
comma, in & the last up stroke is long; separate Q like that of Sertorius 2; 87 mm.—Greek of
Leipzig-Erfurt style (like Schumann).—Lombardic initials identical with those used by Schumann
and Landsberg; the presswork is like the latter.

Type 2, hardly distinguishable from Lotter sen. 12, except by the hyphen, which is single;
the comma is also slightly different; Qu; 93 mm.—Greek type like the preceding.—Large plain
roman M, 17 mm.; not that used by Lotter sen. in 1520.

11571. n. d. [1519.] Oecolampadius: canonici indocti lutherani. [JOHANN von
    Eck.] 4°. P. IX. 168. 61. Type 1, gk.

11572. n. d. Ric. CROCVS: academiae lipsensis encomium. 4°. Type 2, gk.

XXIX. MÜNCHEN.

3. Johann Schobser, second press.
4. Johann Ostendorfer, Hofmaler, and Matthaeus Zeissinger, goldsmith 1505.

iij. JOH. SCHOBSER.

TYPES. Types 3 (early-style square german text, brought from Augsburg, thin ℭ, short double hyphen; 97–98 mm.); 4 (large square church type with fantastic caps.; see the larger type of Burger 22. Short letters 6 mm., 8 lines = 75 mm.); 5 (latin text gothic, italian style, double hyphen; 76 mm.); 6 (large round, like Cornelis of Zierikzee 1; short letters 5½ mm.; 4 ll. = 31 mm.); 7 (large text latin like Ratdolt 7, single hyphen; 94 mm.); for these see part i.— Type 8, large text schwabacher, very like Joh. Otmar 17, but double hyphen, and thin ℭ as 3; 108 mm. The two parts of the hyphen are very far from each other, short, and nearly horizontal; but in 1519 a second sort comes in (both are used thenceforth) the parts of which are so close together as usually to print as one.—Type 9, small text schwabacher, apparently normal, but very little used; double hyphen.—Type 10, small church, like G. Stuchs 6; short letters 4½ mm.; 2 ll. = 14 mm. Double hyphen like the earlier one of type 8.—Type 11 has the caps. (and almost always the a) of 10, but round lowercase; the v is rounded.—Type 12, very like 11, but may be distinguished by (1) a sharp v; (2) a rounded a; (3) italian caps. like those of Dinckmut 3 (Burger 123, colophon); but in 1520 some caps. of 10–11 are found also. Body as 10 or 11.

Type 6, see fig. 26; 8, see fig. 52; 9, see fig. 59; 10, see fig. 22.

DEVICE. a¹ (perhaps not a device at all), an oblong cut with two scutcheons; one bears the arms of Baiern, the other apparently those of Reutlingen.—a², the second scutcheon cut out of the above, and used alone.

INITIALS. α, flourished initials imitative of penwork (cf. those of Theuerdank); from 67 (A), 65 (V) and 50 (H) to 40 (C, E, N) and 37 (M) mm.—β, smaller and thicker, but in a similar style. In 1509 a W with black ground (32 mm.) is used. Other odd initials are calligraphic.

11573. 1501 Feb. 3. Das Buch des hl. röm. Reichs Unterhaltung. [GERMANY.] F°. DA. 513. Types 3, 4, 6; cut; a¹.

11574. 1505. Ang. FVNDIVS: oratio apud Iulium ij. habita. 4°. Types 4, 7.

11575. 1509 May 5. Herzog Albrechts Begängnis zu München. [ALBERT.] F°. Types 3, 4; cut; Δ.

11576. 1510 July 19. Figur und Exempel von eigenem Gericht und sterbenden Menschen. [BÜCHLEIN.] 4°. DA. 673. Types 3, 4; cuts.

11577. 1510. ALBERTVS Magnus: von Heimlichkeiten der Frauen. 4°. Types 3, 4; cut.

11578. n.d. [c. 1510.] Ein hübsches LIED oder Spruch wie der böse Geist seine Botschaft aussand. 4°. W. suppl. i. 57. Types 3, 4; cut. [Gedruckt zu Augspurg.]

11579. 1512 Jan. 15. Ioh. THVRNMAIER: grammatica. 4°. P. VII. 422. 1. Types 3, 4, 5; cut; a².

11580. n.d. [a. 1512 Feb. 24.] Das Einnehmen der Stadt Bressa. [BRESCIA.] 4°. W. 698. Types 3, 4; cut.

11581. 1516 May 19. GEILER: die Passion. F°. DA. 832c. Types 4, 8; cuts.

11582. n.d. [a. 1516 Apr. 23.] Buch der gemeinen Landbote. [BAVARIA.] F°. (Not DA. 843.) Types 4, 8, 9, 10; cuts; α.

11583. n.d. [a. 1516 Apr. 28.] Die neue Erklärung der Landesfreiheit. [BAVARIA.] F°. DA. 846. Types 4, 8; cut; α.

11584. (1516–17.) Joh. SEGER genannt Waldkircher: Practica auf das 1517. Jahr. 4°. Type 8; cut.

11584A. n.d. [c. 1517?] Offenbarungen von JOACHIM und Hildegardis. 4°. W. 931. Types 4, 8; cut.

11585. n. d. [a. 1518 Apr. 23.] Reformation der bairischen Landrechte. [BA-
VARIA.] F°. DA. 906. Types 4, 8, 9, 11; cut, diagr.; αβ. [2 copies on
vellum, 2 on paper.]

11586. [n. b. 1518.] Joh. STAUPITZ: von der Liebe Gottes. 4°. (W. 1148 note.)
Types 4, 8, 11; cut; β.

11587. n. d. [c. 1518?] Das ist jetzt der gemeine und neue GEBRAUCH. 4°. W.
29. Types 4, 8; cut.

11588. n. d. [c. 1519.] Der dreien GLAUBEN die frommsten und bösesten Männer und Frauen. 4°. W. 1394. (DA. 902 note.) Types 4, 8; cuts.

11589. 1519 Sept. 20. ALOFRESANT: wunderliche Prophezeiung oder Weissagung. [For J. Haselberger.] 4°. W. 1160. Types 8, 12; cut; Δ.

11590. 1519 Sept. 20. Von der Kur und Wahl des Königs Karl. [For J.
Haselberger.] 4°. DA. 947. Types 8, 12; cut; βΔ.

11591a. [a. 1520 Apr. 23.] Gerichtsordnung. [BAVARIA.] F°. DA. 993. Types
8, 12; cut; αβ. [On vellum.]

b. [a. 1520 Nov. 25.] Herzoglicher Empfehlungsbrief des vorigen. obl.
Type 8. [Half a folio leaf.]

APPENDIX.

Whether these books are printed by Schobser after 1520 (but this seems unlikely, at least for
the Hirschberg book, no. 11592) or by another printer, perhaps not at München at all, I find no
clear evidence to determine. But the cut on the title of no. 11594 is a copy of Schobser's used in
no. 11582.

TYPES. Type 1 = Schobser 12, but besides caps. from 10-11, it has also some from a fount
like Weissenburger 4.—Type 2 = Schobser 8, but the double hyphen differs. (In no. 11593, however, Schobser's second hyphen is found mixed with this new one; this book also has Schobser's
℃, not found elsewhere in these books.) There are additional sorts of E, S, and flourishes in the
Theuerdank style; 108 mm.—Type 3, largest frakturschrift, like (not =) Schönsperger sen. 12.—
Type 4, intermediate frakturschrift, 140 mm.; cf. Schönsperger sen. 13.—Type 5, text frakturschrift
like Schönsperger sen. 14; double hyphen; 126 mm.—Type 6, small text schwabacher, apparently
= Schobser 9.

INITIALS. α, in fraktur style, 43-47 mm.—β, like α, but smaller; 21-24 mm., mostly 22-23 mm.

11592. [a. 1518 Apr. 10.] Freiheitbrief und Ordnung über das Landgericht
HIRSCHBERG. F°. DA. 906b. Types 1, 2, 3; cut (dated 1518); αβ.

11593. n. d. [c. 1518-19?] Bruder Dietrich: Practica oder Prophezeiung. [THEO-
DERICVS.] 4°. (Not W. 1625-7 or suppl. i. 176.) Types 1, 2.

11594. n. d. [a. 1520 March 26.] Buch der gemeinen Landbote. [BAVARIA.] F°.
DA. 992b? Types 3, 4, 5, 6; cut; α.

11595. n. d. [a. 1516 Apr. 23.] Neue Erklärung der Landesfreiheit. [BAVARIA.]
F°. DA. 846c? Types 3, 4, 5; cut; Δ.

iv. JOH. OSTENDORFER AND M. ZEISSINGER.

Only two books issued in the name of Ostendorfer and Zeissinger are recorded, and it seems
certain that the actual printer was Schobser.

TYPES. Type 1 = Schobser 3.—Type 2 = Schobser 4.

11596. 1505. Eine wunderbarliche wahre Geschichte von einem Landherrn
in Frankreich. [AUBUSSON.] F°. W. 318. Types 1, 2.

WITHOUT PRINTER'S NAME.

All except the following are by Schobser.

1514 [a. Nov. 17]. Des löblichen Hauses Baiern Freiheiten. See no.
11786.

XXX. METZ.

2. Caspar Hochfeder, of Heiligbrunn, from Nürnberg, second press.
3. Caspar Hochfeder, from Krakau, fourth press   1508.

---

ij. CASPAR HOCHFEDER, second press.

TYPES. Type 1*, a recast of 1 on a slightly changed body, with different O (as Koberger 18) and a smaller P; double hyphen, high in the line instead of low; not the same as that used at Krakau; ¶ as at Krakau; 80 mm.—Type 8, large text = Koberger 16; single hyphen; 112 mm. Both these types were taken to Krakau by Hochfeder and not brought back to Metz.

Type 1*, see fig. 36; 8, see fig. 33¹.

11597. n. d. [c. 1501?] Ioh. VRSINVS : modus epistulandi. 4°. H. 16106; Wz. 2025. Types 1*, 8; cut.

iij. CASPAR HOCHFEDER, fourth press.

TYPES. Type 17, large text french-latin, like Gering & Rembolt 10; smaller than TP. XI. 5; 114 mm.—Type 18, small type, like Knoblouch 20, &c.; tailed h, double hyphen, ℂ; 66 mm.— Type 19, larger round church text, like Meurl 1.—Type 20, middle large round, like Ratdolt 9; round h.—Type 21, like 1, but the P shows it to be a Paris fount (as TP. XII. 2); the V however is german. In 1517 with a white ℂ (cf. H. Estienne) and some french capitals from 22. 81 mm.— Type 22, square french-latin large text, smaller than 17 and of earlier style; l.c. like Caillaut 9, caps. like Trepperel 3 (TP. XVI. 8); long double hyphen, ℂ as 24; 99–100 mm.—Type 23, small-text vernacular french, very like Caillaut 11; double hyphen; 80 mm.—Type 24, schwabacher text of Strassburg style, very like Knoblouch 5ᵉ; similar N; at end of no. 11600 mixt with caps. from 22; double hyphen, large ℂ; 99 mm.—Type 25, small type, like Quentell 6, but has open V and round h; a Strassburg fount; double hyphen, ¶; 66 mm.—Type 26, french, very small, like Kerver 14 or Pigouchet 7 (Claudin, HIF. ii. 280, marginalia); double hyphen; 56 mm.

Type 18, see fig. 48; 19, see fig. 30; 20, see fig. 32¹; 21, see fig. 36; 24, see fig. 55; 25, see fig. 46.

DEVICE. What may be a device (of Matth. Häne?) is used at the end of no. 11600, a shield bearing a cross, like the arms of Wien (not those of Metz or Trier): 40 × 34 mm.

INITIAL. An initial P in no. 11599, a man playing on fife and drum; 46 mm.

11598. 1511 Feb. 7. Marchesinus : MAMOTRECTVS. 4°. P. XI. 466. 1ᶜ. Types 17, 18.
11598A. [a. 1512 May 3.] Reliquiae Treueris repertae. [RICHARD.] 4°. P. IX. 191. 320. Types 20, 22.
11599. 1513. Psalterium cum apparatu uulgari. [BIBLE.] 4°. P. VII. 405. 2; DA. 743. Types 17, 19–23; cut; Δ.
11600. 1514 June 3. Ioh. ENEN : medulla gestorum Treuirensium, germ. [For Matthias Häne, Trier.] 4°. W. 826. Types 19, 20, 24; cuts.
11601. 1516 Feb. 4. Le CHEVALIER aux dames. 4°. P. VII. 405. 4. Types 20, 21? 22; cuts.
11602. 1517 July 13. Ioh. ENEN : epitome alias medulla gestorum Treuirorum. [For M. Häne, Trier.] 4°. P. VII. 405. 5. Types 17, 20, 21, 25; cut.
11603. 1517. BARTHOLOMAEVS de Vsingen: regulae congruitatis. 4°. P. VII. 405. 7. Types 20, 25.
11604. n. d. DONATVS nouus pro pueris. 4°. Types 17, 22, 26.

XXXII. HEIDELBERG.

3. Heinrich Knoblochtzer, second press.
4. Jacob Stadelberger   (1512).

iij. H. KNOBLOCHTZER.

TYPES. Types 7 (square church text like Knoblouch 3, lombardic caps., double hyphen; 3 ll.=23 mm.); 8 (text schwabacher, D like S reversed, fraktur forms of b, h, single hyphen; 94 mm.); 10 (small roman like Quentell 13, single hyphen, ℂ with tail turned back; 76 mm.); for these see part i. 10ᴮ is 10 germanised.

Type 7, see fig. 19; 8, see fig. 54; 10, see fig. 11.

INITIALS. α, Maiblumen set as in 1493; S, 38 mm.

11605. (1501.) Pallas SPANGEL: oratio funebris de morte ducissae Margaretae. 4°. P. XI. 426. 3b. Types 7,8,10; cut; α.

11605A. 1501 Dec. 24. Conr. SCHELLIG: Regimen wider die Pestilenz. 4°. W. 206. Types 7,8,10ᴮ; cuts.

iv. JACOB STADELBERGER.

For two books by Stadelberger see DA. 726 [1512], and P. VII. 118. 1 (1513).

XXXIII. REGENSBURG.

4. Paul Kohl   1519.

iv. PAUL KOHL.

See W. 1205 [1519] and 1339, 1340 (suppl. i. 162) [1520]; but in none of these is the printer's name given; it appears first about 1525 (W. 3285, 3286). See also below, no. 12002.

XXXV. MÜNSTER i/W.

2. Lorenz Bornemann   1507 Feb. 20.
3. Dietrich Tzwivel, of Montjoie   1514.
4. Gregorius van Os, of Breda.

ij. LOR. BORNEMANN.

Bornemann, whose first book may have been the Carmen in salutationes euangelicas of Murmellius, which was finished after 1507 Jan. 18 (Ledeboer 263), and whose last books belong to 1510 (Ledeboer 264, 267), inherited or acquired some of Ulrich Zel's material; see Merlo-Zaretzky, Ulrich Zell, p. 37–38 and pl. VI.

TYPES. Type 1=Zel 10. Cf. Tzwivel 1.—Type 2 = Zel 5. Cf. Tzwivel 4.—Type 3, text schwabacher (see Tzwivel 2). For these types see Merlo-Zaretzky, pl. VI. and below, press 3.

DEVICE. That of Zel, with the address cut out; Merlo-Zaretzky, pl. VI.

iij. DIETRICH TZWIVEL.

Apparently successor to Bornemann.

TYPES. Type 1, church text, very like J. Schöffer 5 = Bornemann 1, Zel 10.—Type 2 = Bornemann 3; schwabacher text, like M. von Werden 7 and other Köln types; single hyphen, ¶, D
like S reversed; 97 mm.——Type 3, small type = Zel 4 much worn; single hyphen, ℂ; 67 mm.——
Type 4 = Bornemann 2, Zel 5; latin text gothic with open V; many w.f. caps. from type 3, from
Zel 3, and from other founts: also w.f. h. Single hyphen, rare.

Type 2, see fig. 54; 3, see fig. 47; 4, see fig. 38.

11606. 1514. Ecclesiastes Salomonis. [BIBLE.] 4°. Types 1–4; cut.
11607. 1514. TERENTIVS: Adelphi. 4°. Types 1–4.

iv. GREGORIUS VAN OS.

Only one book by this printer is mentioned (P. VII. 423. 5), and it is undated.

XXXVII. INGOLSTADT.

6. Andreas Lutz   1519 April 25.

vi. ANDREAS LUTZ.

The Oratio of Alberius dated 1519 April 25 (P. VII. 126. 7) is without printer's name: but the
Rolach, no. 11608, which is sine nota, is undoubtedly earlier.

TYPES. Type 1, text schwabacher with stiff straightsided ℂ and tall L like those of Prüss sen.
12, and D like S reversed; 95 mm. In no. 11608 this type has no hyphen or y (for which ij is used);
in 11609, 11610, which must be later, y is found as well as a short double hyphen and a sloping
comma.—Type 2, middle roman; the central point of M is low; ℂ with curved ends, not as in type
1; æ and ę, double hyphen; 5 lines measure 23 mm.—In no. 11610 the first line of the title is
woodcut.

Type 1, see fig. 54; 2, see fig. 8.

BORDER. A, one-piece quarto, a copy of Peypus B (fool and satyr), probably not direct, but
through M. Schürer B. In a shield at the foot are the arms of Öttingen (cf. no. 11609). On the
title of no. 11608 is a cut of S. Catharine supporting the arms of Baiern.

INITIALS. α, calligraphic, 36–37 mm.—β, black or dotted ground, 15 mm., except C, which
is 18 mm.

11608. n. d. Theodericus ROLACH: sermo et tractatulus Fides mea uocatus,
      editus anno 1510; lat.-germ. 4°. Types 1,2; cut; A; α.
11609. 1519. Joh. THURNMAIER: der hochwürdigen Stift Alten Ötting löbliches
      Herkommen. 4°. W. 1163. Type 1; cuts; α.
11610. [a. 1519 July 27.] Ioh. Vdalr. SCHVLHERR: aduersus nugacem F. Mathei
      Hiscoldi epistulam de lipsica disputatione epistula exegetica. 4°. P.
      IX. 121. 148. Types 1,2; A.
11611. 1519 Nov. 13? DIONYSIVS Periegetes: de situ orbis. 4°. P. VII. 126. 6.
      Type 2; cut; β.

XXXIX. HAGENAU.

1. Heinrich Gran.
2. Thomas Anshelm, of Baden, from Tübingen, fourth press   1516 Nov.

---

i. HEINRICH GRAN.

TYPES. Types 4 (large round, exactly as Strassburg xx. 5; like Knoblouch 1, but the hyphen differs); 5 (small text, like Knoblouch 9 or Joh. Schöffer 12; 71 mm. From Jan. 1512 it has some caps., especially T and B, of 9 mixt in it, and ℂ, ¶); 8 (latin text, apparently identical with Strassburg xx. 6; the same hyphen, two forms of C, &c.; 79 mm. 8ᵃ, first found July 1517, has the V mixt with the open form as that of Knoblouch 2, and only one C); 9 (small, as Strassburg xx. 7; like Knoblouch 4, but the hyphen differs; 63 mm.); 10 (as Strassburg xx. 10, see below, 10*); for these see part i.—Type 10*, a recast of 10 on a kerned body (that of type 5), with double hyphen. 10**, again recast, on a full body, with new reversed double hyphen. —Type 12, large text, as Strassburg xx. 9; like Strassburg xv. 2.—Type 13, text schwabacher; A, D, L, like Knoblouch 5, but a double hyphen as type 8; 95–96 mm.—Type 14, small roman, single hyphen; 76 mm. Cf. Knoblouch 13. In one book only (1518 May 31) it has ¶ and ℂ, and some Greek letters like those of Knoblouch's second fount.—Type 15, very small italian gothic, like Renner 6; single hyphen; 61 mm. Cf. S. Otmar 8. Used only in the book dated 1518 May 31.—Type 16, middle roman, like Knoblouch 7; but has a long single hyphen. Greek types: i, very rude, only a few letters found; ij, very like M. Schürer's first fount. A few letters of Knoblouch ij are found in no. 11673.

Type *4, see fig. 24; *5, see fig. 45; *8, see fig. 37; *9, see fig. 46; 10, see fig. 34; 13, see fig. 54; 14, see fig. 11; 16, see fig. 8.

BORDERS. Aa, four-piece quarto border-device, EBM. LXIV. 2; three pieces are a copy of a border used by the younger Prüss.—Bb, four-piece folio border-device, EBM. LXIII. 1, and (much reduced) Butsch I. 73.—Cc, four-piece quarto border-device, EBM. LXVI. 3.—X border = Knoblouch Xᵃᵇ, used only in a book of Dec. 1518 printed for Knoblouch, in whose own books it is not found after 1517.

DEVICES. a–c, see borders A–C.

INITIALS. α, Maiblumen style, letter black; P and Q only; 43–44 mm.—β, Strassburg style, 17 mm.—ɼ, similar to β, 24–5 mm. β and ɼ are perhaps the same as Knoblouch ʜ and ʔ. The only Δ initial is a D, with the figure of a sower, probably from a calendar set (31 mm.; Sept. 1512).

11612. 1501 Aug. 31. Ioh. ᴘᴀʀʀᴇᴠᴛ: textus ueteris artis. [For J. Rinmann.] 4°. P. IX. 465. 6b. Types 4, 8, 9.

11613. 1501 Nov. 22. Paulus ᴡᴀɴɴ: quadragesimale. [For Rinmann.] F°. P. VII. 67. 6. Types 4, 8.

11614. 1501 Dec. 24. ᴍɪᴄʜᴀᴇʟ de Hungaria: quadragesimale biga salutis. [For Rinmann.] 4°. P. VII. 67. 7. Types 4, 5.

11615. 1502 June 10. Pelbartus de Temesvar: sermones pomerii quadragesimales. [ᴘᴇʟʙᴀʀᴛ.—For Rinmann.] F°. P. VII. 67. 10. Types 4, 5.

11616. 1502 June 15. Nicolaus de Gorran: postilla super epistulas Pauli. [ʙɪʙʟᴇ.—For Rinmann.] F°. P. VII. 68. 12. Types 4, 5, 12.

11617. 1502 Aug. 3. Pelbartus de Temesvar: sermones pomerii de tempore. [ᴘᴇʟʙᴀʀᴛ.—For Rinmann.] F°. P. VII. 66. 4; 67. 8? Types 4, 5.

11618. 1503 Jan. 24. Nic. de Orbellis: compendium Scoti super sententias. [ᴅᴜɴs.—For Rinmann.] 4°. P. VII. 68. 15. Types 4, 9, 12.

11619b. 1503 May 27. Bern. de Bustis: rosarium sermonum, pars secunda.
    a. 1503 July 24. id.: eiusdem pars prima. [ʙᴜsᴛ.—For Rinmann.] F°. P. VII. 68. 14. Types 4, 5, 12.

11620. 1503 Dec. 30. Commentarium secundum modernorum doctrinam in HAGE-
    tractatus logicae Petri Hispani i. et iv. [JOHN XXI.—For Rinmann.] NAU.
    4°. P. IX. 466.17b. Types 4,9,12. i. Heinrich
11621. 1504 July 24. Albertus Magnus: postilla super Ioannem. [BIBLE.—For Gran.
    Rinmann.] F°. P. VII. 70.24. Types 4,5,10*,12.
11622. 1504 Oct. 3. Pelbartus de Temesvar: sermones de tempore. [PELBART.
    —For Rinmann.] F°. P. VII. 69.21. Types 4,5.
11623. 1504 Dec. 7. Albertus Magnus: postilla super Lucam. [BIBLE.—For
    Rinmann.] F°. P. VII. 70.23. Types 4,5,10*,12.
11624. 1505 March 17. Albertus Magnus: postilla super Matthaeum. [BIBLE.—
    For Rinmann.] P. VII. 70.26. Types 4,5,10*,12.
11625. 1505 March 17. Albertus Magnus: postilla super Marcum. [BIBLE.—
    For Rinmann.] F°. P. VII. 70.27. Types 4,5,10*,12.
11626. 1505 April 23. Pelbartus de Temesvar: quadragesimale. [PELBART.—
    For Rinmann.] F°. Types 4, 5.
11627. 1505 April 24. Pelbartus: stellarium coronae B.M.V. [PELBART.—For
    Rinmann.] F°. P. XI. 417. 27b. Types 4, 5.
11628a. 1505. Humbertus de Romanis: expositio super regulam Augustini
    (A–P).
      b. 1506 May 31. Hugo de S. Victore: expositio super eandem regulam
    (a–c). [AUGUSTINE.—For Rinmann.] 4°. P. VII. 70. 31. Types 4,5,
    10*,12.
11629. 1506 Feb. 5. MODVS legendi abbreuiaturas. F°. P. IX. 466. 34b. Types
    4, 8.
11630. 1506 Feb. 21. Bern. de Bustis: mariale. [BUSTI.—For Rinmann.] F°.
    P. VII. 71.35. Types 4,5.
    1506 May 31. See 11628b.
11631. 1506 Dec. 7. EVSEBIVS et Baeda: historia ecclesiastica. [For Rinmann.]
    F°. P. VII. 71. 32. Types 4, 8.
11632. 1507 Jan. 15. Aeg. Aurifaber: speculum exemplorum. [CHRISTIANS.—
    For Rinmann.] F°. P. VII. 71.36. Types 4, 8.
11633. 1507 Feb. 10. Paulus WANN: sermones de tempore. [For Rinmann.]
    F°. P. XI. 418.36b. Types 4, 8.
11634. 1507 Aug. 4. Gemma gemmarum. [DICT.—For Rinmann.] 4°. P. VII.
    72. 44; W. 422. Types 4, 9.
11635. 1507 Aug. 26. TORRENTINVS: elucidarius carminum et historiarum. [For
    Rinmann.] 4°. P. VII. 72.43. Types 4,5,9,10*, gk. i.
11636. 1507 Dec. 3. Pelbartus de Temesvar: sermones de sanctis. [PELBART.
    —For Rinmann.] F°. P. VII. 72.40. Types 4,5.
11637. 1508 July 5, 12. HVMBERTVS de Romanis: sermones ad diuersos status.
    [For Rinmann.] F°. P. VII. 73.53. Types 4,5,12.
11638. 1508 Aug. 20. GVIDO de Monte Rocherii: manipulus curatorum. [For
    J. Knoblouch.] 4°. P. VII. 72. 47. Types 4,8.
11639. 1508 Sept. 20. WIMPHELING: adulescentia. [For Knoblouch.] 4°. P.
    VII. 73.48. Types 4,8; cuts.
11640. 1509 Feb. 23. ANGELVS de Clauasio: summa angelica. [For Rinmann
    and Knoblouch.] F°. P. VII. 74.60. Types 4,5.
11641. n.d. [1509.] HIERONYMVS de Villa Vitis (Rebdorf): panis quotidianus de
    tempore. 4°. P. VII. 75.61(1); H. 8658. Types 4,8,12.

11642. 1509 June 19. HIERONYMVS de VillaVitis: panis quotidianus de sanctis. [For Rinmann.] 4°. P. VII. 74. 61(2). Types 4, 8, 12. [First quire by Knoblouch.]

11643. 1509 Aug. 18. HELDENBUCH. [For Knoblouch.] F°. DA. 659. Types 4, 13; cuts.

11644. 1509 Nov. 24. HENRICVS de Herpf: sermones. [For Rinmann.] 4°. P. VII. 75. 62. Types 4, 9, 12.

11645. 1510 March 19. Nic. DENYSE: sermones de sanctis et de festiuitatibus Christi et b. uirginis. [For Rinmann.] 4°. P.VII. 76. 72. Types 4, 9, 12.

11646 a. 1510 June 8. BIEL: sermones de tempore. Types 4, 9, 12.
    b. [1510.] id.: sermones de festiuitatibus Christi. Types 4, 8, 9, 12.
    c. [1510.] id.: sermones de festiuitatibus B.M.V. Types 4, 9, 12.
    d. 1510 July 10. id.: sermones de sanctis. Types 4, 9, 12.
    e. [1510.] id.: sermo passionis dominicae. Types 4, 9, 12. [For Rinmann.] 4°. P. VII. 76. 70.

11647. 1510 Sept. 3. TORRENTINVS: elucidarius. [For Rinmann.] 4°. P.VII. 75. 66. Types 4, 9, 10*, 12.

11648. 1510 Dec. 20. Burlaeus: de VITA et moribus philosophorum. 4°. P.VII. 75. 67. Types 4, 5, 10*, 12.

11649. 1511 Oct. 27. Pelbartus de Temesvar: stellarium coronae B.M.V. [MARY.—For Rinmann.] F°. P.XI. 420. 73b. Types 4, 5, 12.

11650. 1512 Jan. 7. THOMAS Aquinas: secunda secundae. [For Knoblouch.] F°. P.VII. 76. 77 (1). Types 4, 5, 12; α.

11651. 1512 Feb. 13. THOMAS Aquinas: prima secundae. [For Knoblouch.] F°. P.VII. 76. 77 (2). Types 4, 5, 12; α.

11652. 1512 March 24. THOMAS Aquinas: summae pars tertia. [For Knoblouch.] F°. Types 4, 5, 12; α.

11653. 1512 April 28. TORRENTINVS: elucidarius. [For Rinmann.] 4°. P.VII. 76. 74. Types 4, 9, 10*, 12.

11654. 1512 May 7. THOMAS Aquinas: summae pars prima. [For Knoblouch.] F°. Types 4, 5, 12; α.

11655. 1512 June 30. Iac. HENRICHMANNVS: grammaticae institutiones, etc. [For Rinmann.] 4°. P.VII. 77. 78. Types 4, 5, 10*, 12; gk. ij.

11656. 1512 Sept. 7. Ioh. ALTENSTAIG: opus pro conficiundis epistulis, etc. [For Rinmann.] 4°. P.VII. 76. 76. Types 4, 5, 10*, 12, 14, gk. ij; Δ.

11657. 1513 Apr. 4. Ioh. Lud. de VIVALDIS: de ueritate contritionis. [For Rinmann.] 4°. P. VII. 77. 82. Types 4, 9, 10*, 12, 14.

11658. 1513 Nov. 4. HENRICVS de Vrimaria: sermones de sanctis. [For Rinmann.] 4°. P.VII. 77. 84. Types 4, 5, 10**, 12.

11659. 1514 Feb. 15. Iac. HENRICHMANNVS: grammaticae institutiones. [For Rinmann.] 4°. P.VII. 78. 89. Types 4, 5, 10*, 10**, 12, gk. ij.

11660. 1514 Apr. 11. Paulus WANN: sermones de septem uitiis criminalibus. [For Rinmann.] 4°. P.VII. 79. 99. Types 4, 5, 10*, 12; Aa.

11661. 1514 May. GABRIEL de Bareletta: sermones. [For Rinmann.] 4°. P.VII. 78. 90. Types 4, 9, 12; Aa; βɼ.

11662. 1514 Aug. Iac. WIMPHELING: diatriba de proba institutione puerorum. [For Conr. Hist.] 4°. P.VII. 78. 91. Types 4, 5, 12; Aa; ɼ.

11663 a. 1514 Sept. 6. Petrus Hieremiae: sermones uarii. Types 4, 9, 10*, 12; Aa; βɼ.

11663b. 1514 Sept. id.: sermones de sanctis. Types 4, 9, 10*, 12 ; Aa ; βɼ.
    [PETER.—For Rinmann.] 4°. P. VII. 79. 95.
11664. 1514 Oct. BARTHOLOMAEVS Coloniensis: epistula mythologica. [For
    Rinmann.] 4°. P.VII. 79.93. Types 4, 9, 12, 14; Aa; ɼ.
11665. 1514 Nov. Gemma gemmarum. [DICT.—For Rinmann.] 4°. P.IX.469.
    100b; W. 867. Types 4, 9, 12; Aa.
11666a. 1514 Nov. SANCIVS de Porta: sermones de tempore aestiuales (aa–vv).
    Types 4, 5, 10*, 12; Bb; ɼ.
    b. 1515 Jan. id.: sermones de tempore hiemales (a–t). Types 4, 5, 10*,
    12, 14; Bb; ɼ.
    c. 1515 March. id.: mariale (A–Q). Types 4, 5, 10*, 12; Bb; ɼ.
    d. 1515 March 31. id.: sanctorale (Aa–Ll). Types 4, 5, 12; Bb; ɼ. [For
    Rinmann.] F°. P. VII. 79. 98; 80. 109.
11667a. 1515 Feb. 23. Gabr. BIEL : sermones de tempore. Types 4, 9, 10*,
    12; Aa; ɼ.
    b. n. d. id.: sermones de festiuitatibus Christi. Types 4, 8, 9, 12; Aa; ɼ.
    c. n. d. id.: sermones de festiuitatibus b. uirginis. Types 4, 9, 12; Aa; ɼ.
    d. 1515 June 8. id.: sermones de sanctis. Types 4, 9, 12; Aa; ɼ.
    e. 1515 June 28. id.: sermo passionis dominicae. Types 4, 9, 12; Aa; ɼ.
    [For Rinmann.] 4°. P. VII. 80. 105–107.
11668. 1515 Dec. Michael de Hungaria: QVADRAGESIMALE biga salutis. [For
    Rinmann.] 4°. P. VII. 80. 104. Types 4, 9; Aa; ɼ.
11669. 1516 July 31. IACOBVS de Voragine: legenda aurea. [For Rinmann.]
    F°. P. VII. 81. 111. Types 4, 8; Bb; ɼ.
11670. 1517 July 31. Gesta Romanorum. [ROMANS.—For Rinmann.] F°. P.
    IX. 469. 121b. Types 4, 8ᴮ; Bb; ɼ.
11671a. n. d. Gotschalcus HOLLEN: sermones super epistulas Pauli pars hie-
    malis (a–x). Types 4, 5, 10**; Bb; ɼ.
    b. 1517 Aug. 31. id.: pars aestiualis (A–Ii). Types 4, 5, 12; Bb; ɼ. [For
    Rinmann.] F°. P. VII. 82. 124.
11672. 1517 Dec. 13. Ioh. ALTENSTAIG: uocabularius theologiae. [For Rin-
    mann.] F°. P.VII. 82. 122. Types 4, 5, 10*, 10**, 12, 14, gk. ij; Bb; ɼ.
11673. 1518 May 31. IOANNES Gallensis: summa collationum. [By, i.e. for
    Knoblouch and Götz.] 4°. P.VI. 87. 510. Types 4, 9, 10**, 14, 15,
    gk.; Aa; βɼ.
11674. 1518 Dec. 4. Gemma gemmarum. [DICT.—For Rinmann.] 4°. W. 1105.
    Types 4, 9, 12; Aa.
11675. 1518 Dec. 8. Ioh. Glogouiensis: introductorium in tractatum sphaerae
    Ioannis de SACRO BOSCO. [By, i.e. for Knoblouch.] 4°. P.VI. 88. 513.
    Types 4, 8ᴮ, 9, 16; diagr.; ɼ.
11676. 1518 Dec. 30. Herm. TORRENTINVS: elucidarius. [By, i.e. for Knob-
    louch.] 4°. Types 4, 9, 10*, 10**, 12, gk. ij; Aa; ɼ.
11677a. n. d. Sequentiarum interpretatio. Types 4, 9, 10**, 12, 16; Aa; ɼ.
    b. 1519 March 15. Hymni de tempore et sanctis. Types 4, 9, 10**, 12,
    16; Aa; ɼ. [LIT.—For Rinmann.] 4°. P. IX. 470. 158b.
11678. 1519 April 4. Ioh. ALTENSTAIG: de felicitate triplici. [For Rinmann.]
    4°. P.VII. 87. 156. Types 4, 5, 10**, 14, gk. ij; Aa; ɼ.
11679. 1519 Sept. 1. Gul. DVRANDVS: rationale. [For Rinmann.] F°. P. VII.
    87. 157. Types 4, 8ᴮ; βɼ.

147

11680. 1519 Sept. 14. Ioh. ALTENSTAIG: opusculum de amicitia. [For Rinmann.] 4°. P. VII. 87. 158. Types 4, 5, 10**, 14; Cc; ⌐.
11681. 1520 Feb. 29. Gabr. BIEL: sermo passionis dominicae (sermonum pars
v.). [For Rinmann.] 4°. P. VII. 89. 175. Types 4, 9, 12; Cc; β⌐.
11682. 1520 July 5. Pelbartus de Temesvar: stellarium coronae B.M.V. [PEL-
BART.] F°. P. XI. 425. 186b. Types 4, 5, 12; Bb; ⌐. [Partiv.; part i.
dated 1521 Feb. 5; of part ij. 4ff. only, of part iij. none in B.M.]

ij. THOMAS ANSHELM.

TYPES. Types 2, 3, 8, 9, see Pforzheim; 10, 11, 12 see Tübingen.—Type 13 (used in DA. 831,
of 1516), german text schwabacher like Flach jun. 12, Knoblouch 18, &c.; double hyphen, long
sloping comma; a second D (rare) in 1520 like that of Schott 12; 94 mm. Differs from type 1
(Strassburg 1488) in the D, ¶ for ⚏, and the lowercase h. Facs., Muther 184–185.—Type 14,
roman capitals, 10 mm. high. Cf. Miller 13, Grim 11.—Type 15, like 8 (similar caps. and h) but
larger; short letters 4¾ mm.; 20 ll. = 156 mm.—Type 16, rounded canon type in a Lyonnese style
(apparently); cf. Hochfeder 13 (= Haller 3) and Sacon 5 (TP. XXIV. 1). Short letters 8 mm.; 20 ll.
= 252 mm.—Type 17, thin roman caps. like Knoblouch 19 or Schott 14; 7½ mm.—Greek type ij*,
see Tübingen; iij, large capitals, rather thicker than those of 16 (different from the initials in the
Horae); 8 mm.—Hebrew type ij, see Pforzheim; iij, see Tübingen.
Type 13, see fig. 53; 15, see fig. 32¹; 17, see fig. 2.
BORDERS. Border A, see Tübingen.—Border-device Bc, one-piece quarto; EBM. LXI. 1.
—C, folio one-piece, top semicircular on inner side; at foot a bear with boys and fruit.—Of four-piece
borders (X) a folio one signed by Graf is used in Vigerius 1517 and Fulgentius 1520; the Pliny of
Nov. 1518 contains two four-piece folio borders (one piece is common to both); Secerius of Sept.
[1520] has a five-piece quarto border, and the undated Huss, de causa Boemica one in four pieces,
one of which occurs in the Secerius.
DEVICES. b, see Pforzheim; much battered in 1517.—c, see border B.—d = EBM. LXII.
2.—e = EBM. LXII. 4.—f (not in EBM.), a copy of a; the ground is semée with large white dots.
INITIALS. See Paul Heitz, Die Zierinitialen in den Drucken des Thomas Anshelm, Strassburg
1894. α = Heitz Alphabet 3 (33 mm.).—β = Heitz 1 (96–97 mm., except T, 108–9 mm.).—⌐ =
Heitz 2 (47 mm.).—δ = Heitz 5 (45–46 mm.).—є = Heitz 6 (28–29 mm.).—ʒ (not found in these
books; first used in 1519) = Heitz 4. The two 16° Horae have the same initials as the edition of
1514. In March 1517 an I of Strassburg style is found (24 mm.).

11683. 1516 Nov. BARTHOLOMAEVS Coloniensis: epistula mythologica. 4°. P.
VII. 81. 118. Types 8, 11, gk. ij*; Bc.
11684. 1517 Jan. Marcus VIGERIVS: decachordon christianum. [With Ioh.
Albertus, for Joh. Koberger.] F°. P. VII. 83. 125. Types 3, 14;
cuts; X.
11685. 1517 March. REVCHLIN: de arte cabalistica. F°. P. VII. 83. 126. Types
3, 8, 11, 12, 14; cut; Δ.
11686. 1517 July. Val. CYRELEIVS: de laudibus et uituperatione uini et aquae.
4°. P. VII. 83. 129. Types 3, 11, (14), 15.
11687. [1517?] July. MELANCHTHON: de artibus liberalibus oratio. 4°. P. VII.
83. 130. Types 3, 11 [caps.], 14, gk. ij*; A.
11688. 1517. Baptista Mantuanus: bucolica seu adulescentia. 4°. P. VII. 83.
132. Types 3 [caps.], 8, 9, 11, gk. ij*; b [not e, as EBM. copy].
11689. 1518 Jan. Missale Benedictinum. [LIT.] F°. P. VII. 84. 141. Types
3, 8, 15, 16; music; cuts; Y; d; αβ⌐.
11690. 1518 Feb. REVCHLIN: de accentibus et orthographia linguae hebraicae.
4°. P. VII. 85. 143. Types 3, (12), 14, 15, gk. ij*, hb. ij, music; cut; d.
11691. 1518 Feb. Acta iudiciorum inter Iac. Hochstratum et Ioh. Reuchlin.
[JACOBUS.] 4°. P. VII. 84. 142. Types 3, 11, (14), 15, 16,

11692. 1518 Aug. Franc. IRENICVS: Germaniae exegeseos uolumina xij. [For
Joh. Koberger.] F°. P. VII. 85. 146. Types 2, 3, 11, (12), 14, gk. ij*;
diagr.; d; α.

11693. 1518 Aug. Horae B.V.M. secundum consuetudinem romanae curiae,
graece. [LIT.] 16°. P. VII. 85. 147. Types 11, gk. ij*.

11694. 1518 Oct. Luciani dialogi duo, Charon et tyrannus. [LUCIAN.] 4°. P.
VII. 86. 148. Types 3, 14, gk. ij*; A; d.

11695a. 1518 Nov. PLINIVS: naturalis historia. [For Joh. Koberger & Lucas
Alantsee.] Types 3, (12), 14, gk. ij*; X; δε.

  b. 1518 Nov. Ioh. Camers: index Plinianus. [For Lucas Alantsee.]
  Types 3, 11, (12), 14; X; d; δ. F°. P. VII. 86. 149.

11696. 1518 Dec. Iac. Faber: de Maria Magdalena. [LEFÈVRE.] 4°. P.VII. 86.
151. Types 3, 11, (12), 14, gk. ij*; A; ε.

11697. 1519 Jan. MOSES Kimchi: introductorium grammaticae hebraicae. 4°. P.
VII. 88. 160. Types 3, 14, hb. ij, iij; A; d.

11698. 1519 March. ATHANASIVS: de uariis quaestionibus. 4°. P.VII. 88. 163.
Types 3, 17, gk. ij*, hb. ij; d; ε. [Wants last leaf.]

11699. 1519 Apr. CALPVRNIVS et Nemesianus: eclogae. [For Joh. Knoblouch.]
4°. P. VII. 89. 167. Types 3, 9 [caps.], (14), 17, gk. ij; δε.

11700. 1519 Apr. Ioh. Alex. BRASSICANVS: Πᾶν, Omnis. [For Knoblouch.] 4°.
P. VI. 90. 536. Types 3, 9 [caps.], 14, 17, gk. ij*; δ.

11701. 1519 May. REVCHLIN: scenica progymnasmata. 4°. P. VII. 88. 165.
Types 3, 9, 17, gk. ij*; A. [Wants last leaf.]

11702. 1519 May. Illustrium uirorum epistulae. [REVCHLIN.] 4°. (Not P. VII.
88. 164?) Types 3, 9, 11, 17, gk. ij*, hb. ij; A; d; ε. [Wants last leaf.]

11703. 1519 Oct. ERASMVS: collectanea adagiorum ueterum. 4°. P.VII. 89. 168.
Types 9, 11, 17, gk. ij*; ε.

11704. 1519 Dec. ERASMVS: de duplici copia uerborum et rerum. 4°. P.VII. 89.
169. Types 9 [caps.], 11, (14), 17, gk. ij*; A; d; ε.

11705. 1520 Jan. Luciani rhetor. [LUCIAN.] 4°. P. VII. 90. 176. Types 3, 9,
17, gk. ij*; A; d; δ.

11706. [1520?] Jan. Horae B.V.M. secundum consuetudinem romanae curiae.
[LIT.] 16°. Types 9 [caps.], 11, gk. ij*.

11707. 1520 March. Ioh. Franc. Picus: de reformandis moribus oratio. [PICO.] 4°.
P. VII. 90. 177. Types 3, 9 [caps.], (14), 17; A; d; δ.

11708. 1520 March. Luciani fugitiui. [LUCIAN.] 4°. P. VII. 90. 178. Types 3,
9 [caps.], 17; A; d; δ.

11709a. n. d. Iac. HENRICHMANNVS: grammaticae institutiones (a–p). Types 3
[caps.], 8, 9, 11, 17, gk. ij*, hb. ij; Bc.

  b. 1520 June. Bebel: ars uersificandi (A–I). Types 3 [caps.], 8, 9, gk. ij*; f.
  4°. P. VII. 90. 179.

11710. 1520 June. Ξενοφῶντος ἀπολογία Σωκράτους, Ἀγησίλαος, Ἱέρων. [XENOPHON.]
4°. P.VII. 90. 180. Types 11, 17, gk. ij*, iij; A; e; ε.

11711. 1520 Aug. LUTHER: von den guten Werken. 4°. DA. 974 gg. Types 8,
13; A; d.

11712. [1520] Sept. Ioh. SECERIVS: de animae praeparatione in extremo labo-
rantis. 4°. P. VII. 116. 400. Types 3, 9, 11, 17, gk. ij*; X; ε.

11713a. n. d. FVLGENTIVS: opera (a–r). Types 3, 9 [caps.], 11, 17; X; δε.

11713b. 1520. Maxentius: opuscula (A–F). [For the Kobergers.] Types 3,9,
17; C; d; δє. F°. P. VII. 90. 181.

11714. 1520. Pasquillus. S.P.Q.R. [PASQUINO.] 8°. Types (3), 8, 9, 17; є.
[In Aegypto minore excusum.]

11715. n. d. [1520.] HOCHSTRATVS ouans. 4°. (Not P. IX. 179. 188.) Types 3,
11,17; є.

11716. n.d. [1520?] Ioh. Huss: de causa Boemica. [JAN.] 4°. P. IX. 179. 194.
Types 3, 9, 11, 17, gk. ij*; X; δ.

XL. HAMBURG.

1(b). Johann Borchard.

i. JOH. BORCHARD.

Only two books bearing the Hamburg imprint between 1491 and 1523 were known to Lappenberg
(Zur Geschichte der Buchdruckerkunst in Hamburg, p. 5 ff. and 13 ff.). The first (1502), Van der
duldicheyt der vrowen gheheten Griseldis, is without name of printer; the second, De veer utersten,
dated 1510, Tuesday after S. Catharine (Nov. 26) is also described by Panzer, DA. 673b. It bears
the name of Hans Borchard.

TYPES. Type 3 (1502), text schwabacher = Arndes 5 (Lappenberg, p. 7).—Type 4, church
text; type 5 latin text gothic (1510); bad facsimiles of these, Lappenberg, pp. 14, 15. The latter
is perhaps like Arndes 1 (Burger 118). Cf. Dietz 1.

XLIII. FREIBURG i/BR.

3. Johann Schott, from Strassburg, second press   1503 b. July 13.

iij. JOHANN SCHOTT.

TYPES. Type 1, 2, 4, 5, and first greek, see Strassburg xxvi.—Type 6, small schwabacher like
Knoblouch 5, Flach jun. 11, &c.; long single hyphen; 73 mm.
Type 6, see fig. 63*.
DEVICES. c, EBM. II. 4; d, EBM. IV. 6.
INITIALS. α, see Strassburg press 33.

11717. 1503 b. July 13. Greg. REISCH: margarita philosophica. 4°. P. VII. 58.
1; SS. 8. Types 4, 5, gk. i; cuts, diagr.; c, d; α.

11718. 1504 March 16. Greg. REISCH: margarita philosophica. 4°. P. VI. 31.
44; VII. 58. 2; SS. 9. Types 1, 2, 4, 5, 6, gk. i; cuts, diagr.; d; α.

WITHOUT PRINTER'S NAME.

[a. 1502 Aug. 23.] Wimpheling: defensio Germaniae. P. VII. 62. 32.
See no. 9887.

L. TÜBINGEN.

1. Johann Otmar, second press.
2. Thomas Anshelm, of Baden, from Pforzheim, third press   1511 July

i. JOH. OTMAR.

TYPES. Types 7 (large round) and 13 (latin text like Quentell 7 ; double hyphen, 79 mm.); see part i.

Type 7, see fig. 24 ; 13, see fig. 37.

11719. [a. 1501 March 19.] Liber hymnorum in metra nouiter redactorum. [LIT.] 4°. P. VIII. 321. 1; St. 13. Types 7, 13.

ij. THOMAS ANSHELM.

TYPES. Types 3, 8, 9, see Pforzheim. In March 1513 a ¶ and white ℂ begin to be used with 9, and in 1514 with 3.—Type 10, small text schwabacher of normal style, like Miller 8 or Grim 1; double hyphen; short sloping comma; 88 mm.—Type 11, small Aldine roman in the same style as M. Schürer 5, but single hyphen; accents on vowels; 88 mm. Cf. Joh. Schöffer 18, &c.—Type 12, very large roman caps., 14 mm.—Greek ij and hebrew ij (used without vowel-points in 1514), see Pforzheim; Greek ij* seems to be at bottom the same fount as ij, but its character is entirely changed by the addition of a large number of ligatures and other new sorts; it is cast on three bodies, those of types 3, 9 and 11.—Hebrew iij is a small square fount, with vowel-points.

Type 10, see fig. 59 ; 11, see fig. 9.

BORDER. A, the original (or an improved copy) of Prüss jun. A: one-piece quarto.

DEVICE.—b, see Pforzheim.

INITIALS. The only initials found in these books are a calligraphic A (37 mm.) and a black-grounded V (27 mm.), both in no. 11722; a Maiblumen P (36 mm.) with letter black, in no. 11741; in the Horae of 1514 rough plain roman initials of 12 and 8 mm. are found.

11720. 1511 July. Henr. BEBEL: commentaria epistularum conficiendarum. 4°. P. VIII. 322. 5; St. 20. Types 3, 8, 9, gk. ij; b.

11721. 1511 July. BARTHOLOMAEVS Coloniensis: epistula mythologica. 4°. P. VIII. 322. 7; St. 21. Types 3, 8, 9; b.

11722. [a. 1511 Aug. 16.] Joh. REUCHLIN: Augenspiegel. 4°. DA. 694; St. 22. Types 8, 9, 10; diagr.; Δ.

11723. 1511 Sept. Baptista Mantuanus: bucolica seu adulescentia. [SPAGNUOLI.] 4°. P. VIII. 322. 6; St. 23. Types 3, 8, 9; b.

11724. [a. 1512 Feb. 17.] HIPPOCRATES: de praeparatione hominis. 4°. P. VIII. 322. 9; St. 29. Types 3, gk. ij*, hb. iij; b.

11725. 1512 March. Geo. SIMLER: obseruationes de arte grammatica, etc. 4°. P. VIII. 322. 8; St. 27. Types 3, 8, 9, gk. ij*; b.

11726. 1512 March. Rabbi Ioseph Hyssopaeus: lanx argentea. [JOSEPH ben Hanan Ezobi.] 4°. P. VIII. 322. 10; St. 30. Types 3, 9, gk. ij*, hb. iij; b.

11727. [a. 1512 March 22.] Joh. REUCHLIN: eine klare Verständnis ... von den Juden Büchern. 4°. DA. 718; St. 28. Types 8, 10.

11728. 1512 July. Ioh. Franc. Picus: staurostichon. [PICO.] 4°. P. VIII. 323. 12; St. 31. Types 3, 9, gk. ij*; b.

11729. 1512 July. De literis graecis ac diphthongis, etc. [MANUTIUS.] 4°. P. VIII. 322. 11; St. 32. Types 3, 9, gk. ij*, hb. ij, iij; b.

11730. 1512 Oct. REVCHLIN: scenica progymnasmata. 4°. P. VIII. 323. 13; St. 36. Types 3, 9, gk. ij*, music; b.

11731. 1513 March. WIMPHELING: elegantiae maiores. 4°. P.VIII. 324. 18; St.
43. Types 3, 8, 9; b.

11732. 1513 Apr. REVCHLIN: Sergius uel capitis caput. 4°. P.VIII. 324. 19; St.
44. Types 3, 8, 9, gk. ij*; b.

11733. 1513 May. Franc. Philelphus: de educatione liberorum. [FILELFO.] 4°.
P.VIII. 324. 20; St. 47. Types 3, 8, 9.

11734. 1513 July. QuintusCVRTIVSRVFVS: historia Alexandri magni. F°. P.VIII.
324. 21; St. 48. Types 3,9; b.

11735. 1513 Aug. Constantinus Magnus Ioh. Reuchlino interprete. [CONSTAN-
TINE.] 4°. P. VIII. 324. 22; St. 49. Types 3, 11 gk. ij*.

11736. 1514 March. ERASMVS: adagia. [For L. Hornken.] F°. P. VIII. 325. 29;
St. 53. Type 11, gk. ij*.

11737. 1514 March. Clarorum uirorum epistulae ad Ioh. Reuchlinum. [REUCH-
LIN.] 4°. P.VIII. 325. 28; St. 54. Type 11, gk. ij*, hb. ij; b.

11738. 1514 July. ALEXANDER Gallus: doctrinalis pars i. et ij. 4°. P.VIII. 325.
35; St. 56; R. 237. Types 3, 8, 9, gk. ij*; b.

11739. 1514 Aug. Horae B.M.V. secundum consuetudinem romanae curiae,
graece. [LIT.] 16°. St. 59. Type 11, gk. ij*.

11740. [a. 1514 Aug. 16.] Eine wahrhaftige Unterrichtung der Aufruhren in
Württemberg. [WURTEMBERG.] 4°. W. suppl. ij. 452. Types 8, 10.

11741. 1514 [a. Feb. 3]. Ioh. Stöffler: tabulae astronomicae. [EPH.] F°. P.VIII.
325. 33; St. 66. Types 3, 8; Δ. [Imp.]

11742. [a. 1515 Aug. 12.] ATHANASIVS: in librum psalmorum. 4°. P.VIII. 326.
39; St. 78. Types 3, 9 [caps.], 11, gk. ij*; A.

11743. 1516 March. Ioh. NAVCLERVS: memorabilium omnis aetatis chronici
commentarii. [For Conr. Breuning, Kil. Wetzler, Joh. Zuyfel.] F°.
P.VIII. 327. 46; St. 84. Types 3, 8, 11, 12, gk. ij*; cut; b.

LI. DANZIG.

2. Martin Tretter, from Frankfurt a/O, second press   1505.
3. Hans Weinreich, first press?   1520?

For these presses see Dr. P. Schwenke's articles in Dziatzko, Sammlung bibliothekswissen-
schaftlicher Arbeiten, vol. 8 and 13.

---

ij. MARTIN TRETTER.

Type 1, square northern church text=Gothan 3; type 2, small text schwabacher, double
hyphen; 88 mm. Both types brought from Frankfurt a/O. Facs. Schwenke in Dziatzko, ubi supra,
VIII. p. 80.   Eight books or sheets in these types are described by him; one (the only one with
the printer's name) of 1505, one rather later; one of c. 1513, and five of 1520.

iij. HANS WEINREICH?

Type 1, small text schwabacher, not the same as Tretter 2; 92 mm.—Type 2, larger round type
like Weissenburger 4; cf. Halberstadt, Lor. Stuchs, type 2.   Facs. of these types in Schwenke, ubi
supra, opp. p. 64.   Both these types were used by Weinreich at Königsberg in 1524.

LII. PFORZHEIM.

1. Thomas Anshelm, of Baden, second press.

---

i. THOMAS ANSHELM.

TYPES. Type 2 (small schwabacher, as Knoblouch 6); see part i.—Type 3, text roman, like
M. Schürer 8*, Knoblouch 8, Schott 5*, &c., but single hyphen; ę and æ; 109 mm.—Type 4, large
round gothic, angular lowercase; very like Bergmann 2. Short letters 6 mm.—Type 5, text gothic
like G. Stuchs 12, J. Otmar 27, Hüpfüff 7, &c., but probably of french origin; single hyphen; about
83 mm.—Type 6, small french gothic like Koberger 20 or Hölzel 9, but more distinctly french;
round h, double hyphen, 65 mm.—Type 7, middle german roman; double hyphen, ę; 88 mm.;
round comma first used Dec. 1506.—Type 8, middle large, like Ratdolt 9, tailed h; 134 mm.
Facs. (1516) Muther 184, 185.—Type 9, small roman like M. Schürer 4 or Knoblouch 13; ę at first,
single hyphen; 75 mm.; Æ first in Jan. 1511.—Greek types. i. rough, like M. Schürer i; no accents.
—ii. smaller and more cursive; with accents, often omitted in Pforzheim books.—Hebrew types.
i. thin cursive, without vowel-points; 3 lines = 17 mm.—ij, large black square type, with vowel-points.

Type 2, see fig. 63*; 3, see fig. 3; *4, see fig. 25; 5, see fig. 36; 6, see fig. 49; 7, see fig. 8;
8, see fig. 32'; 9, see fig. 11.

DEVICES. a [1505 Aug. 27], see EBM. LXII. 5.—b [1507 July], see EBM. LXII. 3.

INITIALS. Only odd initials are found at this period: in no. 11745 and 11748 a D copied from
the Zeninger-Wagner set, 50 mm.; in no. 11746 a calligraphic C, 35 mm.; in no. 11747 a similar M,
52 mm., large roman capitals (20 mm.) as initials, very numerous, and a Maiblumen A, 32 mm.;
this last is also found in no. 11750; in no. 11752 and later editions of the same book a D of quasi-
Maiblumen style, 29 mm.

11744. 1502. PETRVS de Rosenheim: memorabiles euangelistarum figurae. 4°.
  P.VIII. 226. 1. Type 3; cuts. [... Brantn memorabi-‖les ...]

11745. 1502. PETRVS de Rosenheim: memorabiles euangelistarum figurae. 4°.
  Types 3, 4; cuts; Δ. [... Sebastiani ‖ Brant in ...]

11746. 1502. Facetus lat.-germ. [BRANT.] 4°. W. 221. Types 2, 3, 5, 6; Δ.

11747. 1503 March. HRABANVS Maurus: de laudibus sanctae crucis. F°. P.VIII.
  227. 2. Types 3, 4; cuts, diagr.; Δ.

11748. 1503. PETRVS de Rosenheim: memorabiles euangelistarum figurae. 4°.
  Types 3, 4; cuts; Δ.

11749. 1504 March. Henr. BEBEL: de laudibus Germaniae oratio et opuscula.
  4°. P. VIII. 227. 3. Types 4, 7.

11750. 1504. Ioh. REVCHLIN: liber congestorum de arte praedicandi. 4°. P.VIII.
  227. 4. Types 4, 7; Δ.

11751. 1505 Aug. 27. HRABANVS Maurus: de institutione clericorum. 4°. P.VIII.
  227. 5. Types 4, 7; a.

11752. 1505. PETRVS de Rosenheim: rationarium euangelistarum. 4°. P.VIII.
  228. 8. Types 2, 3, 4, 7; a; Δ.

11753. [a. 1505 Christmas.] Joh. REUCHLIN: deutsche Missive, warum die Juden
  so lang im Elend sind. 4°. DA. 555f; W. 338. Types 2, 4, hb. i; a.

11754. 1506 March 27. Ioh. REVCHLIN: rudimenta hebraica. F°. P.VIII. 228.
  9. Types 3, hb. i, ij; cut; a.

11755. 1506 March 27. Iac. WIMPHELING: apologia pro republica christiana.
  4°. P. VIII. 228. 10. Types 4, 7.

11756. 1506 Sept. Rob. Gaguinus: de arte metrificandi. [GAGUIN.] 4°. P.VIII.
  229. 13. Types 7, 8.

11757. 1506 Dec. Franc. Philelphus: epistulae. [FILELFO.—For Conr. Hist.] 4°. P.VIII. 229. 12. Types 3 [caps], 7, gk. i.

11758. 1507 May. Iac. WIMPHELING: oratio de S. Spiritu. 4°. P.VIII. 229. 16. Types 7, 8.

11759. 1507 July. Ant. GERALDINVS: bucolica. 4°. P. VIII. 229. 18. Types 3, 7, 8; b.

11760. 1507 Sept. Ioh. REVCHLIN: Sergius uel capitis caput. 4°. P. VIII. 229. 19. Types 3, 8, 9, gk. ij; b.

11761. 1507. PETRVS de Rosenheim: rationarium euangelistarum. 4°. P.VIII. 230. 20. Types 2, 3, 7, 8; cuts; b; Δ. [1ᵇ, line 1: Brant.—Wants ff. 3, 4.]

11762. 1507. PETRVS de Rosenheim: rationarium euangelistarum. 4°. Types 3, 7, 8; cuts; b; Δ. [1ᵇ, line 1: brant.]

11763. n.d. [c. 1507.] P. Vergili Maronis bucolica. [VIRGILIVS.] 4°. Types 7, 8.

11764. 1508 March 16. Iac. HENRICHMANNVS: grammaticae institutiones. 4°. P. VIII. 230. 23. Types 3 [caps.], 9, gk. ij, hb. ij; b.

11765. 1508 April. REVCHLIN: Sergius uel capitis caput. 4°. P. VIII. 230. 22. Types 3, 8, 9, gk. ij; b.

11766. 1508. REVCHLIN: liber congestorum de arte praedicandi. 4°. P. VIII. 230. 25. Types 7, 8.

11767. 1508. REVCHLIN: scenica progymnasmata. 4°. P. VIII. 230. 24. Types 3, 7, 8, music.

11768. 1508. Joh. WIDMANN: Rechnung auf allen Kaufmannschaften. 8°. DA. 629. Types 2, 8; cuts, diagr.

11769. 1509 Feb. Henr. BEBEL: commentaria epistularum conficiendarum. 4°. P.VIII. 231. 26. Types 3 [caps.], 8, 9, gk. ij; b.

11770. 1509 Aug. BEBEL: epitome laudum Sueuorum, etc. 4°. P. VIII. 231. 28. Types 3, 8, 9, gk. ij; b.

11771. 1509. Alex. SEITZ: Regiment wider die Böse franzose. 4°. DA. 652. Types 2, 8.

11772. 1510. PETRVS de Rosenheim: rationarium euangelistarum. 4°. P.VIII. 232. 35. Types 3, 8; cuts; b; Δ.

11773. 1511 Jan. WIMPHELING: elegantiae maiores. 4°. P.VIII. 232. 37. Types 3, 8, 9; b.

11774. 1511 March. ALTENSTAIG: uocabularius. 4°. P.VIII. 232. 38. Types 3 [caps.], 8, 9, gk. ij; b.

LIII. LANDSHUT.

1. N. Wurm   [n.b. 1501].
2. Hans Wurm   n.d. [c. 1507?]
3. Johann Weissenburger, from Nürnberg, second press   1513 Dec. 22.

i. N. WURM.
Type 1 = Schobser 3.

11775. [n.b. 1501.] Cronik der Pfalzgrafen. [PALATINATE.] 4°. W. 210. Type 1.

ij. HANS WURM.

For the Ringbüchlein printed by Hans Wurm see Weller 9, who ascribes it to c. 1500, and
Serapeum v. 33, where it is assigned to c. 1507.

iij. JOHANN WEISSENBURGER, second press.

TYPES.   Types 4–7, see Nürnberg.—Type 8, curious small roman; round h, single hyphen,
all caps. out of register; 75 mm.—Type 9, large text schwabacher like Joh. Otmar 17; distinctive ¶,
the two uprights close together; long double hyphen; 107 mm.

Type 9, see fig. 52.

BORDERS.   A, one-piece quarto, a free copy of one used by Froben, with the arms of Baiern and
Landshut.—Bc, one-piece quarto border-device, dated 1519.

DEVICES.   b, see Nürnberg.—c, see border B.   An oblong cut with the arms of Baiern and
Landshut (cf. border A) is not strictly a device, but is used like one; it is found in no. 11783–5,
11791, 11797–8.   The cut with the symbols of the Evangelists, brought from Nürnberg, is used
in no. 11777, 11780, 11782, 11784, 11795, 11796.

INITIALS.   α, see Nürnberg.—β, calligraphic, 35–37 mm.

11776. [a. 1513 March 10.] Electio papae Leonis x. Ordo mansionum in con-
 claui. [LEO X.] 4°. P. VIII. 252. 66? Types 4, 6, 8.

11777. 1513 Dec. 22. MANVALE parochialium sacerdotum. 4°. P. IX. 477. 1.
 Types 4, 6, 7; cut; α.

11778. [a. 1514 March 6.] Ioh. MÜLLER: de uita et honestate clericorum. 4°.
 Types 4, 6, 7.

11779. 1514 March 10. Pharetra fidei catholicae. [CHRISTIANS.] 4°. P. VII.
 131. 2. Types 4, 6, 7.

11780. 1514 April 24. Ioh. Huss: gesta Christi. [JESUS.] 4°. P. VII. 131. 1.
 Types 4, 6, 7; cuts.

11781. 1514 May. Collationes Salomonis et Marcolphi. [SOLOMON.] 4°. Types
 4, 6, 7; cuts.

11782. 1514 June 20. Honorius: ELVCIDARIVS. 4°. P. VII. 131. 3. Types 4,
 6, 7; cut.

11783. 1514 July 19? Canon missae una cum expositione. [LIT.] 4°. P. VII.
 132. 4. Types 4, 6, 7; cut; α.

11784. 1514 July 26. MANVALE parochialium sacerdotum. 4°. P. VII. 132. 5.
 Types 4, 6, 7; cuts; α.

11785. 1514 Oct 22. Pet. Schwicker: in psalmos paenitentiales elucidatio.
 [BIBLE.] 4°. P. VII. 132. 6. Types 4, 6, 7, 8; cut.

11786. 1514 [a. Nov. 17.] Des löblichen Hauses und Fürstentums Baiern Freiheiten. [BAVARIA.] F°. DA. 783. Types 4, 5, 6; cut; β. [Gedruckt zu
 München.]

11787. 1514. Hier. DVNGERSHEYM: de modo discendi et docendi sacra. 4°.
 P. VII. 132. 7. Types 4, 6, 7; cut.

11788. 1514. ARS moriendi. 4°. Types 4, 6, 7; cuts; X.

11789. [n.b. 1515 Feb. 27.] Ios. GRÜNBECK: ad episcopos Frisingensem et
 Ratisponensem exhortatio. 4°. P. VII. 132. 9. Types 4, 6, 8; cut.

11790. [a. 1515 June 15.] Sankt URSULA Schifflein. 4°. DA. 812. Types 4,
 5, 6, 9; cuts.

11791. 1515. Wolfgang MAYER: Christi fasciculus. 4°. P. VII. 132. 10. Types
 4, 6, 8; cut.

11792. 1515 Sept. 4. SALLVSTIVS: opera, germanice. F°. DA. 825. Types 4, 5, 6, 9; cut; β.

11793. 1515 Dec. 14. PLINIVS: panegyricus, germanice. F°. DA. 824. Types 4, 5, 6, 9; cuts; β. [Wants ff. 1–3.]

11794. n. d. [c. 1515.] TVRRECREMATA: de efficacia aquae benedictae. 4°. P. VII. 135. 29. Types 4, 6, 7; cut; b.

11795. n. d. [c. 1515.] HENRICVS de Vrimaria: passio domini explanata. 4°. P. VII. 135. 30. Types 4, 6, 7; cuts.

11796. n.d. [c. 1515.] CVRA pastoralis. 4°. Types 4, 6, 7; cut; α.

11797. n.d.[c.1515.] Chr. SCHEURL: de sacerdotum praestantia. 4°. P.VII. 135. 27. Types 4, 6, 7; cut.

11798. n.d. [c. 1515.] De continentia sacerdotum. [PRIESTS.] 4°. P. IX. 479. 26b. Types 4, 6, 7; cut.

11799. (1515–16.) Simon Eisenmann: Practica deutsch auf das Jahr 1516. [EYSSENMAN.] 4°. W. 936. Types 4, 5, 6, 9; cut.

11800. 1516 Feb. 22. Vita diui Wolfgangi. [WOLFGANG.] 8°. P. IX. 478. 11b. Types 4, 5, 7, 8; cuts.

11801. [a. 1516 Apr. 8.] Ordnung über gemeiner Landschaft in Baiern. [BAVARIA.] F°. DA. 844. Types 4, 6, 9; cut; β.

11802. 1516 June 28. Die neue Erklärung der Landsfreiheit ... [BAVARIA.] F°. DA. 846b. Types 4, 6, 9; cut; β.

11803. n. d. [c. 1516.] Chr. SCHEURL: defensorium sacerdotum. 4°. P.VII. 449. 74. Types 4, 6, 7, 9; A.

11804. [a. 1516 Sept. 1.] Chr. SCHEURL: utilitates missae. 4°. P.XI. 471. 343e. Types 4, 6, 7; A.

11805. 1516 Oct. 13. Vom Klaffern, zwei Büchlein Luciani und Poggii. [LUCIAN.] F°. DA. 856. Types 4, 5, 6, 9; cut; β.

11806. [a. 1516 Dec. 19.] Leo x.: bulla undecimae sessionis praedicatorum diuini uerbi. [ROME.] 4°. Types 4, 6, 7, 9.

11807. [a. 1516 Dec. 19.] Leo x.: bulla super moderatione priuilegiorum fratrum mendicantium. 4°. Types 4, 6, 7, 9.

11808. [a. 1517 Feb. 17.] Hienach folgt wie der Türk den Soldan vertrieben hat. [SALIM I.] 4°. W. 1035. Types 4, 5, 6; cut.

11809. 1517. TRACTATVLVS de his qui ad ecclesias confugiunt. 4°. P. VII. 133. 13. Types 4, 6, 7.

11810. 1518 Aug. 3. Pharetra catholicae fidei. [CHRISTIANS.] 4°. P. VII. 133. 14. Types 4, 6, 7.

11811. 1519 Feb. Vlr. de HUTTEN: Febris, dialogus. 4°. B. xxi. 3; cf. P. IX. 120. 140. Types 4, 5. 6.

11812. 1519. Historie von dem Kaiser Friedrich dem Ersten. [FREDERICK.] 4°. DA. 946; W. 1190. Types 4, 5; cuts; β.

11813. [a. 1519 June 7.] Chronik des Stifts zu SALZBURG. 4°. W. 1176. Types 4, 5, 6; cut.

11814. [n. b. 1519.] Elias CAPREOLVS: de confirmatione christianae fidei. 4°. P. VII. 133. 15. Types 4, 6, 7; Bc.

11815. 1520 Apr. 4. Von dem Sterben ein nutzbarliches Büchlein. [ARS.] 4°. W. 1335. Types 4, 6, 9; cuts; X; b; β.

11816. [a. 1520 June 15.] Bulla Leonis x. contra errores Martini Lutheri. [ROME.] Types 4, 6, 7; cut.

11817. [n.b.1520June.]WieKönigKarlnach Englandgeschifftist.[CHARLESV.]
    4°. DA. 995b? (notW.1658.) Types4,9; cut; β.

11818. 1520. Historia de S. Apollonia. [LIT.] 8°. P.VII. 133. 19. Types 4, 7;
    cut; Y.

11819. n.d.[c. 1520.] Verkündung päpstlicher Prozession. [LEO X.] 4°. Types
    4, 6, 9; cut; β.

LANDS-
HUT.
iij. Johann
Weissen-
burger.

LIV. FRANKFURT AN DER ODER.

i.	Martin Tretter, first press	1502.
2.	Sebastianus Johannes, of Ingolstadt, and Conrad, of Herzo- genaurach	1504 April 22.
3.	Conrad Baumgarten, from Breslau, fourth press	1506.
4.	Ambros Lacher, of Meersburg	1506.
5.	Nicolaus Lamparter and Balthasar Murrer	1507.
6.	Johann Jamer, of Hanau	1509 Oct. 30.
[6*.	Johann Eichorn	1515.]

For the Frankfurt presses see Bauch in Centralblatt für Bibliothekswesen, 1898, pp. 248 ff.; he enumerates no fewer than 75 books of this period.

---

i. MARTIN TRETTER.

Types 1, 2; see Danzig press 2.

iij. CONRAD BAUMGARTEN.

Eighteen books are described by Bauch, ubi supra.

TYPES.   Type 2, fantastic german text, 82 mm., brought from Olmütz (see part i.); without the additional d of 1502.—Type 8, from Breslau; many caps. of types 3, 4 in it at this time.—Type 10, small text, like Bologna vij. 2, Ratdolt 10, Euch. Silber 1, Carcain 1; single hyphen; 68 mm.

DEVICE.   c, from Breslau.

INITIALS.   All single odd letters; calligraphic C, 64 mm. and C, 28 mm. Black-grounded letters; D upside down, used as C, 42 mm., MH on a label inside it; C, 30 mm.; C, 18–19 mm.; C, with grotesque head, 29 mm.; C, diced, 42 mm.; later this last has the black ground cut away.

11820. 1509 Apr. 20. Erasmus Wonsiedel: cursus philosophicus super Aristo-
    telica philosophia. [ARISTOTLE.] F°. P.VII.55.11; Bauch 29. Types
    2, 8, 10; c; Δ.

iv. AMBROS LACHER.

TYPES.   Type 1, a close copy of Peter Schöffer 2 (the larger 1457 Psalter type); short letters 10 mm.—Type 2, small church text, apparently in the Lübeck style; short letters 4½ mm.—Type 3, archaic small text, like Rostock i. 1 (Burger 39), but caps. (of remarkable form) much too large, and all kerned where the type is set solid. Double hyphen; 65 mm. Facs. of all three types, TFS. 1903e.

11821. 1506. Euclidis elementorum libri quattuor. [EUCLID.] 4°. P.VII. 54.1;
    Bauch 7. Types 1, 2, 3; diagr.

157

v. NIC. LAMPARTER AND BALTH. MURRER.

Nine books described by Bauch.

TYPES. Type 1, large round, style of Grüninger 17.—Type 2, roman like Bergmann 1 or one of Rembolt's founts; short sloping comma, also used as hyphen; ę and æ; low us; 102 mm. Cf. also Anshelm 3.—Type 3, larger text, like Gran 10, Grüninger 20 (similar E); with ℭ; 82 mm. —Type 4, small, like Gran 9, Quentell 6, &c.; double hyphen, round h, ¶; 64 mm.

Type 1, see fig. 28; 3, see fig. 34; 4, see fig. 46.

DEVICE. a, contains the trade marks of Lamparter and Murrer on separate shields; 40 × 52 mm.

11822. 1507. CEBES: tabula. 4°. P. IX. 462. 1b; Bauch 11. Types 1, 2; cut.
11823. n. d. HORATIVS: ars poetica. 4°. Types 1, 2, 3.
11824. 1508 Oct. 1. Conr. Wimpina: epithoma problematum circa libros sententiarum. [KOCH.] F°. P. IX. 463. 1c; Bauch 25. Types 1–4; a.

vi. JOH. JAMER.

Twenty-eight books described by Bauch and Weller.
TYPES. Type 1 = Baumgarten 2.—Type 2 = Baumgarten 8.

11825. 1510 [a. July 15.] Vlr. de HVTTEN: in Vedegum Loetzet filium eius querelarum libri duo. 4°. P. VII. 55. 13; Bauch 36. Types 1, 2.

vi*. JOHANN EICHORN.

The only book of this printer cited at this period is an edition of Ioh. de Landshut, Algorismus linealis, described by Wierzbowski, Bibliographia Polonica, no. 914; but it is probably an error, as all Eichorn's work is of a much later date.

LV. WITTENBERG.

1. Henricus Sertorius, from Erfurt, second press   1503 Jan. 18.
2. Wolfgang Stöckel, of München, from Leipzig, second press   1504 (Apr. 20).
3. Johann Rhau, called Grünenberg (of Grünberg?)   1509.
4. Simphorian Reinhart   1512.
5. Melchior Lotter, the younger   (1519–20).

i. HENRICUS SERTORIUS, second press.

Though the name of Sertorius is not found at Wittenberg, the identity of type is certain, and its transfer corresponds with the removal of Marschalk to Wittenberg from Erfurt. The material doubtless belonged more or less to Marschalk; but part at least of the type was in Rhau's hands as early as 1509, and one of the Erfurt cuts appears in a book of 1513 printed by Rhau. No printing for which Marschalk was responsible between 1504 and 1517 has yet come to light, and there is no record of the name of his printer at Wittenberg. Sertorius probably came with Marschalk, but in any case his name helps to show the connexion.

TYPES. Type 1, larger roman, from Erfurt. Cf. Lotter sen. 12.—Type 2, smaller roman, curious; the style is that of 1 but squarer; long single hyphen, short comma, & and us noteworthy; 80–81 mm. Cf. Lotter sen. 13.—Greek type, from Erfurt.

Types 1, 2, see fig. 7.

11826. 1503 Jan. 18. Nic. MARSCHALK: oratio Albiori habita. 4°. P. IX. 65. 1.
 Type 1, gk.
11827. [a. 1504 June 20.] Ioh. de KITSCHER: dialogus de sacri romani Imperii
 rebus. 4°. P. IX. 182. 212. Types 1, 2.

ij. WOLFGANG STÖCKEL, second press.

The Petrus Rauennas appears to have been finished at Leipzig; for the colophon says: Impressum
est hoc opus... quoad primam eius partem in florentissimo studio Wittenbergensi. The only other
recorded book printed by Stöckel at Wittenberg is the Parthenice prima of Bapt. Mantuanus, also
dated 1504; see P. VII. 150. 115.

TYPES. Types 5, 6, from Leipzig.

DEVICE. b, from Leipzig.

11828. 1504 Apr. 20. Petrus Rauennas: compendium iuris canonici. [TOMMAI.]
 F°. P. IX. 65. 2 = VII. 150. 114. Types 5, 6; cut; b.

iij. JOHANN RHAU, CALLED GRÜNENBERG.

Address (1516 Dec.): bei den Augustinern. Panzer records five books printed by him in 1509,
four in 1510. He succeeded to the material of Sertorius; besides the types, the cut in the Batracho-
muomachia (no. 11831) is one used by Sertorius at Erfurt in 1502, and that in Beckmann (no. 11829)
is in the same style. He may be the same as the Ioannes Ru who was printing with Wolf Stürmer at
Erfurt in 1507.

TYPES. Type 1, larger roman = Sertorius 1.—Type 2, smaller roman = Sertorius 2. In 1518
caps. of 7 are mixt with it.—Type 3, round latin text gothic, seemingly = Wolfg. Schenck 3 (similar
M).—Type 4, small text schwabacher, as Hölzel 4, Stöckel 6, &c.; facs. (1509), Muther 252–253;
(1520) Trans. Bibliogr. Soc. III. 13; (1521) Muther 254–255. In 1516 it has short comma, rather
thin ¶, hyphen like Hölzel's; in and after 1518 the comma is longer, the ¶ thicker, the hyphen longer
and lower; this last and the longer comma alone distinguish the type from Stöckel 6.—Type 5, middle
large round, very like Hölzel 2 (same V), but many caps. like Ratdolt 9; facs. (1509), Muther 252–
253.—Type 6, italian text roman, round, badly justified; the hyphen is really double, though
generally clogged so that it seems single : long comma, used also as hyphen, chiefly in caps.; in
1519–20 there is also a very small and low round comma. Small us; ę only, not æ, large thin ¶,
separate Q; the left limb of T is broken as in Hölzel 8; 110 mm.—Type 7, small roman; caps. like
Quentell 13; face smaller than 2; round comma, in one or two books used together with a
sloping one; separate Q, ę always, double hyphen, small ¶; 77 mm.—Type 8, narrow church type
as Stöckel 5; same high hyphen, sometimes reversed; facs. (1520) Trans. Bibliogr. Soc. III. 13;
(1521) Muther 254–255, and (1520) together with some caps. of type 7, Butsch I. 89.—Greek type,
that of Sertorius; cf. W. Schenck's second fount. In and after 1519 it is also found cast on the
body of type 7.

Types *1, *2, see fig. 7 ; 3, see fig. 41 ; 4, see fig. 59 ; 5, see fig. 14² ; 6, see fig. 4 ; 7, see fig. 11 ;
8, see fig. 21.

BORDERS. A, quarto, black ground, apparently cut down and pieced from a larger border;
foliage, with a squirrel and a bird.—B, quarto, white ground; a staghunt. Cut down like A.—C,
one-piece quarto, white, with arms of Sachsen and Wittenberg; at sides a beggar with rosary and a
drinking Silenus.—D, like C, but at sides winged boys playing on the flute and lute.—Ed, white
border-device, with printing press, and monogram in black; facs. Butsch I. 89; Trans. Bibliogr. Soc.
III. 12.

DEVICES. a, oblong, a mountain with a few plants on it; IG; 53 × 60 mm.—b, like a, but a
lower hill quite covered with flowering plants; IG; 53 × 60 mm.—c, upright, black ground; a
monogram surmounted by a thistle; around are interlaced boughs; 62 × 41 mm.—d, see border E.

11829. 1509 [a. March 27]. Otho BECKMAN: panegyricus. 4°. P. IX. 67. 9.
 Types 1, 2, gk.

WITTEN-
BERG.
iij. Johann
Rhau.

11830. 1511. Geo. sibvtvs: Friderici et Ioannis principum torniamenta. 4°.
P. IX. 68. 16. Types 1, 2, gk.; cuts.

11831. 1513 March 4. Βατραχομυομαχία, gr.-lat. [homer.] 4°. P. IX. 69. 19.
Types 1, 2; gk.; cut.

11832. [a. 1515 Jan. 5.] avsonivs: libellus de ludo vij. sapientum. 4°. Type
1, gk.

11833. 1516 Dec. 4. Büchlein von rechter Unterscheide und Verstand. [adam.]
4°. DA. 833 b; W. suppl. i. 128. Types 3, 4, 5; cut.

11834. 1518 [a. May 9]. Andr. bodenstein: ccclxx et apologeticae conclusiones.
4°. P. IX. 72. 40. Types 6, 7, 8.

11835. 1518 July 20. lvther: decem praecepta wittenbergensi praedicata
populo. 4°. P. IX. 71. 33. Types 2, 6, 8; cut; A; a.

11836. 1518 [a. Sept. 14]. Andr. bodenstein: defensio aduersus Eckii mono-
machiam. 4°. P. IX. 72. 41. Types 6, 7. [Woodcut hebrew.]

11837. 1518 [n. b. Nov.]. Ioh. boeschenstain: grammatica hebraica. 4°. P.IX.
72. 44. Types 6, 7; c. [Hebrew all written in.]

11838. [a. 1518 Nov. 28.] lvther: appellatio ad concilium. bs. Types 6, 7.

11839. 1518. Eine deutsche Theologia. [german theology.] 4°. W. 1151. Types
4, 6, 8; cut; a.

11840. 1518. lvther: sermo de digna praeparatione cordis. 4°. P. IX. 71. 32.
Types 4, 6, 8.

11841. 1518. lvther: sermo de triplici iustitia. 4°. P. IX. 71. 31. Types 6, 7.

11842. 1518. lvther: sermo de paenitentia. 4°. P.IX. 71. 30. Types 2, 6; B; b.

11843. 1518. Luther: apologetica responsio contra dogmata quae in M. Egranum
inuulgata sunt. [elevtherivs.] 4°. P. IX. 71. 38. Types 2, 4, 8.

11844. 1518. melanchthon: sermo de corrigendis adulescentiae studiis. 4°. P.
IX. 72. 43. Types 6, 7, gk; c. [Woodcut hebrew.]

11845. (1518.) lvther: resolutiones disputationum de indulgentiarum uirtute.
4°. P. IX. 71. 35. Types 6, 7, 8; cut.

11846. (1518.) lvther: sermo de uirtute excommunicationis. 4°. P.IX. 118.121.
Types 6, 7, 8, gk.

11847. (1519.) Disputatio Eckii et Lutheri Lipsiae futura. [johann.] 4°. P.VII.
211. 732. Types 6, 7, 8. [Preface dated 1518 Dec. 29.]

11848. (1519.) lvther: disputatio et excusatio aduersus criminationes Eckii.
4°. P. IX. 73. 53. Types 6, 7, 8.

11849. [a. 1519 July 21.] melanchthon: epistula de disputatione lipsica. 4°. P.
IX. 74. 58. Types 6 [caps.], 7.

11850. [a. 1519 July 24.] Eckius: epistula ad Iacobum Hochstratum. [johann.]
4°. P. IX. 497. 787c. Type 7.

11851. 1519 [a. Aug. 15]. lvther: resolutiones super propositionibus suis Lipsiae disputatis. 4°. P. IX. 73. 51. Types 6, 7.

11852. [a. 1519 Aug. 15.] lvther: resolutiones…4°. Types 6, 7, 8. [Leaves 1–8
only.]

11853. 1519 Nov. 7. luther: Sermon von dem heiligen Sacrament der Taufe.
4°. DA. 932 uu. Types 4, 8; cut.

11854. 1519. lvther: epistula super expurgatione eckiana. 4°. P. IX. 73. 52.
Types 6, 7, 8; A.

11855. 1519. lvther: ad aegocerotem emserianum additio. 4°. P. IX. 73. 49.
Types 6 [caps.], 7.

11856. (1519.) MELANCHTHON: defensio contra Ioh. Eckium. 4°. P. IX. 74. 59. WITTEN-
BERG.
iij. Johann
Rhau.
Type 6.
11857. 1519. LUTHER: Sermon von dem Sacrament der Busse. 4°. DA. 932p.
Types 4, 8. [Title red; sig. a, b.]
11858. 1519. LUTHER: Sermon von dem Sacrament der Busse. 4°. DA. 932n.
Types 4, 8. [Title black; sig. A, B.]
11859. 1519. LUTHER: Sermon von dem ehelichen Stande. 4°. W. 1243. Types
4, 8.
11860. 1519. LUTHER: Sermon von der Betrachtung des Leidens Christi. 4°.
DA. 932oo. Types 4, 8; cut.
11861. 1519. MELANCHTHON: de rhetorica libri tres. 4°. P. IX. 74. 60. Types 6,
7, 8, gk.; A; c.
11862. n. d. [1519.] Encomium Rubii Longipollii. [NEMO.] 4°. P. IX. 74. 63.
Types 4, 6, 7, 8, gk.; cut.
11863. [a. 1520 May 3.] Epistula Ioannis Eckii sedis papistica e nuntii... [JOHANN.]
4°. P. IX. 123. 156. Types 6, 7.
11864. 1520 [a. May 8]. LUTHER: heilsames Büchlein von der Beichte. 4°. W.
1505. Types 4, 6 [caps.], 8; C.
11865. 1520 [a. May 21]. LUTHER: Predigt von zweierlei Gerechtigkeit. 4°.
DA. 974aa. Types 4, 6 [caps.], 7 [caps.], 8.
11866. 1520 [a. Aug. 19]. Luther: Auslegung des 109. Psalms. [BIBLE.] 4°. DA.
973f. Types 4, 7, 8; D.
11867. (1520 [a. Sept. 6].) LVTHER: epistula ad Leonem x. de libertate christiana. 4°. P. IX. 77. 89. Types 6, 7.
11868. [a. 1520 Sept. 6.] LUTHER: Sendbrief an den Papst Leo. 4°. DA.
974qqq. Types 4, 8.
11869. 1520 Sept. 28. Eine deutsche Theologia. [GERMAN THEOLOGY.] 4°. DA.
969. Types 4, 8; cut.
11870. 1520 [a. Dec. 10]. LUTHER: warum des Papsts Bücher von ihm verbrannt sind. 4°. DA. 974bbb or W. suppl. i. 174. Types 4, 8.
11871. 1520. LVTHER: confitendi ratio. 4°. P. IX. 75. 67. Types 6 [caps.], 7.
11872. 1520. Luther: eine kurze Form der zehn Gebote. [L., Martinus.] 4°. DA.
974n. Types 4, 7 [caps.], 8; C.
11873. 1520. Luther: Sermon von dem Sacrament des Leichnams Christi. [A.,
D.M. L.] 4°. DA. 973pp. Types 4, 8; cuts.
11874. 1520. Luther: Sermon von dem Neuen Testament. [L., Mar.] 4°. W.
1582. Types 4, 8; D.
11875. 1520. Luther: Sermon von dem Neuen Testament. [L., Mar.] 4°. DA.
974yyy. Types 4, 8; C.
11876. 1520. LUTHER: Sermon von dem Gebete und Prozession in der Kreuzwoche. 4°. DA. 974b. Types 4, 8.
11877. 1520. LUTHER: Sermon von dem Wucher. 4°. DA. 973u. Types 4, 7
[caps.], 8; cut.
11878. (1520.) LUTHER: von der Freiheit eines christen Menschen. 4°. DA.
974ttt. Types 4, 8; C.
11879. 1520. Andr. BODENSTEIN: von geweihtem Wasser und Salz. 4°. DA.
988f. Types 4, 8; c.
11880. 1520. Andr. BODENSTEIN: von Vermögen des Ablasses. 4°. DA. 988c.
Types 4, 8; Ed.

11881. (1520.) LUTHER: Appellation an ein christliches freies Concilium ver-
neuert und repetirt. 4°. DA. 974ss; W. 1503. Types 4, 8.

11882. (1520.) Oecolampadius: die verdeutschte Antwort der ungelehrten
lutherischen Domherren. [JOHANN von Eck.] 4°. W. 1609. Types 4, 8.
n. d. [a. 1520.] Eine Klage und Bitte der deutschen Nation... W. 1349.
[Two types, as Trans. Bibl. Soc. III. p. 12.]

iv. SIMPHORIAN REINHART.

For the only book signed by this printer see Weller 680.

v. MELCHIOR LOTTER, THE YOUNGER.

Lotter came to Wittenberg in the spring of 1519 (Trans. Bibl. Soc. III. p. 14); but no book seems
to be dated earlier than 1520.

TYPES. Type 1 = Lotter sen. 2. In one book only (no. 11883) the hyphen is high as that of
Stöckel or J. Rhau.—Type 2 = id. 10.—Type 3 = id. 11.—Type 4 = id. 12.—Type 5 = id. 16 (Butsch
I. 90).—Type 6 = id. 18.—Type 7, large capitals, not pure roman; 12 mm. Facs. Butsch I. 90.
First greek, that of Lotter sen. Second greek, a much ligatured fount in the style of Froben, with
very small capitals.

BORDERS. (All one-piece quarto.) A = Lotter sen. C.—B = id. E.—C has the brazen serpent
device at foot as B, but the arms of Wittenberg at the top. This border is usually found cracked
through at the top, and about halfway through at the bottom (11884, 11888, 11900; not in 11894,
11913, 11915); sometimes there is a further break in the inner line just above the serpent's head
(11889, 11891, 11916); and one book (no. 11914) shows yet more breaks; but unless most of the
books in which this border was used were printed after 1520, these breaks are extremely perplexing,
even supposing that the cracks were mended; for of the three books which show the border unbroken, one (no. 11894) must be later than 1520 Nov. 1. But no. 11900 has the date of printing
1520, and the second state of C. For the third and fourth states there is no definite date.—D,
white; monk and nun at sides, grotesque head at foot; facs. Butsch I. 90 and Trans. Bibl. Soc.
III. p. 15.

INITIALS. α, apparently = Lotter sen. α.—Odd initial: a D, letter black, ground in maiblumen
style, 22 mm. (no. 11885, 11886).

11883. [a. 1520 Jan. 24.] Luther: ad schedulam inhibitionis episcopi Misnensis
responsio. [SCHLEINITZ.] 4°. P. IX. 76. 83. Types 1, 4, 6.

11884. 1520 [a. March 26]. LVTHER: confitendi ratio. 4°. Types 4, 6; C.

11885. 1520 [a. March 29]. LUTHER: von den guten Werken. 4°. W. suppl. i. 175?
Types 1, 3; cut; B; Δ. [1ᵇ, l. 3: Doringen.]

11886. 1520 [a. March 29]. LUTHER: von den guten Werken. DA. 974dd?
Types 1, 3; cut; B; Δ. [1ᵇ, l. 3: Duringē.]

11887. 1520 [a. March 29]. LUTHER: von den guten Werken. 4°. DA. 974cc.
Types 1, 3; cut; B. [Wants last leaf: 1ᵇ, l. 3: Duringen.]

11888. 1520 [n. b. May]. Ioh. VELTKIRCH: confutatio libelli Aug. Alueld, pro
Luthero. 4°. P. IX. 76. 76. Types 5, 6, gk. ij; C.

11889. [a. 1520 June 3.] Vlr. de HVTTEN: epistula ad Lutherum. 4°. P. IX.
77. 90; B. xxx. 1. Types 5, (7), gk. ij; C.

11890. [a. 1520 June 23.] LUTHER: an den christlichen Adel deutscher Nation.
4°. W. 1496. Types 1, 3; α.

11891. [a. 1520 June 23.] LUTHER: an den christlichen Adel... 4°. Types 1, 3; C; α.

11892. [a. 1520 Oct. 17.] Andr. BODENSTEIN: von päpstlicher Heiligkeit. 4°.
DA. 988b. Types 1, 3.

11893. [a. 1520 Oct. 19.] Andr. BODENSTEIN: Appellation zu dem Concilio. 4°.
DA. 988h. Types 1, 3; α.
11894. [a. 1520 Nov. 1.] ERASMVS: epistula ad praesulem moguntinum de
Luthero. 4°. P. VII. 264. 60; cf. ix. 123. 159. Types 5, (7); C.
11895. [a. 1520 Nov. 4.] Andr. BODENSTEIN: welche Bücher biblisch sind. 4°.
DA. 988i. Types 1, 3; α.
11896. [a. 1520 Nov. 17.] LVTHER: appellatio ad concilium denuo repetita. 4°.
P. IX. 77. 84. Types 5, 6 [caps.]; D; α.
11897. 1520 [a. Dec. 10]. LUTHER: warum des Papsts Bücher verbrannt sind. 4°.
W. 1597. Types 1, 3.

11898. 1520. Ὁμήρου Ὀδυσσείας ά-δ'. [HOMER.] 4°. Types 4, 6 [caps.], gk. ij; B.
11899. 1520. MELANCHTHON; declamatiuncula in D. Pauli doctrinam. 4°. P. IX.
76. 80. Types 1, 2, 4, 6, gk. i; cut; α.
11900. 1520. Condemnatio librorum Lutheri per magistros louanienses. [ACAD.]
4°. P. IX. 76. 77. Types 4, 6; C; α.
11901. 1520. Andr. BODENSTEIN: uerba dei quanto candore praedicari debeant.
4°. P. IX. 75. 75. Types 4, 6; cut; α.
11902. 1520. LUTHER: Sermon von der Betrachtung des heiligen Leidens
Christi. 4°. DA. 973ll. Type 3; cut.

11903. (1520.) LVTHER: aduersus execrabilem antichristi bullam. 4°. P. IX.
77. 87. Types 5, 6 [caps.]; α.
11904. (1520.) LUTHER: wider die Bullen des Endchrists. 4°. DA. 974rr. Types
1, 3; α.
11905. (1520.) Andr. BODENSTEIN: Bedingung. 4°. DA. 988l. Types 1, 3; α.
11906. (1520.) LUTHER: von den neuen eckischen Bullen und Lügen. 4°. DA.
974oo. Types 1, 3.
11907. (1520.) LUTHER: von der Freiheit eines christen Menschen. 4°. DA.
974rrr. Types 1, 3; A.
11908. (1520.) LVTHER: assertio omnium articulorum per bullam damnatorum.
4°. P. IX. 77. 88. Types 5, 7, gk. ij; D.
11909. (1520.) Epitoma responsionis ad Lutherum Siluestri Prieratis. [MAZ-
ZOLINI.] 4°. P. IX. 77. 92. Types 5, 6, (7); α.

11910. n.d. [1520.] LUTHER: von dem Papsttum zu Rom. 4°. DA. 974lll. Types 1, 3.
11911. n. d. [1520.] LUTHER: von dem Papsttum zu Rom. 4°. DA. 974kkk.
Types 1, 3; α.
11912. n. d. [1520.] LUTHER: Appellation an ein christliches freies Concilium.
4°. DA. 974xx. Types 1, 3.
11913. n. d. [1520.] LUTHER: Verklärung etlicher Artikel in seinem Sermon
von dem heiligen Sacrament. 4°. W. suppl. i. 173. Types 1, 3; C.
11914. n.d. [1520.] LUTHER: Auslegung deutsch des Vaterunser. 4°. W. 1128.
Types 1, 3; C.
11915. n. d. [1520.] Oecolampadius: canonici indocti lutherani. [JOHANN von
Eck.] 4°. Type 4; C.
11916. n.d. [1520.] LVTHER: de captiuitate babylonica ecclesiae. 4°. P. IX. 76.
79. Type 5; C; α.
11917. n. d. [c. 1520?] Epistula diui Hulderichi de cleri caelibatu. [ULRIC.] 4°.
P. IX. 101. 333. Types 5, 7.

WITTEN-
BERG.
v. Melchior
Lotter, the
Younger.

WITHOUT PRINTER'S NAME.

1503 Jan. 18. Marschalk: oratio	11826.
1518. Luther: apologia contra dogmata	11843.
1519 [a. Aug. 15]. Luther: resolutiones	11851.
1519. Luther: Sermon von der Busse	11858.
1519. Luther: Sermon vom ehelichen Stande	11859.
1519. Luther: Sermon von der Betrachtung des Leidens Christi	11860.
1520. Luther: Sermon von der Betrachtung des Leidens Christi	11902.
1520 [a. Dec. 10]. Luther: warum des Papsts Bücher verbrannt sind	11897.
1520 [a. Dec. 10]. Luther: warum des Papsts Bücher verbrannt sind	11870.
n. d. Epistula diui Hulderici	11917.

LVI. WESSOBRUNN.

1. Lucas Zeissenmair, from Augsburg, second press	1503 Aug. 11.

i. LUCAS ZEISSENMAIR, second press.

Types and initials as at Augsburg.—For the book of 1503 see Weller 262.

11918. 1505 Feb. 10. Ioh. Nider: die vier und zwanzig goldnen Harfen. [CAS-
SIANVS.] F°. DA. 553. Type 2; cut; αβΔ.

LVII. OPPENHEIM.

1. Jacob Köbel, Stadtschreiber [from Heidelberg]	1503?

i. JACOB KÖBEL.

The history of Köbel's press, and the order of his many undated books, are exceptionally hard to
be clear about. The books of 1494 and 1498 (Hain 16219, 1789) are doubtless mythical; DA.
544, dated 1503, seems to rest on doubtful authority; P. VII. 487. 1 is ascribed to the same year;
no. 11919 below also has the date 1503, but is this the year of printing? The use of type 1ᴮ and the
state of the device point to c. 1515; one of the woodcuts is used again slightly more flattened at
the top in 1516 (no. 11934). The text type (type 3) found (in the books here described) again only
in the undated Wirt (no. 11920) does not help us; but the use of a round comma and semicolon,
and of a bastard fount of type 4 in this last (the full-bodied fount is first found in 1516) would in the
case of a less erratic printer point to a late date, c. 1518, for it: yet on the other hand the type of
the marginalia (type 2) is somewhat different in and after 1516 from its state in this book. While
still at Heidelberg Köbel was connected with printing; the preface of Hain *11080 is addressed
to him as responsible for the publication, and a device very like his Oppenheim devices is found
in H. 7401, printed at Heidelberg in 1494; but there seems no reason at present to assign
him a press of his own at that period.

TYPES. Type 1, large round as Grüninger 17; 1ᴮ has a pointed long s and h for use in german
books like those found in Grüninger's fount; but the latin and german forms are often a little mixt
together, especially the s.—Type 2, small, with mixt capitals, like Heinrich of Neuss 4, but has
round h; hyphen single in no. 11919, in 1516-18 double. 65 mm. 2ᴮ, the same type germanised
in the same fashion as type 1.—Type 3, latin text, like Prüss sen. 8; caps. mixt, mostly as Prüss,

Quentell 7 or Drach 13, but it has also caps. of type 7 mixt in it from the first ; double hyphen.
In no. 11919 it has a sloping comma only ; in no. 11920 besides this a round comma, semicolon,
and reversed semicolon are found. 80 mm.—Type 4, square large text, apparently the same as
Drach 25, used at Worms in 1504. In no. 11920 it is cast on the body of 3, and kerned (here called
4*) ; on its reappearance in 1516 it is full-bodied, and has the curly paragraph mark of type 8.—
Type 5, middle roman, with double hyphen, thick ¶, high and rather open us (two forms at least);
remarkable ʒ with the tail curled back, in the earlier books often used with q for que: in 1516 an
equally strange con comes in ; in 1518 round comma and æ œ are first found ; earlier a sloping
comma and ȩ only. Also in 1518 Æ comes in, but it is not a single sort ; 86 mm. 5* has a round
d and pointed (germanised) long s.—Type 6, thin large roman capitals, 8 mm. high. The caps.
used for initials in no. 11919 are different. In 1518 Æ (made out of two sorts) first appears.—
Type 7, small schwabacher, very like Kirchheim ij. 2, Bumgart 5, or Hüpfüff 3.—Type 8, text schwabacher, not distinguishable from Schott 12 except by the h ; paragraph mark with tail bent back ;
92 mm. Facs. of types 1, 5, 6 in Trans. Bibl. Soc. III. p. 75.—Greek type, very little used.

Type *1, see fig. 28 ; 2, see fig. 47 ; 3, see fig. 37 ; 5, see fig. 8 ; 6, see fig. 2 ; 7, see fig. 64 ; 8, see fig. 57.

BORDERS. A, one-piece folio, architectural ; at top two boys with toy windmills ; sill for type
at foot.—B, four-piece quarto ; men in various attitudes.—C, one-piece small quarto, white ; apes
playing amidst foliage.—D, four-piece octavo, dotted black ground, renascence ornament : facs.
Trans. Bibl. Soc. III. p. 75.—E, four-piece quarto ; the design is continuous ; grotesque architec-
ture.—F, four-piece folio, heraldic ; reduced facs., Trans. Bibl. Soc. III. p. 78.

DEVICES. An owl seated on a branch is the printer's trade mark.—a, small, white ground
with blank label.—b, the mark in the initial L of set θ.—c, oblong, black ground powdered with large
dots ; name, &c. on label ; facs. Trans. Bibl. Soc. III. p. 76.—d, small, a shield within a circular
wreath with shaded background.—e, no trade mark ; queen's head in a wreath ; around it : Gedruckt
zu Oppenheim ; the whole in a square.—f, shield with mark held by seated woman : on a label the
letters g i m l h.

INITIALS. α, calligraphic, thin and fancifully curved ; 22–32 mm.—β, calligraphic, heavy,
with grotesque faces ; 25 mm.—Γ, black ground arabesque, 23 mm.—δ, ditto, 12 mm.—ε, ditto,
38 mm.—ʒ, ditto, 18 mm.—Η, ditto, 30 mm.—θ, ditto, 48–51 mm.—ι, black letters on white or
shaded ground, 12 mm.—κ, as Γ–θ, 10 mm. only.—λ, grotesque, white letters, shaded or white
ground ; 28–29 mm.—μ, calligraphic, like α, but larger and freer ; 51–58 mm.—ν, calligraphic,
heavy, 28–29 mm.—ξ, as ι, but 16 mm.—Δ initials are all calligraphic, except a S of french style,
17 mm., first used in a dated book in 1516.—Facs. of Γʒθ, Trans. Bibl. Soc. III. p. 74 ; of εʒθ, all
reduced, Butsch I. 37A, B.

11919. 1503? Defensio bullae Sixtinae siue extrauagantis Grauenimis. [ROME.]
    4°. Types 1^B, 2, 3 ; a ; αβΔ.

11920. n. d. Wigandus WIRT: dialogus apologeticus contra wesalianicam per-
    fidiam. 4°. P. VII. 492. 28. Types 1, 2, 3, 4* ; Γδε.

11921. 1510 [a. Apr. 24]. Iac. WIMPHELING: in Iohannis Keiserspergii mortem
    planctus et lamentatio. 4°. P. VII. 488. 4. Types 5, 6 ; Γδ.

11922. 1512, 1513. Ioh. STOEFFLER: elucidatio fabricae ususque astrolabii. F°.
    P. VII. 488. 7. Types 1, 5, 6, 7, 8 ; cuts, diagr.; A ; bc ; Γεʒθ.

11923. 1514. Ant. de ROSELLIS: summula de quadragesimalibus. 4°. P. VII.
    489. 9. Types 1, 5 ; ʒΗ.

11924. n. d. [c. 1514?] Opusculum de uaticiniis sibyllarum. [SIBYLS.] 4°. Types
    1, 5, 6, 8, gk. ; cuts ; δʒΗικΔ.

11925. n. d. [c. 1514?] Proba Falconia: centones uergiliani. [VIRGILIVS.] 4°.
    Types 1, 5, 7, 8 ; cuts ; δʒΗ.

11926. n. d. [c. 1514?] Opusculum de uariis de Christo testimoniis. [JESUS.] 4°.
    Types 1, 5, 6 ; ʒθ.

11927. 1515. HVGO de Sancto Charo: explicatio missae. 4°. P. VII. 490. 15.
    Types 1, 5 ; cuts ; ʒΗ.

11928. [a. 1515 March 22.] Jac. KOEBEL: ein neu geordnetes Visierbuch. 4°.
    DA. 830. Types 1^B, 5^B, 8 ; diagr.; B ; a ; αΓλΔ.

165

11929. 1515. BAUM und Auslegung der Sippschaft. F°. DA. 813b. Types 1^B,
8; diagr.; A; βλμ.

11930. 1515. Jac. VON MORSSHEIM: Spiegel des Regiments in den Fürstenhöfen.
4°. DA. 827. Types 1^B, 7, 8; cuts; C; a.

11931. n. d. [c. 1515?] HENRICVS de Vrimaria: passio domini explanata. 4°. H.
*7123; P. VII. 492. 27. Types 1, 5, 6; cuts; D; ſȝн.

11932. 1516. Ioh. AQVILA: de potestate et utilitate monetarum. 4°. P. VII.
490. 17. Types 1, 5, 6; cut; ſδȝнθικ.

11933. n. d. [1516.] Gabr. BIEL: de potestate et utilitate monetarum. 4°. P. IX.
551. 17b. Types 1, 5, 6, gk.; cut; X; ȝθιν.

11934. 1516. Iac. Köbel: DIALOGVS libertatis ecclesiasticae defensorius. 4°.
P. VII. 490. 19. Types 1, 5, 6; cuts; ȝ.

11935. 1516. Offenbarung der Sibyllen Weissagungen. [SIBYLS.] 4°. DA.
838c. Types 1, 1^B, 2, 6, 8; cuts; a; αȝнⱸΔ.

11936. 1516. Ioh. AQVILA: de omni ludorum genere. 4°. P. VII. 490. 16. Types
1, 4, 5, 6, gk.; cut; ȝнк.

11937. 1516. KALENDER den Barbirern und gemeinem Volk dienlich. 16°. DA.
860c. Types 1^B, 4, 7, 8; cuts; b.

11938. 1517. Jac. KOEBEL: ein neues Rechenbüchlein (editio secunda). 4°. W.
1057. Types 1^B, 4, 6, 8; diagr.; E; ade; αδιμνⱸ.

11939. 1518 March 24 (— a. Sept. 18). Ioh. Stöffler: calendarium romanum
magnum. [EPH.] F°. P. VII. 491. 21. Types 1, 2, 4, 5, 6, 7; cuts,
diagr.; AF; αΓȝнθιΔ.

11940. 1518 March 24. Joh. Stöffler: der römische Kalender. [EPH.] F°. DA.
925b. [Almost wholly of 1522 ed.; types 1^B, 2^B, 4, 5^B, 7, 8; AF; etc.]

11941. 1518. ALBERTVS Magnus: de mineralibus. 4°. P. VII. 491. 22. Types
1, 4, 5 [round comma from sig. K to end, but ẹ], 6, 8, gk.; cuts; f; ȝнⱸ.

11942. n. d. [c. 1518.] Poggius: modus epistulandi. [BRACCIOLINI.] 4°. Types
1, 4, 5 [with round comma], 6; н.

11943. n. d. [c. 1520?] Jac. KOEBEL: ein neues Gedicht wie die Landbe-
scheisser … die Einfältigen … betrügen. 4°. Types 1^B, 2^B, 8; cuts; νⱸΔ.

11944. n. d. [a. 1520?] Kalender neu geordnet. [EPH.] 4°. W. 704. Types 1^B,
2^B, 4, 8; cuts, diagr.; Y; βινⱸ.

LVIII. WORMS.

1. Peter Drach, from Speier, second press   1504 Apr. 15.
[1*. Peter Schöffer, the younger, from Mainz, second press 1518.]
2. Hans, of Erfurt, from Augsburg, second press   1520 [a. Sept. 26].

---

i. PETER DRACH.

TYPES. Types 13, 16, from Speier. Type 25, remarkable square large text on a kerned body
(that of 26); mostly a reduced copy of 19. Cf. Köbel 4.—Type 26, text schwabacher, very like
Prüss sen. 12, but the L and double hyphen are different; mixt D (one is the S reversed). 94 mm.

11945. 1504 Apr. 15. Psalterium latino-germanicum cum glossis Nicolai de
Lyra. [BIBLE.] 4°. DA. 545. Types 13, 16, 25, 26.

[i*. PETER SCHÖFFER.

See DA. 924 for a notice of a book printed at Worms by Schöffer in 1518; but seeing that no other book seems to be cited of an earlier date than 1525 (Weller 3414, 3681) the right date is perhaps 1528. Cf. P. IX. 102. 2.]

ij. HANS, OF ERFURT.

TYPES. Types 1, 2, from Augsburg.

11946. [a. 1520 Sept. 26.] Ioh. SCHNAITPECKH: Rede, aus Latein ins Teutsch gezogen. 4°. W. 1455; cf. P. IX. 102. 1. Types 1, 2; Δ.

LIX. KONSTANZ.

1. Johann Schäffler (from Ulm? fourth press?)   1506 Jan. 26.

---

i. JOH. SCHÄFFLER.

Books printed by Schäffler (who may or may not be the Ulm-Freising printer of the same name) bear dates of 1506 Jan. 26 (W. 368), 1507 June 8 (DA. 597b), 1515 March 20 (W. 901), and 1517 June 27 (DA. 863).

TYPES. Type 1, text schwabacher, very like Schönsperger jun. 2, with different E from that used in all save one of his books.—Type 2, large type, as Schönsperger jun. 1, but single not double hyphen. In no. 11949 the text is in this type: the sigs. and directors are in what seems to be type 1, but the C and E are different.

Type 1, see fig. 52; 2, see fig. 27.

INITIAL. P, in no. 11949, large, black ground, Augsburg style; 49 mm.

11947. [n.b. 1507.] Iac. MENNEL: Chronica hapsburgensia. F°. W. 406. Types 1, 2; Y.

11948. [a. 1507 Aug. 14.] Kaiserliches Mandat wider Deutsche im französischen Dienst. [GERMANY.] obl. W. 403. Type 1.

11949. n.d. Donatus minor. [PARTES.] 4°. Types 1? 2; Δ.

LX. DUTENSTEIN.

1. Wilhelm Schaffener, from Strassburg, second press ... 1506 Midlent (about March 22).

---

i. WILHELM SCHAFFENER.

The only book printed at Dutenstein, which is 8 kil. from Lahr in Baden (where Schaffener was printing 1514–15) is a Plenarium, described by Panzer, DA. 564.

LXI. SCHNEEBERG.

1. Georg Stuchs, of Sulzbach, from Nürnberg, second press ... 1506 April 28.

i. GEORG STUCHS.

Two books professedly printed at Schneeberg are recorded; they were finished within three days of each other.   For the Missale Hauelbergense of 1506 Apr. 28 see Weale, Bibl. Liturg. (1886) p. 74; for the Missale Caminense, ib. p. 48.   If, as seems probable, the Schneeberg in question is the town of that name near Zwickau Stuchs can hardly have gone thither only to print the missals of two dioceses so remote.

LXII. BRAUNSCHWEIG.

1. Johann Dorn   1506 July.

i. JOHANN DORN.

Books of Dorn's printing are recorded for the years 1506, 1507, 1509, 1511 (P. XI. 390. 1); and none thenceforward till 1516 (P. IX. 416. 1b, 1c) and 1517, after which he vanishes.   He is possibly identical with the Oxford bookseller John Dorne, whose Daybook has been printed by Mr. Madan, as the dates agree.   In 1507 he speaks of his as a noua officina, so that 1506 is probably the true beginning of his press, and not 1502, as has been supposed (C. L. Grotefend, Geschichte der Buchdruckereien in den Hannoverschen und Braunschweigischen Landen, 1840).

TYPES.   Type 1, canon of northern style; short letters 11 mm.—Type 2, broad church type like Thanner 2; 10 ll. = 81 mm.—Type 3, small text schwabacher, perhaps identical with Stendal i. 2 (Burger 119, no. 2); it has the same C, E (as Öglin 3, J. Otmar 18) and ⲤⳊ, but two other sorts of ⲤⳊ also; single hyphen. 89 mm.—Type 4, text schwabacher, resembling Riedrer 1 (Burger 132), but many noteworthy caps., C E M L Q T, &c. A similar E is used by Arndes in his type 5. Upright double hyphen, long comma; ⲤⳊ with tail turned back. 92 mm. Facs., Grotefend, ubi supra, pl. III.—Type 5, small text latin, like Froschauer 5; long single hyphen; V from type 3 common; 70–71 mm.—Type 6, archaistic Italian roman text; the same face as Marschalk-Winter 3, but 98 mm. only; it has besides the round comma a long sloping comma reversed.

Type 2, see fig. 17; 3, see fig. 60; 5, see fig. 45; 6, see fig. 5.

INITIALS.   α, like Arndes α, but 18 mm. only.—β, like Arndes Γ; 35 mm. (D, A only in 1506 July.)—A calligraphic R, 36 mm., in 1507.

11950. 1506 July 15. Dath boke der hilgen Ewangelien. [BIBLE.] F°. DA. 566.
     Types 1, 2, 3; cuts; αβ.

11951. 1507. REMIGIVS siue dominus quae pars. 4°. Types 1, 2, 4; cut; αΔ.

11952. 1509. Henr. BEBEL: latinum idioma. 4°. Types 1, 4, 5; cut; α.

11953. 1517 Nov. 12. Ioh. BRANDES: distichoneomenion abaci. 4°. P. VI. 343.
     2. Types 2, 6; cut.

LXIII. OTTOBEUREN.

1. Press of the Benedictine Abbey of SS. Alexander and Theodore 1509 Sept. 1.

For this press see an article in Wissenschaftliche Studien und Mitteilungen aus den Benedik-
tiner Orden, 2. Jahrg., Bd. 2, p. 313 ff.

TYPES. Type 1, rough roman capitals, not those of type 3.—Type 2, text gothic, like Greif or
Kunne 5 ; æ, œ, made out of two sorts filed together ; 89 mm. Facs. of types 1, 2, TFS. 1901I.—
Type 3, roman, text size ; double hyphen, short sloping comma, ℮, ℭ ; separate Q with short flat
tail ; remarkable 3 ; 110 mm.—Greek and hebrew (with points), both rough.

INITIALS. α, quasi-calligraphic (see TFS. 1901I), 26–28 mm.—A similar H, 20 mm. ; a
black-grounded V, 21 mm., and an E, black on white ground, 19 mm.

11954. 1511 Oct. 10. PASSIO septem fratrum, etc. 4°. P. VII. 494. 2. Types 1,
    2, gk., hb. ; αΔ.

11955. 1513. Christoph. STADION : oratio in synodo ad clerum habita. 4°. P. VII.
    494. 3. Type 3 ; cut ; α.

LXIV. FRANKFURT AM MAIN.

1. Beatus (Batt) Murner, of Strassburg   1511.

---

i. BEATUS MURNER.

For this press see M. Sondheim, Die ältesten frankfurter Drucke, 1885 ; here quoted as So.

TYPES. All are reproduced by Sondheim.—Type 1, latin text gothic, like G. Stuchs 12, but
rather open ; double hyphen, short sloping comma ; ¶. 91 mm.—Type 2, large round.—Type 3,
French text, resembling Levet 3 ; straight-ended ℭ. 100 mm.

Type 1, see fig. 36 ; 2, see fig. 24.

11956. 1511. Tho. MURNER : ludus studentium friburgensium. 4°. P. VII. 51.
    3 ; So. 1. Types 1, 2 ; cuts.

11957. 1511. Tho. MURNER : arma patientiae. 4°. P. XI. 415. 3b ; So. 2. Types
    1, 2 ; cuts.

11958. n. d. [1512.] Ritus et celebratio phase iudaeorum, a Tho. Murnero tra-
    ducta. [JEWS.] 4°. P. VII. 51. 4 (2) ; So. 3. Types 1, 2 ; cuts.

11959. 1512. Benedicite iudaeorum, Tho. Murnero interprete. [JEWS.] 4°. P.
    VII. 51. 4 (1) ; So. 4. Types 1, 2 ; cuts.

11960. n. d. [1512.] Der Juden Benedicite. [JEWS.] DA. 718b ; So. 5. Types
    1, 2 ; cut.

11961. 1512. Tho. MURNER : der Schelmen Zunft. 4°. DA. 738 ; So. 6. Types
    1, 2 ; cuts ; XY.

11962. 1512. Tho. MURNER : ludus studentium friburgensium. 4°. So. 9. Types
    2, 3 ; cuts.

LXV. BADEN.

1. Reinhard Beck, from Strassburg, second press   1511 Nov. 20.

i. REINHARD BECK, second press.

TYPES. Types 1, 2 ; see Strassburg press 34.—Type 5, small roman＝Strassburg xiv. 16.
DEVICE. a, see EBM. XV. 2 : cf. M. Maler's border A.
INITIALS.—δ, black ground with arabesque ornament, letter shaded.   Only P, S found ;
32 mm.

11963. 1511 Dec. 24. Ioh. MOTIS: apologia mulierum. 4°. P. VI. 54. 239. Types
     1, 2, 5; a; δ.

LXVI. DURLACH.

1. Nicolaus Keibs, frater Ordinis S. Iohannis, plebanus in Durlach   1512.

i. NICOLAUS KEIBS.

For the only dated book from this press, the Passio Christi ab Vdalrico Vannio metrice exarata
of 1512, see P. VIII. 332. 1.
TYPES. Type 1, text schwabacher, like that of Hans von Erfurt; mixt with roman caps. (A O P
Q R) ; tall C, low L, D like S reversed, I from a latin (Strassburg ?) type.   94 mm.

11964. n. d. Vita sanctae Adelhaidis. [ADELAIDE.] 4°. Type 1; cut.
11965. n. d. [c. 1516?] Mariae uirginitatis castitas ... F°. Type 1; cut. [One
     leaf; Print Room.]

LXVII. LAHR.

1. Wilhelm Schaffener, from Strassburg, fourth press   1514 Nov. 1.

i. WILHELM SCHAFFENER.

TYPES. Types 1, 3, see Strassburg press 31.—Type 4, smaller church type＝Basel vij. 3 (Burger
58, smallest type) ; the I of the fount is always used as A and replaced by a w.f. I.—Type 5, large
round, narrower than 2.—Type 6, small latin text, of the Basel-French kind, like Koberger 20
or Anshelm 6, with a w.f. W much too big.   65 mm. (See fig. 49.)
BORDER.   A four-piece border identical with that used by the younger Prüss for his Philelphus
of 1513.
INITIALS.   One A, 31 mm., of curious style; called α.

11966. 1514 Nov. 1. Gemma gemmarum. [DICT.] 4°. W. 866; SSf. 5. Types
     4, 5, 6; X; α.
11967. 1515 Feb. 22. TORRENTINVS: elucidarius carminum et historiarum. 4°.
     Types 1, 4, 5, 6; X; α.

170

LXVIII. HALBERSTADT.

i. LORENZ STUCHS.

An article by one Schmidt on Halberstadt printing appeared in 1891 in a Festschrift zur Jubelfeier der Doelleschen Buchdruckerei.

TYPES. Type 1, round church text = Meurl 1 ; 170 mm.—Type 2, smaller church on the body of 1 = Meurl 2.—Type 3, square canon like Quentell 9, Knoblouch 12, &c.; short letters 9 mm.—Type 4, rounded canon, short letters 7 mm. No capitals known.—Type 5, square larger church text as Prüss sen. 15.

Type 1, see fig. 30 ; 2, see fig. 31² ; 3, see fig. 15 ; 4, see fig. 23 ; 5, see fig. 16.

BORDER. A, one-piece folio ; signed C D (?) and dated 1520.

INITIALS. α, black ground, 42 mm.—Also a canon T (sacrifice of Isaac) ; 59 mm.

11968. 1520. Missale Benedictinum de obseruantia per Germaniam. F°. Types 1–5; cuts; αΔ. [Wants eight leaves.]

LXIX. SCHLETTSTADT.

i. LAZARUS SCHÜRER.

The date of Schürer's coming to Schlettstadt is limited by the Aesop of Aug. 1519 (no. 10256), at which time he was still at Strassburg.

TYPES. Type 1, text roman = M. Schürer 8*.—Type 2, small roman = M. Schürer 4, but has a long single hyphen, very low down and almost horizontal.—Type 3, very large roman caps. = M. Schürer 12.—Type 4, smaller roman caps. = M. Schürer 13.—Type 5, middle roman = M. Schürer 1.—Type 6, small aldine roman = M. Schürer 5. Greek type = M. Schürer iij*, but mostly on large body.

Type 1, see fig. 3 ; 2, see fig. 11 ; 4, see fig. 1 ; 5, see fig. 8 ; 6, see fig. 9.

BORDERS. A, four-piece, a close copy of Cratander B.—B = M. Schürer D.—C = M. Schürer C.—D = M. Schürer E. Two X borders are used : X¹ = M. Schürer X¹ᵇ. X² is made up of the top and bottom of A with the sides of B.

DEVICE. a = M. Schürer e with the lettering cut out, and L. Schürer's name inserted in type ; EBM. LXXVI. 2.

11969. (1519) Dec. Hermannus de Noua Aquila : epistula Germaniae studiosorum ad Carolum Aug. [NUENARE.] 4°. P. VIII. 290. 3. Types 1, 2 [caps.], 3, 4.

       1520 Jan. Horatius : epodon liber. P. VI. 94. 573. Types (3), 4, 5. See no. 10257.

11970. 1520 Feb. CATO : disticha de moribus, etc. 4°. P. VIII. 291. 17. Types 2, (3), 5 ; A.

11971. 1520 Feb. Laur. VALLA : elegantiae. 4°. P. VIII. 290. 6. Types 2, (3), 4, 6, gk.; X¹.

11972. [a. 1520 Feb. 20.] Ioh. Fr. COTTA Lambergius (Pirckheimer) : Eccius dedolatus. 4°. P. IX. 122. 152. Types 1, 2, 4, gk.; A.

SCHLETT-
STADT.
i. Lazarus
Schürer.

11973. 1520 [a. May 1.] PRVDENTIVS: hymnus de miraculis Christi. F°. P.
VIII. 291. 14. Types 1, 2, (3), 4, 6; B; a.

11974. 1520 May. Otto BRVNFELS: confutatio sophistices. 4°. P.VIII. 291. 9.
Types 1, (3), 4, gk.; C; a.

11975. 1520 May. WIMPHELING: pragmaticae sanctionis medulla excerpta. 4°.
P. VIII. 290. 7. Types 1, (3), 4, 5, gk.; A; a.

11976. 1520 June. Ioh. Lud. VIVES: aduersus pseudodialecticos; Pompeius
fugiens. 4°. P.VIII. 291. 11. Types 1, 2, (3), 4; A; a. [Wants quire B.]

11977. [a. 1520 July.] Nic. de CLEMANGIIS: de corrupto ecclesiae statu. 4°. P.
IX. 169. 76. Types 1, 2, (3), 4.

11978. 1520 Aug. ERASMVS: parabolae. 4°. P. X. 27. 6b. Types (3), 4, 6,
gk.; A; a.

11979. 1520. Elementale introductorium in declinationes graecas. [GREEK
DECLENSIONS.] 4°. P.VIII. 291. 16. Types 2, 4, 5, gk.

11980. 1520. Conr. Nastadiensis: dialogus de funere Calliopes. [NESEN.] 8°.
Types 4, 6, gk.

11981. n. d. [1520.] Vlr. de Hutten: HOCHSTRATVS ouans. 4°. P.VI. 384. 334.
Types 1, 2, (3), 4.

11982. n. d. Iac. WIMPHELING: Ad Leonem x. carmen contra prodigos in scorta.
4°. SSr. 148. Types 2 [caps.], 4, 5, 6; D.

11983. n. d. [n. b. 1519.] Andr. BODENSTEIN: ccclxx. et apologeticae conclusiones. 4°. P. IX. 73. 56. Types 2, 4, 5, 6, gk.; X².

LXX. MEISSEN.

1. Melchior Lotter, the elder, from Leipzig, second press . . .   1520 Feb. 14.

---

i. MELCHIOR LOTTER.

The following book was printed at Meissen, tempore pestilitatis in aula episcopali.   Cf. the
similar instance of Reinhard Beck at Baden.
TYPES.   Types 2, 14, from Leipzig, q.v.

11984. 1520 Feb. 14. Breuiarius Misnensis. [LIT.] 8°. P.VII. 214. 753. Types
2, 14; cut. [Woodcut music.]

LXXI. HALLE.

1. Printer of Heiligthumsbüchlein 1520.

---

i. PRINTER OF HEILIGTHUMSBÜCHLEIN.

TYPES. Type 1, narrow church, like Lotter sen. 2 or G. Stuchs 5; single hyphen.—Type 2, small text schwabacher, normal; short double hyphen, short comma; 91 mm.
Type 1, see fig. 21; 2, see fig. 59.

11985. 1520. Verzeichnis der Heiligthümer der Stiftkirchen zu Halle. [MAURICE.] 4°. DA. 999; W. 1653. Types 1, 2; cuts. [Wants 4 leaves.]

PLACE AND PRINTER UNKNOWN.

A. GROUPS.

Group 1. [Basel or Strassburg.]
Type 1, square church text like Prüss sen. 13 or Quentell 10, but W, w, from a rounder type, like J. Schöffer 5; a V from a large round type is also used for W. Two forms of D as in Knoblouch 3.—Type 2, text schwabacher like J. Schöffer 7, Cratander 6, Knoblouch 18, &c.; double hyphen, ¶; 92 mm.
Type 1, see fig. 18; 2, see fig. 53.

11986. n.d. [n.b. 1509.] Ioh. VETTER: die wahre Historie von den vier Ketzern Prediger Ordens. 4°. DA. 642 (1)? Types 1, 2.
11987. [1520.] LUTHER: eine kurze Form der zehn Gebote. 4°. W. 1514. Types 1, 2.

Group 2. [Köln?]
Type 1, archaistic text roman like J. Schöffer 19, but single hyphen (as a fount of Adam Petri; Heil's type of 1521 has it double); capitals rather out of keeping; 110 mm.—Type 2, large round like Ratdolt 9 or Koberger 14; no h in these books.—Type 3, large text like Koberger 16, Hölzel 12.—Type 4, small roman like Quentell 13; single hyphen. About 80 mm.—Type 5, roman capitals used as initials; 15 mm. high.—Greek type of the later Basel-Strassburg-Köln style.—Initial: a calligraphic versal like Prüss sen. β; 30 mm.
Type 1, see fig. 5; 2, see fig. 32'; 3, see fig. 33'; 4, see fig. 11.

11988. n. d. [1519?] Ex obscurorum uirorum salibus cribratus dialogus. [GRATIVS.] 4°. (P. IX. 119. 134, note.) Type 1; Δ.
11989. [n. b. 1520.] Nic. Quadus: flores ex diuersis libris Hochstrati collecti. [IACOBVS.] 4°. P. IX. 191. 310. Types 1-5, gk.; Y.

Group 3. [Probably after 1520, both types being used in W. 2032 (1522) and W. 3194 (1524).]
Type 1, square church text in the style of Quentell 10, but rather narrow and very rough.—Type 2, small text schwabacher, normal; long double hyphen, very short comma, thick ¶. 90 mm. In no. 11992 a few letters of a roman type are found in it.—Initials. α, curious small calligraphic, like some used by Pamphilus Gengenbach; 21 mm.
Type 1, see fig. 18; 2, see fig. 59.

11990. n. d. Diss büchlein gibt dir zu verston Was etlich priester hondt gethon...
    [BUECHLEIN.] 4°. W. 1334. Types 1, 2; cut.

11991. n. d. KLAGEREDE eines jungen Mönchs über seine Kutte. 4°. W. 1453.
    Types 1, 2; cut (a copy of that in no. 11997). [Imp.]

11992. n. d. Vom Gewalt und Haupte der Kirche ein Gespräch. [PETER.] 4°.
    W. 1318. Types 1, 2; cuts; α.

B. SINGLE BOOKS.

i. Books in German.

Type 1, smaller rounded church text like Miller 11 ; but the A is of Mainz form ; short letters
4½ mm.—Type 2, text schwabacher; D like S reversed, long comma also used as hyphen, thin saw-
edge ℂ; 91 mm. The text for which these types are used is dated from Augsburg, signed and filled
up in MS. Apparently from a private press.

Type 3, text schwabacher, Strassburg style, D like S reversed; long comma used also as hyphen;
95 mm.

Type 4, square church text, very rough, but like Schönsperger sen. 4; short letters 5 mm.—Type
5, text schwabacher, with fraktur forms; L and D like Prüss sen. 12 ; short comma, no hyphen;
very badly cast and printed. 100 mm.—Initial, a curious calligraphic D, 30 mm. The first letter
is dated from Landshut, the second from München. This also seems to be from a private press.

Type 6, small narrow church text, rough ; curious capitals. Short letters 4 mm.—Type 7, small
text schwabacher, with long double hyphen and an odd kind of spiral leaf-ornament. 91 mm.

Type 8, square church text of Basel style; capitals like Koberger 11, but latin lowercase.—Type
9, text schwabacher, very like M. Schürer 15, except the L ; D, H, are like his ; thick ¶. 94 mm.
Initial O of Strassburg style, dotted ground ; 18 mm. Cf. no. 11991.

Type 1, see fig. 31¹; 2, 3, 5, see fig. 54 ; 4, see fig. 19 ; 7, see fig. 59 ; 9, see fig. 56.

11993. [a. 1510 March 14.] Hans von AUERSPERG: Entschuldigung und wahr-
    hafte Verantwortung. 4°. Types 1, 2.

11994. [a. 1515 April 10.] Ordnung und Regiment des Fürstentums Württem-
    berg. [WURTEMBERG.] F°. W. 956 (2). Type 3.

11995. [a. 1515 Dec. 24.] SABINA Herzogin v. Württemberg: Ausschreibung
    an die Landschaft. 4°. Types 4, 5; Δ.

11996. n. d. [1520.] Ulr. von HUTTEN: Anzeigung wie sich die Päpste gegen
    den Kaisern gehalten haben. 4°. W. 1410; B. xxxv. 6. Types 6, 7.

11997. n. d. [a. 1520?] KLAGEREDE eines jungen Mönches über seine Kutte. 4°.
    (Not W. 1453.) Types 8, 9; cut; Δ.

ij. Latin books in Roman type.

Type 10, text roman, like Lotter 12 ; short double hyphen, no comma, æ not ę. 97 mm.—Type
11, smaller roman, very like Sertorius 2, except the hyphen, which is double. 83 mm.—Border A,
one-piece, striped ground ; birds, flowers and butterflies. Initials, perhaps by the same hand, of
three sizes ; α, 26 mm., I (men) ; β, 22 mm., I (beasts) ; γ, 17–18 mm., G, T (boys). Leipzig or
Erfurt ?

Type 12, middle roman, very like M. Schürer or Morhard 1; the M is similar, but single hyphen
only ; round comma, thick ¶. 88 mm.—Type 13, small roman like M. Schürer 4. The lombardic
I on leaf 1ᵇ does not look like Strassburg work.

Type 10, see fig. 6; 11, see fig. 7²; 12, see fig. 8 ; 13, see fig. 11.

11998. n. d. [c. 1510?] SAVONAROLA: expositio in psalmos Miserere et In te
    domine speraui. 4°. Types 10, 11; A; αβγ.

11999. n. d. [c. 1519?] Dialogus inter Iulium ij. et Petrum ad caeli fores. [JULIUS.]
    8°. Types 12, 13.

iij. Latin books in Gothic type.

Type 14, narrow church text, not unlike G. Stuchs 5, but slightly taller; short letters 5½ mm.—Type 15, curious small latin gothic; M very distinctive; some capitals like those of Arndes 4*, though much smaller. Round h, no hyphen; us ranges with the short letters. 10 lines [on vellum], 35½ mm. These types belong to North Germany, perhaps Lübeck.

Type 16, curious latin text gothic like Knoblouch 14, Kistler 5 and Landen 4, but differs from all these in its double hyphen. These three and Cornelis of Zierikzee 6 (only found in small quantities and much mixt) are the only identified founts of this style. Single and double hyphen, ¶ like Kistler 5. 79 mm. Strassburg or Köln?

Type 17, text schwabacher, with a wrong-fount (latin) R. Three lines only, and three capitals M, O, R; no hyphen. Extraordinary printing; every u not printed wrongly for n (it begins: O insiguem . . . See title-register) has umlaut or the broadening sign. Printed at Regensburg by Paul Kohl?

Type 18, small narrow church text like G. Stuchs 6; short letters 4 mm.—Type 19, small text schwabacher, normal; double hyphen, thick ¶. 89 mm.

Type 20, square angular church text, thick ¶, short letters 5½ mm. F, the only capital, is of curious style; the other capitals used are lombardic.—Type 21, small text schwabacher, small face; D resembles that of Kerner 1 or Baumgarten 9, though of smaller size; wrong fount V of Lübeck style, odd Q, double hyphen; 5 lines = 21 mm. Northern Germany.

Type 14, see fig. 21; *16, see fig. 39; 18, see fig. 22; 19, see fig. 59.

12000. (1502.) Raym. Peraudi: literae indulgentiarum. [ROME.] obl. Types 17, 18. [On vellum.]

12001. [a. 1504 July.] Liber constitutionum fratrum praedicatorum, etc. [AUGUSTINE.] 4°. Type 19. [Title wanting.]

12002. [n.b. 1519.] Capella beatae Mariae pulchrae Ratisbonae. bs. Type 20. [Print Room.]

12003. n.d. [c. 1519–20.] NEMO: encomium Rubii Longipolli apud Lipsim. 4°. P. IX. 74. 63. Types 21, 22; cut.

12004. (1520.) Formula confraternitatis fratrum heremitarum S. Ioannis Baptistae de claustro Viterbii. [JOHN.] obl. Types 23, 24; cut. [Two editions, probably printed on one sheet; the cut is different in each.]

Presses have been wrongly assigned to the following towns during the years
1501–1520.

ZWIEFALTEN.

An edition of Bebel's opuscula said to be printed at Zwiefalten in 1504 by Leonardus Clemens appears in Weislinger's catalogue of the library of the house of S. John of Jerusalem at Strassburg (1749), and the entry is copied by Panzer (IX. 103). Steiff (Der erste Buchdruck in Tübingen, p. 233) has shown that this entry referred to an imperfect copy of Grüninger's edition of 1508.

MINDELHEIM.

Panzer (VII. 406. 1) quotes from Hennings an edition of Altenstaig, de felicitate triplici, as printed in 1518 at Mindelheim. This appears to be an error. The Hagenau edition of 1519 has on the last printed page (the colophon being on the preceding page) a letter from the author dated: Ex Mindelhaim Anno 1518, and the mistake probably arose from these words, which are the last in the book.

STECHELBERG.

The book (Ulrich von Hutten's opuscula, Sept. 1519, P. VIII. 299. 1) which purports to be excusum in arce Stekelberk, is in reality the work of Joh. Schöffer: see no. 9866, and the reference there given to Böcking's Index Huttenianus.

Rosentaler, Caspar. Schwaz.

Schlick, Arnold. Speier.

Schregel, Sixtus. Augsburg.

Wacker, Joh. Salzburg.

Wagner, Joh. Regensburg.
  1519 June 10. Odofrancus: de Ratis-
    bona   10775

Wetzler, Kilian. Tübingen.
  1516 March. Nauclerus, commentarii 11743

Widmann, Johann. Augsburg.
  1507. Gessler, formulare   10702
  1508. Imitatio Christi, germ.   10705

Zuyfel, Joh. Tübingen.
  1516 March. Nauclerus, commentarii 11743

TITLE-INDEX TO BOOKS WITHOUT IMPRINT.

1. Dated Books.

2. Undated Books.

185

A A

TYPE-REGISTER.

[Abbreviations used : b, bastard type, i.e. body too large for face. c, circa. d, double hyphen. k, kerned, i.e. body too small for face. n, no hyphen. s, single hyphen. An asterisk denotes the actual type in each group which was photographed for the figure (in the Illustrations to this Type-Register) to which a reference is given.

In other references the superior number (e.g. Burger 63²) is used where more than one type is shown in the facsimile referred to; and ¹ means the largest, ² the next in size, and so on. References to facsimiles given in the text are as a rule not repeated here.]

A. ROMAN TYPES.

a. Large capitals.

1. Over 8 mm.

Schumann	7	[17]
Heil	4	[15]
No. 10954	14	[15]
No. 11988–9	5	[15]
Knoblouch	17	[14]
Schott	13	[14]
M. Schürer	12	[14]
L. Schürer	3	[14]
Schürer counterfeit	2	[14]
Prüss jun.	8	[14]
Anshelm	12	[14]
J. Schöffer	22	[13]
S. Otmar	12	[13]
Grim	4	[13]
Lotter jun.	7	[12]
Gymnicus	3	[10]
Miller	13	[10]
Grim	11	[10]
Anshelm	14	[10]
Striblita	2	[8½]

2. Thick, 8 mm. [fig. 1.]

*J. Schöffer	15
M. Schürer	13
L. Schürer	4
Prüss jun.	11
Morhard	2
Landen	7
Cervicornus	3
Elisabeth	3
Heil	5
No. 10608	4
No. 10954–5	15
Heinrich of Neuss	7
Kaiser	2

3. Thin, 8–7 mm. [fig. 2.]

(Flach, 1521)		[8]
*Ratdolt	21	[8]
S. Otmar	6	[8]
Miller	1	[8]
Köbel	6	[8]
Anshelm	17	[7½]
Knoblouch	19	[7]
Schott	14	[7]

4. Under 7 mm.

Gymnicus	4	[5½]
Grim	10	[5½]

b. Text size.

i. German style.

1. Double hyphen [fig. 3].

*Schott	5*	[110]
Öglin	8	[109]
Schumann	9	[109]
M. Schürer	8*	[108]
L. Schürer	1	[108]
Beck	12	[108]
Miller	2	[108]
Grim	7	[108]
Grüninger	26	[105]
Heil	2	[104]
Prüss sen.	18	[100]
Knoblouch	8	[100]
M. Schürer	8	[100]
Schott	5	[98–9]
Quentell	12	[95]

2. Single hyphen.

Anshelm	3	[109]
Cervicornus	4	[107]

ij. Italian style.

1. Broken T, double hyphen [fig. 4].

Rhau	6	[110]
G. Stuchs	19	[98–9]
*Hölzel	8	[98–9]
J. Stuchs	5	[98–9]

2. Unbroken T, double hyphen.

J. Otmar [a]	19	[106]
Öglin	1	[106]
S. Otmar	1	[106]
Peypus	3	[102]

3. Unbroken T, single hyphen.

Nürnberg xxi.	1	[102]
Weissenburger	1	[102]

iij. French style, single hyphen [b].

Lamparter and		
Murrer	2	[102]

iv. Archaistic founts [fig. 5].

*J. Schöffer	19	[112, d]
(Heil, 1521)		[110, d]

[a] No hyphen till 1509. [b] Cf. Bergmann 1, and types of Rembolt, H. Estienne, &c.

No. 11988–9 — 1 [110, s]
Marschalk-Winter — 3 [108, n]
Dorn — 6 [98, n]

v. Leipzig-Erfurt styles.
  1. Lotter variety [fig. 6].
    No. 11998 — 10 [97, d]
    *Lotter sen. — 12 [95, d]
    Lotter jun. — 4 [95, d]
    Landsberg — 8 [95, d]
    Thanner — 7 [94, d]
    Schumann — 3 [92, d]
    No. 11572 — 2 [93, s]
  2. Sertorius variety; 109 mm., single hyphen [fig. 7¹].
    Sertorius — 1
    Marschalk-Winter — 1
    *Rhau — 1
    Knapp — 5

vi. Unclassed.
    Ottobeuren — 3 [110]
    Ottobeuren [a] — 1 [caps.]

c. Middle types.
  i. German style [¶ mostly; M varies; fig. 8].
    1. Double hyphen.
    Morhard — 1 [93]
    M. Schürer — 1 [92]
    L. Schürer — 5 [92]
    Heil — 3 [92]
    No. 10956 — 17 [92]
    Lutz — 2 [92? ¶]
    Grüninger — 22 [89]
    No. 10608 — 5 [88]
    Miller — 3 [88]
    Schumann — 5 [88]
    Anshelm — 7 [88]
    J. Schöffer [b] — 12 [87]
    Hüpfüff — 10 [87]
    Knoblouch [c] — 7 [87]
    Schott — 7 [87]
    Grim — 5 [87]
    No. 10339 — 3 bis [86]
    Prüss sen. — 14 [86]
    Flach — 4 [86]
    Beck — 7 [86; ¶]
    Schürer counterfeit — 1 [86]
    Prüss jun. [d] — 2 [86]
    Köbel — 5 [86]
    Gymnicus — 5 [?]
    No. 10607 — 1 [?]
    2. Mixt hyphens.
    *J. Schöffer [e] — 12 [87]
    Knoblouch [f] — 7 [87]

    3. Single hyphen.
    Kaiser — 1 [88–9]
    Gymnicus — 1 [88]
    No. 11998 — 12 [88]
    Cervicornus — 1 [87–8]
    Elisabeth — 1 [87–8]
    Prüss jun. [g] — 2 [86]
    No. 11570 — 1 [?]
    Gran — 16 [?]
  ij. Italian style, round h, 91 mm. [Burger 5[12].]
    Ratdolt — 8
    J. Otmar — 20
  iij. Erfurt (Schenck) style, double hyphen.
    W. Schenck — 1 [86]
    Maler — 3 [86]
    Paul of Hachenburg — 3 [83]
  iv. Smaller Sertorius style.
    1. 80–81 mm., single hyphen [fig. 7²].
    Sertorius — 2
    Marschalk-Winter — 2
    *Rhau — 2
    2. Double hyphen.
    No. 11998 — 11 [83]
    Lotter sen. — 13 [80]
  v. Unclassed; double hyphen, 87 mm.
    No. 11570 — 1

d. Aldine and Capcasa styles.
  i. Aldine style [fig. 9].
    J. Schöffer — 18 [88, d]
    Anshelm — 11 [88, d]
    Lotter sen. — 16 [88, d]
    Lotter jun. — 5 [88, d]
    *M. Schürer — 5 [76–7, d]
    L. Schürer — 6 [76–7, d]
    Gymnicus — 2 [67, s]
  ij. Capcasa style [fig. 10].
    *No. 10953 — 13 [90–91, d]
    No. 10954–5 — 16 [88–9, s]
    Hölzel — 13 [86, s]
    J. Stuchs — 6 [86, s]
    Cornelis of Zierikzee — 9 [82, d]
    J. Otmar — 25 [82, s]
    Öglin — 2 [82, s]
    S. Otmar — 2 [82, s]

e. Small roman founts.
  i. German style [fig. 11].
    1. Single hyphen.
    No. 11988–9 — 4 [c. 80]
    Beck — 5 [79]
    (Flach, 1521) — [78]
    Schott — 4* [77]

[a] TFS. 1901 l.   [b] Before 1518.   [c] Before 1515 Aug.   [d] Before 1520.   [e] From 1518.
[f] From 1515 Aug.   [g] In 1520.

B B

<table>
<tr><td>

*M. Schürer [a]   4 [77]
L. Schürer   2 [77]
Knoblouch   13 [76]
No. 10608   6 [76]
Gran   14 [76]
Knoblochtzer   10 [76]
Prüss sen.   16 [75]
Prüss jun.   3 [75]
Anshelm   9 [75]
Schott [b]   4 [73]
2. Mixt hyphens.
   Grim   6 [75]
   Schott [c]   4 [73]
3. Double hyphen.
   M. Schürer [d]   4 [77]
   Rhau   7 [77]
   Miller   4 [74]
   Quentell   13 [72]
   J. Schöffer   16 [66]
   Schumann   8 [65]
   Grüninger   23 [63-4]
   Heil   1 [?]
   Cervicornus   5 [caps., b]
   No. 11999   13 [?]
4. M different.
   α. Heinrich of Neuss   6 [76, d]
   Cervicornus   2 [71, s]
   Elisabeth   2 [71, s]
   β. Lotter sen.   18 [66]
   Lotter jun.   6 [66]

ij. Italian style.
   Nürnberg xxi.   5 [78, n]
   Peypus   4 [74, d]

iij. Various.
   Weissenburger   8 [75]
   Lotter sen.   17 [75]
   No. 11570   2 [73-4, d]
   Gymnicus   7 [63, d]
   No. 11187   15 [caps.]
f. Italic founts.
   i. Earlier style [fig. 12].
     Schott   15

   ij. Later style [fig. 13].
     *J. Schöffer   21 [88]
     Knoblouch   22 [92]
     Heil   6 [?]

   iij. Abnormal.
     Striblita   1 [93]

B. SQUARE CHURCH TYPES.
a. Canon.
   i. Nürnberg style, 11 mm. [fig. 14[1].]
     G. Stuchs   15

</td><td>

*Hölzel   7
Nürnberg xxi.   2
G. Schenck   3
Weissenburger   6
W. Huber   4
J. Stuchs   4
Peypus   5
Gutknecht   3
Lotter sen.   3
Stöckel   9
Kachelofen   11
Schumann   1
ij. Leipzig-Erfurt style, 10 mm. [fig. 14B.]
   W. Schenck   7
   Knapp   1
   *Maler   6
   Landsberg   7
   Thanner   3
   Dyon   3 [9 mm.]
iij. Strassburg-Köln style, 9-10 mm. [e]
       [fig. 15.]
   *Prüss sen.   4
   Strassburg xv.   8
   Hüpfüff   4
   Knoblouch   12
   Flach   5
   M. Schürer   7
   Schott   10
   Beck   4
   Kerner   2
   Zel   7
   Quentell   9
   Martin of Werden   5
   Cornelis of Zierikzee   8
   Heinrich of Neuss   1
   Kruffter   3
   Schönsperger sen.   5
   J. Otmar   22
   Ramminger   5
   Drach   21
   L. Stuchs   3
iv. Northern styles (various).
   Dorn   1 [11]
   Dietz   2 [9]
   Ludwig of Renchen [f]   1 [8]
   Martin of Werden   6 [8]
   Math. Brandiss   7 [7]
v. Various [fig. 31[1]].
   *Weissenburger   5 bis [11]
   Paul of Hachenburg   2 [11]
   Pfeil [g]   23 [10]
   Lacher [h]   1 [10]
   P. Schöffer sen. [i]   2 [9]
   J. Schöffer   6 [9]

</td></tr>
</table>

[a] To 1513.   [b] In 1504.   [c] In 1503.   [d] From 1515.   [e] Burger 43[1], 16[1].   [f] Burger 16[2]; cf. 69[1].   [g] Burger 105(1).   [h] T.F.S. 1903e[1].   [i] Druckschriften 61-3.

Schöffer appendix 5 [7]
P. Schöffer sen. 1 [7]
J. Schöffer 13 [7]

b. Intermediate, or large text, 6½ mm.[a]
[fig. 16.]
*Prüss sen. 15
Wähinger 1
Beck 6
Prüss jun. 10
G. Stuchs 10
W. Huber 6
L. Stuchs 5

c. Text sizes (6–4 mm.).
i. Broad styles.
1. Leipzig northern style, 5 mm.[b]
[fig. 17.]
W. Schenck 2
(Knapp[c] 2)
Jac. Winter 1
Landsberg 5
*Thanner 2
Dorn 2

2. Northern styles, various.
Pfeil[d] 10 [6]
Arndes[e] 7 [5¼]
Math. Brandiss[f] 10 [5¼]
Tretter 1 [?]
Borchard 4 [?]
Ludwig of Renchen[g] 2 [5]
Dietz 3 [5]
Arndes[e] 8 [4¾, b]
Math. Brandiss[f] 9 [4¾, b]
Pfeil[d] 11 [4¾, b]
Lacher 2
Dietz 4 [4]

3. Mainz styles, 5 and 4 mm.[h]
α. P. Schöffer sen. 7
J. Schöffer 5
Schöffer appendix 1
Zel 10
Arndt of Aachen 1
Bornemann 1
Tzwivel 1
β. Heumann 1
Schmidt 3
γ. P. Schöffer sen. 9 [4]
J. Schöffer 4 [4]

ij. Middle width, Strassburg-Köln style.
1. Square capitals, 5 mm.[i] [fig. 18.]
α. *Prüss sen. 13
Hüpfüff 11
Knoblouch 3

Flach 10
M. Schürer 9
Beck 1
Prüss jun. 1
Quentell 10
Kruffter 2
Drach 19
Schmidt 1
β. No. 11986–7 1
No. 11990–92 1

2. Rounded or mixt capitals, 5 mm.[k]
[fig. 19.]
Hüpfüff 1
Kistler 3
Knoblouch 3[B]
Schott 2
page 52, after 10343 8
Bumgart 8
Landen 7
*Martin of Werden 7
Spot 3 ?
Schönsperger sen. 4
J. Otmar 21
Zeissenmair 1
No. 10949 1
Greif 9
Knoblochtzer 7
No. 11995 4

3. Square, rounded or mixt caps., 4 mm.[l]
[fig. 20.]
*Prüss sen. 17 [b]
Beck 3
Prüss jun. 9
(Koelhoff sen. 14)
Quentell 14
Heinrich of Neuss 2
Gutschaiff 1
J. Otmar 23
Drach 22 [b]
No. 11996 6

iij. Narrow styles.
1. Nürnberg-Leipzig style, 5 mm.[m]
[fig. 21.]
*G. Stuchs 5
W. Schenck 6
(Knapp[n] 2)
Maler 1
Lotter sen. 2
Stöckel 5
Thanner 4
Schumann 2
Rhau 8
Lotter jun. 1

[a] Burger 117[1] ; Druckschriften 71. [b] Burger 131(2)[1]. [c] Caps. only. [d–f] These types correspond as large and small text respectively. [g] Burger 69[2]. [h] Burger 75[1]; Druckschriften 27[1]. [i] Cf. TP. XXXVII. 9. [k] Burger 43[3], 96[1]. [l] Burger 43[3], 16[4]. [m] Burger 117[2], 35[1]. [n] Lower-case only.

Pfeil 21
Dietz 7
Marschalk-Winter 6
Halle 1
2. Same style, 4 mm. [a] [fig. 22.]
G. Stuchs 6 [b]
*Hölzel 3
Ambr. Huber 1
G. Schenck 1
Weissenburger 2
W. Huber 7
No. 11186 10
Lotter sen. 8
Schobser 10
Pfeil 22 [b]
Dyon 4
No. 12003 18
iv. Basel styles (various).
Schaffener [b] 3 [5]
G. Stuchs 11 [5]
No. 11997 8 [5]
Schaffener [b] 4 [4]
v. Miscellaneous.
Schobser [c] 4 [6]
Ostendorfer 2 [6]
No. 12000 14 [5½]
No. 12004 20 [5½]

C. ROUNDED CHURCH AND HEADING TYPES.

a. Canon types.
i. Augsburg-Nürnberg style.
1. Normal [fig. 23].
No. 11183 3 [9]
Miller 5 [8½]
No. 10951 4 [8½]
Grim 9 [8]
*Hölzel 6 [8]
Meurl 3 [8]
Nürnberg xxi. 6 [8]
J. Stuchs 7 [8]
No. 11186 9 [8]
Pfeil 18 [8]
L. Stuchs 4 [7]
2. Otmar-Öglin variety, 8 mm.
J. Otmar 26
Öglin 6
S. Otmar 3
Ramminger 1
ij. Various.
Grüninger 19 [8½]
Hüpfüff 3 bis [8½]
Ratdolt [italian] 11 [7]
Anshelm [lyonnese] [d] 16 [8]

b. Heading types.
1. Normal style, 6 mm. [e] [fig. 63[1].]
*Flach 1
Hüpfüff 8
No. 10338–9 2
2. Normal, 5 mm. [f] [fig. 24.]
Strassburg xx. 5
(Schaffener 2)
Flach 7
Knoblouch 1
M. Schürer 2
Schott 9
Beck 11
Schönsperger sen. 7
J. Otmar 14
Öglin 4
Hans of Erfurt 1
S. Otmar 7
No. 10953 12
No. 10957A 18
Hist 6
Dietz 6
Marschalk-Winter 4
Stöckel 2
*Gran 4
J. Otmar 7
B. Murner 2
3. Bergmann (french) style [g] [fig. 25].
*Anshelm 4 [6]
(Baumgarten 5) [5½]
4. Sorg style [h] [fig. 26].
*Cornelis of Zierikzee 1 [5]
Gutschaiff 3 ?
Schobser 6 [5½]
5. Froschauer style [fig. 27].
Landen 5
Grim 15 ? [5]
Froschauer 6 [5]
*Schönsperger jun. 1 [5]
Kunne 7 [5]
Schäffler 2 [5½]
6. Grüninger style (4–4½ mm.) [fig. 28].
Grüninger 17
Kerner 3
Bumgart 3
Landen 1
Cornelis of Zierikzee 7
Lamparter & Murrer 1
*Köbel 1
7. Germanised founts.
α. M. Schürer 14
Schott 9 [a]
Koberger 11
β. Grüninger [i] 17
Köbel 1 [a]

[a] Burger 117[3], 35[2].　[b] Cf. TP. XXI. 2; Burger 58.　[c] Burger 22[1].　[d] Cf. TP. XXIV. 1.　[e] Cf. TP. XII. 7; XXXV. 1, 4.　[f] Cf. TP. VIII. 5.　[g] TP. XII. 7.　[h] Burger 154[1].　[i] After 1506.

8. Nadler-Öglin style, 4 mm. [fig. 29.]
   Öglin   5
   *Nadler   1
   Grim   13
   Schönsperger jun. 5
   (W. Huber   2)

9. Various, 5 mm.
   Strassburg xv.[a]   1
   Schaffener [narrow] 5
   Ratdolt[b] [italian] 12

c. Church text.
 i. Augsburg-Nürnberg style.
  1. Larger text, 5 mm. [fig. 30.]
   Öglin   10
   Miller   10
   No. 10951   7
   *Hölzel   10
   Schleiffer   1
   Meurl   1
   No. 11187   12
   Hochfeder   19
   L. Stuchs   1
  2. Smaller text, 4 mm. [fig. 31².]
   Öglin   9
   Miller   11
   Grim   3
   Sittich   2
   No. 10951   5
   No. 10952   10
   Hölzel   15
   Meurl   2
   Nürnberg xxi.   3
   *Weissenburger 4
   W. Huber   3
   Dyon   1
   Peypus   1
   Gutknecht   4
   No. 11187   13
   Pfeil   19
   Weinreich   2
   L. Stuchs   2
   (No. 11993   1)
  3. As last, with different capitals, 4 mm.[c]
                   [fig. 14².]
   G. Stuchs   16
   *Hölzel   2
   J. Stuchs   2
   Gutknecht   1
   Rhau   5
  4. Other founts of the same class, 4 mm.
   W. Huber   2
   No. 11183   4

   Schobser   11
   Schobser   12
   Schobser appendix 1

ij. Ratdolt-Koberger style.
  1. Larger text, tailed h, 5 mm.
   Grüninger   31
   Anshelm   15
  2. Smaller text, tailed h, 4 mm. [fig. 32¹.]
   Knoblouch   16
   Froschauer   4
   *Ratdolt   9
   Ramminger   3
   Anshelm   8
  3. As 2, but round h.
   Koberger   14
   Hochfeder   20
   Baumgarten   8
  4. Form of h unknown.
   J. Schöffer   20
   No. 11988-9   2

iij. Strassburg style; tailed h; 4 mm.[d]
   [Prüss sen.   7]
   Beck   14
   Prüss jun.   5

iv. Italian small text; 3½–3 mm.[e] [fig. 32².]
   *Ratdolt   13
   G. Stuchs   17
   J. Stuchs   3
   Baumgarten   6

v. Köln fifteenth-century.
   [Guldenschaff 2]
   Martin of Werden 2

D. LATIN TEXT TYPES.

a. Large text and text size. [110–75 mm.]
 i. Older large text.
  1. Like Burger 74.
   Joh. Schöffer   1 [118–9]
   Spot   1
  2. Like Burger 70.
   Martin of Werden 1 [110]
  3. Like WP. 1 (smaller Mainz text).
   J. Schöffer   2 [92]

ij. Koberger-Basel large text.
  1. As Koberger 16[f] [fig. 33¹].
   *Pfeil   13 [110]
   (Pfeil   20)
   G. Stuchs   7 [107]
   Hölzel   12

[a] Burger 149[1].   [b] Burger 5[2]; cf. TP. XVIII. 5.   [c] TFS. 1901 xx[1].   [d] Burger 77[1].
[e] Cf. TP. XVIII. 4; Burger 5[4], 154[3].   [f] WP. 20[1].

Hochfeder 8 [112]
No. 11988–9 3
2. As Koberger 15 [fig. 33²]. [a]
*Pfeil 14 [110,b]
G. Stuchs 8 [107, b]

iij. Strassburg-Speier large text.
Grüninger 27 [90, k]
Drach 23 [112]
Hist 4 [89]

iv. Grüninger bible-text.
1. As Grüninger 20 [fig. 34].
Strassburg xv. 7 [90]
*Koberger 25 [82]
Lamparter and Murrer 3 [82]
2. With different E.
Prüss sen. 20 [87]
Strassburg xx. 10
Beck 9
Gran [10]

v. Basel-Paris-Strassburg style[b].
1. Larger text [Burger 149²].
Strassburg xv. 2 [91]
Strassburg xx. 9
Gran 12
2. Smaller text [Burger 149³].
Strassburg xv. 3 [91]

vi. Augsburg large text [fig. 35].
Ratdolt 22 [107]
Öglin 11
*Miller 6 [104]
Grim 2
Gutknecht 5 ?[b]
No. 11183 5
Stöckel 8 [97]

vij. Basel-Nürnberg text.
1. German variety[c] [fig. 36].
Murner 1 [91]
Pfeil 24 [87]
J. Otmar 27 [85]
S. Otmar 9 [85]
G. Stuchs 12 [84]
Ambr. Huber 2 [82]
*J. Stuchs 9 [82]
Hüpfüff 7 [82]
Gutknecht 6 [81]
W. Huber 5 [80]
Hochfeder 1* [80]
Kunne 8 [79–80]
2. French variety[d].
Hochfeder 21 [81]
Anshelm 5 [c. 83]

viij. Strassburg-Köln text.
1. Quentell-Prüss variety[e] [fig. 37].
Heumann 2 [81–82]
(Grüninger 25 [80])
[Prüss sen. 8]
Strassburg xv.[f] 4 [79]
Strassburg xx. 6 [79]
Schaffener 1 [81]
Beck 15 [80]
Prüss jun. 7 [80]
Quentell 7 [80]
Martin of Werden 3 [80]
J. Otmar 13 [79]
Drach 13 [81]
*Gran 8 [79]
Köbel 3 [80]
2. Zel-Flach variety[g] [fig. 38].
J. Schöffer 8 [80–81]
Schöffer appendix 2
Prüss sen. (?) 21 [83]
Knoblouch 2 [81]
*Flach 3 [81]
M. Schürer 3 [80–81]
(Schott [differs] 8 [83])
Zel 5 [81]
Cornelis of Zierikzee 2 [81]
No. 10607 2
Stöckel 1 [82]
Bornemann 2 [81]
Tzwivel 4 [81]

ix. Strassburg-anonymous style.
1. Larger text.
Knoblouch 11 [105]
Beck 10
2. Smaller text [fig. 39].
Kistler 5 [78]
Knoblouch 14 [78]
Landen 4 [78]
Cornelis of Zierikzee 6
*No. 12001 16 [79]

x. Augsburg-Leipzig style.
1. Large face.
Lotter sen. 12 bis [81]
2. Middle face[h] [fig. 40].
Schleiffer 2 [83]
Meurl 4 [83]
*Weissenburger 7 [82]
Landsberg 6 [82]
Peypus 6 [76]
Grim 8 [76]
J. Otmar 16 [75]
Miller 12 [74]
Lotter sen. 1 [72]

[a] WP. 20²; TFS. 1901 xx². [b] Cf. Burger 59; Bocard 1, Baligault 1, Kesler 4, Richel 7, Valdarfer 8, &c. [c] Cf. Furter 1, Koberger 18, &c. [d] Cf. TP. XII. 2. [e] Burger 44. [f] The E differs. [g] Burger 141 (1, 2). [h] Burger 133², 150².

J. Otmar   15 [70–71]
S. Otmar   4 [70–71]
3. Small face.
    Lotter sen.   2 [72, b]
xi. Various smaller groups.
  1. Large text, round, c. 108mm. [a]
    Lotter sen.   10
    Lotter jun.   2
  2. Large text, northern style [fig. 51¹].
    *Lotter sen.   6 [97]
    No. 10951   8
  3. Large text, square.
    Drach   25 [94, k]
    Köbel   4
  4. Reutlingen-Memmingen text [Burger 81¹; WP. 89, 92].
    Greif   5* [92]
    Ottobeuren   2 [89]
  5. Erfurt round text [fig. 41].
    W. Schenck   9 [88]
    Knapp   6
    *Maler   5
    W. Schenck   3 [86]
    Rhau   3
  6. Kesler-Richel text [fig. 42].
    No. 10338   3 [83]
    *Hölzel   1 [80]
  7. Koelhoff-Pafraet text [b].
    Bumgart   10 [82]
    Heinrich of Neuss   3 [80]
xij. Single text types.
    Ratdolt   20, 20ᴮ [106]
    Lotter sen.   15 [86, k]
    Baumgarten   7 [83]
    Schumann   4 [79]
    J. Schöffer   11
    Schönsperger sen.   15
xiij. Foreign styles.
  1. Italian founts.
    α. [Burger 5⁵.] [c]
      Schobser   7 [94]
      Ratdolt   7 [92]
    β. (law text.)
      M. Schürer   10 [90]
    γ. [WP. 206, text.]
      Corn. of Zierikzee   3
    δ. [Burger 81².] [d]
      Paul of Hachenburg   3 [81]
    ε. [Burger 5⁷.]
      Ratdolt   4 [76]
    ζ. [Burger 118.]
      Schobser   5 [76]
      Dietz   1
      Borchard   5?

2. French vernacular founts.
    Hochfeder   17 [114]
    Hochfeder   22 [99–100]
    Murner   3 [100]
3. Dutch.
  α. Larger [MT. 108 b 1].
    Bumgart   9
  β. Smaller [MT. 110 a].
    Zel   11
    Ludwig of Renchen   8
    Bumgart   6 [98]
b. Small text [c. 75–68mm.].
 i. Stuchs-Zainer style [e] [fig. 43].
    Schönsperger sen.   8 [76]
    *G. Stuchs   13 [72]
    Hölzel   11 [72]
 ij. Froben-Vietor style [fig. 44].
    *Koberger   19 [74]
    Hüpfüff   9 [72]
 iij. Strassburg-Köln style.
  1. Flach-Quentell variety; tailed h.
    Flach   2 [74]
    Knoblouch   10 [74]
    Quentell   5 [72]
  2. Normal, with round h [fig. 45]. [f]
    J. Schöffer   9 [71–2]
    Schöffer appendix   3
    Prüss sen.   11 [71]
    Strassburg xv.   6 [70]
    Hüpfüff   6 [70]
    Knoblouch   9 [71]
    Knoblouch   15 [70]
    Schott   11 [71]
    Beck   8 [71]
    Prüss jun.   6 [71]
    No. 10337   1 [71]
    Froschauer   5 [74]
    Hist   5 [72]
    Stöckel   3 [73–4]
    *Gran   5 [71]
    Dorn   5 [70–71]
iv. Single types.
    Landen   6 [78]
    No. 10951   9 [74]
    No. 12000   15 [c. 72]
    Lacher   3 [65]
v. Foreign styles.
  1. Italian founts.
    S. Otmar   13 [75]
    M. Schürer   11 [70]
    Ratdolt [g]   15 [69]
    A. Huber   3

[a] Cf. Burger 14². [b] Burger 16⁵; MT. 64 e 2³. [c] Cf. Burger 131(2)³ and 143(2); WP. 204, 211. [d] Cf. Burger 131(2)³. [e] Cf. Burger 131(1)³ and 154³. [f] Burger 144³. [g] Burger 5³.

2. French founts (α Paris, β Lyon).
  α. Hochfeder   23 [80]
  β. Peypus   7 [73]

c. Small types [from c. 65 mm.].
  i. Strassburg-Köln style.
    1. Round h, double hyphen [fig. 46].
      Schönsperger jun.   4 [66–7]
      Landen   2 [66]
      J. Schöffer   17 [64]
      Schöffer appendix   2
      Knoblouch   4 [64]
      Drach   24 [64]
      C. Hist   7
      Lamparter & Murrer   4 [64]
      Strassburg xx.   7 [63]
      *Gran   9 [63]
    2. Round h, single hyphen.
      Prüss sen.   10 [65]
      Beck   10
    3. Tailed h, double hyphen.
      Quentell [a]   6 [63]
    4. Tailed h, single hyphen.
      Bumgart   1 [63]
      Martin of Werden [b]   4 [63]
      Cervicornus   6
    5. Mixt h, double hyphen.
      Quentell [c]   6 [63]
      Cornelis of Zierikzee   5 [63]
    6. Mixt h, single hyphen.
      Martin of Werden [d]   4 [63]
    7. Similar fount with open V (round h).
      Hochfeder   25 [66]
    8. With different capitals [fig. 47].
      [Zel   4 (67)]
      Tzwivel   3 [67]
      Köbel   2 [65]
      No. 10607   3 [64]
      Heumann   3 [c. 63–4]
      *Heinrich of Neuss   4 [63]
  ij. Quasi-french, tailed h, double hyphen
                [fig. 48].
      Knoblouch   20 [71]
      *Hölzel   14 [68]
      J. Stuchs   10 [68]
      Lotter sen.   14 [67]
      Grüninger   30 [66]
      Hochfeder   18 [66]
  iij. Basel-French [e], round h [fig. 49].
      Schaffener   6 [65]
      Anshelm   6 [65]
      *Koberger   20 [63]
      Hölzel   9 [60–61]

iv. Smaller groups.
  1. like MT. 79 d 2.
    S. Otmar   8 [60]
    Gran   15 [61]
  2. Broad round types [fig. 50].
    *W. Schenck   8 [65]
    Knapp   4 ?
    Maler   4
    W. Schenck   4 [64]
    Thanner   5 [63]
  3. Leipzig founts [fig. 51²].
    *Lotter sen.   7 [61–2]
    Stöckel   7
    Kachelofen   10
    Schumann   6
v. Very small types.
    Grüninger   28 [55]
    Grüninger   4
vi. Foreign styles.
  1. Italian [f] [Burger 5⁹].
    Baumgarten   10 [68]
    Jamer   2
    Ratdolt   10 [65]
    Schleiffer   3 [60]
  2. French (α Paris, β Lyon).
    α. Gymnicus   6 [63]
       Hochfeder   26 [56]
    β. Grüninger   29 [60–61]

E. VERNACULAR GERMAN TYPES.

a. Large text.
  i. Normal [fig. 52].
    No. 10957A   19 [112]
    Knoblouch   21 [108]
    *J. Otmar   17 [108]
    Öglin appendix   13 [108]
    S. Otmar   10 [108]
    Schobser   8 [108]
    Schobser appendix   2 [108]
    Dyon   2 [107]
    Weissenburger   9 [107]
    Prüss sen.   19 [106]
    Hüpfüff   12 [106]
    Beck   2 [106]
    Schönsperger sen.   6 [104]
    Zeissenmair   2 [104]
    No. 11181   1
    No. 11185   8
    Greif   13
  ij. Older and abnormal founts.
    Math. Brandiss   6 [120]
    Hüpfüff [g]   5 [112]

---

[a] To 1509.   [b] After 1501.   [c] From 1510.   [d] In 1501.   [e] Cf. Joh. v. Amorbach 19, Kesler 6, Furter 4; Levet 6, Bocard 2, &c. TP. XVI. 4, XVII. 4.   [f] Cf. E. Silber 1, Carcain 1, Adam of Rottweil 3, Lorenzo di Alopa 1, D. de Lapis 2, &c.   [g] TFS. 1902b.

Schobser 3 [97-8]
Ostendorfer 1 [97-8]
N. Wurm 1 [97-8]
Ramminger 4

b. Text size.
 i. Normal[a].
  1. With D^1, H^1 [fig. 53].
   J. Schöffer[b] 7 [94-5]
   Ramminger 2 [94]
   Flach 12 [92-3]
   *Knoblouch 18 [92]
   No. 11986-7 2 [92]
   Arndes[c] 5 [91]
   Borchard 3
   Konstanz 1 [91]
   J. Otmar 24 [90]
   S. Otmar 5 [90]
   Schönsperger jun. 2 [89]
   Miller 7 [88]
   Öglin appendix 14
  2. With D^1, H^2 [Burger 75].
   Schmidt 2 [95]
   J. Schöffer 3 [91]
  3. With D^1, D^2, H^2.
   Drach 26 [94]
  4. With D^1, D^3, H^1.
   Anshelm 13 [94]
  5. With D^2, H^1.
   Hans of Erfurt 2 [89]
  6. With D^2, H^2 [fig. 54].
   No. 11995 5 [100]
   Spot 2 [98]
   *Hüpfüff 2^B [97]
   Gutschaiff 2 [97]
   Bornemann 3 [97]
   Tzwivel 2
   Heinrich of Neuss 5 [96-7]
   Arndt of Aachen 2 [96-7]
   Kruffter 1 [96-7]
   Gran 13 [95-6]
   Prüss sen.[d] 12 [95]
   Lutz 1 [95]
   No. 11994 3 [95]
   Grüninger 5 [94]
   Landen 3 [94]
   Knoblochtzer 8 [94]
   Durlach 1 [94]
   Knoblouch 5 [93]
   Flach 6 [93]
   Ludwig of Renchen 4 [92]
   Sittich 1 [91]
   No. 11993 2 [91]

Hist 2 [88]
Bumgart 7
  7. With D^3, H^2.
   Hochfeder 24 [99]
   Hüpfüff 2^A, 2^C [97]
   Prüss sen.[e] 12 [95]
   Beck[f] 13 [95]
   Prüss jun. 4 [95]
   No. 10342 5 [95]
   Flach 9 [94-5]
   M. Schürer 6 [94-5]
   Knoblouch 5^B, 5^D [93]
   Flach 8 [92]
  8. With D^3, H^2, H^4.
   Beck[g] 13
  9. With D^3, H^3 [fig. 55].
   *Schott 1 [97-8]
   Kistler 4 [96]
   No. 10340-41 4 [95]
   Knoblouch 5^c [93]
   page 52, after 10343 7 [93]
  10. With D^3, H^4 [fig. 56].
   *M. Schürer 15 [95]
   No. 10343 6 [95]
   No. 11997 9 [94]
 ij. Abnormal.
  1. Schott style [D^3, H^1; fig. 57].
   Schmidt 4 [97]
   Heumann 4 [c. 95]
   *Schott 12 [95-6]
   Dietz 5 [92]
   Marschalk-Winter 5?
   Köbel 8 [92]
   Martin of Werden 8
  2. Lotter style [fig. 58].
   *Lotter sen. 11 [91-2]
   Lotter jun. 3
   Thanner 6
  3. Various.
   Kerner [D^2] 1 [94-5]
   Dorn [D^1 H^1] 4 [92]
   Baumgarten [D^4 H^1] 9 [91]
   Froschauer [$D^2 D^5 H^5$] 3 [90]
   No. 12002 17
c. Small text.
 i. Normal[h].
  1. C^1, E^1, double hyphen [fig. 59].
   Weinreich 1 [92]
   Halle 2 [91]
   No. 11996 7 [91]
   No. 11990-92 2 [90]
   Öglin 7 [89]

---

[a] D^1, H^1, as in fig. 53; D^2, H^2, as in fig. 54; D^3, H^3, as in fig. 55 (and D^3, fig. 56); H^4, as in fig. 56.
[b] Druckschriften 27^2. [c] Burger 71^3, Druckschriften 26^8. [d] Till 1508. [e] From 1508.
[f] Before 1519. [g] In 1519-1520. [h] Called Swedish in the early Oxford specimens. C^1, E^1, as in fig. 59; C^2, as in fig. 60-62; E^2, as in fig. 60; E^3, as in fig. 61; E^4, as in fig. 62.

C C

Sittich 3 [89]
Miller 8 [89]
G. Stuchs 18 [89]
*Hölzel 4 [89]
Nürnberg xxi. 4 [89]
Weissenburger 5 [89]
J. Stuchs 1 [89]
Peypus 2 [89]
Gutknecht 2 [89]
Dyon 5 [89]
Stöckel 6 [89]
Rhau 4 [89]
No. 12003 19 [89]
No. 10950 3 [88–9]
No. 11187 14 [88–9]
Nadler 2 [88]
No. 10951 [no E] 6 [88]
Koberger 26 [88]
W. Huber 1 [88]
No. 11183 6 [88; ℭ]
No. 11186 11 [88; ¶]
Knapp 3 [88]
Anshelm 10 [88]
Tretter 2 [88]
Pfeil 25 [87]
Grim 1 [87]
No 10952 11 [87]
W. Schenck 5 [87]
Maler 2 [87]
No. 11184 7
Schobser 9
Schobser appendix 6

2. C^1, E^1, single hyphen.
Lotter sen. 4 [89]
Kachelofen 12 [89]
Thanner 1 [88]

3. With C^2, E^1 and different O, Q, T.
No. 11181 2 [88]

4. With C^2, E^2 [fig. 60] [a].
J. Otmar 18 [89]
S. Otmar 11 [89]
Dorn 3 [89]
Schönsperger sen. 9 [88]
*Öglin 3 [88]
Kunne 6 [87]
No. 10949 2 [86]

5. With C^2, E^3 [fig. 61].
G. Schenck 2 [88]
*Weissenburger 3 [88]

6. With C^2, E^3, E^4.
Schönsperger sen. 16 [75, k]

7. With C^2, E^4 [fig. 62].
Jac. Winter 2 [85–6]
*Landsberg [b] 1 [87]

ij. Abnormal and various.
No. 12004 21 [c. 84]
Baumgarten 2 [82]
Jamer 1 [82]
Math. Brandiss 8

d. Small schwabacher founts.
i. Normal [c] style [fig. 63^2].
Knoblouch 6 [78]
Wähinger 2 [78]
Anshelm 2 [78]
*Flach 11 [77]
Kerner 4 [75]
Schott 6 [73]
Hölzel 5 [c. 71–2]
J. Schöffer 14
Öglin appendix 14
Miller 9

ij. Kirchheim style [d] [fig. 64].
J. Schöffer 10 [82]
Hüpfüff 3 [82]
*Bumgart 5 [81]
Quentell 15 [80]
Köbel 7

iij. Various.
J. Stuchs 8

e. Frakturschrift [3, fig. 65; 4, fig. 66].
1. Schönsperger sen. [e] 12
Schobser appendix 3
2. Schönsperger sen. [f] 13 [152]
Schobser appendix 4 [140]
3. Schobser appendix 5 [126]
*Schönsperger sen. 14 [118]
4. *Grim 14 [106]
Grim 12 [95]

[a] Burger 119^2. [b] O, Q, T, as no. 11181 (Ec. i. 3). [c] Called Islandic in the early Oxford specimens. [d] Burger 96^2 and 47. [e] Druckschriften 1. [f] Druckschriften 2.

QVITATVM COLLECTA
NEA· IN AEDIBVS IO
ANNIS SCHOEFFER
MOGVNCIACI· AN

Fig. 1. Mainz, J. Schöffer, type 15.   From no. 9875.   [Aa 2.]

LVCIANO·EVGILI
ANO·FILIO·CARIS
SIMO·VIXIT·ANNOS·
XIX·LVCIANVS·ING·
PATER·FECIT·S·S·

Fig. 2. Augsburg, E. Ratdolt, type 21.   From no. 10645.   [Aa 3.]

plurimū funt fubituri fermonis. Reteximus enim
uniuerfam philofophiā humano quæfitā igenio :
Ariftoteleācꝗ maxime in libra appēdimus. Quā
ob rem multas in me conflandas effe calūnias nõ
fum animi dubius. Sed præftat mea quidē fentē⸗
tia:a veritate contra vanitatez ftare contumelijs
preffum / cꝗ a vanitate contra veritatez laudibus
onuftū. Sunt & alia. Necꝗ em conficio noftrarū
catalogū lucubrationū: quibus fi aliquid ocij da⸗
bitur:& imponi extrema manus poterit : & cura
ri/üt in Germaniā ufcꝗ perferant tui gratia. Quē
& nomine litterarꝝ/& veteris amicitię non diligi
modo a nobis/fed amari fcias : plus etiam cꝗ tute
ipfe uncꝗ arbitrareris. Vale. Romæ Idibus Nouē
bris. M D XII.

Fig. 3. Strassburg, J. Schott, type 5*.   From no. 10273.   [Ab. i. 1.]

Dum fuas Titan reuõcat quadrigas
Tercius iam iam folitos ad ortus
Et refurgentis domini ftatuta
          Tranfijt hora
Mane.feftino pede Magdalena
Ad fepulti Sarcophagum tonantis
Pergit.amiffi gemebunda patris
          Orphanitate.
Ad facrum velox vbi venit antrum
Et caui faxi tenebras ocellis
Luftrat intentus.reperitcꝗ nufquam
          Corpus Iefu.
Heu meum.clamat.lachrymans Iefum
Quis tulit?diras etiam fubirem
Præfidum portas.raperemcꝗ raptum
          Certa.virago.

Fig. 4. Nürnberg, H. Hölzel, type 8.   From no. 11003.   [Ab. ij. 1.]

Dum stupet in uacuo quem forte feriret Erasmus
Nec Lea,nec uitulus,musca nec ulla fuit.
EIVSDEM IN LEVM·
Cui studiä,& castos mores hæc tempora debent
Qui tibi non mundo uiuere Christe docet.
Laudat Apostolici quem tota corona Senatus
Quem charum patres Orbis & Vrbis habent.
De quò nemo,nisi indoctus,nisi pessimus audet.
Quä quæ de uera R elligione,loqui.
Qua tu fronte audes illum reprehendere quem tu
Si decies uiuas Nestora,non referes?

Fig. 5. Mainz, J. Schöffer, type 19.   From no. 9873.   [Ab. iv.]

ablatiuo scilicet & actõ Sub signis tertiȩ phalangis mili
tabät Di,Dis,Re,Se,An & con.Eratq̃ eoꝝ proprium
officium cõpositionë facere in usum militü, nanq̃ tunc
dies quadragesimæ erät. At qui noïa omïa in suas acies
distributa, pulcherrimo ordine ꝓcedebät, videlicet sub
stätiua & similiter Adiectiua,ꝓpria,Appellatiua & par
titiua. Post quæ Cõparatiua,Suplatiua,Possessiua,Pa
tronymica, Gëtilia,Numeralia & Multiplicia,Singula
eorü distinguebant per declinatiões quinq̃,scilicet pri
mä,secunda,tertiä quartä & quintä,Quoꝝ arma erant
species,genera,nüeri,figurȩ & casus,   His igitur om
nibus in vnü coactis,Rex nominü Poeta,copias & iße
suas deduxit in eandë planicië Coniunctionü,posuitq̃
castra ab altera parte prȩdicti fluminis Siue, ita vt tätos
exercitus vnicus diuideret alueus fluminis Vnde, & fie
bat vt inter aquatores non leuia interdü prȩlia inirentur

Fig. 6. Leipzig, M. Lotter, type 12.   From no. 11352.   [Ab. v. 1.]

Thiloninus Philymnus. poeta preclariſſ.
Reip. Herfurdienſis principi & Archiſo⸗
pho Ioáni Vuerlichio:& Flauio Materno
ytriuſq; Theoſophiæ conſecraneo⸗amicis
ac patronis ſuis Salutē & fœlicitatē
optat .

Obtulerūt mihi aliquis & muſaꝝ & mei amātes ꝑclariſſ.
Reip. litterariæ princeps Ioannes Vuerlichi: ac ſpectatæ
homo probitatis Flaui Materne: patroni & amici opt .
Batrachomiomachiā Homeri(eius ſc oσ ιϒɛΝɛτοτ σο
Φωτατοσ και θɛοσ ΠαΝτωΝ τωΝ ΠοιꝗτωΝ qui ſuit oīm
poetaꝝ ſapientiſſ & deus)carmia ut docta & eruditiõe
plena⸗ſic ſacera & ſalſa. Quod opᵍ qum pellegiſſem re⸗
legiſſemq; ſragmēta potius quā integrū libellū offendi :
anio nāq; reputaui bonā partē (max. ubi pallados oꝛo)
deeſſe: ad eū quē ſuperioribus annis licet neq; ꝑ vngue

Fig. 7. Wittenberg, J. Rhau, types 1 and 2.   From no. 11831.   [Ab. v. 2 ; Ac. iv. 1.]

cis, Ceruſſæ, baccarū lauri, Aluminis, boli Armeniæ, Ci
nabaris, Minij, Corallij, Salis uſti, Viridis æris, Scorię plū
bi, plumbi uſti, Rubiginis ferri, Reſinæ uulgaris, & Tere
binthinæ. Oleorum optime omnium laurinū, deinde ſim
plex, Roſaceum, Terebinthinum, & magno effectu Iuni⸗
perinum, ac Nardinū. Adipes, Suillus, Anſerinus, Vrſi⸗
nus, humanus, melinus. Item pingue ex ungula bouilla,
Butyrū præſertim quod menſe Maio coactum eſſet, me⸗
dulla ceruí, ſepum hircinum, ceruinumᵹ, mel Roſaceū,

Fig. 8. Mainz, J. Schöffer, type 12.   From no. 9865.   [Ac. i.]

vitam, quaſi quoddā ſpeculū intuētes, ab opeꝝ ſimul & ſer
monū turpitudine ſe penitus auertant. Nam ſi quis delin⸗
quētes obiurgat filios, tum is in eoſdē illabatur errores, hic
ignorare videt, ſub illoꝝ noie ſua ſe incuſare crimina. Et
vt ſuccincte dicā. Qui vita improbe degūt, ꝗ nullam in ſer
uos aut liberos increpādi licétiam agunt. Et vbi impudēs
eſt ſenectus, ibi & inuerecūdos eſſe iuuenes eſt neceſſe. Ad
comparandā igiꝛ ſibijs modeſtiā dandā opera eſt, ut omnia
pro reꝝ conuenientia perficiant. Imitemur aūt potiſſimū
Euridicen, quæ ꝗuis illyrica, & barbariſſima foret mulie⸗
rū, ad erudiēdos tamē liberos, ꝗ ꝗ in ætate iā prouecta, ſtu
diū ac diſciplinam attigit. Hacten⁹ ex Plutarcho de liberis
educādis.   Subijtiā. M. Catonis exemplū ab eodē in illius
vita memoratū. M. Cato filiū, quū primū per ætatem intel
ligere potuit, literis erudiuit, tam & ſi Chilonē gratioſum
ſeruum Grámaticum haberet, qui compluribus pueris lu
dum aperuerat, indignum, vt ipſe phibet, ratus filium ſuū,

Fig. 9. Strassburg, M. Schürer, type 5.   From no. 10202.   [Ad. i.]
206

Ecciana modeſtia quam iactat:parcat tot milibus ſanctorũ.
Cum vſḡ ad noſtra tempora durarit eccleſia Greca: & ſine
dubio vſḡ hodie durat & durabit.Nõ eñ Chriſtus accepit
medium terræ Romanę ſed omnesſines terrę in poſſeſſionẽ
& hereditatem a patre Pſal.ii.
AD SEPTIMVM Quod ex Hieronymo de ſummo ſacer⸗
dote oppoſuit:meã reſponſionẽ dixit eſſe euaſionẽ.Ideo con
firmaturus dictum ſuñ adiecit.Cur B.Hiero.Damaſum Pi
ſcatoris ſucceſſorem dicat & cathedrę Petri vult aſſociari.
Illud diuiñ citãs.Mat.xvi.Super illã petrã fundatam eccle
ſiam ſcio:Qđ ita reliquis eccleſiis appropriari nõ poteſt.Et
deide cõplorat,Hieroſolymitanę,Antiochenę, Alexãdrinę,
tandem & Bohemicę caſum. Et qđ eodẽ Hiero. reſte apud
ſolos Romanos incorrupta patrum ſeruaretur auctoritas.
RESPONDEO & rogo dñm Doctorem egregiũ velit di⸗
cta patrũ allegare ſecundũ conſcientiã,Ne p Theologis vi⸗

Fig. 10. Augsburg, without name of place or printer, type 13.   From no. 10953.   [Ad. ij.]

QVOT SVNT EXITVS SVPERLATIVI

Octo ſunt ſuplatiui nominis exitus.ſ.Rimus.ſimus,quæ ſuntfre
quãtiores.Limus ſimus,nimus,timus,ximus,remus.

VNDE FORMATVR SVPERLATIVVM IN RIMVS⸗

Suplatiuũ in rimus formaſa nominatiuo in er finito,rimus ad⸗
iecta,vt pauprimus a paup,tenerrimus a tener.Sic creberrimus,p
ſperrimus.valetudine,pſperrima vtor,celerrimus,a creber,proſp
celer.Q aũt Neſtor inqt a celer celeriſſimus,antiquitati det.Preter
dexter dextimus,& a ſiniſter ſiniſtimus.Maturrimus vo & ſaturri⸗
mus a nominatiuis exolcus ſunt matur & ſatur.Quoꝝ loco latini
maturus & ſaturus dicũt,ꝗ recta ſuplatiua habẽ maturiſſim⁹ et ſa⸗
turiſſimus.Corne.Ta.Robur ætatis ꝗ̃ maturrimũ p̃cari.Similr̃ ve
terrimus a veter,deterrimus a deter recta ſuplatiua ſunt,q & hodie
latinitati militant,ita celeberrim⁹ ſaluberrimus,acerrim⁹.a celeber
ſaluber,acer deducta.

Fig. 11. Strassburg, M. Schürer, type 4.   From no. 10200.   [Ae. i. 1.]

qua per discipulum proditus est, & captus, accepit
panem, & gratijs actis deo, fregit panem, ac dixit:
Sumite, edite, hoc est meum corpus, quod pro nobis
frangitur omnibus impartiendum . Hoc quod me
facere uidetis , posthac & nos faciatis in memo/
riam mei. Videtis hic cum præceptore suo simul
omnes accumbere, mensam ac cibum esse cõmunem
omnibus, ne Iudam quidem proditorem à consor/
tio mensæ semotū, panem eundē in omnes ex æquo
distributum. Dominus sic egit cum suis discipulis,
& nos despicitis fratres, & eiusdem religionis cõ/
sortes? Ad eundem modum, post distributum pa/
nem, & poculū sumpsit in manus, cœna iam pera/
cta, dicens: Hoc poculum, nouum est testamentū,
per meum sanguinem:ex hoc quoties bibetis, in me/
moriam mei facite. Hic igitur de eodem poculo bi/
bebant omnes, & inter nos diuites ebrij sunt, pau
peres sitiunt. Christus hoc conuiuiū mortis suæ cõ
memorationem, & æterni fœderis symbolum esse
uoluit, cum nunc per luxum ac dissensionem apud
nos celebretur. Mysticus est panis , cuius ex æquo
participes esse debent omnes acrosanctum est po
culum ad omnes æque pertinens, haudquaquā paratū
ad placandam corporis sitim, sed ad arcanæ rēi re/
praefentationē,

Fig. 12. Basel, J. Froben. Erasmus, paraphrasis in epist. Pauli
ad Romanos, etc.   1519 April.   [Af. i.]

qñ clunibus erat atris, totusq; hispidus, sub arbore quadam cubantem, aggre
di conarentur correptos, uinctosq; de claua à tergo (quo more lepores à uenatoribus portari solent) suspensos, materni uaticinij fidem impleuisse. Quid
uero non dicamus & hunc Eduardum in clunatrum incidisse, dum Erasmo ne
gocium facessit, qui auderfarios suos sic uincit, sic omnibus presidijs spoliat,
ut eo respectu Marsyas ab Apolline uestitus, non excoriatus uideri queat.
Quæ cum ita sint uix credas quàm moueat stultitia hominis, cum publicū totius ætatis dedecus interpreter, esse quibus displiceat Erasmus, esse qui mordere audeāt, tot modis pietati iuxta ac optimis studijs utilem, ut si omnium, quæ
annos abhinc sexaginta uixerunt, labores conferas, æquilibrium non sint facturi. Et spectabunt hæc ociosi bonarum literarū amatores, quibus caput suum utiumq; iampridē deuouit Erasmus? Non credo sane, Tu itaq; Eobane mi
iucundissime fac agas Misenum Acoliden, quo non præstantior alter, Aere
ciere uiros Martemq; accendere cantu, cane nobis classicum, ut undiq; irru

Fig. 13. Mainz, J. Schöffer, type 13.   From no. 9873.   [Af. ij.]

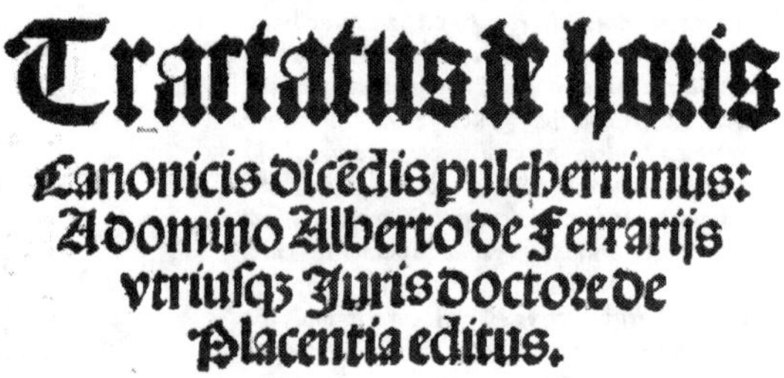

Trattatus de horis

Canonicis dicēdis pulcherrimus:
A domino Alberto de Ferrarijs
vtriusq̄ Iuris doctore de
Placentia editus.

Fig. 14. Nürnberg, H. Hölzel, types 7 and 2.   From no. 10984.   [Ba. i; Cc. i. 3.]

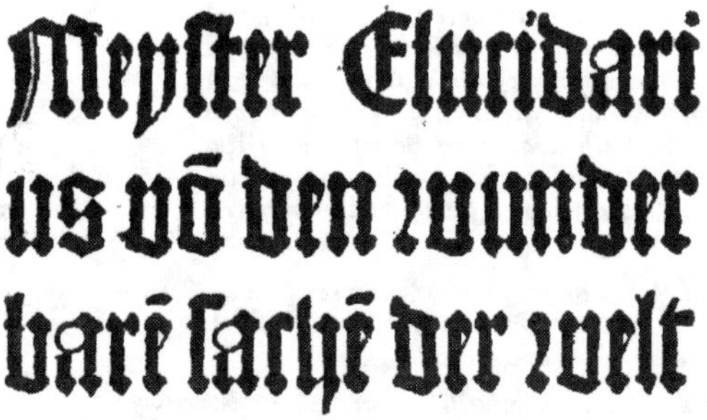

Meyster Elucidari
us vō den wunder
barē sachē der welt

Fig. 14B. Erfurt, M. Maler, type 6.   From no. 11249.   [Ba. ij.]

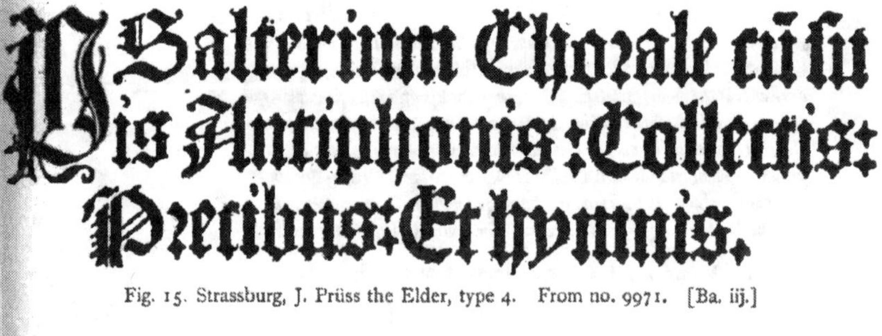

PSalterium Chorale cū su
is Antiphonis:Collectis:
Precibus:Et hymnis.

Fig. 15. Strassburg, J. Prüss the Elder, type 4.   From no. 9971.   [Ba. iij.]

In nomine dñi Incipit plalterium chozale
scðm ritum inlignis ecclie Constantien.
A prima dñica octobris vlcp ad aduentum
dñi. et ab octau a ephie vlcp ad.xl. in domini
cis diebus.Ad matutinas Inuitatorium.

Fig. 16. Strassburg, J. Prüss the Elder, type 15.   From no. 9971.   [Bb.]

Acerdotis Petri he
di libzi tres de Gene
ribus amozis: luculēte et eru-

Fig. 17. Leipzig, J. Thanner, type 2.   From no. 11398.   [Bc. i. 1.]

turba dicens.Tolle hūc:1 di
mitte nobis barrabā. Qui
erat,ppter seditionē quandā
factā in ciuitate 1 homicidiū
millus ī carcerē. Itez aūt pi
latus locutus est ad eos: vo
lens dimittere iesum. At illi
lucclamabāt dicētes. Cruci
fige:crucifige eū Ille aūt ter
tio dixit ad illos. Quid enī
mali fecit iste:Nullā causam
mozis iuenio ī eo.Cozripiā
ergo illū 1 dimittā. At illi in

Fig. 18. Strassburg, J. Prüss the Elder, type 13.   From no. 9988.   [Bc. ij. 1]

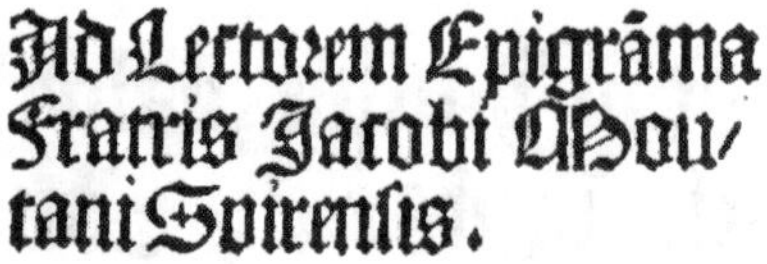

Ad Lectorem Epigráma
Fratris Jacobi Mou/
tani Spirensis.

Fig. 19. Köln, Martin of Werden, type 7.   From no. 10527.   [Bc. ij. 2.]

ᵹciliét. Ø. Ite missa est. Feria.
Duxit eos dñs i spe vf.
all'a: ꝫ inimicos eoꝛ ope
ruit mare all'a all'a all'a
pš. Attendite popule meus legé
meá: inclinare auré vestrã in ver
ba oꝛis mei. Gl'a i eꝫ. Colt
Mps sempiterne de⁹: ꝗ

Fig. 20. Strassburg, J. Prüss the Elder, type 17.   From no. 9988.   [Bc. ij. 3.]

excidet: ꝫ in igné mittet. Et
interrogabãt eü turbe dicé
tes. Quid ergo faciem⁹: Re
spondens auté dicebat illis.
Qui habet duas tunicas. det
nõ habenti: ꝫ ꝗ habet escas.
similiter faciat. Venerüt auté
ꝫ publicani. vt baptisarenf:
ꝫ dixerüt ad illü. Magister.
quid faciemus: At ille dixit
ad eos. Nihil ampli'. ꝙ ꝗd
cõstitutü est vobis faciatis.

Fig. 21. Nürnberg, G. Stuchs, type 5.   From no. 11084.   [Bc. iij. 1.]

Nobis quoq; peccatoribus famulis tuis de
multitudine miserationu tuaru sperauti-
bus partem aliqua ⁊ societate donare digne
ris cu tuis sanctis apostolis ⁊ martyribus.
Cum Johanne. Stephano. Mathia. Bar-
naba. Ignatio. Alexadro. Marcellino. Pe
tro. Felicitate. Perpetua. Agatha. Lucia.
Agna. Cecilia. Anastasia et cum omnibus
sanctis tuis intra quoru nos consortiu. non
estimator meriti. sed venie quesumus largi

Fig. 22. Nürnberg, H. Hölzel, type 3.   From no. 10973.   [Bc. iij. 2.]

Expositio Misse do-
mini Hugonis Car
dinalis ordinis
Predicatoru.

Fig. 23. Nürnberg, H. Hölzel, type 6.   From no. 11013.   [Ca. i. 1.]

Textus veteris artis .s.
Isagogarum Porphirii.
predicametoru Aristotelis
simul cuz duobus libris pe
ribermenias eiusdem.

Item

Exercitata circa hoc scdm

Fig. 24. Hagenau, H. Gran, type 4.   From no. 11612.   [Cb 2].

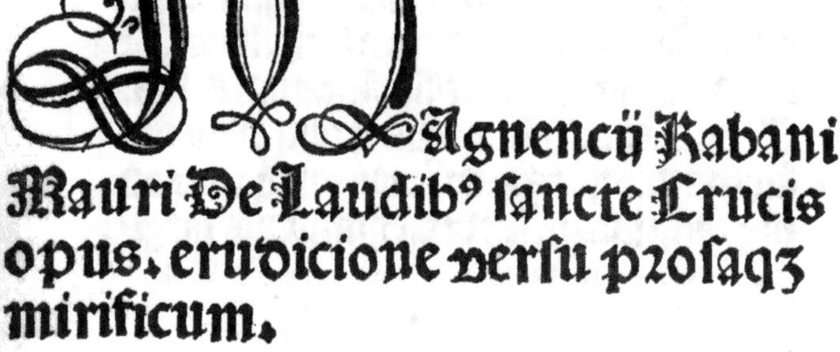

Fig. 25. Pforzheim, T. Anshelm, type 4.   From no. 11747.   [Cb 3.]

Fig. 26. Köln, Cornelis of Zierikzee, type 1 (2, 5).   From no. 10540.   [Cb 4.]

Fig. 27. Augsburg, J. Schönsperger the Younger, type 1.   From no. 10733.   [Cb 5.]

De numero Sibyllarum.
Caput. II.
Arro in libris rerum di/

Fig. 28. Oppenheim, J. Köbel, type 1.   From no. 11924.   [Cb 6.]

Ein Freihait des
Sermons Bebst
lichen ablas vnnd
gnad belangent
Doctoris Mar
tini Luther

Fig. 29. Augsburg, G. Nadler, type 1.   From no. 10863.   [Cb 8.]

ire trans fretū. Et accedens
vnᵒ scriba: ait illi. Magister:
sequar te quocunqz ieris. Et
dicit ei iesus. Uulpes foueas
habēt ⁊ volucres celi nidos:
filius aūt hois nō habet vbi
caput suū reclinet. Alius aūt
de discipulis suis ait illi. Dñe:
pmitte me primū ire: et sepeli
re patrē meū. Jesus aūt ait il
li. Sequere me: ⁊ dimitte mor
tuos sepelire mortuos suos.

Fig. 30. Nürnberg, H. Hölzel, type 10.   From no. 11016.   [Cc. i. 1.]

De cõtinentia sa
cerdotũ. Sub hac questio
ne noua. Vtrũ Papa
possit cũ sacerdo=
te dispensare
vt nubat.

Fig. 31. Nürnberg, J. Weissenburger, types 5 bis and 4.   From no. 11053.   [Ba. v; Cc. i. 2.]

Decollatio iohãnis baptiste Jn
troitus. Gloria z honore. Oratio.
Ancti iohannis baptiste z
martyrz tui dñe quesumᵘ
venerãda festiuitas salutarz auxi
lij nobis pstet effectũ. p. Lectio.
Expectatio. Graduale. Dñe pue
nisti. Alleluia. Justi epulenf. Segñ.
Sallite regi nro:psallite psal/
lite psallite prudenter. Nam
psalterium est iocundum cum cytha/
ra. Nato virginis quo psallens natus
sterilis. Cytharaz carnis percussit in
domo domini. Qum quod sonabaz

Fig. 32. Augsburg, E. Ratdolt, types 9 and 13.   From no. 10651.   [Cc. ij. 2; Cc. iv.]

sito fraudulento non donares: Mirã/
da ergo est sed z timenda dei paciẽtia. q̃
cum te sublimi imperio quod mortales
magni estimant preesse oĩbus voluit.
tu tamẽ tãtis beneficijs eius ingratus.
rebus visibilib⁹ attribuis:quod cõferre
debueras illi⁹ digne maiestati. Tu autẽ
O mater.nostra ter sancta quater ꝗ̃ bea/ ℞.
ta. Cũ prece deuota famulãtũ suscipe vota. ℣.
Jam xp̃o iuncta sponsoq̃z tuo copulata. Cũ p̃c̃e
M achina penalis nutu Jn tercio noct .añ
dispacta tonãtis.martire nil lesa redit orco mil/
lia cesa.Ps̃. Cãtate j.Añ. Martyr vt ora/
uit gladiũ subiit.etbera scandit.spõsus.bonor
q̃z datur.cum xp̃o deliciat.Ps̃. Dñs regna
uit exultet.Añ. Virginis ex oleo quod ma/
nat corpore sacro.certa medela datur morbi ge
nus omñe fugat.Ps̃. Cãtate.ij.℣. Audi filia.

Fig. 33. Bamberg, J. Pfeil, types 13 and 14.   From no. 10344.   [Da. ij. 1 ; Da. ij. 2.]

mC.S.De baptismate Jobãnis in iorda/
ne:z de xp̃i baptismate.   LII
In diebꝫ autẽ illis venit iohãnes ba/
i   ptista‖p̃dicans in deserto iudee:z di/
cens‖Penitẽtiam agite:appropinq̃
bit eñ regnũ celor.Hic est eñ de quo dictũ
est p esaiam propheram:dicentẽ ‖Vox clamã
tis in deserto parate viam dñi:rectas faci/
te semitas eius. Jp̃e autẽ iohãnes habebat
vestimentũ de pilis cameloꝛ:z zonam pelli
ceam circa lumbos suos.Esca aũt eius erat
locuste z mel siluestre.‖Tũc exibãt ad eum
hierosolyma z ois iudea:z ois r̃gio circa ior
danẽ ‖z baptizabãt ab eo i iordane pfitẽtes
pctã sua.‖Videns autem multos pharizeo
rum z saduceoꝛũ venientes ad baptismum
suũ:dixit eis.‖Progenies viperaꝛ:quis de
monstrabit vobis fugere a ventura ira? Fa

Luce.3. a
Johã.1. a

Esa.40.a
Mar.1.a.
Luce.3. a
Johã.1. c
Mar.1.a.
B

Luce.3. a
Johã.3. e
Luce.3.b.
isra.23. d.

Fig. 34. Nürnberg, A. Koberger, type 25.   From no. 10958.   [Da. iv. 1.]

Disiunctiua est illa in qua coniun-
gitur duae cathegoricae per hãc
cõiunctione vel / vt Sortes currit
vel Plato disputat. Ad veritatem
disiunctiuae sufficit alterã parte esse
verã/vt Hõ est aial/vel equus est
lapis. tame permittit ꝙ vtraqз sit
vera/sed nõ ita proprie/vt Hõ est
anial vel equus est hinnibilis. Ad
falsitatem eius requiritur vtraqз
partem esse falsam/ vt Homo est
asinus vel equus est lapis.

Fig. 35. Augsburg, J. Miller, type 6. From no. 10833. [Da. vi.]

tame ex fide siue opere operante. cũ amplioris auctoritatisfit sa-
cerdotij noue legis ministeriũ. Nulli dubiũ quin ecclesia catho-
lica christi sacerdotio sublimata z tãte potestatis locupletata mu
nere. possit instituere multa sacramentalia. ꝗ ex totius ecclesie fide
z meritis efficatiore z pfusiore habebũt virtutis operatione. Ce-
terũ si aqua expiatiõis in lege veteri p ministros moysi cinere vi-
tuli in se cõsperfa tãte efficatie dica� fuisse vt ꝙlm sanctificaret?
quãtomagis aqua benedicta in christi nofe diuinis pcibus nõ per
moysi ministros. sed iesu christi ministros sctificata. Qui igif ecclesiã sanctã catholicã amplioris dignitatis et potestatis credit
esse ꝗ sinagogã. incũctãter credere debet hec ecclesie sacramentalia nõ inania. sed ad ea ad ꝗ p ecclesiã deputata verace z efficace
diuinitus cõtinere virtute. Instituta aũt legif ꝗl in principio na-
scentis ecclesie. Ut em legif tam in decreto de cõse. di. iij. c. aquã
sale. In cronicis summoꝛ pontificũ tam Uincetij hystorialis ꝗ
Martini fratrũ sacri ordinis pdicatoꝛ. Alexander primus z mar
tyr qui sedit in cathedra Petri Anno a passione dñi. lxxxiij. fuit

Fig. 36. Nürnberg, J. Stuchs, type 9. From no. 11097. [Da. vij. 1.]

Inest autẽ contrarietas in relatione vt virtus vicio con-
trariũ est. cũ sit vtrunqз horum ad aliquid. z disciplina igno-
rantie. Nõ autẽ oĩb relatiuis inest ꝑtrarietas. duplici enim
nibil est cõtrariũ: neqз triplici. neqз vlli tallũ. Uidenf aũt
magis et minus relatiua suscipere. Simile em magis z minus dicif: z inequale magis z min dicif. cũ vtruqз sit relati-
uum. simile em alicui simile dicif. z inequale alicui inequale
Non autẽ omnia relatiua suscipiunt magis z minus. Duplex enim non dicitur magis et minus duplex. nec aliquid
talium.

Fig. 37. Hagenau, H. Gran, type 8. From no. 11612. [Da. viij. 1.]

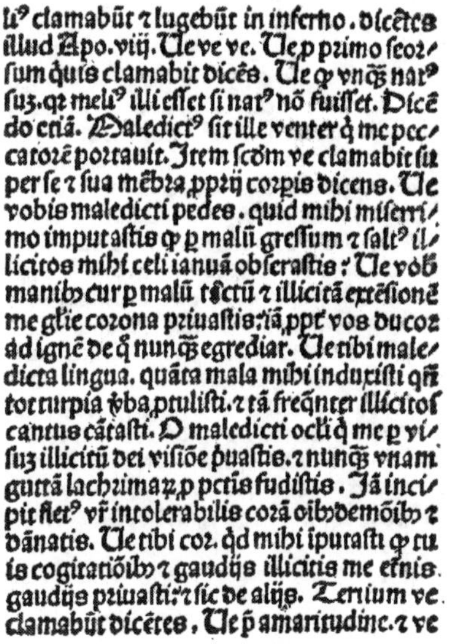

lı⁹ clamabūt ꝛ lugebūt in inferno. dicētes
illud Apo. viij. Ue ve ve. Ue p primo seor-
sum quis clamabit dicēs. Ue ꝙ vnq̄ nat⁹
sum. qꝛ meli⁹ illi esset si nat⁹ nō fuisset. Dicē
do etiā. Maledict⁹ sit ille venter q̄ me pec-
catorē portauit. Item scd̄m ve clamabit su
per se ꝛ sua mēbra ꝓprij corporis dicens. Ue
vobis maledicti pedes. quid mihi miserri-
mo imputastis ꝙ ꝑ malū gressum ꝛ salt⁹ illicitos mihi celi ianuā obserastis: Ue vob̄
manib⁹ cur ꝑ malū tactū ꝛ illicitā extēsionē
me glie corona priuastis: iā ꝓpt vos ducor
ad ignē de q̄ nunq̄ egrediar. Ue tibi male-
dicta lingua. quāta mala mihi induxisti q̄n
tot turpia ṽba ptulisti. ꝛ tā freq̄nter illicitos
cantus cātasti. O maledicti oculi q̄ me ꝑ vi-
sum illicitū dei visiōe ꝑuastis. ꝛ nunq̄ vnam
guttā lachrimaꝝ ꝓ pctis fudistis. Iā incipit flet⁹ vñ intolerabilis corā oib⁹ demōib⁹ ꝛ
dānatis. Ue tibi cor. q̄d mihi iputasti ꝙ tu
is cogitatiōib⁹ ꝛ gaudijs illicitis me etnis
gaudijs priuasti: ꝛ sic de alijs. Tertium ve
clamabūt dicētes. Ue ꝑ amaritudine. ꝛ ve

Fig. 38. Strassburg, M. Flach, type 3. From no. 10141. [Da. viij. 2.]

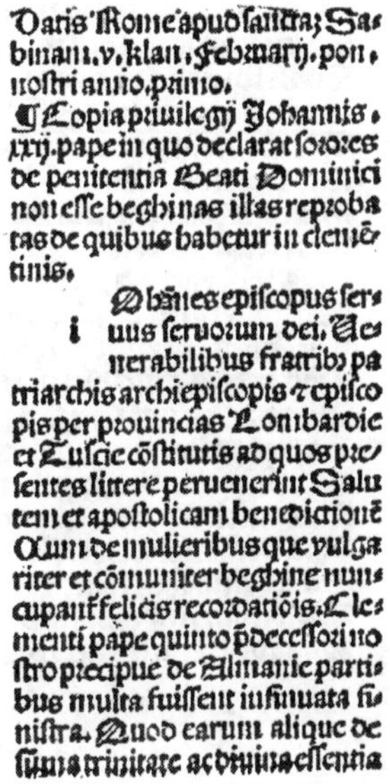

Datis Rome apud sanctā Sa-
binam. v. klan. Februarij. pon-
nostri anno primo.
¶ Copia priuilegij Johannis
xxij. pape in quo declarat sorores
de penitentia Beati Dominici
non esse beghinas illas reproba
tas de quibus habetur in clemē
tinis.
Johānes episcopus ser-
uus seruorum dei. Ue-
nerabilibus fratrib⁹ pa
triarchis archiepiscopis ꝛ episco
pis per prouincias Lombardie
et Tuscie cōstitutis ad quos pre-
sentes litteree peruenerint Salu
tem et apostolicam benedictionē
Cum de mulieribus que vulga
riter et cōmuniter beghine nun-
cupant felicis recordatiōis Cle-
menti pape quinto ꝑdecessori no
stro precipue de Almanie partibus multa fuissent insinuata si-
nistra. Quod earum alique de
summa trinitate ac diuina essentia

Fig. 39. Place and printer unknown, type 16. From no. 12001. [Da. ix. 2.]

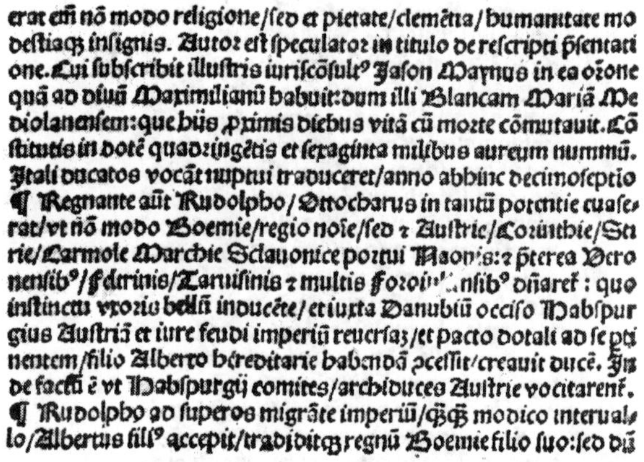

erat eñ nõ modo religione/sed et pietate/clemẽtia/humanitate mo
destiaqz insignis. Autor est speculator in titulo de rescripti psentati
one. Cui subscribit illustris iuriscõsult° Iason Maynus in ea orone
quã ad diuũ Maximilianũ habuit: dum illi Blancam Mariã Me
diolanensem: que hiis primis diebus vitã cũ morte cõmutauit. Cõ
stitutis in dotẽ quadringẽtis et sexaginta milibus aureum nummũ.
Itali ducatos vocãt nuptui traduceret/anno abhinc decimoseptio
¶ Regnante aũt Rudolpho/Ottocarus in tantũ potentie euase-
rat/vt nõ modo Boemie/regio nosie/sed et Austrie/Corinthie/Sti
rie/Carniole Marchie Sclauonice portui Naonis: et pterea Vero
nensib°/fdtrinis/Taruisinis et multis foroi..nsib° dñaret: quo
instinctu vxoris bellũ inducẽte/et iuxta Danubiũ occiso Habspur
gius Austriã et iure feudi imperiũ reuersaz/et pacto dotali ad se ptí
nentem/filio Alberto hereditarie habendã pcessit/creauit ducẽ. In
de factũ e vt Habspurgij comites/archiduces Austrie vocitarent.
¶ Rudolpho ad superos migrãte imperiũ/ĝ modico interual-
lo/Albertus fili° accepit/tradiditqz regnũ Boemie filio suo: sed dũ

Fig. 40. Nürnberg-Landshut, J. Weissenburger, type 7.　From no. 11803.　[Da. x. 2.]

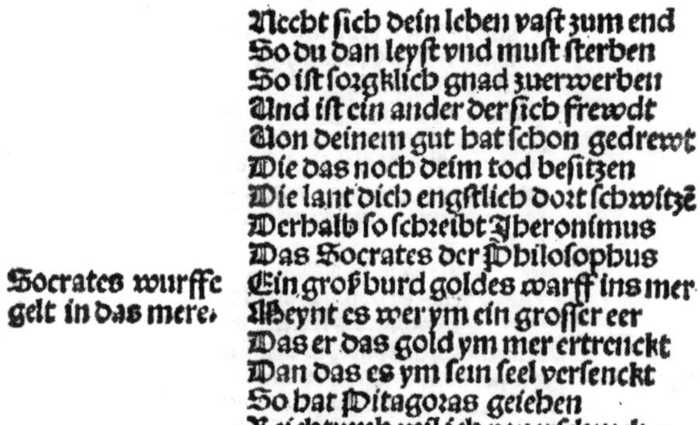

Necht sich dein leben vast zum end
So du dan leyst vnd must sterben
So ist sorgklich gnad zuerwerben
Und ist ein ander der sich frewdt
Von deinem gut hat schon gedrewt
Wie das noch deim tod besitzen
Wie lant dich engstlich dort schwitzẽ
Derhalb so schreibt Jheronimus
Das Socrates der Philosophus
Ein groß burd goldes warff ins mer
Weynt es wer ym ein grosser eer
Das er das gold ym mer ertrenckt
Wan das es ym sein seel versenckt
So hat Pitagoras geleben
Reichtumb wil sich ye verschmeben
Das mich ab zeucht von miltẽ mud
Und der karckheit erfullen thut
Da Curius sein feindt vermeindt
Wolt man mit gelt sie han vereindt
Das wolt er nit vnd sprach zu erst

Socrates wurffe
gelt in das mere.

Fig. 41. Erfurt, M. Maler, type 5.　From no. 11244.　[Da. xi. 5.]

nõnunqz suis pcharis fratribus interloquedũ referret)nisi ferrũ
ignitũ. Modũ itacz expressit in eo. Proprıũ calorẽ et vigiorẽ habet ignis: bec tamẽ ferro cõmunicat: ferrũ vo babet ppriã figurã
z magnitudinẽ: que siliter igni nõ negat. Sic in ista visione duoz
corporũ vnus locus z duplex effigies apparebat: in qua xps ostẽ-
dere voluit quomodo esset vnũ in actu cõsecratiõis cũ sacerdote.
¶ Sequit. Noui z eterni testamẽti. Nouũ dicit respectu vcteris
testamenti. Eternũ vo: id est ppetuũ a parte post: quia eternaliter
durabit z nõ reuocabit. ¶ Sequit. Mysteriũ fidei: id est sacramẽtũ secretũ fidei: qd põt referri ad passionẽ z mortẽ xpi: que fuit san
ctissimũ sacramẽtũ sub figura vcteris testamẽti absconsum: z fide
antiquoꝛũ patrũ precognitũ: tancz mysteriũ regalis et generalis
redemptionis nature humane. ¶ Sequit. Qui p vobis z multis

Fig. 42. Nürnberg, H. Hölzel, type 1.   From no. 10973.   [Da. xi. 6.]

Timoris tres sunt filie
          ·Prima   Timoꝛ pene
          Secũda   Est   Timoꝛ offense
          Tercia   Timoꝛ reuerentie
Timoꝛ superbie filia est dyaboli
Timoꝛem animabus incutit crebra missio iaculoꝛum
Timoꝛ moꝛtis concupiscentiã extinguit
Timoꝛ apprebensionẽ babet potentie seu iustide
Timoꝛ et pudoꝛ a sapientia diuina oꝛiuntur
Timoꝛ duplex est
                    Plenitudo   Sapientie
                    Gloꝛia   Senum
Timoꝛ   Fons   Est   Modestie
                    Thesaurus   Dei
                    Sumus
                    Viuimus
Totumqd   Mouemur   Est dei donũ dei beneficium
                    Boni babemus
                    Bonifacimus

Fig. 43. Nürnberg, G. Stuchs, type 13.   From no. 2275 (part i).   [Db. i.]

gnũ buiꝰ sodomite extincte sunt in nocte natiuita
tis xpi. Aug. Deo in carne aduentente oẽs bostes
nature sodomitas intellige moꝛte reproba z subita
perijsse. Ad designãdum q in bũana natura a minõ
nuncz inueniri deberet tale pcrm. quã naturã filius
dei dignificauit cũ bõ natus sit. Et sciendũ q tales
sodomite sunt pessimi boies. vñ Geñ. xiij. bomies
aũt sodomite erãt pessimi z pcaõꝛes coꝛã do nimis
Itẽ grauitas illius pcti ptz ex vindicta ſõcurſiõis
dncz ciuitatũ. z Ray. dicit. boc viciũ qz detestabile
sit ptz p penã sodomitis inflictã. In q vindicta at-
tendẽdũ est q dñs nõ solũ voluit punire nocẽtes. ſ
etiã innocẽtes puulos. ſ. vniꝰ diei. z in b est pullus
pueris ne diutiꝰ viuẽtes exẽpla patz seqrent z gra
uius dãnarent. Et etiã circũlacẽtes regiões punire
voluit. Nec solũ boies imo etiã aialia z terrenascẽ
tia. ſpamcz terrã destruxit puertẽdo eã in mare moꝛ
tuũ in q nibil viuit. nec auis nec piscis. Vñ Gene.
xix. Dñs pluit sup sodomã z gomoꝛrã ignem et sul
pbur de celo. z ſõuertit ciuitates bas z omnẽ circa

Fig. 44. Nürnberg, A. Koberger, type 19.   From no. 10960.   [Db. ij.]

220

facere nõ intẽdit.ſz vult ꝙ ea boniſ opibꝰ addã/
ramꝰ.vt inꝗt ſctꝰ Bona.i.ij.diſt.rij.ar.j.q.ij.
Ideo inꝗt Paulꝰ.ij.Tim.ij. Nõ coꝛonabit ni
ſi ꝗ legitie certauerit.ſ.ꝗ tẽtatõeſ :aduerſitateſ
ꭓ tribulatõeſ mũdi ꭓ diaboli. Neceſſe ergo eſt
in hac vita noſ aduerſa tolerare ſi volumꝰ ꝓ
ſpiritatẽ ẽternã ꝓmereri. Vt etiã inꝗt Mgr̃ ſen.
in.ij.di.rrir.ꭓ ſctꝰ Bona.eiuſdẽ libꝛi diſt.rrr.
ar.j.q.j. Ideo ſcriptũ eſt Ecſ.riij.ꭓ fuerũt ✝ba
Pauli que ibi recitat ſctꝰ Lucaſ. Per mꝉtaſ
tribulatõeſ opoꝛtꝫ noſ intrare in regnũ celoꝛ
rũ. Idcirco ad heremitaſ Aug.inquit. Qui ex/
ceptuſ fuerit a paſſiõe flagelloꝛ :exceptꝰ erit a
numero gloꝛificatoꝛ. Et Hiero.ad Julianuꝫ
ait. Difficile imo impoſſibile eſt vt ꝓſentibꝰ ꭓ fu
:turiſ qſ fruatur boniſ:vt hic ventrẽ ꭓ illic mẽ
tem impleat: vt de delicijſ trãſeat ad delitiaſ:
vt in vtroꝗ ſeculo ꝓmuſ ſit:vt i celo ꭓ in terra
gloꝛioſuſ appareat. Iſtõ.quoꝗ in li.de ſũ.bo.
dicit. Si dulciſ ꝗrimꝰ neceſſe eſt vt puſ amaꝛ/
ta toleremuſ. Ideo inꝗt Paulꝰ Heb.rij.Per
patientiã curramꝰ ad ꝓpoſitũ nob certamẽ. Et
hoc ſufficiat ꝓ ſecũda ꝑte noſtri ſermõiſ.
Parſ tertia de diſtinctiõe patiẽtie.

Fig. 45. Hagenau, H. Gran, type 5.   From no. 11619.   [Db. iij. 2.]

Arguitur.j.   Arguitur ꝓmo. Hre ꞓriũ ꭓ ſuſcipe magꝭ ꭓ minꝰ ꝗueniũt relatiuiſ. Pro/
Reſponſio   bat ꝑ Ariſto.ꝓbiſ.ꝗ allegatꝭ a ꝓncipio. Rñr ſm Antboniũ andree.ꭓ Frã
ciſꝰ maro.ꝙ Ariſto.i hiſ ꝓbiſ nihil deꞇmiat ſm ꝓpriã opinionẽ. ſz h lo/
cutꝰ ẽ ſm opinionẽ Platõiſ. Et ſignt dic Antboniꝰ andree.ꝙ Ariſto. ni/
hil videt deꞇmiare de relatiuiſ ſm ſuã opinionẽ ꝓpriam añ illã ꝓtẽ textꝰ
ꝗ incipit ſic. Hꝫ aũt qõem. Vel dr.ꝙ ipe loꝗt de relatiuiſ ſm vict. ꝗ etiaꝫ
reperiunt i alijſ ꝓdicamẽtꝭ.ꭓ ſic eẽnt ꝓprie ꝓmo mõ relatiuiſ ſm vict. Vl̃ dr
ꝙ hre ꞓriũ vt ſuſcipe magꝭ ꭓ miꝰ ꝗueiat relatiõi nõ ꝑ ſe rõne ſue eẽntie in/
quãtũ ipoꝛtãt reſpectu ſz ꝑ accnſ ꭓ fũdamntatr̃ vt ſilitudo ſuſcipit magiſ
nõ rõne reſpectꝰ ſed rõne ſui fundamnti.ſ.albediſ.ſz tñ nõ ꝗueit oibꝰ.
Arguitur.2.   Ar ſcdo. In vnoꝗꝫ ꝓdicamnto ẽ vna ꝓma ꞓrietaſ.ꝗ i adaliꝗd etiã ẽ ꞓrie/
Reſponſio   taſ. Añſ eſt pbi.ꝓmo phyſicoꝛ. Rñr ꝙ pbſ loꝗt de ꞓrietate large victa.
ꭓ vult ꝙ qõlibet generaliſſimũ diuidat ꝑ duaſ dñaſ vel ſpẽſ imediataſ
ꝗ ſm eadẽ rõem nõ poſſint veriſicari de eodẽ. ꭓ h ẽ veꝛ ꝗ ꝗlibꝫ ꝓdicamnto.
Arguitur.3.   Ar tertio. Qualitati ꝗueit hre ꞓriũ ꭓ ſuſcipe magꝭ ꭓ minꝰ vt pbſ dicit.
Et oiſ ꝗlitaſ ẽ relatio.ꝗ relatõi ꝗueit hre ꞓriũ ꭓ ſuſcipe magꝭ ꭓ minꝰ. Te/
net ꝗña ſyllogiſtice i diſamiſ. Dioꝛ pbaꞇ. Oiſ ꝗlitaſ eſt eadẽ vel diuer/
ſa.ꝗ oiſ ꝗlitaſ eſt relatio. Tenet ꝗña a ſpẽ ad genꝰ. Rñr ꝙ illa ſit vera ex
Reſponſio   rigoꝛe verboꝛ. relatõi reali ꝗueit hre ꞓriũ ꭓ ſic argumẽtũ pbat tñ forma/
liter ꝑ ſe loꝗndo tñc nõ ẽ vera ſic victũ eſt de ꝗnctitate.nã licꝫ relatio habet
ꞓriũ nõ tñ inꝗntũ eſt relatio ſed inꝗntũ eſt ꝗlitaſ. Et h voluit pbſ.

Fig. 46. Hagenau, H. Gran, type 9.   From no. 11612.   [Dc. i. 1.]

pus christi:vinū in sanguinē transmutat. Nonne z Aaron qui Moysi ad
bibitus fuit in ministerium sacerdos fuit.vt habetur Numeri.xviii. Ps.
Moyses z Aaron in sacerdotibus eius.Tu autem z filij tui custodite zc.
An non Moysi tussit dominus deus Numeri.xx.Loquimini ad petram
coram eis z ille dabit aquas. Si igitur verbis Moysi dei tamen virtute
sarum durissimū in aquam versum est:quāto magis id credere debes de no-
stris sacerdotibus.Ps.Conuertit petraz in stagna aquaruz z rupes in fon
tes.Credis quoqz ꝙ baculus Moysi conuersus est in serpentez viuū z rus
sum ille in baculum aridum z siccum.Exod.iiii. Dixit ergo ad eum quid ē
in manu tua Respondit.Virga.Dixit dominus:ꝓiice eam in terram pro
iecit z versa est in colubrum ita vt fugeret Moyses. Credisitez ꝙ ex arido
costa quā dominus tullit de latere Ade.Eua facta est homo plenus carne z
sanguine.Genes.ij.Cunqzobdormiuisset tulit vnaz de costis eius z reple-
uit carnem pro ea. hoc nunc os ex ossibus meis.Sed z illud non minⁱ vxo
rem loth mutatam fuisse ob diffidentiaz z incredulitatem in cautem durissi
mam.Genes.xix. Respidensqz vxor eius.post se:vsa est in statuā salis zc.
Jam vero audisti insuper o Judee que moysi precepit deus z aaron vt scz
petris loquerentur Numeri.xx.Et loquimini ad petram coram eis z illa
dabit aquas.profecto:hec verba quibus Moyses iussu atqz imperio domini petris locutus est:non poterant esse inefficatia.hoc est sine vi atqz vir
tute:que petram durissimā vertere in aquam mollissimā.non equidem da
vehementer eam moyses percusserit.Numeri.xx.Cūqz eleuasset moyses ma
num percutiens virga bis silicem:z gresse sunt aque largissime. sed virtute
potius que in verbis erat:facile effectum est vt ex petra fluerent aque.

Fig. 47. Köln, Heinrich of Neuss, type 4.   From no. 10560.   [Dc. i. 8.]

Sacrum habet.S.T.Pater beatissime z pontifex Max.Sacrum inquā
z admirabilē modū facili libello apertū.Quo oīm conditor sacerdotis
ministerio:eternū numen:z sub cibo leuissimo suis fidelibus celeste z an
gelicū tribuit alimentū. Qui dum p egregiū virū.F.de Laziginis:als
Accursio ꝑbitatis morū et oīm scientiarū amatorē.E.S.T.Reuerēter
porrigit:illum supplico benigne sumere dignet.Is em literarū apostos
licarum scriptor:tue eximie potestatis z celsitudinis splendor:p scripta
z varia doctorum opera vniuerso mundo eterno cum cōmemoratu:ma-
gis ac magis luceat:ingenue cupit z optat.Quare nris de cōcilio z sups
ma potestate tua opusculis z alias:quoatsupstes sumus.T.S.ꝓtegens
te illā(solo veritatis intuitu)indesinēter:referare satagimus.Et valeat
S.T.ea semp valitudine:quam queat exoptare felicius.

Impressum Nuremberge p acuratissimum Bibliopolam
Hieronymum Hoeltzel.die.5.Mensis Februarij.Sa-
lutis Anno.Millesimoquingētesimodecimosexto.

Fig. 48. Nürnberg, H. Hölzel, type 14.   From no. 11015.   [Dc. ij.]

Genesis.Exo.Leui.Numerorum.Deuteronomi.
Post Josue. Judicū.Ruth.Regū.Paralip.Esdre.
Tobias. Judith.Hester.Job.Dauiticusꝫ.
Uerba dat Eccle.Cantat.Sapit.Ecclesiastic.
Esai.Hieremi.Baruch.Ezech.Danielꝫ
Ose. Jobel.Amos.Abdi.Jonas.Miche.Naum.Aba
Sophon.Aggeus.zacha.Malachias.Machabeus.
    Mattheus.Marcus.Lucas.postremo Johannes.
Roma.Corin.Galat.Eph.Philippen.Colosenses.
Thessal et Timotheus.Tytus.Philemon.Hebreus
Et Actus.Jacob.Petrus.Johan.et Judas.Apoc.
            Fluit

Fig. 49. Nürnberg, A. Koberger, type 20.   From no. 10958.   [Dc. iij.]

Utrū Realis sit differentia inter res naturales et artificiales
Utrū Differentia pbi inter artificialia et naturalia sit bene data
Utrum Figura sit realiter distincta a re figurata
Utrum Natura per pbm sit bene diffinita.
Utrū In substantijs materialibus forme substantiales principalius sint pdu-
ctiue suarū opationum quam qualitates
Utrum Mathematicus differat a pbisico
Utrum Scientie medie magis sint pbisice quam mathematice
Utrum Finis sit causa
Utrum Pater sit causa filij.
Utrum Diffinitio fortune sit bona
Utrum Fortuna et casus sint cause agentes
Utrum Natura pducens monstrum intendat monstrum
Utrū Necessitas in opationibus naturalibus pueniat expte materie vel finis

Fig. 50. Erfurt, W. Schenck, type 8.   From no. 11226.   [Dc. iv. 2.]

rio plis ..si q lo
qnt in vob?. Ite
r. Qui vos audit
me audit ꝫc. (Sz
dico Mudd non
audieri) Ly.i.ba
bēt excusationem
sue infidelitatis p
pter desicerū pub-
licatiōis.q.d.non
ad qd inducit au
ctoritatem pphete
dauid.q habeb in
psal.rviij (Et qdē
Gor.i.certe(si om
nē terrā)quātum
ad fras medias.
(exiuit sonꝰ).i.fa-
ma(eorū.ꝫ i fines
orbis terre).i.in
terras extremas.
(Cba eorū).i.pdi-
catio vel auditus
pdicatiōis eorū.
Ominꝰpos-
sedit me ab
initio viarū suaꝗ
anteꝗ quicꝗ ꝫc.
In festo cōceptio
nis beate virgis
marie pro episto-
la presens lectio ꝫm secu-
lectio principaliter expo-

lai epi ꝫ cōfes. Epist. Ecce sa.
magnꝰ ꝫc. qre infra i cōi scto
rū de pfes.   In festo pceptio
nis vgis marie. Prouer. viij.
Dominꝰ possedit
me ab initio viarū suarū atꝙ
qcꝙ faceret a pncipio. ab eter
no ordinata sum ꝫ ex antiqs.
anteꝙ terra fieret. Necdum
erāt abyssi. ꝫ ego iam cōcepta
erā. Nec dū fontes aquarum
eruperant. necdū mōtes gra-
ui mole constiterāt Ante oēs
colles ego parturiebar. Adhuc terrā nō fecerat ꝫ flumia
ꝫ cardines orbis tre Qn ppa
rabat celos aderā. Qn certa
lege et giro vallabat abyssos

eterno ordinata
sum ꝫc. Necdum
erāt abyssi. et ego
iam cōcepta eraꝫ
nec dum fontes
aquarum erupe-
rant).s. de locis
subterraneis (nec
dum mōtes gra-
ui mole pstiterāt)
.i. sup terrā pla-
nā eleuati(añ oēs
col. ego ptur).i.
pcedeba a secūdi
tate pina (adhuc
terrā nō fe. ꝫ flu.)
ꝫi. creaturā visibi
lē(ꝫ cardi. orbis
tre).i. ptes mūdi
pncipales. q sunt
oriēs ꝫ occidens.
austr et aquilo.
(Qñ ppa. et. ade
rā)indiuisa enī st
opa trinitatis et
ideo filius qui est
sapientia genita
semp operat cum
patre. vt ꝫ Job. v
Pater meus vsꝗ
mō operat et ego
lege et giro vallabat
tates vbi congregate

la presens lectio ꝫm seculares legit. que
lectio principaliter exponitur de eterna
sapientia que christus est filius Marie
virginis. Donor aut filij est bonor ma-

operor (qñ certa lege et giro vallabat
abyssos).i. cōcauitates vbi congregate
sunt aque. vt appareret arida habita-
tioni hominū animaliū terrestriū apta.

Fig. 51. Leipzig, M. Lotter, types 6 and 7 (also 2).   From no. 11330.   [Da. xi. 2 ; Dc. iv. 3.]

müſt dich laſſen vnd erſterben dein
ſelbs zů grundt. Er ſprach du ſoldt
mir nachuolgen. Der knecht geedt
ſeim herren nach. nit vor. Nitt nach
des knechtes willen. beſunder nach
des herren willen. Vnd het wir nit
mer leere. dann das wir ſehen wie
diener vnnd dienerin ſo wenig ires
willen mügen haben Wañ alzeit ir
fleiß ir macht geet zů ires herrñ wil
len vnnd dienſt in aller weiß. Das
waitzen korn můß ſterbñ. ſoll es an
ders ſein frucht bringenn. du můſt
deines aigen willens zů grunt ſter
ben. Der menſch ſolt auch alſo gar
ſein ſelbs vnnd ſeines aygenn wil‑
lens aufgeen. vñ als er ſich got võ
innen gibt. ſo ſolt er ſin als ob er nie
willen het genõmen. Ain junkfraw

Fig. 52. Augsburg, J. Otmar, type 17.   From no. 10670.   [Ea. i.]

erloßt in auch vß dem kercker/vnd füert
ſie beid in ein hauß/da warē chriſtē men‑
ſchen iñ. Da ſprach d engel zů in/die men
ſchen ſollent ir am chriſtē glauben ſterckē
vnd beleybent viertzig tag bey in/dz the‑
ten ſie/vnd lertē ſie mit groſſem fleyß den
waren chriſten glaubē. Vnd des morgēs
ward dem richter geſagt dz ſanct Peter
hin wår/vnd wår der kercker noch ver‑
ſperret/ des erſchrack d richter Serenus
ſeer/vñ thet im gar zorn/vñ hieß Archen
num fragē wo Marcellinus hinkomen
wår. Da ſprach Archennus. Ein engel
gottes bracht im ſein gewand/vnd hieß
in mit im vß dem kercker geen/der kerck‑
er ward aber nye vffgethon. Da dz der
richter erhort/da ſprach er. vff mein eyd
ich verſpert ir keinen nymer mer/vñ ließ
zůhand Archenno ſein haupt abſchlahē
da für ſein ſeel zů den ewigē freüdē. Dar
nach nam ein Heid Archennus tochter.
die hieß Candida/die ſant Peter võ dem

Fig. 53. Strassburg, J. Knoblouch, type 18.   From no. 10114.   [Eb. i. i.]

Sie yetzt wölln wol auß reiben
So mit nit hinfür sie treiben
Sollichen grossen übermüt
Kein man ward ir nie gnüg güt
Sie ist gewesen so mechtig vnd reich
Gschribn ein herrin mörs. vnd ertreich
Welches den Bapst verdrossen hat
Auch die keiserlich maiestat
Deßgleichen den künig von franckreich
Den hochmeister von Rhodis des gleich
Künig von Hyspan vnd Arragon
Der wil der braut gaben gar schon
Also das yedem würt sein teil
Was die junckfraw hat das ist feil
Wer die junckfraw sey wil ich sagen
Venesia welch vor tagen
Mit schalck verretrey ist kummen
Hat dem Bapst das sein genommen
Auch den herren von österreich.

Fig. 54. Strassburg, M. Hüpfüff, type 2ᴮ.   From no. 10025.   [Eb. i. 6.]

Que fiunt propria flu. men. ven. poñe marina.
Hec dabit arboribus. sed fructibus hoc sociamus.
Mas oleaster erit. dumus et rubus associabis.
Hoc siler est herba: siler hic donat tibi vina.
Hec sit auelana nux glans castanea ficus.
Triplex mobilibus gen̄us ut vult ars sociamus.
De genere nominum prime declinatio/
nis. Capitulum tredecimum.
a   manet in prima mulier. des mammona pasca
Neutris. et manna neutrum/mulierqz polenta.
Adria plancta maribus dabis atqz coniecta.
De genere noīm. secunde declinatiōis. Cap. xiiij.

Fig. 55. Strassburg-Freiburg, J. Schott, type 1.   From no. 11718.   [Eb. i. 9.]

wölcher nutz nit allein minder dañ der coſtẽ/ ſunder
auch vngewiß iſt. Aber du wilt dardurch den gemei
nen nutz fürdern. Nun kan ð gemein nutz durch kei/
nen weg ee vnnd übler zergeen dañ durch den krieg/
vñ ee du den krieg recht anfaheſt/ ſo haſt du deinem
vatterland mer geſchadt/ dañ du nutz ſein möchteſt
ſo du obligen würdeſt. Du erſchöpffſt deiner vnder/
thon reychtumb/du beleidigſt die heüſer mitt becla/
gung der erwürgten/vnd fülleſt alle ding voller mör
derſcher böſzwicht/dieben/ vnd junckfrawſchwecher
ein ſolche letze gibt ð krieg. Vnd wañ dir vor gebürt
her der gantzẽ Gallien zů nieſſen/ ſo ſchleüſt du dich
ſelbſt alſo vſz von vilen gegenten. Haſtu die deinen
recht lieb/ſo ſoltu vil mer zůuor ein ſolch meinūg be/
dencken/warūb vnderwürff ich mein blůend jugent
allẽ übel. Warūb wolt ich ſouil erbarer frawen irer

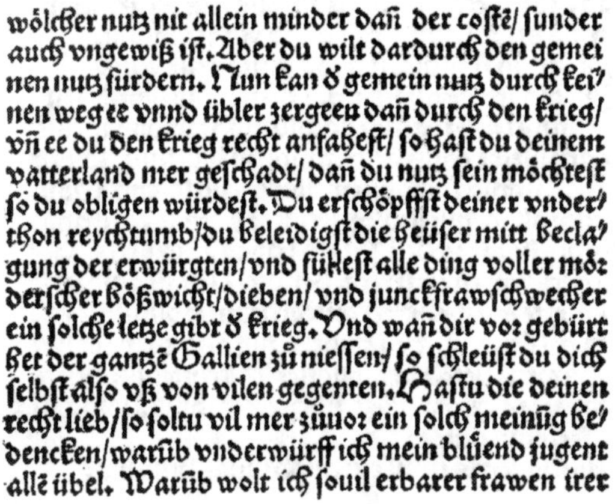

Fig. 56. Strassburg, M. Schürer, type 15. From no. 10259. [Eb. i. 10.]

¶ Darnoch im jar tauſent vierhundert vnd zwey vnd vier/
zig brachten die Venediger ſouil zů wegen/das gedochter
hertzog Philips Maria/ in krafft eins vertrags bezwung
en wardt/ſein baſtardt tochter genant Blanca/ dem Fran/
ciſco Sfortie/ eim haubtman einer kleinen geſelſchafft/ zůr
Ee/auch Cremona vnd daſſelbig land darumb zů heyradt
ſteür zegeben. Das ſelbig mitſampt der frawen die Vene/
diger an ſich namen. Aber Franciſcus Sfortia erobert das
aller wider/do er ſich hertzog zů Meylandt machte mit ge
walt freuelich/vnd zů abbruch des huſzes Orlyentz/dem ſo
lichs von recht zůgehört. Dañ die ſelb zeyt kundten die Frã
tzoſzen darzů nit thůn/ von des kryegs wegen ſo jnen do ze/
mal von den Engellendiſchen begegnet. Alſo hat ein yeder
abzenemen/wie vñ welcher maſſzen ſich die Venediger be/
fliſſen haben die gantze welt zů betrůben/ vnnd jren eygenen
nutz mit andererleüt ſchaden geſůcht.

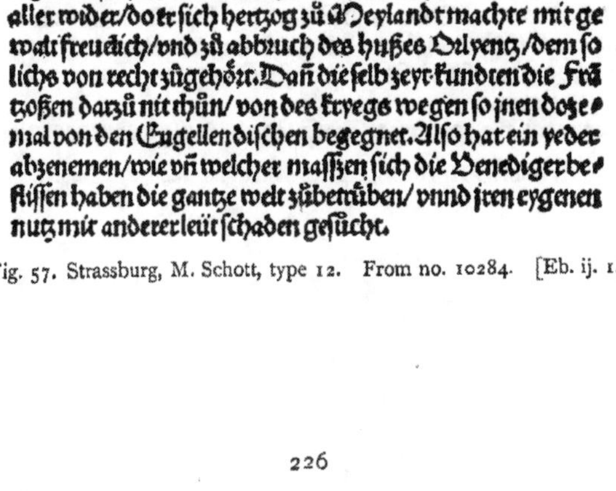

Fig. 57. Strassburg, M. Schott, type 12. From no. 10284. [Eb. ij. 1.]

Itaq̈ Propertio crede: q̈ amoris tela expt⁹inquit.
Durius in terris nihil est: quod viuat/amante:
Nec modo si sapias: quod minus esse velis.
Intellexisti ñe q̈d sit amor: An cupis plurib⁹ tibi
Aluz definiri: Est amor poculũ illud: in quo mellis
perparũ inest: fellis atq̈ absinthij plurimũ. Probe
Naso: Impia sub dulci melle venena latent. Quid
est amor aliud/nisi idoloꝝ seruit⁹: Deũ Cecili⁹amo
rem appellauit: ⁊ deũ Plato: quẽ ⁊ Dicearch⁹Pe
ripathetic⁹ob eã cãm reprehendit. Nũ igit amor erit
de⁹: Certe erit ijs de⁹: q̈ amori dediti/obliuiscũk sui.
Nam cui q̈s seruit/deũ habz. Quisq̈s ⁊ eñ vitia sua
adorãs/atq̈ pctã: vt ait noster Hieronym⁹: deũ ce
pit habere: a quo vict⁹est. O q̈ execrabilis idoloꝝ:q̈
dura seruitus amor:
Durius in terris nihil est: quod viuat/amante:

Fig. 58. Leipzig, M. Lotter, type 11.   From no. 11342.   [Eb. ij. 2.]

¶Item nach im Reyt der groß meyster von Franckreich/herr
Karel von Amboisa auff einen grossen hengst köstlicher dann
keyner vnder dem hauffen/außgenomen den konig/der auch in
seiner hant fueret ein ploß schwert als ein Siger vnd stathalter
des konigs.

¶Item darnach Reyt gantz allain auff einem Maul der hoch
wirdig in got herr vnd vater der Cardinal võ Amboisa Legat
in Franckreich. Nach ime zohen Vier Cardinel/mit namen der
Cardinal von sant Seuerin/Der Cardinal final/Der Cardinal
von puie/Der Cardinal von Albi/Vñ nach den Reyt ein grosse anzal von Ertzbischofen/Bischofen/Abt/prothonotarij vñ
ander Prelaten.
Itẽ darnach Reyten die potschafft so zu dẽ konig gesant waren

Fig. 59. Nürnberg, H. Hölzel, type 4.   From no. 10985.   [Ec. i. 1.]

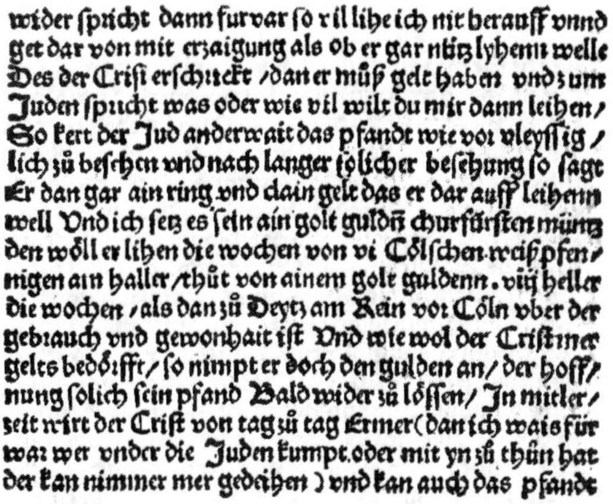

wider spricht dann furvar so vil libe ich nit berauff vnnd
get dar von mit erzaigung als ob er gar ntitz lyhenn welle
Des der Crist erschtickt /dan er müß gelt haben vnd zum
Juden spricht was oder wie vil wilt du mir dann leihen/
So kert der Jud anderwait das pfandt wie vor vleyssig/
lich zü besehen vnd nach langer solicher besehung so sage
Er dan gar ain ring vnd clain gelt das er dar auff leihenn
well Vnd ich setz es sein ain golt guldin churfürsten müntz
den wöll er lihen die wochen von vi Cölschen weiß pfen-
nigen ain haller /thüt von ainem golt guldenn . viij heller
die wochen /als dan zü Deytz am Rain vor Cöln vber der
gebrauch vnd gewonhait ist Vnd wie wol der Cristner
gelts bedörfft/ so nimpt er doch den gulden an/ der hoff-
nung solich sein pfand Bald wider zü lössen/ In mitler-
zeit wirt der Crist von tag zü tag Ermer(dan ich wais für
war wer vnder die Juden kumpt.oder mit yn zü thün hat
der kan nimmer mer gedeihen) vnd kan auch das pfande

Fig. 60. Augsburg, E. Öglin, type 3.   From no. 10706.   [Ec. i. 4.]

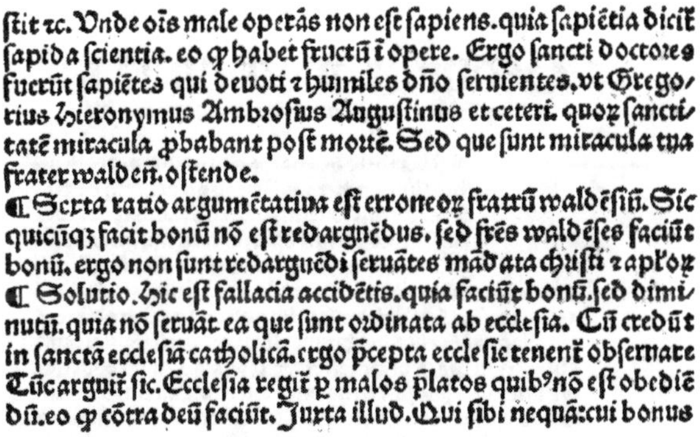

stit rc. Vnde ois male operas non est sapiens.quia sapiētia diciť
sapida scientia. eo cp habet fructū i opere. Ergo sancti doctores
fuerūt sapiētes qui deuoti z humiles dño seruientes.vt Gregorius Hieronymus Ambrosius Augustinus et ceteri. quoz sancti-
tatē miracula pbabant post mortē. Sed que sunt miracula tua
frater waldeñ. ostende.
℩ Sexta ratio argumētatiua est erroneoz fratrū waldēsiu. Sic
quicūqz facit bonū nō est redargnēdus. sed frēs waldēses faciūt
bonū. ergo non sunt redargucdi seruātes mādata chisti z aploz
℩ Solutio. Hic est fallacia accidētis. quia faciūt bonū.sed dimi-
nutū. quia nō seruāt ea que sunt ordinata ab ecclesia. Cū credūt
in sanctā ecclesiā catholicā. ergo pcepta ecclesie tenenť obseruate
Tūc arguiť sic. Ecclesia regiť p malos platos quib⁹ nō est obediē
dū.eo cp cōtra deū faciūt. Juxta illud.Qui sibi nequā:cui bonus

Fig. 61. Nürnberg, J. Weissenburger, type 3.   From no. 11043.   [Ec. i. 5.]

228

nus de tue pstantie laudib' memoratissuz rogo. Concurret
(vt sit)ad spectaculu pzimi pfertim operis : no solu vulgus
ineptu Sed et alertes homines. Postq vndiq pspectauerit
No dubite quin aliqui viri sint pzobitate venerabiles : me tt
integre atq scientie opus nostrum non redarguentes quos
tibi commendo . Nec de futuros homines qui suis viperinis
linguis hoc danare veluti Scorpionis veneno intoricareq
studebut Et nisi innouationem magni perpetui ozbis sum-
mus Jupiter caducis hominibus exemisset innouare nitere
tur . Hoc munusculum (non ex me inuentum Sed ex alijs
congestum et compoztatum)tibi et alijs huius cultozibus
non hijs offero . Quo vbi rigozosi certaminis gradusmagi-
sterij glozioius triumphatoz euaderes : defatigatum animuz
in hoc vt amenitatis campo suauissimis flozibus et odozi-
bus compto recrees . Tuisq studiosis germanis legendum
et relegendum mandes . Nemo ambigit vna cum ceteris
studosissimis maximum fructum inde nacturos . Vale

Fig. 62. Leipzig, M. Landsberg, type 1.   From no. 11277.   [Ec. i. 7.]

Sequitur anathomia me
bzoz contentoz. Et primo de anathomia zyrbi.

Estat videre de anathomia ztentoz/hec mem
bza sunt numero.x.Primu qd occurrit est zyr-
bus.Scdm intestina.Tertiu stomach'.Quar
tu splen.Quintu epar.Sextu misinteriu.Se
ptimu renes.Octauum vesica.Nonu testiculi
z vasa spermatica/z matrix muliez.Decimu est virga cu
collo zvesica.De zyrbo aut primo qd opter videre est loc'
eius.locus em eius in homine est/qz cooperit stomachum
abinteriozi pte/z oia intestina.z lz in alijs non cooperiat
oia intestina/hoc fuit qz bo inter cetera aialia eiusde quan
titatis est debiliozis digestiue frtutis/z etia qz intestina no
ciuis exteriozibus sunt magis disposita/ppter cutem ei'
subtiliozis esse z minus pilosam.Et hoc etia potest patere
fm q sit eius iuuamentu.Juuametu em ei' est principaliter pfortare szutez digestiua stomachi/z interioz/reuer

Fig. 63. Strassburg, M. Flach, types 1 and 11.   From no. 10150.   [Cb. i; Ed. i.]

gesaztßartest. Jtē dzymaill off veirmaill
im dagßß saltu vpsetzen suyreclichen ent/
gßeen ßouerdie. ¶ Die dzytte ocuōg sal die
syn/du salt dencken van eynichem goiden
wāne du die zijt ßaist leedich/ Wār du salt
vp eynē igligen dacß ßain eyne sunderlige
materie van wilcßer du dencken salt duck
maill/vn zo wilcßer du dynē zo ganck ßa/
uest. ¶ Wāt sondagßß sal die materie syn
vam ßemelreich Maendācß vam iunxstē
oirdell. Oyinstachas vā den waildade gotz
Goedestags vam doide. Donrestags van
den pynen der ßellen. Vrydags vam lyden
vnsers ßeren. Saterstags vā vnser lieuer
frauwen vū vā dynen eygßenen sunden.
Auer ßie mit saltu alldage dat lyden vn/
sers ßeren mit der materien des dags vnd
vā den waildaden gotz ßauen in dyme ge/
decßtnisse. vnd zo yederen desen zyden/zo
metten/primen/tertien/sexten/nonen rc.
saltu vam lyden assodaniger vren/myt en
wielzijt van der materien des dags ouerr
dencken Jst dartu alsus doßest dyne dyn/

Fig. 64. Köln, H. Bumgart, type 5. From
no. 10482. [Ed. ij.]

SVnder dein hilff vnd be/
schirmungñ fleüch ich
O du allerhayligste Junnck/
fraw Mariā ein mütter aller/
gnaden / aller Barmhertzig/
kait ein trösterin allerbetrüb/
ten hertzen / verschmech nitt
mein gebet in meiner grossen
not/sonder erledige mich von
aller ferlichayt vnnd hilff mir
auß aller meiner widerwertig/
kait. ¶ Der versickel.
¶ In aller meiner trüebsall
vnnd angst/ kum mir zühilff

Fig. 65. Augsburg, J. Schönsperger the Elder,
type 14. From no. 10938. [Ee 3.]

Sem. nun wie halt wir vns Par. wie du wild wie
wol ich noch erschrockē bin vō dem/so ich vō dir geseßē
hab vñ noch teglich sich Sem. schweig ich will dich
hin für noch baß erschreckē Par. O warer gott kain
schedlichere pestilentz ist in ð welt dañ der haußfeind.
Calix. nun gang hin mein mûter gib trostũg deinem
hauß vnd wider ker bald darnach/vnd bring daß trost
dem meinen Cele. Gotbeleib mit dir Calix. vnd er
behût dich vnd sey dein belaiter.

Argument der Andern Würckung
Nach abschid Celestine von Calixsto haim zû gon/ber

Fig. 66. Augsburg, S. Grim and M. Wirsung, type 14. From no. 10925A. [Ee 4.]

REGISTER OF PRINTERS.

[Where the second date is left blank, the printer continued his work after 1520. For publishers see p. 177.]

TABLE OF AUTHORS

Altenstaig, Ioh.: opusculum de amicitia
Hag. 1519 11680
—— uocabularius Pforzh. 1511 11774
—— —— Str. 1515 10323
—— —— Hag. 1517 11672
Alter. Die zehn Alter dieser Welt
Augsb. 1518 10741
—— —— Memm. 1519 11265
Altväterleben Str. 1513 10034
—— Str. 1516 9939
Alveld, Aug.: diuino iure institutum
esse ut caput ecclesiae sit papa
n.p.d. 10608
—— malagma optimum n.p.d. 11313
—— sermo de confessione Sacramentali
n.p.d. 11315
—— Sermon wider Luther
Leipz. 1520 11498
—— super sede apostolica
Leipz. 1520 11567
—— Büchlein vom päpstlichen Stuhl
n.p.d. 11560
—— tractatus de communione sub
utraque specie n.p.d. 11502
An den grossmächtigsten...Adel deut-
scher Nation Str. 1520 9959
Andreae, Ioh.: lectura super arboribus
Nürnb. 1506 10983
—— summa super secundo decretalium
n.p.d. 10547d
—— summa super quarto decretalium
Köln n.d. 10547f
Andreas de Escobar: modus confitendi
Nürnb. 1506 11044
—— —— Augsb. 1507 10627
—— —— Nürnb. 1508 10993
—— —— Augsb. 1513 10631
—— —— Augsb. 1519 10634
Andrelinus, Faustus: de moralibus in-
tellectualibusque uirtutibus
Str. 1509 10168
—— ecloga moralissima Str. 1513 10217
—— ex amorum libris uersus selecti
n.p.d. 10449
Andronicus, Tranquillus Parthenius:
oratio de laudibus eloquentiae
Leipz. 1518 11368
Angeltugenden, die vier Str. 1515 10038
Angelus, anachorita. See Fundius.
Angelus de Clauasio: summa angelica
Hag. 1509 11640
—— —— Str. 1513 10302
Angliara, Juan de: die Schiffung mit
dem Lande der goldnen Insel
n.p.d. 10858
Anguilbertus, Tho.: mensa philoso-
phica Köln 1508 10550
Anna, S. Legenda S. Annae Str. 1501 10044
—— —— Leipz. 1505 11328
—— —— germanice Str. 1501 10045

Anna, S. Legenda, germ. Str. 1509 10024
—— Vinetum b. Annae Köln 1507 10511
Annius, Ioh.: glossa super apocalypsim
Köln 1507 10512
Anschlag der Türken wider die Christen-
heit Str. 1502 10046
Antichristus. Von des Endchrists Le-
ben Erfurt 1516 11245
—— —— Str. n.d. 10013
Antwort der Herren Herzog Ruprechts
Verwandten n.p.d. 11274b
Anzeigung der Blutschweissung des
Dorns von der Krone Christi n.p.d. 10872
Anzeigung wie sich die Päpste gegen die
Kaiser gehalten haben. See Hutten,
Ulr. von.
Apocalypsis cum figuris Hier. Greff
Str. 1502 9964
—— idem germanice n.p.d.? 9963
—— cum figuris Dureri Nürnb. 1511 11002
Apollonia, historia de Sancta
Landsh. 1520 11818
Apologia sacrae scripturae
Nürnb. 1511 11004
Apuleius, Lucius: floridorum libri
Str. 1516 10242
Aquila, Ioh.: de omni ludorum genere
Opp. 1516 11936
—— de potestate et utilitate monetarum
Opp. 1516 11932
Aquinas, Thomas. See Thomas.
Arator: actus apostolorum n.p.d. 11345
Arcimboldus, Ioh. Ang.: literae
indulgentiarum n.p.d. (1517) 10454
—— —— n.p.d. (1517) 10455
Aristoteles, Salomon, Samson n.p.d. 10941
Aristoteles: de anima Augsb. 1520 10914
—— de caelo, de generatione, etc.
Augsb. 1519 10900
—— ethica Leipz. 1501 11267
—— organon Augsb. 1516-7 10836
—— physica Augsb. 1518 10873
—— problemata Köln 1506 10409
—— —— n.p.d. 10569
—— See also Auctoritates.
Armandus de Bellouisu: declaratio
difficilium terminorum Köln 1502 10363
Arnaldus de Villanoua: regimen
sanitatis salernitanum. See Regimen.
—— von Bereitung der Weine
Str. 1512 10029
—— —— Augsb. n.d. 10748
Arnoldus de Tungris: refutatio articulorum Reuchlini Köln 1512 10440
Ars moriendi Nürnb. 1512 11064
—— Landsh. 1514 11788
—— Nürnb. n.d. 11057
—— germ. Leipz. 1507 11332
—— germ. Landsh. 1520 11815
Ars notariatus n.p.d. 10547c

Ars notariatus, germ.   Nürnb. 1502   11036
Articuli siue propositiones de iudaico
  fauore. See Arnoldus de Tungris.
Articuli tractati inter legatum et conuen-
  tum imperii, 1501   n.p.d.   10469
Aruernus, Gulielmus. See Gulielmus.
Ascensius, Iodocus Badius. See Badius.
Athanasius : de uariis quaestionibus
                        Hag. 1519   11698
—— in librum psalmorum Tüb. n.d.   11742
Aubanus, Ioh. Boemus. See Boemus
  Aubanus.
Aubusson, Pierre d'. See Wunder-
  barliche wahre Geschichte...
Auctoritates Aristotelis et aliorum
                        Leipz. 1510   11455
Auctoritates Aristotelis   n.p. 1503   10376
Auentinus, Ioh. See Thurnmaier.
Auersberg, Hans von : Entschuldigung
                             n.p.d.   11993
Aufruhren in Württemberg, Unterricht-
  ung der   Tüb. n.d.   11740
Aufsatzung und Ordnung auf den
  Reichstag zu Köln, 1512   n.p.d.   10712
Augsburg. Brief des Rats an den
  Kaiser, 1508   n.p.d.   10649
Augsburger Reichstag, 1510
                        Augsb. n.d.   10709
Augustinus, Aurelius: de doctrina chri-
  stiana   Leipz. 1515   11359
—— de essentia diuinitatis
                        Leipz. 1509   11421
—— manuale de aspiratione hominis
  ad deum   Köln 1507   10513
Augustinus de Leonissa : sermones
                        Köln 1503   10542
Auianus, Flauius: apologus adulescen-
  tulis utilissimus   Leipz. 1509   11452
Auisamentum de concubinariis non ab-
  soluendis. See Wimpheling.
Auitus, Alcimus : libri sex
                        [Str.] 1507   9903
Aura scholarium pharetra
                        Augsb. 1502   10616
Aurelius Victor, Sextus : de uiris illu-
  stribus   Köln 1505   10390
Aurifaber, Aegidius: speculum exem-
  plorum   Hag. 1507   11632
Aursperg. See Auersberg.
Auslegung der Sippschaft Opp. 1515   11929
Ausonius : opera   Leipz. 1515   11505A
Ausschreiben der Stadt Worms wider
  Franz von Sickingen   n.p.d.   9857
Ausschreibung von Herzogin Sabina
                             n.p.d.   11995
Ausschreien und Eröffnung der Bündnis
  zwischen Julio ij. und dem Kaiser
                             n.p.d.   11008
Auszug etlicher Practica und Prophe-
  zeien   n.p.d.   11187

Auszug etlicher Sendbriefe von wegen
  einer neugefundenen Insel
                        Nürnb. 1520   11135
Auszug gen Rom Kaiser Friedrichs...
                        Augsb. 1503   10660
Badius, Iodocus : de epistulis compo-
  nendis   n.p.d.   10976
—— nauiculae stultiferae Str. 1502   9961
Baeda : historia ecclesiastica (1506).
  See Eusebius.
Baiern. Freiheiten (1514)
                  München [Landsh.] 1514   11786
—— Gerichtsordnung (1520) n.p.d.   11591a
—— Landbote, Buch der gemeinen
  (1516)   n.p.d.   11582
—— —— (1520)   n.p.d.   11594
—— Landesfreiheit, Erklärung der
  (1508)   n.p.d.   10672
—— —— (1516)   Landsh. 1516   11802
—— ——   München n.d.   11583
—— —— (1520)   n.p.d.   11595
—— Landrechte, Reformation der
                             n.p.d.   11585
Bambergische Halsgerichtsordnung
                  Mainz 1508 (Apr.)   9848
——   Mainz 1508 (Oct.)   9851
——   Mainz 1510   9853
Bandellus, Vinc.: constitutiones fra-
  trum praedicatorum   n.p.d.   12001
Baptista de Salis. See Trovamala.
Baptista Mantuanus: bucolica seu adu-
  lescentia   Str. 1503   9967
——   Köln 1510   10433
——   Tüb. 1511   11723
——   Hag. 1517   11688
—— carmen in laudem Ioannis baptistae   Leipz. 1505   11411
—— contra poetas impudice loquentes
                        Str. 1501   10135b
—— de calamitatibus mundi
                        Str. 1501   10135c
——   Str. 1518   10115d
—— de fortuna Marchionis Mantuae
                        Str. 1510   10178
—— de patientia   [Str.] n.d.   10183
—— eclogae   Erfurt 1501   11218
——   Leipz. 1510   11454
—— elegiae duae   Leipz. 1505   11443
—— fasti   Str. 1518   10253
—— Georgius   Str. 1510   10182
—— parthenice prima et secunda
                        Str. 1501   10135a
—— parthenice prima Leipz. 1508   11282
——   Leipz. 1510   11422
——   Str. 1518   10115a
—— parthenice secunda Köln 1510   10434
——   Leipz. 1510   11288
——   Str. 1518   10115b
——   Leipz. 1519   11534
—— parthenice tertia Leipz. 1516   11362

237

Claudianus, Cl.: de raptu Prosérpinae
Nürnb. 1518 11128
Clemangiis, Nic. de: de corrupto eccle-
siae statu n.p.d. 11977
Clichtoueus, Iod.: dogma moralium
philosophorum Str. 1512 10198
Clusa, Iacobus de. See Iacobus.
Coccinius, Mich.: de imperii transla-
tione n.p.d. 9900
——— de rebus in Italia gestis n.p.d. 9923
Cochlaeus, Ioh.: grammatica
Str. 1515 10324
——— musica Köln 1507 10488
——— tetrachordum musicae
Nürnb. 1512 11089
Collationes Salomonis et Marcolphi
Landsh. 1514 11781
——— n.p.d. 10438
Collenutius, Pand.: Agenoria, Alethia
Leipz. 1506 11416
——— Alethia n.p.d. 11293
——— apologi quattuor Str. 1511 10195
Columella: de cultu hortorum liber xi.
Erfurt 1510 11237
Columna, Aegidius. See Aegidius Ro-
manus.
Comestor, Petrus. See Petrus.
Commentarium in tractatus logicae
Petri Hispani i. et iv. Hag. 1503 11620
Compendiosa capitis physici declaratio
Leipz. 1510 11456
Compendium theologicae ueritatis
Köln 1503 10370
——— Köln 1506 10408
Complexion der Menschen, Büchlein
von Augsb. 1512 10735
——— Str. 1516 10105
Computus nouus astrologiae fundamen-
tum continens Leipz. 1504 11401
——— Leipz. 1506 11415
——— n.p.d. 10398
Computus nouus ecclesiasticus
n.p. 1515 11507
Concordia curatorum et fratrum men-
dicantium n.p.d. 9966
Condemnatio librorum Lutheri per
magistros Louanienses
Wittenb. 1520 11900
Confraternitas S. Ioannis Baptistae
Viterbii n.p.d. 12004
Conradus Nastadiensis: dialogus de
funere Calliopes n.p. 1520 11980
Conradus Noricus: Aderlasstafel lip-
sensis n.p.d. 11049
——— Practica lipsensis auf 1515
n.p.d. 11183
Constantinus Magnus Ioh. Reuchlino
interprete Tüb. 1513 11735
Constitutiones fratrum praedicatorum
n.p.d. 12001

Contemptu mundi, Liber de
Str. 1510 10073
Continentia sacerdotum Nürnb. 1510 11053
——— Landsh. n.d. 11798
Conuersio S. Albani n.p.d. 10503
Conuocatio generalis concilii
Nürnb. 1512 11065g
Copei der Absagung wider H. Albrecht
und H. Wolfgang n.p.d. 10975
Copia articulorum conclusorum inter
legatum et conuentum imperii, 1501
n.p.d. 10469
Cordiale seu quattuor nouissima
Köln 1506 10403
Cordus, Euricius: contra Thilonium
Philymnum defensio Erfurt 1515 11235
——— epigrammata Erfurt 1517 11246
Cornelius Nepos: uitae imperatorum
Str. 1511 10186
——— uita Catonis Str. 1505 9973
Coruinus, Laur.: compendiosa carmi-
num structura Köln 1508 10518
——— dialogus de mentis saluberrima
persuasione Leipz. 1516 11511
——— hortulus elegantiarum
Breslau 1503 11210A
——— ——— Leipz. 1503 11393
——— ——— Leipz. 1512 11347
——— ——— Augsb. 1516 10757
——— ——— Str. 1516 10097
——— latinum idioma Nürnb. 1508 11050
——— ——— Leipz. 1511 11426
——— ——— Nürnb. 1518 11148
Coruinus, Maximus: oratio in concilio
lateranensi [Nürnb. 1512] 11065d
——— oratio sanctissimi foederis
Leipz. n.d. 11292
Cotta Lambergius, Ioh. Fr.: Eccius de-
dolatus n.p.d. 11253
——— ——— n.p.d. 11972
Cracouiensis, Petrus. See Petrus.
Crates: epistulae Nürnb. 1501 11023
Crescentiis, Petrus de: opus ruralium
commodorum, germanice Str. 1518 10286
Crocus, Ric.: academiae lipsensis en-
comium n.p.d. 11572
——— tabulae graecas literas discere
cupientibus utiles Leipz. 1516 11512
Cube, Joh. von. See Hortus sanitatis.
Cupiner, Christoph.: elegantissimae
annotationes Leipz. 1507 11331
Cura clericalis Köln 1509 10524
Cura pastoralis Landsh. n.d. 11796
——— Nürnb. 1513 11071
Cursius, Petrus: panegyris de foedere
(Nürnb. 1512) 11065f
Cursus b. Mariae, etc. n.p.d. 10696
Cursus philosophicus compendiosis-
simus. See Wonsiedel, E.
Curtius, Quintus. See Quintus Curtius.

Cybeleius, Val.: de laudibus uini et
   aquae   Hag. 1517 11686
Cymon, Historie von   Str. 1516 9940
Cyprianus : de contemnenda morte
     Köln 1518 10602
Cyrillus: speculum sapientiae
     Köln n.d. 10546
Danielis somniorum interpretatio
     Leipz. 1507 11334
Datus, Aug.: elegantiolae Str. 1504 10008
—— epistula amoris leuitatem impro-
bans   n.p.d. 11342
De compassione uirginis Mariae
     Magdeb. 1513 11259
De continentia sacerdotum
     Nürnb. 1510 11053
——   Landsh. n.d. 11798
Defideconcubinarum. See Olearius, P.
De fraternitate septem gaudiorum b.
Mariae   n.p.d. 10494
De generibus ebriosorum n.p. 1516 9860
——   n.p.d. 11741
De gloriosissimae imperatricis nostrae
conceptione sermo Nürnb. 1503 11038
De his qui ad ecclesias confugiunt
     Landsh. 1517 11809
De laude et utilitate studii Augsb. 1501 10614
De literis graecis et diphthongis
     Tüb. 1512 11729
De ora antarctica   Str. 1505 10011
De quattuor heresiarchis ordinis prae-
dicatorum   n.p.d. 10026
——   n.p.d. 11076
—— germ.   n.p.d. 11075
—— germ.   n.p.d. 11986
—— niedersächsisch   n.p.d. 11213
De uisitatione B. V. Mariae carmen
     n.p.d. 11451
De unitate ecclesiae seruanda
     Mainz 1520 9868
Decisio quaestionis de audientia missae
     n.p.d. 11066
Declaratio compendiosa capitis physici
     Leipz. 1510 11456
Defensio bullae sixtinae per Alexandrum
vi. reuisae   [Opp.] 1503? 11919
Denyse, Nic.: sermones de sanctis, etc.
     Hag. 1510 11645
Der drei Glauben die frommsten und
bösesten Männer und Frauen
     Augsb. 1518 10931
——   München n.d. 11588
Des Loblichen haus vnd furstenthumbs
Obern vnd nidern Bayren freiheyten
     München [Landsh.] 1514 11786
Despauterius, Ioh.: ars uersificatoria
     Str. 1512 10205
—— syntaxis   Str. 1515 10226
Desponsatio et coronatio Friderici iij.
     Augsb. 1503 10620

Deutsche Theologia Wittenb. 1518 11839
——   n. p. 1518 10766
——   Leipz. 1519 11297
——   Str. 1519 10124
——   Augsb. 1520 10793
——   Str. 1520 10130
——   Wittenb. 1520 11869
Deutsche Theologia. See also Büch-
lein von rechter Unterscheide.
Deutsches Requiem über die verbrannte
Bulle   n.p.d. 10318
——   n.p.d. 10922
——   n.p.d. 10944
Dialogus ex obscurorum uirorum salibus
cribratus   n.p.d. 11988
Dialogus libertatis ecclesiasticae defen-
sorius   Opp. 1516 11934
Dialogus philosophiae Nürnb. 1509 11051
Dialogus quomodo Iulius ij. caeli fores
pulsauit, etc.   n.p.d. 10331
——   n.p.d. 11999
Dialogus Salomonis et Marcolphi
     Landsh. 1514 11781
——   n.p.d. 10438
Dietrich, Bruder: Practica oder Prophe-
zeiung   n.p.d. 11593
Dietrich von Münster: Spiegel der
christen Menschen Köln 1501 10559
Dinkelsbühl, Nicolaus de. See Nicolaus.
Dionysius Areopagita: opera
     Str. 1502-3 9997
Dionysius Nestor: uocabula Str. 1507 9982
Dionysius Periegetes: de situ orbis
     Ingolstadt 1519 11611
Directorium concubinariorum
     Köln 1508 10420
——   Köln 1509 10431
Directorium Constantiense
     Augsb. 1501 10640
Directorium ecclesiasticum pro anno
1511-12   n.p.d. 11195
Directorium missae Moguntinum
     Mainz 1508 9850
Discipulus. See Herolt, Ioh.
Disputatio Eckii et Carolostadii
     n.p. 1519 11251
Disputatio Eckii et Lutheri Lipsiae
futura   n.p. (1519) 11847
Disputatio inter Lutherum et Eckium
Lipsiae habita   n.p.d. 10953
Diss büchlin saget wie die zwen durch-
lüchtigsten herren ... Str. 1509 9914
Distichoneomenionabaci. See Brandes,
Ioh.
Diurnale Frisingense Augsb. 1507 10647
Doctor Keiserspergs Paternoster. See
Geiler.
Dogma moralium philosophorum
     Str. 1512 10198
Dominus quae pars Köln 1502 10471

Gengenbach, Pamph.: die zehn Alter
dieser Welt   Memm. 1519   11265
Georgius de Gemmingen: annotatiun-
cula pro confessoribus   Str. 1509   10173
Georgius de Hungaria: de ritu et
moribus turcorum   n.p.d.   10552
Georgius Trapezuntius: dialectica
                        Str. 1509   10170
——— ———   Str. 1513   10218
Geraldinus, Ant.: bucolica
                        Pforzh. 1507   11759
Gericht des sterbenden Menschen
                        München 1510   11576
Gerichtsordnung in Baiern (1520)
                        n.p.d.   11591a
Germaniae Wimphelingianae defensio
                        n.p.d.   9999
Gern, Hans: Lied von der böhmischen
Schlacht   n.p.d.   10610
Gersdorf, Hans von: Wundarznei
                        Str. 1517   10285
Gerson, Ioh.: opera   Str. 1514   10085
—— operum pars iv.   Str. 1502   10139
—— de cognitione peccatorum
                        Memm. 1502   11262
—— —— (tractatuli) Memm. 1502   11263
—— ——   Augsb. 1503   10619
—— ——   Augsb. 1519   10635
—— modus uiuendi christifidelium
                        Köln 1510   10565
—— sermo de passione domini
                        Str. 1509   10167A
——— ———   Str. 1510   10176
Gertrudis diuae uirginis officium
                        Köln 1513   10480
Gesangbuch   Augsb. 1512   10710
Geschichte des grossen Alexanders
                        Str. 1514   10037
Geschichte von einem Landherrn in
Frankreich   München 1505   11596
Geschichten von geistlichen Weibsper-
sonen   n.p.d.   10968
Gesetze. Fünf andächtiger Gesetze
neue Gedichte   Augsb. n.d.   10698
Gesetze, Etliche, der Stadt Leipzig
                        Leipz. n.d.   11414
Gespräch vom Gewalt und Haupt der
Kirchen   n.p.d.   11992
Gessler, Henr.: Formulare und deut-
sche Rhetorica   Augsb. 1507   10702
——— ———   Str. 1519   10122
Gesta proxime per portugalenses in
India   Köln 1507   10487
——— ———   Nürnb. 1507   11048
Gesta romanorum   Hag. 1517   11670
Gezeitigung aus dem Heere vor
Terebona   n.p.d.   10713
———   n.p.d.   11012
Gilgengart einer christlichen Seele
                        n.p.d.   10938

Giraldus, Lilius Greg.: syntagma de
musis   Str. 1511   10188
——— ———   Str. 1512   10199
Glaser, Hans: Spruch von dem Krieg
                        n.p.d.   10009
Glauben. Der drei Glauben die frömm-
sten und bösesten Männer und Frauen
                        Augsb. 1518   10931
——— ———   München n.d.   11588
Globus mundi   Str. 1509   9917
Glogouiensis, Ioannes. See Ioannes.
Gnaden, Buch geistlicher Leipz. 1503   11323
Gnidius, Matth.: defensio Christia-
norum de cruce   n.p.d.   10299
Goldene Bulle, die   n.p.d.   11199
Gorinchem, Henricus de. See Henricus.
Gorran, Nicolaus de: postilla super
epistulas Pauli   Hag. 1502   11616
Gottfried von Bouillon, Geschichte von
                        Augsb. 1502   10656
———   Leipz. 1518   11476
Gouda, Gulielmus de. See Gulielmus.
Grammaticarum institutionum enchiri-
dion   Köln 1516   10538
Grapaldus, Franc. Mar.: de partibus
aedium   Str. 1508   9986
Gratius, Ortuinus: lamentationes ob-
scurorum uirorum Köln 1518 Mar.   10460
                        Köln 1518 Aug.   10462
Gregoriana super nouum testamentum
                        Str. 1516   10099
Gregorius Nazianzenus: de amandis
pauperibus   Augsb. 1519   10895
—— libelli   Str. 1508   10059
—— sermones   Augsb. 1519   10901
Gregorius Thaumaturgus: periphrasis in
Ecclesiasten   Augsb. 1520   10919
Gregorius Tifernas: opuscula
                        Str. 1509   10171
Gresemundus, Theod.: carmen de his-
toria uiolatae crucis   Str. 1514   10305
—— uersiculi. See Germaniae Wimphelingianae defensio
Grieninger, Henr.: de generibus nominum   Augsb. 1517   10761
Grosse Legende S. Hedwigis
                        Breslau 1504   11211
Grosseteste, Rob.: de physicis lineis
angulis figuris   Nürnb. 1503   11039
Gruitroedius, Ioh.: Lauacrum conscientiae   Köln 1501   10499
                        Köln 1506   10410
Grünbeck, Joseph: ad episcopos exhortatio   n.p.d.   11789
—— libellus de mentulagra n.p.d.   11256
—— speculum naturalis caelestis propheticae uisionis   Nürnb. 1508   11082
—— —— germanice Nürnb. 1508   11083
Gualtherus, Phil.: Alexandreis
                        Str. 1513   10303

Luther, Martin : confitendi ratio, germ.
(heilsames Büchlein von der Beichte)
Wittenb. 1520   11864
—— —— germ.   n.p.d.   10805
—— contra malignum Ioh. Eckii iudicium   n.p.d.   11389
—— de captiuitate babylonica ecclesiae
n.p.d.   10297
—— ——   n.p.d.   10954
—— ——   n.p.d.   11916
—— —— germ. (von der babyloni-
schen Gefängnis der Kirchen) n.p.d.   10298
—— —— germ.   n.p.d.   10806
—— decem praecepta wittenbergensi
praedicata populo Wittenb. 1518   11835
—— ——   Leipz. 1519   11537
—— —— —— germ. (der zehn Gebote eine
nützliche Erklärung) Augsb. 1520   10789
—— disputatio et excusatio aduersus
criminationes Ioh. Eckii
n.p. (1519)   11848
—— ——   n.p.d.   11299
—— disputatio inter Lutherum et
Eckium   n.p.d.   10953
—— epistula ad Leonem X. de libertate
christiana   n.p. (1520)   11867
—— —— germ. (von der Freiheit eines
christen Menschen)   n.p. (1520)   11878
—— ——   n.p. (1520)   11907
—— ——   n.p.d.   10316
—— —— germ. (Sendbrief an Leo X.)
n.p.d.   10868
—— ——   n.p.d.   11868
—— epistula de disputatione sua, etc.
n.p.d.   10778
—— epistula super expurgatione ecciana   Wittenb. 1519   11854
—— Erklärung etlicher Artikel in seinem Sermon von dem heiligen Sacrament   n.p.d.   10812
—— ——   n.p.d.   11174
—— ——   n.p.d.   11500
—— ——   n.p.d.   11501
—— ——   n.p.d.   11913
—— explanatio orationis dominicae.
See above : Auslegung deutsch des
Vaterunser.
—— Freiheit des Sermons päpstlichen
Ablass und Gnade belangend
n.p. 1518   11151
—— ——   n.p. (1518)   11526
—— ——   Augsb. 1520   10863
—— ——   n.p.d.   10952
—— ——   n.p.d.   11152
—— gute trostliche Predigt von der
würdigen Bereitung zum Sacrament.
See below : Sermo de digna praeparatione...
—— heilsames Büchlein von der
Beichte. See above : Confitendi ratio.

Luther, Martin : in epistulam Pauli ad
Galatas commentarius   n.p.d.   11386
—— kurze Form das Paternoster zu
verstehen   n.p. 1520   10157
—— ——   n.p.d.   10639
—— ——   n.p.d.   11162
—— kurze Form der zehn Gebote, etc.
Augsb. 1520   10790
—— ——   Nürnb. 1520   11137
—— ——   Wittenb. 1520   11872
—— ——   n.p.d.   11166
—— ——   n.p.d.   11987
—— kurze Unterweisung wie man
beichten soll   Leipz. 1519   11385
—— ——   Leipz. 1520   11490
—— ——   Leipz. 1520   11491
—— ——   n.p. 1520   10799
—— ——   n.p.d.   10638
—— ——   n.p.d.   11164
—— ohne Ablass von Rom kann man
doch selig werden   n.p.d.   10942
—— ——   n.p.d.   10943
—— Predigt von dem ehlichen Stande.
See below : Sermon, etc.
—— Predigt von zweierlei Gerechtigkeit   Wittenb. 1520   11865
—— ——   n.p. 1520   10796
—— resolutio super propositione sua
decima tertia de potestate papae
Leipz. 1519   11383
—— ——   n.p.d.   10821
—— resolutiones disputationum de indulgentiarum uirtute Leipz. 1518   11366
—— ——   n.p. (1518)   11845
—— ——   n.p. 1519   10254
—— resolutiones super propositionibus
suis Lipsiae disputatis Augsb. 1519   10907
—— ——   Leipz. 1519   11485
—— ——   Wittenb. 1519   11851
—— ——   n.p.d.   11852
—— Sendbrief an Leo X.   See above :
Epistula ad Leonem X.
—— sermo de digna praeparatione cordis pro suscipiendo sacramentum eucharistiae   Wittenb. 1518   11840
—— ——   Augsb. 1519   10773
—— ——   n.p.d.   11298
—— ——   n.p.d.   11530
—— ——   n.p.d.   11531
—— —— germ. (gute trostliche Predigt von der würdigen Bereitung zum
Sacrament)   Augsb. 1518   10768
—— —— germ.   Augsb. 1520   10786
—— —— germ.   n.p.d.   11160
—— —— germ.   n.p.d.   11161
—— —— germ.   n.p.d.   11532
—— sermo de paenitentia
Leipz. 1518   11372
—— ——   Leipz. 1518   11520
—— ——   Wittenb. 1518   11842

Luther, Martin: sermo de paenitentia
          Augsb. n.d. 10811
—— Sermo de praeparatione ad moriendum. See below: Sermon von der
Bereitung zum Sterben.
—— sermo de triplici iustitia
          Wittenb. 1518 11841
—— ——   Leipz. 1519 11544
          n.p.d. 11296
—— sermo de uirtute excommunicationis   Leipz. 1518 11474
—— ——   n.p. (1518) 10771
—— ——   n.p. (1518) 11846
—— ——   Leipz. 1519 11542
          n.p.d. 11305
—— Sermon geprediget zu Leipzig am
Tag Petri und Pauli   n.p.d. 10637
—— ——   n.p.d. 10857
—— ——   n.p.d. 11157
—— Sermon von dem Ablass und
Gnade   n.p. 1518 11149
—— ——   n.p. 1518 11475
—— ——   n.p. 1518 11525
—— ——   Breslau 1519 11212
—— ——   Leipz. 1520 11493
—— ——   n.p. 1520 10864
          n.p.d. 11150
—— Sermon von dem Banne
          Augsb. 1520 10860
—— ——   Leipz. 1520 11489
—— ——   Leipz. 1520 11564
—— ——   n.p. 1520 10797
—— ——   n.p.d. 10160
—— ——   n.p.d. 11169
—— Sermon von dem ehlichen Stande
          Augsb. 1519 10776
—— ——   Leipz. 1519 11482
—— ——   Wittenb. 1519 11859
—— ——   Augsb. 1520 10794
—— ——   Augsb. 1520 10859
—— Sermon v.d. Gebete und Prozes-
sion in der Kreuzwoche Leipz. 1519 11481
—— ——   Leipz. 1520 11488
—— ——   Wittenb. 1520 11876
—— ——   n.p.d. 10809
—— ——   n.p.d. 10810
—— ——   n.p.d. 11170
—— Sermon von dem heiligen hoch-
würdigen Sacrament der Taufe
          Wittenb. 1519 11853
—— ——   Augsb. 1520 10784
—— ——   Leipz. 1520 11486
—— ——   Leipz. 1520 11487
—— ——   Str. 1520 10158
—— ——   n.p.d. 10808
—— ——   n.p.d. 11172
—— ——   n.p.d. 11173
—— Sermon von dem hochwürdigen
Sacrament des Leichnams Christi
          Augsb. 1520 10782

Luther, Martin: Sermon von dem hoch-
würdigen Sacrament des Leichnams
Christi   Leipz. 1520 11551
—— ——   Wittenb. 1520 11873
—— ——   n.p.d. 11158
—— ——   n.p.d. 11159
—— Sermon von dem neuen Testa-
mente   Augsb. 1520 10792
—— ——   Nürnb. 1520 11138
—— ——   Wittenb. 1520 11874
—— ——   Wittenb. 1520 11875
—— ——   n.p. 1520 10802
—— Sermon von dem Sacrament der
Busse   Leipz. 1519 11384
—— ——   Wittenb. 1519 11857
—— ——   Wittenb. 1519 11858
—— ——   Augsb. 1520 10795
—— ——   n.p.d. 10159
—— ——   n.p.d. 10814
—— ——   n.p.d. 11171
—— Sermon von dem Wucher (A)
          Leipz. 1519 11543
—— ——   Str. 1520 10155
—— Sermon von dem Wucher (B)
          Augsb. 1520 10803
—— ——   Augsb. 1520 10861
—— ——   Wittenb. 1520 11877
—— ——   n.p.d. 11175
—— Sermon von der Bereitung zum
Sterben   Augsb. 1520 10862
—— ——   Leipz. 1520 11492
—— ——   n.p.d. 10815
—— ——   n.p.d. 10816
—— ——   n.p.d. 11167
—— ——   n.p.d. 11168
—— ——   n.p.d. 11388
—— —— lat. (sermo de praeparatione
ad moriendum)   Leipz. 1520 11563
—— Sermon v.d. Betrachtung des heiligen Leidens Christi Leipz. 1519 11381
—— ——   Wittenb. 1519 11860
—— ——   Wittenb. 1520 11902
—— ——   n.p.d. 10817
—— ——   n.p.d. 10818
—— ——   n.p.d. 10865
—— sieben Busspsalmen mit einer
deutschen Auslegung Leipz. 1518 11439
—— ——   Leipz. 1519 11440
—— ——   Str. 1519 10335
—— ——   Leipz. 1520 11441
—— tessaradecas consolatoria
          Augsb. 1520 10804
—— ——   Leipz. 1520 11561
—— —— germ. (trostliches Büchlein)
          Augsb. 1520 10800
—— —— germ. Augsb. 1520 10801
—— —— germ. Leipz. 1520 11562
—— theses xcv   n.p. 1517 11017
—— trostliches Büchlein. See above:
Tessaradecas.

Ouidius: de tribus puellis, etc. n.p.d. 10558
—— Oenone Paridi Leipz. 1505 11412
Paenitentionarius lat. et germ. n.p.d. 10978
Palaephatus: de non credendis historicis
                              Str. 1517 10246
Paltz, Ioh. de: celifodina Erfurt 1502 11219
——— ———   Leipz. 1504 11273
——— ———   Leipz. 1511 11291
——— ——— germ. (die himmlische
  Fundgrube)   Augsb. 1506 10626
——— germ.   Str. 1517 10334
—— supplementum celifodinae
                           Erfurt 1504 11221
——— ———   Leipz. 1510 11286
Panis quotidianus. See Hieronymus
  de Villa Vitis.
Panormitanus, Abbas. See Nicolaus
  Panormitanus.
Papsttume, Von dem   n.p. 1520   9958
Parreut, Ioh. : textus ueteris artis
                            Hag. 1501 11612
Partes orationis quot sunt. See
  Donatus minor.
Parthenius Andronicus, Tranquillus.
  See Andronicus.
Paruulus philosophiae naturalis
                           Leipz. 1512 11427
Pascha iudaeorum. See Ritus.
Pasquillus (In Aegypto minori excusus)
                           n.p. 1520 11714
Passio domini nostri   Str. 1513 10036
—— See also Ringmann, M.
Passio septem fratrum filiorum sanctae
  Felicitatis   Ottob. 1511 11954
Passion oder Leiden Christi. See
  Ringmann, M.
Passion zu teutsch   Augsb. 1514 10631A
Passionael to dude   Lübeck 1507 11209
Patriarcharum duodecim testamenta
                              n.p.d. 10856
Patriarchatus, archiepiscopatus, episco-
  patus   Augsb. 1505 10663
Paulinus, S. Reliquiae ecclesiae S.
  Paulini Treuiris   n.p.d. 11510
Paulus Aegineta: praecepta salubria
                              Str. 1511 10187
Peckham, Ioh.: perspectiua communis
                           Leipz. 1504 11272
Pelbartus de Temesvar: sermones de
  sanctis   Hag. 1507 11636
—— sermones pomerii de tempore
                           Hag. 1502 11617
——— ———   Hag. 1504 11622
—— sermones pomerii quadragesimales
                           Hag. 1502 11615
——— ———   Hag. 1505 11626
—— stellarium coronae B.V M.
                        Augsb. 1502 10658
——— ———   Hag. 1505 11627
——— ———   Hag. 1511 11649

Pelbartus de Temesvar: stellarium
  coronae B.V.M.   Hag. 1520 11682
Pennaforti, Raymundus de. See Ray-
  mundus.
Pentzeldt, Thomas : modus studendi
                           Leipz. 1504 11408
Peraudi, Raym.: epistulae ad romani
  imperii senatores   n.p.d. 11318
—— legenda x. milium martyrum
                           Köln 1503 10473
—— literae indulgentiarum (1502)
                              n.p.d. 12000
——— ——— (1502)   n.p.d. 10350
Perottus, Nic.: cornu copiae Str. 1506 9979
Persius: saturae   Leipz. 1516 11364
——— ———   Str. 1517 10112
Perutilis repetitio capituli Omnis utrius-
  que sexus   Leipz. 1517 11468
Pestilentia. Imago Christi ad pestilen-
  tiam fugandam   n.p.d. 10681
Petrarcha, Franc.: remedia aduersae
  fortunae   Leipz. 1504 11400
Petrus Comestor: historia scholastica
                              Str. 1503 10001
Petrus Cracouiensis: computus eccle-
  siasticus et astronomicus n.p. 1501 10539
Petrus de Rosenheim: memorabiles
  euangelistarum figurae Pforzh. 1502 11744
——— ———   Pforzh. 1502 11745
——— ———   Pforzh. 1503 11748
——— ———   Pforzh. 1505 11752
——— ———   Pforzh. 1507 11761
——— ———   Pforzh. 1507 11762
——— ———   Pforzh. 1510 11772
Petrus Hieremiae: sermones
                           Hag. 1514 11663
Petrus Hispanus: commentarium in
  tractatus logicae eius i. et iv.
                           Hag. 1503 11620
Petrus Mosellanus. See Mosellanus.
Petrus Rauennas: artificiosa memoria
                              n.p.d. 11394
—— aurea opuscula   Erfurt 1503 11220
——— ———   Köln 1506 10411
——— ———   Köln 1508 10424
—— compendium iuris canonici
                        Wittenb. 1504 11828
Peurbachius, Geo.: institutiones arith-
  meticae   Nürnb. 1513 11070
—— quadratum geometricum
                        Nürnb. 1516 11101
Peutinger, Conr.: inscriptiones romanae
  in Augusta Vindelicorum
                           Mainz 1520   9869
—— romanae uetustatis fragmenta in
  Augusta   Augsb. 1505 10645
—— sermones de Germaniae antiquitatibus   Str. n.d.   9978
Pfalzgrafen, Chronik der
                        Landsh. n.d. 11775

Politianus, Ang.: epistulae eius et
aliorum   Str. 1513   10214
———— silua cui titulus Rusticus
                            Leipz. 1512   11429
Pomerium sermonum. See Pelbartus
de Temesvar.
Pontanus, Ioh. Iouianus: amorum libri
                            Str. 1515   10094
Porcia, Iacobus: de liberorum educa-
tione   Str. 1510   10267
Porta, Santius de. See Santius.
Practica deutsch gezogen aus der Lehre
Sibyllae   Speier n.d.   11204
                    Speier n.d.   11205
Practica Iohannis Rossschwanz
                            n.p.d.   10023
Pressa. See Brescia.
Prierio, Siluester de. See Siluester.
Proba, Falconia: centones uergiliani
                            Opp. n.d.   11925
Probatissimorum ecclesiae doctorum
sententiae   n.p.d.   10590
————   n.p.d.   10601
Probus, Aemilius.   See Cornelius
Nepos.
Probus, Val.: de literis antiquis n.p.d.   9878
Proles, Andr.: Lehre wie man sich
halten soll bei der Taufe
                            Augsb. 1511   10746
Prophet in Persia Sophey genannt
                            Nürnb. n.d.   11086
Prudentius: hymnus de miraculis
Christi   Schlettst. 1520   11973
———— psychomachia   Augsb. 1506   10697
Psalmi paenitentiales cum argumentis
Iac. Fabri   Köln 1519   10467
Psalmi paenitentiales heb. lat. germ.
                            Augsb. 1520   10917
Psalterium   Mainz 1502   9842
————   Köln 1508   10517
————   Mainz 1516   9859
Psalterium cantica et hymni
                            n.p. 1515   10308
Psalterium chorale Constantiense
                            n.p.d.   9971
Psalterium lat.-germ.   Worms 1504   11945
————   Str. 1506   9980
————   Str. 1508   10064
————   Köln 1509   10478
————   Metz 1513   11599
Psalterium tetraglottum   Köln 1518   10598
Ptolemaeus: geographia   Str. 1513   10271
———— ————   Nürnb. 1514   11095
———— ————   Str. 1520   10289
Purgatorium detractorum
                            Köln 1509   10429
Purliliarum, Iacobus comes.   See
Porcia.
Pusculus, Hub.: Simonidos libri ij.
                            Augsb. 1511   10683

Quadus, Nic.: flores ex libris Iac.
Hochstrati collecti   n.p.d.   11989
Quaestiones naturales philosophorum
                            Köln n.d.   10555
Quattuor nouissima. See Cordiale.
Quercu, Simon de: opusculum musicae
                            Nürnb. 1513   11072
Qui sequitur me. See Imitatio Christi.
Quintilianus: institutiones oratoriae,
liber i.   Leipz. 1518   11472
Quintus Curtius: gesta Alexandri
                            Tüb. 1513   11734
Quintus Curtius Rufus: historia Alex-
andri   Str. 1518   10252
Rabanus Maurus: de institutione cleri-
corum   Pforzh. 1505   11751
———— de laudibus sanctae crucis
                            Pforzh. 1503   11747
Radinus Todiscus, Tho.: ad principes
Germaniae aduersus Lutherum
                            Köln 1520   10468
Rampegollis, Ant.: aurea biblia
                            Köln 1505   10544
———— ————   Str. 1509   10172
———— ————   Str. 1516   10096
Ratbüchlein   n.p.d.   10333
Ratisbona. See Regensburg.
Rauennas, Petrus. See Petrus.
Raymundus de Pennaforti: summula
sacramentorum   Str. 1504   10047
———— ————   Köln 1506   10400
———— ————   Köln 1508   10416
Raymundus de Sabunde. See Sa-
bunde.
Rebdorf, Hieronymus de.   See Hie-
ronymus de Villa Vitis.
Rechter Weg von Lissabon gen Kalikut
                            n.p.d.   10966
————   n.p.d.   11047
Rede der Botschafter der Venediger
an den Kaiser   n.p.d.   11074
Reformation der Bairischen Landrechte
(1518)   n.p.d.   11585
Reformation der Stadt Frankfurt am
Main   Mainz 1509   9852
Reformation der Stadt Worms
                            n.p. 1513   10082
Reformation Kaiser Sigmunds
                            Str. 1520   10262
Refrigerium animae peccatricis n.p.d.   10530
Regensburg. De capella beatae Mariae
pulchrae Ratisbonae   n.p.d.   12002
———— Von der neuen Kapelle in Re-
gensburg   n.p.d.   11020
Regimen sanitatis salernitanum
                            Köln 1507   10548
Regiomontanus, Ioannes. See Ioannes.
Region. Von der neugefundenen
Region   n.p.d.   10982
Regula ordinis sancti Benedicti n.p.d.   9883

Regulae grammaticales antiquorum
                        Augsb. 1501   10615
Reichs Unterhaltung, Buch des
                        München 1501 11573
Reichstag zu Augsburg 1510
                        Augsb. n.d.   10709
—— zu Köln, 1512   n.p.d.   10712
—— zu Konstanz, 1507   n.p.d.   10629
Reinhardus de Laudenburg.   See
    Laudenburg.
Reisch, Greg. : margarita philosophica
                        Freib. 1503   11717
——— ———   Str. 1504   9891
——— ———   n.p. 1504   11718
——— ———   Str. 1508   9907
——— ———   Str. 1512   9924
——— ———   Str. 1515   9935
Reitterius, Conr. : mortilogus
                        Augsb. 1508   10703
Reliquiae cum indulgentiis S. Maximini
    Treueris   n.p.d.   11509
Reliquiae et indulgentiae S. Paulini
    Treueris   n.p.d.   11510
Reliquiae Treueris inuentae anno 1512
                        n.p.d.   11598A
Remigius siue dominus quae pars
                        Köln 1502   10471
———   Braunsch. 1507 11951
Repgow, Eyke von.   See Eyke.
Requiem der verbrannten Bullen.   See
    Deutsches Requiem.
Resolutio lutheriana...   See Luther.
Reuchlin, Joh. : Augenspiegel n.p.d.   11722
—— congesta de arte praedicandi
                        Pforzh. 1504 11750
——— ———   Pforzh. 1508 11766
—— de accentibus et orthographia
    hebraica   Hag. 1518   11690
—— de arte cabalistica Hag. 1517   11685
—— deutsche Missive, warum die
    Juden im Elend sind Pforzh. n.d.   11753
—— klare Verständnis von den Juden-
    büchern   n.p.d.   11727
—— rudimenta hebraica
                        Pforzh. 1506 11754
—— scenica progymnasmata
                        Pforzh. 1508 11767
——— ———   Tüb. 1512   11730
——— ———   Leipz. 1515   11435
——— ———   Hag. 1519   11701
—— Sergius uel capitis caput
                        Pforzh. 1507 11760
——— ———   Pforzh. 1508 11765
——— ———   Tüb. 1513   11732
—— See also Epistulae ; Vocabularius
    breuiloquus.
Reuelationes Mechtildis et Gertrudis
                        Leipz. 1510   11424
Reynmann, Leonh. : Natiuität-Kalen-
    der   Nürnb. 1515   11117

Rhau, Georg : enchiridion musicae
                        Leipz. 1518   11524
—— enchiridion utriusque musicae
                        Leipz. [1520] 11549a
Rhegius, Vrbanus : de dignitate sacer-
    dotum   Augsb. 1519   10847
Rhinoceros von Alb. Dürer gezeichnet
                        n.p. [1515]   11184
———   n.p. [1515]   11185
Ribsch, Henr.   See Rybisch.
Ricardus archiep. Treuirensis. Reliquiae
    ab eo inuentae anno 1512 n.p.d.   11598A
Ricardus de Monte Crucis. See Monte
    Crucis.
Ricardus de Sancto Victore : de
    duodecim patriarchis Str. 1516   10325
—— de trinitate   Nürnb. 1518   11127
Ricius, Paulus : apologetica ad eckiana
    responsa narratio   n.p.d.   10912
—— de anima caeli   Augsb. 1519   10893
—— de anima caeli aduersus Eckium
    examinatio   Augsb. 1519   10899b
—— de mosaicae sanctionis edictis
                        Augsb. 1515   10825a
—— de nouem doctrinarum ordinibus
                        Augsb. 1515   10825d
—— in apostolorum symbolum dia-
    logus   Augsb. 1514   10823
—— in cabalistarum eruditionem
    isagoge   Augsb. 1515   10825c
—— in psalmum primum meditatio
                        Augsb. 1519   10899c
—— in psalmum i. commentariolum
                        Augsb. 1519   10910
—— portae lucis   Augsb. 1516   10835
—— sal foederis   Augsb. 1514   10825b
—— talmudica commentariola
                        Augsb. 1519   10899a
Riedrer, Friedrich : Spiegel der wahren
    Rhetorik   Str. 1509   9991
Ringbüchlein   n.p.d.   10033
Ringmann, Matthias : passio domini
    nostri   Str. 1507   10057
——— ———   Str. 1507   10058
——— ———   Str. 1508   10063
——— —— germ.   Str. 1506   10050
——— —— germ.   Str. 1509   10070
Ritter. Der weise Ritter Str. 1514   9934
Rituale.   See Agenda ; Obsequiale.
Ritus et celebratio paschae iudaeorum
                        n.p.d.   11958
Robertus Linconiensis. See Grosseteste.
Rodericus Zamorensis : speculum uitae
    humanae   Str. 1507   9981
Rojas, Fernando de.   See Celestina.
Rolach, Theodoricus : fides mea n.p.d. 11608
Romanis, Humbertus de : expositio su-
    per regulam Augustini Hag. 1505   11628a
—— sermones ad diuersos status
                        Hag. 1508   11637

Tanstetter, Geo. : Kalender auf 1513
n.p.d. 10749
————— 1514 n.p.d. 10750
————— 1514 n.p.d. 11093
Tauler, Ioh. : sermones, germ.
Augsb. 1508 10670
Teckendorf. Von Tegkendorff das
geschicht n.p.d. 10807
Temesvar, Pelbartus de. See Pelbartus.
Tengler, Ulr. : Laienspiegel
Augsb. 1509 10675
———— —— Str. 1510 10027
———— —— Augsb. 1511 10686
———— —— Augsb. 1512 10691
———— —— Str. 1518 10121
Terentius : comoediae Str. 1503 9889
———— —— Str. 1503 9965
———— —— Str. 1511 9921
———— —— Mainz 1520 9870
———— adelphi Münster 1514 11606
Testamenta duodecim patriarcharum
n.p.d. 10856
Testimonia de Christo uaria
Opp. n.d. 11926
Tetzel, Joh. : Vorlegung wider Luthers
Sermon von Ablass und Gnade
n.p.d. 11372A
Teutsch Kalender Str. 1504 10006
Teutsch Kalender mit Figuren
Augsb. 1510 10630
Teutsches Requiem. See Deutsches
Requiem.
Text des Passions oder Leidens Christi.
See Ringmann, M.
Textus sequentiarum. See Sequen-
tiarum textus.
Themeswar, Pelbartus de. See Pel-
bartus.
Theobaldus: physiologus Köln 1502 10361
Theodericus de Thuringia : Cronica
Sankt Elisabeth Erfurt 1520 11254
Theologia teutsch. See Deutsche
Theologia.
Theramo, Iacobus de. See Iacobus.
Thesaurus animae e reuelationibus
Brigittae collectus Köln 1517 10458
Theuerdank. See Pfinzing, Melchior.
Thomas a Kempis : hortulus rosarum
Köln 1513 10481
———— See also Imitatio.
Thomas Aquinas : confessionale
Köln 1508 10516
———— de ente et essentia n.p.d. 11392
———— de sacramento eucharistiae
Leipz. 1505 11444
———— de ueritate catholicae fidei
Köln 1501 10358
———— summa, pars prima Aug. 1512 11654
———— —— prima secundae
Köln 1512 10442

Thomas Aquinas : summa, prima
secundae Hag. 1512 11651
———— ———— secunda secundae
Hag. 1512 11650
———— ———— tertia Hag. 1512 11652
Thorelle, Historie von Str. n.d. 10106A
Thurnmaier, Ioh. : grammatica
München 1512 11579
———— grammatica noua Nürnb. 1513 11067
———— n.p. 1513 10951
———— Henrici iv. imp. uita
Augsb. 1518 10881
———— historia et antiquitates Otingae
Nürnb. 1518 11104
———— des hochwürdigen Stifts Alten Öting
Herkommen Ingolst. 1519 11609
———— musicae rudimenta Augsb. 1516 10834
Tibulli Propertii Catulli carmina
Erfurt 1513 11240
Tifernas, Gregorius. See Gregorius.
Titelbüchlein Nürnb. 1513 11069
Tobiae liber. See Matthaeus Vindo-
cinensis.
Todischus, Tho. Radinus. See Ra-
dinus Todiscus.
Tollat, Ioh. : margarita medicinae
Str. 1508 10022
———— —— Str. 1512 10145
Torrentinus, Herm. : elucidarius car-
minum Hag. 1507 11635
———— —— Hag. 1510 11647
———— —— Hag. 1512 11653
———— —— Str. 1513–14 10304
———— —— Lahr 1515 11967
———— —— [Hag.] 1518 11676
Tractat wie durch Gottfried von
Bouillon das gelobte Land gewon-
nen ist Leipz. 1518 11476
———— Nürnb. n.d. 11146
Tractätlein von dem sterbenden Men-
schen [Memm.] n.d. 11263
Tractatulus de his qui ad ecclesias con-
fugiunt Landsh. 1517 11809
Tractatus contra Waldenses n.p.d. 11043
Tractatus de festis B.V.M. celebrandis
n.p. 1508 10668
Tractatus de ritu et moribus turcorum
n.p.d. 10552
Tragedia von Calisto und Melibea
Augsb. 1520 10925A
Tranquillus Parthenius Andronicus.
See Andronicus.
Transiluanus, Max. See Maximilianus.
Trapezuntius, Georgius. See Georgius.
Trebellius, Wigandus : concordia cura-
torum n.p.d. 9966
Tritheim, Ioh. : Compendium annalium
regum Francorum Mainz 1515 9858
———— de purissima conceptione B.V.
Mariae Str. 1506 10016

Villa Vitis, Hieronymus de. See Hieronymus.
Vindocinensis, Matthaeus. See Matthaeus.
Vinetum beatae Annae Köln 1507 10511
Viola sanctorum Str. 1516 10043
Vipera, Mercurius: de disciplinarum laudibus Str. 1520 10129
—— de diuino et uero numine Str. 1520 10128
Virdung, Joh.: Auslegung über die wunderbaren Zeichen Speier n.d. 11203
—— Practica teutsch Str. 1503 10005
Virgilius Wellendorfer. See Wellendorfer.
Visitatio. De uisitatione beatae Mariae carmen n.p.d. 11451
Vita diui Brunonis n.p.d. 10498
Vita diui Wolfgangi Landsh. 1516 11800
Vita sanctae Adelhaidis Durlach n.d. 11964
Vita sancti Albani n.p.d. 10503
Vitas patrum, germ. Str. 1513 10034
—— Str. 1516 9939
Vitellius, Erasmus: oratio in conuentu Augustensi Augsb. n.d. 10843
Viterbiensis claustri confraternitas n.p.d. 12004
Viualdis, Ioh. Lud. de: de ueritate contritionis Hag. 1513 11657
Vives, Ioh. Lud.: aduersus pseudodialecticos; Pompeius fugiens Schlettst. 1520 11976
Ulrich, S., Leben Augsb. 1516 10756
Unterhaltung. Buch des H. R. Reichs Unterhaltung München 1501 11573
Unterrichtung der Aufrühren in Württemberg Tüb. n.d. 11740
Unterscheide und Vorstand, Büchlein von Wittenb. 1516 11833
Vocabula ex probatissimis auctoribus Augsb. 1518 10772
Vocabula pro iuuenibus Nürnb. 1508 10994
Vocabularius breuiloquus Str. 1504 10002
Vocabularius gemma gemmarum. See Gemma.
Vocabularius poeticus. See Torrentinus, H. (Elucidarius.)
Vocabularius quattuor linguarum Augsb. 1516 10719
Vocabularius rerum. See Brack, W.
Vocabularius teutonico-latinus Str. 1515 10042
Vocabularius uariorum terminorum Str. 1502 9962
Vochs, Ioh.: de pestilentia anni praesentis Magdeb. 1507 11257
Voerda, Nicasius de. See Nicasius.
Von dem christlichen Streit zu Lissabon geschehen n.p.d. 10019

Von dem ehelichen Stande Augsb. n.d. 10739
—— Augsb. n.d. 10744
Von dem Gewalt und Haupt der Kirchen ein Gespräch n.p.d. 11992
Von dem neuen Propheten in Persia Sophey genannt Nürnb. n.d. 11086
Von dem Sterben. See Ars Moriendi.
Von den Almosen n.p.d. 10731
—— n.p.d. 10948
Von der Kur und Wahl des Königs Karl München 1519 11590
Von der neugefundenen Region n.p.d. 10613
—— n.p.d. 10982
Von der unchristlichen Handlung des Königs von Portugal wider die Christen n.p.d. 11046
Von des Endkrists Leben. See Antichristus.
Von Sibylla Weissagung n.p.d. 11178
Von Tegkendorff das geschicht n.p.d. 10807
Voragine, Iacobus de: legenda aurea Str. 1502 9998
—— —— n.p. 1503 10000
—— —— Hag. 1516 11669
—— —— germ. Str. 1517 10114
—— —— niedersächsisch Lübeck 1507 11209
Vratislauiensis, Michael. See Michael.
Vrimaria, Henr. de. See Henricus.
Vrsinus, Ioh.: modus epistulandi n.p.d. 11597
Vrspergensis abbatis chronicon Augsb. 1515 10829A
Ursula-Bruderschaft zu Braunau n.p.d. 11034
Ursula-Schifflein n.p.d. 11790
Vsingen, Barthol. de. See Bartholomaeus.
Vsuardus: martyrologium Köln n.d. 10497
Wächter, der, an der Zinnen lag n.p.d. 10632
Wahrhaftige Historie von Kaiser Friedrich i. Augsb. 1519 10940
—— Landsh. 1519 11812
Wahrhaftige Sage oder Rede vom Rock Christi Nürnb. 1512 11062
—— Str. 1512 10031
Wahrhaftige Unterrichtung der Aufrühren in Württemberg Tüb. n.d. 11740
Waldkircher, Joh. See Seger.
Waldseemüller, M. See Hylacomylus.
Wälsche Gattung, die Str. 1513 10218A
Wandalino, Ioannes de Sancto. See Ioannes.
Wann, Paulus: quadragesimale Hag. 1501 11613
—— sermones de septem uitiis Hag. 1514 11660

OXFORD   PRINTED BY
HORACE HART AT THE
UNIVERSITY PRESS